MOBILE COMPUTING FOR DUMMIES®

by Cliff Roth

IDG Books Worldwide, Inc.
An International Data Group Company

Foster City, CA ♦ Chicago, IL ♦ Indianapolis, IN ♦ Southlake, TX

Mobile Computing For Dummies®

Published by
IDG Books Worldwide, Inc.
An International Data Group Company
919 E. Hillsdale Blvd.
Suite 400
Foster City, CA 94404
www.idgbooks.com (IDG Books Worldwide Web site)
www.dummies.com (Dummies Press Web site)

Library of Congress Catalog Card No.: 97-73302

ISBN: 0-7645-0151-8

Printed in the United States of America

10 9 8 7 6 5 4 3 2 1

1A/RS/QY/ZX/IN

Distributed in the United States by IDG Books Worldwide, Inc.

Distributed by Macmillan Canada for Canada; by Transworld Publishers Limited in the United Kingdom; by IDG Norge Books for Norway; by IDG Sweden Books for Sweden; by Woodslane Pty. Ltd. for Australia; by Woodslane Enterprises Ltd. for New Zealand; by Longman Singapore Publishers Ltd. for Singapore, Malaysia, Thailand, and Indonesia; by Simron Pty. Ltd. for South Africa; by Toppan Company Ltd. for Japan; by Distribuidora Cuspide for Argentina; by Livraria Cultura for Brazil; by Ediciencia S.A. for Ecuador; by Addison-Wesley Publishing Company for Korea; by Ediciones ZETA S.C.R. Ltda. for Peru; by WS Computer Publishing Corporation, Inc., for the Philippines; by Unalis Corporation for Taiwan; by Contemporanea de Ediciones for Venezuela; by Computer Book & Magazine Store for Puerto Rico; by Express Computer Distributors for the Caribbean and West Indies. Authorized Sales Agent: Anthony Rudkin Associates for the Middle East and North Africa.

For general information on IDG Books Worldwide's books in the U.S., please call our Consumer Customer Service department at 800-762-2974. For reseller information, including discounts and premium sales, please call our Reseller Customer Service department at 800-434-3422.

For information on where to purchase IDG Books Worldwide's books outside the U.S., please contact our International Sales department at 415-655-3200 or fax 415-655-3295.

For information on foreign language translations, please contact our Foreign & Subsidiary Rights department at 415-655-3021 or fax 415-655-3281.

For sales inquiries and special prices for bulk quantities, please contact our Sales department at 415-655-3200 or write to the address above.

For information on using IDG Books Worldwide's books in the classroom or for ordering examination copies, please contact our Educational Sales department at 800-434-2086 or fax 817-251-8174.

For press review copies, author interviews, or other publicity information, please contact our Public Relations department at 415-655-3000 or fax 415-655-3299.

For authorization to photocopy items for corporate, personal, or educational use, please contact Copyright Clearance Center, 222 Rosewood Drive, Danvers, MA 01923, or fax 508-750-4470.

is a trademark under exclusive license to IDG Books Worldwide, Inc., from International Data Group, Inc.

About the Author

Cliff Roth has been writing about — and using — laptop computers since 1984, when his first articles on the subject appeared in the (now defunct) magazine *Pico*. He was a columnist for *PC LapTop* magazine for the better part of a decade, and has also written about computers and technology for dozens of publications including *The New York Times, The Washington Post, Rolling Stone, New Media, Home Office Computing,* and *Gist,* an online magazine where he is Technology Editor.

Besides mobile computers, Cliff's avocation is low budget video and film-making — he has written a book on the subject, writes regularly for *Video* magazine about camcorders and digital video technology, and in his spare time has been producing a feature length 16mm film, tentatively titled, *The Stoned Channel.*

Cliff lives in New York with his wife Debbie and son Gerry.

Dedication

To my son Gerry, and wife Debbie, who patiently let me ignore them while working at home to write this book. (Gerry — sorry I didn't let you bang on the keyboard while I was writing this. Someday you'll understand.)

Author's Acknowledgments

I'll skip the guys that invented the transistor and integrated circuits and jump to the people who I have had personal contact with.

Let me start out thanking my dear friend and colleague, Michael Goldstein, who as former editor of *PC LapTop* magazine (since renamed to *Portable Computing*) loved to joke that my first laptop computer, circa 1984 (see Introduction), could cut and paste text just as fast as today's supercharged Pentium models. Ditto for numerous other magazine and online editors who have nurtured me along the way, with a special mention for Jonathan Greenberg, whose flexibility and zest for life also helped make this book possible.

Specific thanks for help in producing this book go to Ronnie Abraham for research assistance, to Frank Preuss for technical review and insights, and to Clark Scheffy the project editor for keeping me on track and in focus. There's also a whole slew of other people from IDG books listed on the reverse side of this page, and special thanks to Frank Douglas for help interfacing with them.

Perhaps the biggest thanks go to all the companies (and their hard working public relations agencies) whose products this book revolves around. I'll spare you their names — see the Appendix for a list — they really do make some pretty nifty stuff.

Publisher's Acknowledgments

We're proud of this book; please send us your comments about it by using the IDG Books Worldwide Registration Card at the back of the book or by e-mailing us at feedback dummies@idgbooks.com. Some of the people who helped bring this book to market include the following:

Acquisitions, Development, and Editorial

Project Editor: Clark Scheffy

Acquisitions Editor: Gareth Hancock

Product Development Director: Mary Bednarek

Associate Permissions Editor: Heather H. Dismore

Copy Editor: Christa J. Carroll

Technical Editor: Frank Preuss

Editorial Manager: Mary C. Corder

Editorial Assistant: Chris Collins

Special Help: Barb Terry

Production

Project Coordinator: E. Shawn Aylsworth

Layout and Graphics: Cameron Booker, Lou Boudreau, Linda M. Boyer, Angela F. Hunckler, Tom Missler, Heather N. Pearson, Brent Savage

Proofreaders: Kathleen Prata, Christine Berman, Joel K. Draper, Robert Springer, Karen York

Indexer: Lynnzee Elze Spense

General and Administrative

IDG Books Worldwide, Inc.: John Kilcullen, CEO; Steven Berkowitz, President and Publisher

IDG Books Technology Publishing: Brenda McLaughlin, Senior Vice President and Group Publisher

Dummies Technology Press and Dummies Editorial: Diane Graves Steele, Vice President and Associate Publisher; Judith A. Taylor, Product Marketing Manager; Kristin A. Cocks, Editorial Director; Mary Bednarek, Acquisitions and Product Development Director

Dummies Trade Press: Kathleen A. Welton, Vice President and Publisher

IDG Books Production for Dummies Press: Beth Jenkins, Production Director; Cindy L. Phipps, Manager of Project Coordination, Production Proofreading, and Indexing; Kathie S. Schutte, Supervisor of Page Layout; Shelley Lea, Supervisor of Graphics and Design; Debbie J. Gates, Production Systems Specialist; Robert Springer, Supervisor of Proofreading; Debbie Stailey, Special Projects Coordinator; Tony Augsburger, Supervisor of Reprints and Bluelines; Leslie Popplewell, Media Archive Coordinator

Dummies Packaging and Book Design: Patti Sandez, Packaging Specialist; Lance Kayser, Packaging Assistant; Kavish + Kavish, Cover Design

♦

The publisher would like to give special thanks to Patrick J. McGovern, without whom this book would not have been possible.

♦

Contents at a Glance

Cartoons at a Glance

By Rich Tennant

The 5th Wave — By Rich Tennant

"OF COURSE, IT'S PORTABLE SIR. LOOK, HERE'S THE HANDLE."

page 5

The 5th Wave — By Rich Tennant

Ever the innovator, Larry beta-tests the Personal Belt Buckle Assistant/Wireless Fax

Hold on a second, Stu, I'm getting a fax.

page 125

The 5th Wave — By Rich Tennant

FIRED YOU

"NIFTY CHART, FRANK, BUT NOT ENTIRELY NECESSARY."

page 219

The 5th Wave — By Rich Tennant

"YOU KNOW, IF WE CAN ALL KEEP THE TITTERING DOWN, I, FOR ONE, WOULD LIKE TO HEAR MORE ABOUT KEN'S NEW POINTING DEVICE FOR NOTEBOOKS."

page 267

The 5th Wave — By Rich Tennant

COMPUTERS

"A PORTABLE COMPUTER? YOU'D BETTER TALK TO OLD BOB OVER THERE. HE'S OWNED A PORTABLE LONGER THAN ANYONE HERE."

page 349

Fax: 508-546-7747 • E-mail: the5wave@tiac.net

Table of Contents

Introduction

· ·

*W*elcome to the world of mobile computing! The freedom and
capabilities of today's laptop, notebook, and handheld are truly
mind-boggling. However, when the proverbial cows finally do come home,
it's what you can *do* with these computers that counts — not how sexy the
technology is. And so, in this book, I focus on the exciting and useful side of
portable computers — the things that are cool, but actually work — and
avoid some of the high-tech hype.

For me, laptop computers have provided the freedom to work practically
anywhere. Back in the 1980s, when I was a budding young writer, I bought
my first computer — a laptop model made by Bondwell that weighed in at
twelve pounds, had no hard drive, and ran the CP/M operating system (the
forerunner of DOS, and great-grandfather to Windows 95).

What I remember most about that old laptop is not any of its technical
features, rather the places I went with it. Like the time my girlfriend — now
my wife — and I went to Mexico for a couple of weeks and I paid for the trip
by writing a how-to on video production while I was there. Now, I'm writing
these very words on the deck of our summer cabin — a little mountain
retreat with a nice view and plenty of fresh air. The notebook computer I'm
using is several generations beyond that old Bondwell (it's a lightning-fast
150 MHz Pentium). If I sound like I'm bragging because (thanks to notebook
computers) I get to work in a nice place, I apologize. However, I've got to tell
you — it's my answer to the critics out there who contend that mobile
computing is turning people into 24-hour-a-day employees — always on call,
always working, always computing, and always connected.

True, the portable computer can allow you to become some kind of
cyberslave/raging automaton kind of thing, but don't blame the machines.
These new technologies are also creating fantastic new opportunities for
people to work at home, to work on their own schedules, to work more
productively, and to make work more enjoyable. The mobile computer is
quite simply about *freedom*.

About This Book

I organized this book with one thing foremost in my mind: making it easy for you to figure out *how* to do whatever it is you *want* to do with a mobile computer, all with the least amount of hassle and confusion. Of course, most of the stuff that you end up doing with a notebook computer is pretty similar to what you can do with a desktop machine — that's part of the point of owning a portable computer, anyway, isn't it? You get a mobile computer so you are no longer tied to a desktop computer and whatever dingy room it happens to be in. In any case, I don't spend much time telling you how to do the basic computing tasks that you can do on a desktop computer. Instead, I focus mainly on the stuff you can do with a mobile computer that is unique to, or associated with mobile computing. If you want to join the tribe of work where you want to work, follow your own schedule, freewheeling computer road warriors, you are reading the right book!

The Nickel Tour

Before I tell you what you can expect to find in this book, let me tell you what (hopefully) you don't find: technical gibberish, confusing procedures, and what I consider the worst offense of computer books: equal treatment of simple and complex solutions. As much as possible, I try to explain the approach most people take to work through a particular mobile computing situation, and why. If one method of doing something is ridiculously complicated, while another method is much simpler, I want you to know that.

Part I: The Portable Universe

These chapters cover what I consider the most basic stuff about mobile computers — the different types of notebook and pocket-sized computers available, how to choose between them, the key features to look for, common accessories such as fax/modem cards, and how to get the most out of your notebook computer battery.

Part II: Staying Connected

All the basic ways that you may want to communicate with your mobile computer, or to exchange files with your desktop computer, are covered here — including synchronizing your mobile computer with your desktop computer, mobile e-mail, Web browsing, maintaining software on two computers, and gaining remote access to your desktop machine.

Part III: Taking Your Show on the Road

Lots of people use notebook computers to put on presentations, and the chapters in this section are devoted to helping you get acquainted with the various display options (such as LCD projectors and projection panels), as well as some of the considerations that go into authoring and distributing multimedia.

Part IV: Going to the Next Level

What do you do if you're in a hotel room and you are having trouble dialing into your online service? How do you connect to a Local Area Network (LAN) at your office? How do you install and configure PCMCIA/PC card accessory devices? What is the sound of one hand clapping? I cover these and other, more advanced topics, such as wireless communications, here.

Part V: The Part of Tens

The Part of Tens is a de rigueur (and handy) feature of the _...For Dummies_ series, and this book is no exception. In this part, I provide some concise, practical tips to make your battery last longer and to aid you in your travels. The Part of Tens also includes the Appendix (if someone hasn't had to have it removed) where you can find out how to contact the various campanies I mention in this book, as well as how to locate other companies and organizations that can help you put icing on your mobile computing cake. True, the Appendix doesn't normally go in The Part of Tens, but my Appendix has about ten pages, so my editor let it slip by. If you ever need just the straight, simple answers on a given topic, The Part of Tens is the place.

Icons Are Cool!

The most fun part of writing this book was getting to use the official _...For Dummies_ icons. I think they do a great job of helping you sift through reading which — hard as I try to make it engaging and lighthearted — can get pretty dense. Here are the icons I use, and what I mean by them:

I try to identify particularly useful stuff with a tip, so if you're just skimming a section and you need to quickly glean some helpful advice, look for this icon.

Sometimes the topics I bring up are, by necessity, flirting with some form of danger — such as accidentally erasing important files, making a computer network vulnerable to attack, or ordering the fish dinner on an airplane trip. This icon is intended to warn you of such instances. However, as long as you pay special and careful attention to warnings, you will have no problems at all.

You don't need to read these sections to do whatever it is you're trying to figure out, but if you want to understand some of the technical background of the subject at hand, you find it here.

It never hurts to emphasize key points, and sometimes something covered in depth in one chapter needs to be summarized elsewhere so that things make sense in a self-contained way. So when you see the Remember icon, you know that you can find a friendly and helpful reminder that may be useful for what you're trying to do.

Mobile Computing Awaits You

Okay, since you've read this far, let me guess your interest:

- ✔ You're thinking about buying a notebook or pocket computer.

- ✔ You just bought a portable computer and want to figure out what to do with it.

- ✔ You've had a laptop computer for years and want to start communicating and doing more advanced things.

- ✔ You're killing time in a bookstore waiting for a friend, or for the rain to stop.

Well, I can't stop the rain, but I can show you how to get the most out of your portable computer — or at least that's my goal in writing this book. So by all means . . . read on!

Part I
The Portable Universe

"OF COURSE, IT'S PORTABLE SIR. LOOK, HERE'S THE HANDLE."

In this part . . .

Buying and getting started using a mobile computer is what these first eight chapters are about. I cover such specifics as choosing between a notebook or pocket-sized computer, selecting features, understanding how to maximize your battery run time, using modems and other peripherals that hook up to your mobile computer, and tips on traveling with a mobile computer.

You can come away from this part feeling refreshed, invigorated, and ready to smell really good. Ooops — I've been writing copy for too many soap commercials. No, what I mean to say is: You can come away from this part feeling powerful, alive, and ready to use your mobile computer to rule the world!

Chapter 1

So You Want to Buy a Portable Computer?

. . . .

In This Chapter

▶ Figuring out which type of computer to buy

▶ Dealing with the future needs issue

▶ Coordinating with desktop computer equipment

. . . .

1 know of nothing else quite like that feeling of being on the road with a computer. Granted, today's notebook computers are not quite the full-service companions envisioned by science fiction. Your notebook is not likely to reach the level of the infamous HAL computer in *2001: A Space Odyssey,* but when you're in a hotel room with a notebook computer, it does provide you with a valuable link to the outside world, and it's the only one that you can personalize.

For many people, the portable computer is an extension of the office, and for many others, it *is* the office. This chapter and the next can help you understand the various types of portable computers, and the main features you can expect to find on notebook computers. Of course, I want to write a book that will (hopefully) remain on store shelves for more than a month, so I can speak here only in general terms about the types of computers and features to look for, and how much they cost. As you narrow down your search to particular makes and models, I highly recommend that you look at current magazine reviews to help guide your final decision. Two outstanding magazines in particular are *PC Portables* (formerly *PC LapTop,* and published by L.F.P. Inc.) — which also has a Web site at www.pcportablesmag.com — and *Mobile Computing & Communications* (published by Curtco Freedom Group). These magazines specialize in publishing hands-on reviews written by real people — just like me (indeed, I've written enough of them over the years) — that often point out the odd quirks and convenience features that make one model different from another.

Identifying Your Needs

I'm the first to admit that, beyond all their utility, portable computers are cool. They represent super high-tech that, if not cheap, is at least affordable to many people. I suspect that a lot of people buy these computers not quite knowing what they're going to do with them. Nonetheless, these portable marvels can do so much that they wind up becoming indispensable companions for most people.

How will you use your notebook computer?

For many people, the main use for a portable computer is likely to be the same stuff you use a desktop machine for — word processing, spreadsheets, databases, and address books. However, in this book, I don't spend much time with those more general applications. Instead, I cover in detail some of the more specialized things that you may need to do with your portable computer, such as travel, put on presentations, or communicate via phone lines from around the world.

If you're setting out as a road warrior, a computer address book — known more formally as *contact management software* — should be one of your first software acquisitions. Act! from Symantec, Ecco Pro from NetManage, and GoldMine from GoldMine Software are the most well-known contenders in this category. These programs also include calendar features that help you keep your schedule of appointments on your computer, and some can even automatically schedule meetings with coworkers. Microsoft also includes similar software, called Outlook 97, with their Office 97 suite.

If you use a contact manager, periodically copy your address book file to a floppy disk and keep it in a separate place from your notebook computer, just in case the unthinkable happens.

If scheduling appointments and keeping track of names and telephone numbers are actually your main uses for a portable computer, then you're an excellent candidate for a smaller, pocket-sized model. Though not nearly as versatile as large notebook machines, almost all of the pocket-sized computers have good contact management software, and some can retrieve e-mail over the phone line, or even work as pocket pagers (see Chapters 7 and 21).

What brand of computer should you buy?

The decision you make as to what kind of computer you get ultimately has to come down to what you want to do with it, and your personal tastes and preferences. The fact is, most computers come from good brands. Sure, you can make better or worse decisions about which particular one to buy, but if it runs as promised and doesn't fall apart during the two-year life span that I think is reasonable to expect for a notebook, then don't obsess over finding the best one. No single such model exists. This market is highly competitive, and you have many choices that are all extremely similar. So base your decision on these factors:

✔ **Personal preferences.** Do you like the keyboard, pointing system, and other features? See in Chapter 2 for a more detailed discussion of features.

✔ **Warranty.** Consider the length of the warranty period, the quality of its coverage (is it a no-questions-asked approach?), who pays for shipping, and the manufacturer's reputation for honoring the warranty.

✔ **Technical Support.** Does the manufacturer offer a toll-free, 24-hour tech support line?

✔ **Status.** If you expect to use your computer to show presentations to potential clients, the brand and type of computer you're using is likely to be a frequent topic of chitchat while you're setting up. Even though you may not feel that status is an issue, your client may — just as driving someone to lunch in some beat-up hoopdie makes a different impression from a late model deluxe-interior roadster.

Don't purchase an extended warranty service plan — unless money is no object. If you do purchase one of these plans, try to buy it directly from the computer's manufacturer, rather than from a store or independent insurance company — the manufacturer has easier access to parts and knows the machine inside out.

Will the notebook computer be a main or secondary unit?

The next question you need to ask yourself is this: Is your notebook computer going to be the main computer that you rely on to do most of your work, or do you already have a desktop machine that functions as your main machine and you now want to add a notebook to your cyber empire for occasional use while traveling, or to take work home or to the library?

If your notebook (or other portable) computer is to be your main computer, then you have to be able to run all the software you may ev_r want to use on it. My usual advice is "buy for today" — meaning, if you don't know why you need some fancy feature, don't pay extra for it.

If you're starting from scratch, buying your first computer and the first software to go with it, take a look at the software packages you think that you need and see what they recommend as the minimum hardware specifications. If you know what system your software needs to run smoothly, you have a base for determining your notebook computer's specifications. However, note that you are usually best off if you get more memory and a faster processor speed than what the software engineers consider the minimum. On the minimum system, the program is likely to run sluggishly, especially if you keep several different applications open at the same time (such as if you keep a word processor, spreadsheet, and e-mail open, while playing audio CDs from the computer's CD-ROM drive).

The only really accurate way to know how much processor speed and memory constitute enough for the software you intend to run is to test that very same software up and running on another machine with comparable specifications.

If your notebook computer is your second computer and you expect to continue using a desktop machine as well, then you have many more choices. The question of whether your notebook computer should be equal to or inferior to your desktop machine in processing power cuts both ways. On the one hand, having a more powerful desktop machine to perform your most intensive computing frees you up to carry a *much* less expensive (and lighter weight) notebook. With remote computing software, explained in Chapter 13, you can even remote control the desktop machine from the notebook and perform tasks the notebook can't handle by itself — the actual *computing* takes place on your more powerful desktop, and you see what it's doing on your notebook.

On the other hand, if you work on a state-of-the-art desktop computer, you may feel that every time you use a less powerful notebook machine, it feels like you are trying to run a relay race with a garden slug. If you want to run the same applications on both a desktop and notebook computer, my advice is to get comparable specifications (processor speed and memory) on each. Using a slow machine when you are used to a desktop speed demon can leave you tearing your hair out.

In any event, if you buy a notebook computer as a second computer to work in tandem with your desktop machine, you need to think a bit about how you want them to work together. Ideally, you have a desktop and notebook computer that are both equipped with infrared communication ports (IrDA — see Chapter 2), so they can exchange data without needing any connecting wires or hookup.

Also, you generally have a much easier time if both of your computers are based on the same operating system — usually Windows 95 or Macintosh. On the other hand, for small businesses, having one computer of each type may maximize your compatibility with the outside world, and perhaps even different departments at your office, though it minimizes your compatibility between the two computers you most likely need to use.

Having two machines from the same manufacturer does not necessarily make the computers any more compatible than if you mix and match brands, as long as they are on the same operating system.

What type of portable computer should you buy?

If you're not quite sure what sort of portable computer to get, my advice — obviously generic — is to buy a notebook PC with a built in CD-ROM and floppy drive. This is today's standard issue portable computer. The standard issue may not be the smallest and lightest, but it's definitely the most versatile in terms of being able to install new software, transfer files to other computers, and run multimedia.

If size and weight are of great concern to you, however, you may want to consider the smaller subnotebook type computers, or even the pocket-sized palmtop models. You may ultimately decide to buy two portable computers to carry with you on your travels — a pocket model for keeping track of appointments and a notebook model for writing reports, e-mail, and so on (you can even exchange data between them, so that, for example, the address books on both computers are always up-to-date — see Chapter 9).

The following sections are a small trip back in history to help give you a rundown of the main characteristics that broadly distinguish the various categories of portable computers. It ain't no E-ticket ride, but it still gives me a small thrill.

Laptops

Laptop is the name given to the first generation of truly mobile computers, and it has come to have two meanings — a portable computer bigger than a notebook, or the generic category of portable computers. The earliest computers to qualify as laptops weighed around 12 pounds. In this book, I use the term *laptop* generically to denote modern notebook type computers — probably out of an old and hard-to-break habit, though you still hear the term fairly frequently.

Notebooks

As laptop computers evolved, the industry parlance began to include *note-book* to describe the new smaller, lighter units. Originally, notebook computers were supposed to have the same dimensions as a standard 8 $\frac{1}{2}$ x 11-inch page (depth and width, respectively), but the addition of CD-ROM drives has fudged this guideline a bit, and some so-called notebooks are as big as 10 x 12 inches. Most new models have built-in floppy disk drives as well as CD-ROM drives, but with some of the smaller models you only get one of these drives — sometimes they're swappable (see Chapter 2).

The keyboards on most notebook computers are full-sized, which means that the spacing between keys is the same as what you find on a desktop computer keyboard (that is, for the alphabet and number keys, but not for punctuation and cursor control). Most notebooks have a wrist rest in front of the keyboard, as shown in Figure 1-1. Notebook computer screens are usually color, with at least 640 x 480 resolution and sometimes higher. Most notebooks weigh between five and seven pounds. You may find me simply calling a notebook computer a notebook — you can be sure that I'm not talking about an actual paper notebook but rather slipping into the slang of the computer road warrior and just saying, "notebook," dig?

Subnotebooks

The term *subnotebook* was adopted to describe computers that are smaller than 8 1/2 x 11 inches, generally weigh less than five pounds, and usually have no wrist rest in front (the subnotebook body doesn't have enough room, as shown in Figure 1-2). The keyboards on subnotebooks are not always full-sized, and sometimes the amount of key travel (how far each key goes down) is limited as well. All this keyboard stuff may seem irrelevant, but it's kind of like driving someone else's car — if you switch between a desktop and a subnotebook, you may feel like you're typing with all thumbs at first.

Subnotebooks usually lack a built-in floppy disk drive — the computer, by itself, has only a hard drive, and you must attach an accessory floppy drive, usually supplied with the computer, if you want to use floppies. But sub-notebooks usually do have color screens with full 640 x 480 VGA (Video Graphics Adapter) resolution.

Figure 1-1:
These models from Toshiba and IBM have built-in floppy and CD-ROM drives, and wrist rests.

Figure 1-2:
IBM's
ThinkPad
365X (on the
left) weighs
5.9 pounds,
and
Toshiba's
mini-sized
Libretto 50
CT (a
palmtop
computer),
weighs just
1.9 pounds.

Palmtops

The *palmtop* category includes the smallest subnotebooks, with miniature keyboards and displays. Some people use the term *palmtop* to describe what I would call *pocket computers* — in my definition, a palmtop is different from a pocket computer because it has a built-in hard drive, and has the ability to run full scale operating systems such as Windows 95 (such as Toshiba's Libretto 50 CT, shown in Figure 1-3).

Pocket computers

Pocket computer is the generic way to describe what manufacturers variously call handheld PCs (HPCs), PDAs (Personal Digital Assistants), and pocket computers. These computers are all much smaller than even subnotebooks — they're intended to fit into a pocket, though with some models you'd need quite a pocket. Pocket computers never have full-sized keyboards — instead, you find the keys squished together, and if you're used to touch typing, these keyboards can be very uncomfortable for entering anything longer than short notes. The screens are usually monochrome (not color) and have less detail than larger computers, with a resolution of 320 x 240 (one-fourth the regular 640 x 480 VGA resolution found on notebooks).

Most people use pocket computers for keeping track of appointments and address books. Many pocket computers have touch-sensitive screens (allowing you to use your finger instead of a mouse or other pointing device), and most that do also allow you to jot down notes using a stylus — this feature is called *digital ink.* Some models can send and receive e-mail and faxes. The most sophisticated units, called *pen computers,* can read your handwriting and convert it to standard computer text. See Chapter 7 for more on these handheld marvels.

What platform do you want — PC versus PowerBook (Mac)?

By most estimates, more than 90 percent of notebook computers are based on what is commonly called the *PC platform* — they use microprocessors made by Intel or clones (such as AMD or Cyrix), and they are designed to run the Windows 3.*x*, Windows 95, or the older DOS operating systems from Microsoft. This overall configuration is commonly referred to as the *IBM-compatible platform,* though at this point, IBM's share of the overall market for IBM-compatible notebook computes is not very big. Other major manufacturers of IBM-compatible notebook computers include Compaq, Toshiba, Sharp, Hewlett-Packard, Texas Instruments, AST, NEC, Samsung, and Hitachi. You can also get numerous brands sold only via mail-order (that's through the *direct channel* in industry jargon), including Dell, WinBook, Gateway 2000, and Micron. All these brands — and just about every other brand of notebook computer, with one exception — run the Windows 95 operating system, which usually comes already installed. If you have an older model, your computer may run one of the Windows 95 predecessors — Windows 3.11, Windows 3.1, or DOS.

The one exception I mention in the previous paragraph is Apple. Apple's main line of notebook computers is called the PowerBook line, and these portables, (Model 3400 is shown in Figure 1-3) are based on Motorola microprocessor chips. They are designed to run the Macintosh operating system — the same operating system used in Apple's desktop computer.

Figure 1-3:
Apple
PowerBook
notebook
computers
run the
Macintosh
operating
system.
Courtesy of
Apple
Computer,
Inc.
Photographer:
John
Greenleigh.

Technologically, the PowerBook line deserves a lot of credit for the advancement of mobile computing. The innovative PowerBooks were the first to introduce the wrist-saving, and very comfortable wrist-rest design, with the keyboard pushed back, and a pointing system up front and center. This design is now pretty standard on all PC-compatible notebooks. Apple PowerBooks also pioneered the use of advanced lithium-ion battery technology, and built-in SCSI interface jacks that offer higher-speed connections and more flexibility for hooking up external devices. However, the technical details are minor, almost irrelevant factors in the decision of whether to buy a PowerBook. Primarily, the decision is based on which operating system you want to use — Windows 95 or Macintosh.

The vast majority of notebook computer buyers never even think about this choice, and just automatically buy PC-compatibles for a variety of reasons — to be compatible with office computers (which are overwhelmingly PC, not Apple), because they're already familiar with Windows software, or simply because the vast majority of available models are not Macintosh. The fact that, practically speaking, just one source for Macintosh computers exists is also a concern to some buyers, especially for corporate fleets — what would happen if Apple stopped making them? Yes, Apple has recently allowed Macintosh clones to be built, but they're expensive and mainly of interest to advanced users. Nevertheless, you have plenty of good reasons to buy a PowerBook, including:

✔ You already use a Macintosh desktop computer.

✔ You see desktop publishing, multimedia production, high-end video editing, or graphics work as your main use for the computer.

✔ You need to hook up a lot of external equipment, such as storage devices, audio/visual, or music equipment, that requires the SCSI connector.

✔ You are new to computers, and have a very good friend or relative who is guiding you and is a Macintosh devotee.

Prior to Windows 95, the Macintosh operating system had a big advantage over the DOS and Windows 3.*x* systems in that it was easier to use, and much easier to install and configure new hardware and software. That difference has almost (though admittedly, not entirely) disappeared with Windows 95, which offers fairly consistent plug-and-play installation for most new devices, such as PCMCIA/PC card accessories.

Part of the difference in ease of use stems from the fact that the PC platform is an *open standard,* meaning that anyone can copy and build devices for it. Apple, by contrast, maintains tight control over the Macintosh platform, and only recently began allowing other companies to produce Mac clones.

With extra software called SoftWindows from Insignia, you can get a Macintosh computer, such as a PowerBook, to run Windows 95 software and, in essence, emulate a PC. The only problem with this solution is that the extra layer of software takes its toll on the amount of time it takes to process information, so a 240 MHz PowerBook may seem to run Windows 95 only as fast as a 133 or 150 MHz native PC.

Besides the Macintosh operating system used in PowerBooks, Apple also markets another operating system for mobile computers known as the Newton operating system. Newton is used in both Apple pen-based Newton MessagePad pocket computers, and in the Apple eMate no-frills notebook computer that's aimed at the educational market. I cover both of these alternatives in more detail in Chapter 7.

Shopping Tips for the Value-Conscious

If you have unlimited resources to spend and want to burn through a lot of money quickly, you've come to the right place — my address is in the back of the book and you can make all checks payable to Cliff Roth. On the other hand, if you want to at least get *something* for your money, mobile computing provides you plenty of opportunity to pay through the nose for equipment that quickly becomes obsolete. You pay the most money when:

- ✔ You insist on getting the absolute newest and fastest microprocessor chip available
- ✔ You demand an extremely high-resolution active matrix LCD (Liquid Crystal Display) screen
- ✔ You want the absolute fastest CD-ROM drive available
- ✔ You need the computer loaded with very large amounts of memory (RAM)

On the other hand, if you're interested in getting the best value for your money, here's my advice:

- ✔ **Buy a notebook equipped with the third or fourth fastest processor chip currently available.** This alone can save you several thousand dollars, and the difference in performance, for many applications such as word processing, is negligible. Plus, if you already have a desktop computer and you can use remote computing software (see Chapter 13), you can come close to the processor speed of your desktop.
- ✔ **Don't be sucked in by fancy technical frills you don't understand and don't need.**

- ✔ **Make do with a humble hard drive size.** (Compared to whatever sizes are commonplace in desktop units, notebooks are perennially a step behind in the base-unit hard drive size.)

- ✔ **Closely compare the technical specs of the models you're considering, and choose the brand that is less expensive for a given set of specs.**

- ✔ **Consider buying a mail-order brand** — but be sure that they offer a money back guarantee, offer a decent warranty, and are reputable.

- ✔ **Don't purchase an extended warranty** — unless it covers physical damage from drops and mishandling.

A Word about Obsolescence

How long can you expect your notebook computer to last? The answer probably depends on how badly you want to stay current with the latest computer technology. From the point of view of being able to run the most recent operating system release and the newest software, figure about two to four years. I can guarantee you that your notebook computer will start showing signs of age, in terms of its specifications, within a year after you get it. The ongoing introduction of new computer processor chips — ever faster, ever more powerful — is relentless.

If you adopt the attitude that you're probably going to replace your notebook computer every two years just to stay up-to-date, then the way you choose a computer may change. For one thing, you don't need to be as concerned about the long-term durability of the computer. For another, you can abandon the mindset that even though a humbler computer may satisfy your needs today, you want to buy something more powerful so that it will be there for you when you need it tomorrow. I believe in *just-in-time* computer buying — if you don't know why you need more power, you probably don't need it, and by the time you do, it will be a lot cheaper.

Knowing How to Adjust

No, I'm not talking about working out the kinks in your back — I'm talking about using the adjustments you're given to make your notebook computer appear better. I cannot tell you how many times I've seen people comment that someone else's computer seemed better for some reason, but the thing they were admiring was something they could just as easily do on their own computer — like making the pointer appear bigger.

If you are shopping for a computer in a store, understanding how to make these adjustments can help you distinguish between those things that really make different models different and the minor differences in the way they happen to be set on the display model. If you already have a notebook computer, getting it adjusted right may spare you the expense of junking it for a new one.

The most important adjustments of all are the screen viewing angle, the contrast and brightness controls, the volume, and the computer's suspend mode — I cover these adjustments in Chapters 2 and 4. Note that no notebook screens — not even the best — look good in bright outdoor sunlight. Having familiarity with these adjustments can mean the difference between seeing the screen, or having it appear totally washed out.

Understanding how to adjust the pointing system also makes a big difference in how easy using the computer appears to be. One of the most common complaints about touchpad pointing systems is that they're hard to control — the pointer seems to move wildly around the screen like a chicken without a head. You can slow it down — in Windows 95, you find this adjustment in the Mouse section of the Control Panel (see the next tip to find out how to get there).

If you're having trouble seeing your pointer (arrow) on the screen, you can make it appear bigger and add trails so that when you move it you can see the motion more distinctly. I highly recommend enabling the mouse trails feature for just about all notebook computers. If you're working in Windows 95, follow these steps:

1. **Choose Start⇨Settings⇨Control Panel to get to the area of Windows 95 where most of the basic adjustments to the computer itself are made.**

   A panel appears with numerous icons for things like printers, modems, mouse, keyboard, and so on.

2. **Find the mouse icon and double-click it.**

   A new dialog box appears that says Mouse Properties along the top and has several tabs, one of which says Pointers.

3. **Click the Pointers tab.**

   Near the top is a selection for Scheme.

4. **Click the down-arrow button just to the right of this selection, and scroll down the list until you find Windows Standard (extra large), as shown in Figure 1-4.**

   This scheme makes the mouse arrow appear bigger (and easier to see).

Figure 1-4:
Selecting
the
Windows
Standard
(extra large)
Scheme
makes the
arrow
appear
bigger on
your
notebook's
screen.

5. **Click the Motion tab near the top of the panel to add trails to the pointer.**

6. **Click the box next to the phrase** Show Pointer trails, **to put a check mark in the box.**

   This adds the trails to the mouse arrow.

7. **Drag the slider immediately beneath** Show Pointer trails **all the way to the right, toward the word** Long, **to make the trails appear most prominently.**

8. **Click OK to save the settings.**

   The dialog box closes.

9. **Click the x in the box in the upper right corner of the Control Panel to close the Control Panel.**

Chapter 2

What to Look for When Buying a Notebook

- -

In This Chapter

▶ Figuring out which features matter to you

▶ Choosing which type of screen is best for you

▶ Comparing the different mouse pointing systems

▶ Do the connections in back of the computer matter?

- -

*I*f you're like me, you do your research after you already made your big purchase, which means you very likely just bought a new notebook computer and are now looking here to figure out what you got (or didn't get, as the case may be). If you're actually reading this prior to making a purchase decision, fantastic! I hope this section helps you muddle through all the terminology and choices you face in purchasing a notebook computer.

The few things this chapter does not cover in much detail are battery, AC adapter/charger, and power management information, which may all significantly influence your purchase decision. Batteries and adapter/chargers are so varied and fun to read about that they get their own chapter, Chapter 3. Power management issues and the various types available are covered in Chapter 4.

The Spiritual Side of Choosing a Notebook Computer

Before you dive into all the technological mumbo jumbo that the various manufacturers use to confuse their customers and occasionally tout their products, let me first make a few points that speak more to the personal, spiritual side of buying a notebook computer.

✔ **The perfect computer is a modern myth.** The industry offers too many similar choices for just one model to be right for you.

✔ **How long your new computer lasts is probably more dependent on your need to stay up-to-date than on how advanced a model you buy today.** Even a computer with the most advanced processor chip stays top-of-the-line for only a few extra months — just until the manufacturers release new models. My advice is to buy the computer power you need for today and then buy a new computer when you need additional power to do your work.

✔ **Be careful if you buy an unknown mail-order computer.** Look for sturdy construction, covers for the jacks and ports in the back, a solid feel, and a money-back guarantee, and always pay by credit card to protect yourself in case of a dispute.

✔ **The advantages of buying brand-name equipment can in some cases be an illusion.** Sometimes the biggest companies price their products very aggressively to gain market share. Sometimes you get an integrated package with audio, modem, and other built-in devices that already have everything installed and working reliably and with great tech support. However, the biggest companies have been known to produce shoddy merchandise, and sometimes their customer support involves waiting for long periods of time.

✔ **Take manufacturer claims of upgradability with a grain of salt, especially for microprocessor chips.** Designing equipment for connecting to devices that don't yet exist is very difficult. Two exceptions are memory upgrades and hard drive replacements. However, the procedures for upgrading are not any fun, so I advise you to get as much memory and as big a drive as you think you need.

Size and Weight, Size and Weight, Size and Weight

They say that only three things matter in real estate: location, location, location. For notebook computers, the only three things that matter are bulk, bulk, bulk. Of course, saying that only bulk matters is a bit of an exaggeration, but look at it this way: All notebook computers are about some degree of compromise — you sacrifice a bit of what you get with a desktop machine to make it fit in a small, lightweight, portable box.

Of course, only you can decide how much of a premium you're willing to pay for a smaller, lighter computer — both in terms of cost and in sacrificed features. Most people end up buying notebook computers that are considerably bigger and heavier than the absolutely smallest models. Just how much extra bulk you're willing to accept in your notebook computer may depend on numerous factors — not the least of which is who is paying for it, how much computer you can afford, and what features you can't sacrifice for lighter weight. Here are some other key questions to keep in mind:

- ✔ **How often do you expect to carry the computer?** If you need to carry the computer only from rental cars to airplanes to hotel rooms to rental cars to airplanes, you can probably accept a considerably heavier computer than, say, if you plan to trek through Nepal for a month and use the computer to keep a diary.

- ✔ **How much do you expect to use the computer when you're lugging it along?** I have several times taken a computer along on a trip to a convention in Las Vegas, ambitiously thinking I'd get some work done. Sitting on the plane going home, I'd realize I never once even turned the computer on.

- ✔ **How important is the size of the display?** Generally speaking, a computer with a bigger screen will be bigger (and heavier) than a comparable model with a smaller display.

- ✔ **How important is the quality of the display?** Active matrix screens weigh more than comparably sized dual-scan models and use up the battery faster. But the picture looks clearer, due to active matrix's superior contrast ratio, and is more visible when using the computer outdoors during the day. Passive matrix screens look more washed out — kind of milky — when compared with active matrix.

- ✔ **How long do you expect to need to run the computer on battery power before you can recharge?** If you anticipate using your mobile computer on long transatlantic and coast-to-coast flights, you're probably a candidate for a notebook computer that lets you keep two batteries installed at the same time. See Chapters 3 and 4 for more about batteries and power management.

- ✔ **How much does a difference such as five pounds versus seven pounds matter to you?** Sometimes the additional features you get with a slightly heavier notebook computer far outweigh (no pun intended) the advantages of a lighter model.

Remember to include the size and weight of the battery and AC adapter/ charger in your consideration of each computer model. See Chapters 3 and 4, which cover battery issues and power management in depth.

The Usual Suspects

Besides the aspects of a notebook computer that are really different from desktop models such as the size, weight, display type (all covered in this chapter), and battery technology (covered in Chapter 3), your purchase decision may be influenced by many of the concerns relevant to all computers. I'm talking about features that every computer salesperson thinks will hook you into buying his or her computer — things like the processor speed and memory, and a few confusing acronyms like PCMCIA and CD-ROM. In this section, I tell you what they all mean. Read on if you want to tell the salesperson to sell you the computer *you* want instead of the one he or she thinks is cool.

Processor

Also called the *CPU* (Central Processing Unit), *microprocessor,* or *computer chip,* the processor is the electronic brain that runs the whole show. Most current notebook PCs use Pentium processor chips or their equivalents. Earlier generations of processor chips, in order of descending power, include the 486, 386, 286, and 8086 series — these numbers were designated by Intel, the biggest computer chip manufacturer. In fact, the Pentium is just the 586 chip after Intel attached a nifty trademarked name to it. Intel, however, is not the only chip manufacturer, and you may run into a variety of 586 chips that don't bear the trademarked Pentium name. AMD is Intel's main competitor, and their K6 processor chip is considered by some pundits to be better than the state-of-the-art Intel Pentium II with MMX chips (see the Technical Stuff that follows). Apple PowerBook computers use the Motorola PowerPC line of microprocessor chips. The pocket computers discussed in Chapter 7 usually use simpler RISC-based processors from various other brands. (RISC stands for Reduced Instruction Set Computing.)

Intel's MMX technology is an addition to its Pentium microprocessor chips that improves the performance when running multimedia applications. The improvement is very slight when running existing software that was not written with MMX in mind. However, as new software is written especially for MMX, experts say that you can expect about a 50 percent improvement in performance when running multimedia. If you do mostly stuff like word processing and spreadsheets, MMX doesn't make any difference.

Processors within a given generation (say, for example, all the various Pentium chips) are rated by their speeds, measured in megahertz (MHz). The speed simply refers to the number of individual computations the computer can process in a minute, and thus how quickly the computer responds to your actions. The fastest chips usually appear in new desktop computers several months before they're available in notebook computers. When new, faster chips first come out, you pay a considerable premium for them — the cost of the computer may rise as much as $1,000 if it includes the latest chip, which may even be as little as 30 percent faster than the next fastest model. (As I write this book, Pentium chips range in speed from 90 MHz to 300 MHz, and PowerPC chips go up to 300 MHz, too. By the time you read this, things will have changed!)

Chip manufacturers offer special low-power versions of their microprocessors for use in notebook computers. These are commonly referred to as *low-voltage* or *mobile microprocessors*. These chips not only use less power, but also sometimes take up less space, thus allowing for more compact notebook designs. Unfortunately, these mobile microprocessors are perennially a few months to a year or more behind the top-performing chips that are available for desktop machines. Some notebook manufacturers get around this lag by using the same chips that desktop computers use, but these chips tend to consume more power and lack the advanced power management features built into mobile microprocessors.

Faster speed is not always better in a notebook computer. In addition to the high price tag, speed usually comes at the expense of battery run time. If you are drooling for that lightning-fast latest chip, make sure that the battery life of the computer is acceptable (even the fastest chip won't make your work go so quickly that decent battery life is no longer important).

Memory

Along with processor speed, your computer's *RAM* (Random Access Memory) is one of the main features that determines overall performance. RAM is where your software gets loaded after you launch it, and the operation of the computer, in essence, is a constant back-and-forth exchange of data between the microprocessor and RAM. The more RAM you have, the more software and data you can have ready for instant access — when the computer runs out of RAM, it starts storing temporary information on the hard drive, slowing down performance. Having more RAM also speeds up operations where the computer must sift through a lot of data, such as when running database software.

RAM is measured in units called megabytes, or MB for short (1 megabyte equals a million bytes and is just a measure of the invisible information units flowing through your computer). Most notebook computers currently come with 16MB of RAM; older models have 4MB or 8MB. 16MB is generally considered the minimum to run Windows 95 properly, and 32MB is becoming quite common as this book is being prepared. Most notebooks have slots for adding more RAM — you can typically add up to 40, 64, or 80MB. Some computers use standard inline memory modules (the same type used in desktop machines) for this upgrade, but most use special modules offered uniquely for the particular computer model.

EDO RAM (EDO stands for Extended Data Output) offers faster speed, compared to non-EDO RAM — meaning the microprocessor can get information in and out of memory faster.

You're always best off buying as much RAM at the time of initial purchase as you think you'll ever need — yes, you can always add more later, but the project can be a hassle. Besides the trouble of installing it, you may have problems just finding a place that sells the kind of memory modules your notebook uses. And though I generally recommend buying only what you need for today, additional RAM is pretty cheap and may affect overall performance much more than slight differences in processor speeds.

So how do you know how much RAM you need? Keeping numerous applications open at the same time requires having more memory available. You also want more memory if you need to run graphics or multimedia programs. Word-processing and spreadsheet programs can usually get by with the minimum widely recommended memory for an operating system — meaning, the minimum that most experts agree on, which is 16MB for Windows 95, though Microsoft claims 8 is enough. You may want to ask knowledgeable friends or business associates how much they think is sufficient — especially if they are already running the same kind of software that you intend to use.

Disk drives

All notebook computers incorporate a hard drive. For notebook computers, hard drive capacity, which is always on the increase, is in the ballpark of one to two *gigabytes* (or *GB* for short — 1GB equals a billion bytes) at the time I write this book. Besides capacity, hard drives vary in speed, that is, how quickly they can access the information you need. As with microprocessors, the hard drives available for notebook computers are usually a bit behind what you can get for desktop machines. The challenge of miniaturizing and keeping power consumption low in computer components keeps the special drives used in notebook computers perennially a step behind desktops.

Besides the amount of data they can hold, the performance of disk drives is also measured by how quickly they can access data. The faster the access, generally referred to as *seek time,* the faster your computer runs.

Most, but not all notebook computers also incorporate a standard 3¹/₂-inch floppy drive. The really small computers that have omitted the floppy drive to reduce size and weight are commonly called *subnotebooks.* You can (and often need to), of course, still use a floppy drive with a subnotebook, but you must attach it to a port on the back of the computer as an accessory.

The 3¹/₂-inch floppy drive is almost always for disks with 1.44MB capacity. Even if you do most of your computing using the hard drive, you still need the floppy to install new software (unless it's on CD-ROM) and to easily transfer files to another computer (see Chapter 9).

A small number of notebook computers have even more exotic disk drives built in, such as higher capacity magneto-optical disk drives that can store as much on a single disk as a CD-ROM. Magneto-optical technology, in general, offers much higher capacity in a size that's similar to today's floppies and CD-ROMs, and unlike recordable CD-ROMs, you can re-record on the disks over and over again. However, these drives are expensive, typically adding over $500 to the cost of the computer, and they're not compatible with other computers (unless they too have a similar magneto-optical drive — several different types exist). These disk drives can be useful if your company is involved in multimedia production, or in other situations where you may need to quickly switch between large volumes of data, but most notebook computer users can do without them.

One new notebook innovation that you may want to consider, however, is the built-in Zip disk drive. Some notebook models offer this as an option for the bays where you can also install a floppy drive, CD-ROM, or spare battery. The Zip disk format, created by Iomega, holds 100MB per disk and is widely used in desktop publishing to hold large graphics files. They're also useful for making backups of your computer's hard drive. Each blank disk costs less than $20.

CD-ROM and DVD-ROM

Though it adds a bit of bulk and costs extra, a computer with a built-in *CD-ROM* drive has a lot of advantages (CD-ROM stands for Compact Disc–Read-Only Memory — Read-Only because you typically can't save data on a CD-ROM). Of course, a CD-ROM is useful for running multimedia software, but it can also make installing new software a lot easier and quicker. Without a CD-ROM drive, you may find yourself jockeying over a dozen floppies for some applications, and in fact, some software such as the latest version of CorelDRAW! (a graphics suite) comes only on CD-ROM. In addition, many businesses, maybe yours, produce custom CD-ROMs that contain catalogs, presentations, or other data for employees.

Though CD-ROMs are read-only, you can buy special drives, called CD-ROM recorders (shortened to *CD-R drive*) or *CD burners* as they are called by those in the know, that let you save information onto a special type of compact disc called CD-Recordable (CD-R). The blank discs cost under $10 each and hold up to 650MB. You can record onto each disc only once — the recording process is permanent. Currently, to use this technology with notebook computers, you have to buy an external CD-R unit, and it usually requires a SCSI port connection (which you can add via a PCMCIA/PC card). In the future, CD-R drives may replace the current playback-only devices commonly found in notebook computers.

The main distinguishing feature of a CD-ROM drive is its access speed, expressed as a multiplier of the original audio CD speed — with numbers like 6x, 8x, 12x, and 16x.

For entertainment, you can always use your CD-ROM drive to play standard audio CDs, too. In the future, CD-ROM drives will probably be replaced by higher capacity *DVD-ROM* (Digital Video Disc–Read-Only Memory) drives — DVD-ROM drives will play not just audio CDs, but also new digital video discs as well.

Display Screens

Just about all new notebook computers come equipped with color LCD screens (some older models have black and white). LCD stands for *liquid crystal display* — a system that works by controlling whether light can pass through, or gets blocked, at hundreds of thousands of individual points, known as *pixels,* on the screen. The source of light is not the LCD panel itself: A *backlight* behind the LCD panel provides the illumination. Hence, the backlight actually controls the overall brightness of the display.

Most notebook screens have two adjustments: one for brightness and one for contrast. I prefer computers that have separate dials or sliders for each control, but many notebook manufacturers prefer to make these adjustments available via function keys. On some models, you can adjust only the contrast.

Because notebook screens are notoriously difficult to read in bright outdoor light, you may wonder why not just install a more powerful backlight to brighten up the image? The reason is that because these panels have a somewhat limited *contrast ratio* (a measure of the difference between the brightest and darkest spots in the picture), the screen image appears washed out when the backlight is too bright. As a result, the range of brightness adjustment available with most LCD screens is fairly limited.

Although the brightness adjustment goes from minimum to maximum, the contrast adjustment is not so simple. I generally find that the maximum contrast (the picture looking the least washed out) is achieved with the control set somewhere in the middle of its range — not the far end. Try adjusting the brightness first and then playing with the contrast to find the best setting.

The size and quality of the screen are major factors in the overall cost of a notebook computer. For screens of a given type, the bigger the screen size (measured diagonally), the more you pay.

Active matrix versus dual scan

LCD screens come in two different varieties: *active matrix* and *passive matrix*. Active matrix screens, also called *TFT* (Thin Film Transistor), are higher quality and more expensive than the passive matrix type. Active matrix screens have a better picture because they have a wider *contrast ratio* (the difference between the brightest and darkest areas of the screen) than passive matrix models. Active matrix screens universally look better than passive matrix (dual scan) models, but they also cost more and use up battery power at a faster rate.

Passive matrix screens are commonly called *dual scan screens,* or sometimes *DST* (Dual Scan Twisted), or *super-twisted* screens. Since their introduction, passive matrix screens have improved via *dual scan* and *super-twist* technology (the sidebar later in this section has the hideous details). The latest passive matrix LCD screens are commonly referred to as *dual scan screens.* They are less expensive and available in larger (up to 12.3 inches) sizes for much lower prices than active matrix screens. Passive matrix screens look very good, but they're just a notch below active matrix models because they have a narrower contrast range.

How does LCD work?

In a *passive matrix screen,* each pixel is sent electricity from along the edges of the display, but no actual circuitry is placed at the pixels themselves. The electric charge coming from the edge of the display triggers the liquid crystal molecules to act like shutters or prisms, and stop light (produce a black image) or act like a prism and refract light (produce a colored image). The *super-twisted LCD* twists the liquid crystal molecules (the LCD molecules look like twisted strands of hair under a microscope), which makes the shutter or prism action have higher contrast (a bigger difference between the open and closed positions) compared with the earlier LCD screens. The *dual scan* technology, introduced in the early 1990s, also improves the contrast by splitting the screen in half and refreshing the data sent to each half twice as often. These improvements make the dual-scan passive matrix screen almost, but not quite, as good as an active matrix model.

The increased contrast in active matrix screens is achieved by giving each pixel (dot of light on the screen) its own microscopic switching circuit, right next to the actual pixel. These circuits are made from thin film transistors, which is where *TFT* comes from. By putting these little electronic switches right next to each pixel, rather than at the edges of the screen, a higher amount of electricity can be used to control each pixel, and the electrical level can be maintained until the next time the screen information for that particular pixel gets refreshed, thus making the shutter action of the liquid crystal molecule even more effective.

You can get many notebook computer models with either type of screen — paying extra for the active matrix version is just like ordering a bigger hard drive. Is the active matrix screen worth the extra money given how you intend to use your computer? That's something only you can decide. Here are some questions and points to keep in mind:

- ✔ **What's your overall price range?** In my view, you hardly have any reason to skimp on the display if you plan to buy a $4,000 computer, but in the under $2,000 price range, the difference between active matrix and passive matrix becomes a much more significant part of the overall cost.

- ✔ **Do you expect to mostly do word-processing and spreadsheet work in indoor situations, such as on a plane or in a library?** Passive matrix screens are perfectly adequate for most business and writing work.

- ✔ **Will you be using the computer just for yourself, or will you be showing the screen to other people (such as when making presentations to potential clients)?** You may want to get an active matrix screen to be sure that you can show off the best-quality images and charts.

- ✔ **Do you plan to look at many photographs or video clips? Do you plan to use your notebook for graphics work?** If so, the high-quality images you get with active matrix screens may be worth the extra cost.

- ✔ **How much do you want to be able to use your computer outdoors?** Active matrix screens are slightly more readable and tend to look less washed out when viewed in the midday sun.

Screen resolution and color depth

Besides the size of the screen and the type of LCD technology (active or passive, as I describe in the previous section), the *resolution* and *color depth* are the other major factors that determine screen quality.

Most color LCD computer screens built into notebooks have standard VGA (Video Graphics Adapter) picture resolution — that's 640 × 480 *pixels* (individual dots of light on the screen). But many models have higher resolution, such as Super-VGA (SVGA for short), which displays 800 × 600 pixels. The higher resolution of SVGA displays allows you to work with smaller fonts (typefaces), thus fitting more text on the screen at a time. In addition, SVGA shows pictures and graphics with finer detail.

Like conventional computer screens, you can also operate a *high-res* (another name for SVGA) LCD monitor at the lower 640 × 480 resolution. However, unlike conventional CRT monitors (Cathode Ray Tube, the type that look like TVs), a high-res LCD may look pretty funky at the lower resolution setting. (You can find complete instructions for changing your display resolution in Chapter 17.) Also, note that some multimedia CD-ROMs do not fill the entire screen when they run on an 800 × 600 LCD.

Don't attempt to set the LCD to a higher resolution than it is capable of handling, or you may end up in a situation in which your picture appears all messed up and you have to call for service.

The *color depth* is perhaps the most subtle aspect of picture quality. Color depth refers to the number of different colors the screen is capable of producing. Any color LCD screen can give you red, but one with more color depth can give you brick red, candy apple red, and cherry red, instead of a mix of red, orange, and black dots to approximate the more flavorful shades. Although just about all conventional CRT computer monitors are capable of displaying about 16 million colors, most notebook LCD screens have more limited capabilities. Some early color LCD screens were limited to 16 or 64 colors, but most newer notebooks have screens with at least 256 colors, and commonly 32,000 or 65,000 colors. The very best LCD screens can match a traditional monitor and deliver 16 million colors, but these screens come at a higher cost than screens with less color depth.

What difference does the number of colors make? For word processing or spreadsheets, it doesn't make much difference at all — in fact, 16 colors is usually sufficient. However, the color depth (number of colors) makes a big difference in how good images, especially photographs, look.

Most notebook screens have the same shape as a traditional desktop computer screen, which is a third wider than it is high (in techno-speak, that's a 1.33:1 *aspect ratio*). Some older screens mystically appear more squished, even though the standard 640×480 VGA display has the same aspect ratio of 1.33:1.

As the next generation of TV sets is going wide-screen, so too may notebooks. Sharp Electronics, which makes more than half of all the screens used in notebook computers, recently introduced a new wide-screen notebook computer design, shown in Figure 2-1, with 1024×600 pixels — you can use it, for example, to simultaneously view two documents side by side, making cut and paste operations easier.

Bad pixels

Manufacturers of LCD screens have a hard time getting every single pixel to work properly — in tech parlance, this is called the *yield problem*. Notebook computer displays usually have a few (typically between two and ten) *bad pixels* — these are tiny points of detail on the screen that don't work. Typically, they're stuck in the illuminated mode, which means you usually detect them only when you look at a nearly all-black screen.

Manufacturers have a complex rating system for determining how many bad pixels they allow to go out on each screen. A bad pixel in the center, for example, is considered a bigger defect than a bad pixel in the corner.

Figure 2-1:
Sharp's
innovative
WideNote
provides a
wider
screen
that's
perfect
when you
want to
view two
documents.

Just as certain upscale restaurants may get first crack at the freshest fish in the fish market, certain notebook computer manufacturers may get better-quality screens due to their clout, or they may agree to pay more for screens with fewer defects (and pass on the extra cost to you, of course).

Do Touch! (Keyboard Feel Is Everything)

The feel, or *action,* of a computer keyboard is the main way that two computers with otherwise identical specifications can have vastly different personalities. As a professional writer, I sometimes spend entire days typing away on a notebook computer, so keyboard feel is of particular importance to me.

You really need to spend time with a computer to get a good idea of how well you like the keyboard. Besides the feel of the keys themselves, you need to consider the comfort of the wrist rest and the ease of use of the pointer device. If the front edge of the computer, where your wrists rest (except on the smallest subnotebook models) is not gently curved, your wrists may ache at the point where they contact the edge of the computer's case.

For those concerned about ergonomics issues — and I count myself among this crowd — the fact that the keyboard and display are joined at the hip, so to speak, means you can never precisely adjust your posture when using a notebook the way you can with a desktop system, because you almost always end up looking down rather than straight across at the screen. If this posture bothers you (it will if you do a lot of writing), I highly recommend that you purchase an external keyboard for your notebook. Then — at least when you're not traveling with it — you can prop up the notebook on a shelf or a stack of books so that the screen is a foot or more higher than the external keyboard. Incidentally, while on the subject of health and safety, I should point out that one potential advantage of notebook computers, over desktops, is that unlike traditional CRT (desktop) monitors, the LCD display screens emit no X-rays.

I like keyboards that have a distinctive click to them as they go down. I like to both feel the click in my fingers, and hear it. I absolutely hate keyboards that attempt to make an electronic clicking sound each time a key is depressed — these systems lack the tactile feedback, which is just as important as the sound.

Besides tactile and audible feedback, keyboards also vary in the size and layout of the keys, as well as the amount of key travel. In my opinion, keyboards with the best feel have *full travel* keys, that is, they go down the same distance as the keys on a typical desktop computer keyboard — 3 mm. In order to save space, many notebook computers have keys that don't travel the full 3 mm.

Almost all notebook computers claim to have a *full width* keyboard, but take this claim with a grain of salt. Yes, such keyboards usually have the same size letter and number keys, with the same spacing, as you find on a full-sized desktop keyboard. But note that just about all the other keys are squished together. In particular, the space bar along the bottom is considerably shorter than what you find on a desktop keyboard in order to create space for the Ctrl and Alt keys (see Figure 2-2).

Pay particular attention to the size of the Shift and Enter keys. If these keys are too small, you may find yourself accidentally hitting other nearby keys. Another consideration is whether the keyboard has Ctrl and Alt keys on both the left and right sides of the space bar. Other notebook computer keyboard variables include the location of the cursor control keys; the Page Up, Page Down, Home, and End keys (sometimes these are combined with cursor control arrow keys); and the Insert and Delete keys.

I personally hate keyboards that place the Insert key next to anything important, because I inevitably accidentally press it and then find myself typing over something else.

Figure 2-2:
Keyboard
layout can
vary
considerably
among
notebook
computers.
Notice the
differences
in the space
bar and
Shift keys.

Shift key

Space bar

To save space, notebook computer keyboards don't have separate numeric keypads on the right as desktop keyboards do. However, for the die-hard bean counters out there, almost all notebook keyboards incorporate an *embedded numeric keypad.* When you hit the *Num Lock* button, a group of letter keys located below the 7, 8, and 9 keys (on top) become number keys. The letter U becomes 4, I becomes 5, O is 6, J is 1, K is 2, L is 3, and M is 0. These numbers are usually marked in a different color on the keys.

As with the display, the need to have a full-width keyboard puts a certain physical limit on how small a notebook computer can be made. IBM's butterfly keyboard design, which unfolds for use, offers an innovative way around size limitations, but even IBM's butterfly computers are clearly in the subnotebook camp. Ultimately, the keyboard, more than anything else, distinguishes these notebook and subnotebook models from the smaller palmtop, PDA (Personal Digital Assistant), organizer, and handheld PC category, which I cover in Chapter 7.

Your Pointing Device

Most notebook computers incorporate a built-in pointing device to take the place of the mouse that you use with most desktop computers. Your preference for a particular pointing device should be a big factor in your decision to purchase a particular notebook computer model. I give you a rundown of the main systems, with my subjective comments, but your own feelings about the ease of use and comfort of each device are your best guide.

In some of these sections, I mention particular features that you can turn on or off in the Control Panel. You can get to your pointer features with these steps:

1. **Choose Start⇨Settings⇨Control Panel.**

2. **Double-click the mouse icon, or the icon that represents your particular pointer device, if one exists.**

3. **Enable or disable any features you want to customize.**

TrackPoint

TrackPoint is my favorite type of pointing device. It looks like a little rubber eraser from the back end of a pencil, located in the middle of the keyboard, between the G and H keys (see Figure 2-3). It works a lot like a joystick — you push it up, down, and sideways as needed, and the arrow (cursor) floats across the screen accordingly. Two buttons located below the space bar function as the left and right mouse buttons.

Figure 2-3:
The
TrackPoint
pointing
system
found on
many
models is
my personal
favorite.

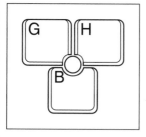

I like the TrackPoint because I don't have to take my hands off the keyboard. And unlike other pointer systems, I find that I rarely move it by accident. Many computer models come with different colors and textures for the rubber nub.

Trackball

The trackball is a very comfortable, easy-to-use system consisting of a ball that rolls around and moves the cursor in the corresponding direction. Actually, I like trackballs so much that I use one on my desktop machine instead of a mouse. On notebook computers, the trackball is usually located just below the spacebar. You use your fingers to move the cursor, and either thumb to rotate the trackball. As with touch pad systems, the left and right mouse buttons are usually located just in front of the trackball (closer to the front edge of the computer).

Trackballs feel great when you first use them, but over time they can get gritty, and the movements of the cursor can become irregular or sluggish. The problem is that dirt gets into the trackball mechanism. You can usually remove the ball from the mechanism and clean things out. If you're not extremely careful, though, you may knock out a tiny spring or other vital mechanical component when you clean out a trackball.

Because they require maintenance (cleaning), and because they are somewhat expensive, trackballs are becoming less popular with notebook manufacturers.

Touch pad

The touch pad has rapidly become the most common pointing system in notebook computers, though personally I'm not too fond of it. Manufacturers like the touch pad system because it has no moving parts, nothing to clean out, is cheap to make, and less prone to breakdowns than many other systems. The pad is typically a rectangle, shaped like the notebook's screen, and measures about 3 inches diagonally. You drag your finger across the pad to move the cursor wherever you want it to go on the screen. Like any pointing system, it takes some getting used to, at first.

The place where you put your finger down on the pad becomes the point where you pick up the arrow (cursor) — it's not where you want it to end up. You have to keep your finger pressed down and drag it to the place where want to click. Therefore, you want to leave room for your finger to move. If you need to move the cursor up to the top of the screen, for example, then start you finger near the bottom of the pad so you have room to move up without hitting the edge.

I have a zillion reasons why I don't like the touchpad. I find that I constantly hit the edge of the pad and have to let go of the cursor, reposition my finger, and then pick up the cursor again to move it more. Just as with an ordinary mouse, you can adjust the sensitivity so that the pointer moves further with slighter touch. But when I adjust it like that, I find that I lose control, and it moves wildly.

But my repositioning complaint is minor compared to my biggest gripe: I tend to lose data with the touch pad when my hand accidentally brushes against it as I type. (I think that I inadvertently highlight things, and then the next character I type deletes them.) This problem actually happened while writing this book (see whether you can find missing chunks of text).

Though the trend is clearly towards the touch pad becoming almost universal in notebook computers, a few holdouts exist among the major manufacturers, including, most notably, IBM. Some mail-order companies, such as

WinBook (see the Appendix) offer a choice of pointing systems when you order their computers — the choices include TrackPoint, trackball, or touch pad.

A touch pad feature usually installed as the default lets you click the mouse button from the touch pad by quickly tapping on the pad so that you don't have to remove your finger from the pad to make a menu selection. Below the touch pad are regular left and right mouse buttons. I highly recommend that you disable this touch pad tapping feature and use only the regular buttons. See the beginning of this section for instructions.

The problem with this feature is that it's very easy to accidentally trigger. I have found myself accidentally activating all sorts of obscure features in my word processor, because my hand brushed against the pad for an instant.

Another touch pad feature, also commonly set up as the default, and that can also be confusing, is called the *virtual scroll bar*. The right edge of the pad mimics the scroll bar you find in many software programs, allowing you to easily move up or down through text or a spreadsheet without having to move the cursor over to the onscreen scroll bar. If you find while you use the touchpad that you suddenly start moving up or down through text, you probably touched the virtual scroll bar by accident.

No Noise Is Good Noise

Notebook computers tend to make noise in three distinct ways:

- ✔ From the clicking of the keys as you type
- ✔ From the whirring of the cooling fan that keeps the guts cool
- ✔ From the beeps and alarms that you hear when the computer boots up, and then, most annoying (but perhaps helpful), as the battery charge gets low

Some people like to hear a distinct click each time a key goes down — especially touch typists who don't look at the screen. But if you are a student using a notebook computer to write up research in a library, a computer with a noisy keyboard may get you kicked out.

Similarly, some people may love to have a loud beeping alarm go off when their battery still has ten minutes of juice left. Sure, some may love it.

But let me tell you about the times when I'm working while my 2-year-old son Gerry is napping ten feet away. Having a loud low-battery warning alarm go off at 110 decibels (okay, I'm exaggerating) is the last thing I want my computer to do. For me, a more gentle visual warning, like a flashing light, is enough.

Unfortunately, you have no way to fairly judge the musical subtleties of a computer in a crowded computer superstore. Also note that sometimes a computer's fan, the musical nuance of which can be quite loud and unpleasant depending on the model, sometimes doesn't come on until after an hour or two of use.

Connections and Card Slots

The back of most notebook computers is typically filled with about a half-dozen special connectors of various shapes, sizes, and genders (plugs or jacks). These connections, sometimes called *ports,* provide physical links to external devices such as keyboards, monitors, telephone lines, and a host of other hardware options (see Figure 2-4). Some computers also have a new style of wireless connection that uses infrared light, much like a remote control for a television, to connect to external devices. Most notebooks also have *PCMCIA* (Personal Computer Memory Card International Association) slots, also called *PC card* slots for adding a modem, network interface, or other special-function cards.

Keyboard, keypad, mouse

Most notebook computers let you hook up an external keyboard and mouse or other pointing device via a small keyboard jack whose technical name is *PS/2 style keyboard port.* This feature is especially useful if your computer's keyboard is not that comfortable, and you do a lot of writing from a fixed location such as a vacation home or a home office. Students who want the portability of a notebook for library work as well as a comfortable home office may find adding a keyboard a big help (that's how this book was written — using my trusty IBM external keyboard plugged into a variety of notebook models). A full-sized keyboard can be as little as $20 at many office supply stores.

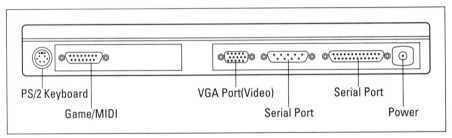

Figure 2-4:
The rear panel of a typical computer showing the various ports.

PS/2 Keyboard

Game/MIDI

VGA Port(Video)

Serial Port

Serial Port

Power

If you do a lot of number crunching, you may alternately want to use the computer's keyboard jack to plug in a numeric keypad. Though a bit clunky as a dangling attachment to take on the road, the numeric keypad offers a very good solution to the lack of calculator-style number keys on notebook computers.

Some computers have a separate jack for hooking up a mouse. Technically this jack, which looks identical to the keyboard jack, is called a *PS/2 style mouse port*. If a notebook computer has only one jack for both keyboard or mouse, you can usually hook up an adapter that provides separate connections for each. Alternatively, you can opt for a mouse with a serial port connection.

If you really want to expand on this idea of adding a keyboard and mouse to your notebook, take a look at Chapter 6, which covers *expansion stations*.

Serial port

The serial port is useful for hooking up to external modems, an external pointing device, and for connecting to a zillion and one other oddball computer devices like pocket organizers, bar code readers, and video editing controllers.

The serial port gets its name from the fact that it sends and receives data one bit at a time, in a series. It is thus inherently less efficient than the parallel port, which moves data in chunks of eight bits at a time.

The serial ports you find on laptop computers are almost all the more compact 9-pin variety. Many modems and other devices use a larger 25-pin connection. You can readily adapt from 9-pin to 25-pin via a standard adapter sold at all computer stores (it costs about $5). The device you want to use may even come with its own adapter.

When you buy a 9-pin to 25-pin serial port adapter, be sure that it is the right gender — a male *plug* has pins, a female *socket* (or *jack*) has holes — for the specific connection you need. Unlike most of the other connections on the back, the serial port built into most notebook computers is a male connection.

Though the vast majority of notebook computers have just a single serial port, you may run across a few models with two. Most notebook users probably don't even need one, let alone two, but advanced users may get into a situation where they need to add multiple extra hardware devices. For instance, if you expect to use your notebook computer for presentation, music, or video applications, you may need to use any number of specialized devices that require a serial port connection. Fortunately, many devices intended specifically for notebook computers are being reconstructed as PC card (PCMCIA) connections, thus alleviating the need for additional serial ports. I discuss PC cards (PCMCIAs) a bit later in this chapter, and in full detail in Chapter 23.

Printer port

The printer port has two aliases — *parallel port* and *Centronics port*. Both mean the same thing, though you should know that Centronics, the company that helped standardize the parallel port, also makes other connectors. The parallel port is capable of transferring data at faster rates than the serial port (8 bits at a time as opposed to 1 bit at time).

The parallel port is nearly universal for printer connections with the one exception of Macintosh computers. Also, because of its higher speed, the parallel connection is common on many other optional accessories. These include

✔ external disk drives (such as Iomega Zip disks)

✔ scanners (including portable business card models)

✔ audio expansion systems (powered speakers)

✔ tape backup devices

✔ data transfer software (such as LapLink — see Chapter 9)

✔ multimedia and MIDI music devices

Many of these same devices can be hooked up other ways — external disk systems, such as Iomega's Zip drives, for example, comes in three versions: parallel port, SCSI, or PCMCIA/PC Card. However, the parallel port is still often the way to go if you need to use a device with both your notebook and a desktop computer. Though most desktop systems use SCSI for hooking up many devices, the portable versions of these devices commonly resort to the parallel port because every single notebook PC has one. (See the "SCSI" section in this chapter for more on SCSI connections.)

Most notebooks include just one single parallel port connection. However, some notebook manufacturers offer expansion stations or port replicators that have a second parallel port, or let you install a standard desktop-sized card to add one.

Like most of the other connectors mentioned here, the parallel port has also gone through a number of revisions over the years. The newest version is called ECP/EPP (Extended Capabilitie Port/Enhanced Parallel Port), and it facilitates the fastest data transfers for external devices such as disk drives.

Infrared port (IrDA)

The *infrared port,* also called the IrDA port, uses the newest form of data communications. Amazingly, the infrared port does not use wires for the connection. Instead, IR ports use a beam of invisible (infrared) light to send data across a space, just like a television remote control. IrDA stands for Infrared Data Association, an industry trade group set up to establish standards across brands and platforms. IrDA ports are widely available on both PC and Macintosh notebook computers, as well as most pocket computers, including the Apple Newton and Sharp Zaurus lines. The IrDA port usually looks like a dark red plastic window located in the front or rear of the computer.

IrDA has thus far come in two versions. IrDA 1.0, the first, can achieve data speeds of 115 Kbps. IrDA 1.1, sometimes called *Fast IR,* is what you find on most new notebooks, and runs at a blazing 4 million bps. Most IrDAs operate over just a short range — three feet is about the maximum — and the two IrDA device windows must be facing each other.

Technically, IrDA operates serially (one bit at a time), but it runs so fast that you get data speeds near what you get with a parallel port. If you have a printer that also has an infrared port, you can print documents by simply placing a notebook computer a few feet from the printer.

IrDA ports are also fantastic for exchanging information between two notebook computers — especially two identical notebook models. You can easily keep files in sync with your collaborators, coworkers, or managers without a mess of cables. Newer versions of file exchange software such as LapLink include the ability to exchange data via infrared (see Chapter 9 for more information).

SCSI port

SCSI stands for Small Computer System Interface and has been around almost since day one of personal computing. Yet the SCSI port is still a rarity on PC notebooks, though it is standard on Apple Macintosh PowerBook computers. SCSI has two big advantages over the serial and parallel ports: First, it is fast — several versions of SCSI have appeared over the years, but the newest SCSI-II version commonly included in notebooks, is capable of speeds up to 5 Mbps. Second, SCSI devices can be daisy chained together so that up to seven different peripherals can be connected to a single port. (A *daisy chain* is a type of connection that allows you to link devices together using only one port on your computer — the first device in the chain connects to the computer, and then the second device to the first device, and so on.) SCSI connections are commonly used for tape drives, external hard drives, scanners, and external audio and video equipment. Fortunately, if you need to add a SCSI port to your notebook computer, you can add it with a special PCMCIA/PC card.

USB port

USB stands for Universal Serial Bus, and this new port promises to someday replace many of the other ports on the computer — possibly all of them. The USB port itself looks like a miniature horizontal strip, about the same size as a keyboard jack. But what this port can do is far more powerful: It can transfer data at a rate of 12 million bps, and one single port can connect to up to 127 different devices in a daisy chain. The very same port can thus simultaneously connect an external keyboard, mouse, printer, disk drive, and just about any other external devices you can dream up.

The USB port can thus replace the ports for keyboard, mouse, parallel, serial, and even SCSI. And unlike SCSI, which requires manually setting addresses for each device in a chain, USB has been designed from the ground up as totally plug-and-play. Just hook up another device in the daisy chain, and it is automatically configured to work with your system. You can even add and remove USB devices from the chain while everything is turned on (a feature known as *hot swappable*).

If it actually replaces the existing assortment of ports, USB may ultimately produce a big savings in rear panel real estate. Thanks to USB, pocket computers may someday be able to do everything a larger-sized notebook can do. However, for the time being, expect a USB port to appear as an addition to the usual jacks until the USB ports become widely available on external devices.

MIDI/game port

The MIDI or game 15-pin port looks like a bigger version of the serial or VGA ports and is included on many notebook computers. The game port lets you connect a joystick or similar game controller device as well as MIDI devices. MIDI stands for Musical Instrument Digital Interface and is widely used throughout the world of electronic music and recording — including keyboards, drum machines, and even tape recorders and direct-to-disk recording. MIDI is also sometimes used for synchronizing and controlling audio/video equipment in big-scale multimedia presentations.

VGA monitor port

Just about all notebook computers have an external VGA monitor port so that you can hook the computer up to a conventional CRT (TV-like) computer monitor. Most computers let you see the image simultaneously on the notebook's screen and on the external monitor, but you may need to invoke a special *simulscan* feature. Simulscan is covered in much more detail in Chapter 17, along with other display devices that hook up to the VGA monitor port, such as:

- scan converters (to display on a conventional TV)
- projection panels for use with overhead projectors
- LCD and CRT projectors

Many notebook computers have the ability to configure the VGA port to operate at higher resolution or color depth than the built-in LCD screen is capable of handling. Again, see Chapter 17 for all you need to know on external display stuff.

Video output jack

These jacks are variously called *NTSC line out, video out,* or *S-video out.* They allow you to hook the notebook computer directly to a regular TV. This feature is useful for putting on presentations, but be forewarned — the display you see on the TV set isn't nearly as sharp as the computer screen.

Technically, if you have a video output jack on a computer, it already has a built-in *scan converter,* a device that I cover in Chapter 17. The video output jack usually takes the form of an RCA-type phono jack (the same kind used for stereo equipment) that connects to the TV monitor's video input jack (usually colored yellow). Note that the TV must have *line input* jacks, in addition to the antenna jack, and that getting the audio to play through the TV speakers requires a separate hookup (see Chapter 17). Some notebooks have an S-video jack output — this hooks up to most better-quality big-screen TV sets and provides a slightly higher-quality picture signal than the standard phono jack connection.

PCMCIA/PC card expansion slots

The PCMCIA (Personal Computer Memory Interface Adapter, often shortened to PC card) expansion slot allows you to add a modem, a LAN (Local Area Network) interface, audio adapter, video capture, or numerous other devices to your notebook computer. Most notebook computers come with at least one, and often two PCMCIA slots to accommodate the various types and sizes of PCMCIA/PC cards. For a detailed description of PCMCIAs, or PC cards, see Chapter 23.

Like just about every other connection listed in this chapter, the PCMCIA/PC card slots have evolved since their introduction in the early '90s. The first version, Release 1.0, was only for memory cards, whereas versions 2.0 and 2.1 accommodate disk drives, LAN (Local Area Network) adapters, modems, and wireless devices. Version 3.0 adds support for multifunction cards, like combo LAN/modem cards. The newest feature is called *zoomed video* — this allows direct access to the notebook computer's video system and helps improve video performance when you hook up video-related devices, such as MPEG playback cards.

Proprietary connection

Some manufacturers offer their own proprietary ports for sliding the computer into a *docking* or *expansion station,* or *port replicator.* These optional accessories are covered in more detail in Chapter 6.

Telephone

Some notebook computers come equipped with built-in modems, saving you the expense of tying up one of the PCMCIA slots with a modem card. Such computers provide one or two telephone jacks built right into the computer's case. When you have two telephone jacks on your computer, one is for the fax/modem, and the other is to optionally plug in an extension phone.

Note that sometimes a computer has a phone jack but no modem inside to back it up — for example, if a built-in modem is optionally available, but you decline the option. The manufacturer may find that including the jacks on all their computers is cheaper rather than retooling different plastic cases for different models.

Audio

Many notebook computers, including just about all that also come equipped with a CD-ROM drive, incorporate a built-in audio adapter and speaker(s). Three mini-jack ($^1/_8$-inch phono) connections are usually provided:

- microphone input
- line input
- headphone output

The various jacks are usually indicated by cryptic symbols that bear a vague resemblance to the function of the jack (see Figure 2-5).

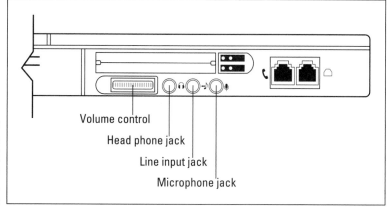

Figure 2-5:
A typical
audio
section.

Volume control

Head phone jack

Line input jack

Microphone jack

The headphone output also works as a connection to powered speaker systems.

The quality of the audio systems built into notebook computers can vary widely. Most are generically described as *16-bit* systems — although Pentium and PowerPC processors are 32-bit chips. In the world of digital audio, 16 bits is all you need unless you're involved in professional recording applications. Regular CD audio, for example, is 16 bits and by most accounts, sounds terrific.

Though most notebook computers can indeed be used as digital audio recorders, don't expect CD sound quality. Many notebook manufacturers skimp on the audio, especially on the input side — sometimes for recording, the system is only 8 bits. Though audio output is almost always stereo, the input jack(s) is often monaural. And the notebook computer's hard drive may not be fast enough to record reliably at the highest quality that the audio system theoretically permits (such as 16-bit stereo with 44.1 kHz sampling speed, which is the spec for audio CDs).

Most notebook computers have pretty wimpy built-in amplifiers, with output power typically in the ballpark of one-half to one watt, and with speakers that are rarely bigger than an inch in diameter. If your computer has a CD-ROM, and you hook up a pair of powered speakers — the same type you use with portable cassette players — you can transform it into a great little hotel room stereo system. See Chapter 18 for more on hooking up external speakers.

Besides the audio connectors, pay attention to how a computer's volume control is set up. I prefer a physical, old-fashioned dial or slider, but many computers have software controlled adjustments that require pressing function (Fn) keys or clicking an icon. In the worst case, the computer loses your volume setting every time you turn the computer off.

Windows 95 has its own software-based volume control that works in series with the computer's hardware (or function key) volume control. In other words, if either one of these volume controls is set to minimum, you don't hear anything, and to get maximum volume, you must set both to maximum. To find the Windows 95 volume control, look for an icon showing a yellow speaker, with little lines coming out of it in the lower right corner of your notebook's screen, and double-click it (or choose Start⇨Settings⇨ Control Panel and look for the Multimedia icon, double-click it, and then click the Audio tab at the top of the panel, and you see the volume control).

Power Adapter

All notebook computers sold in the U.S. come with an AC power adapter/charger. It plugs into a special jack on the back of the computer and is usually the same or a similar type to what you find on portable audio tape players and other portable equipment.

Use only the exact power adapter supplied with your computer! If you plug another AC adapter into your computer, severe permanent damage may result. If you lose or destroy your AC adapter and need to get a replacement, find one with exactly the same voltage rating, at least the same (or more) amperage, and the same polarity on the plug.

The AC adapter both recharges the battery and powers the computer directly from a wall outlet. Some can do both at the same time, but the computer usually charges much more slowly if you're using it while you charge. See Chapter 3 for more information about your computer's battery and charger.

Chapter 3
Batteries: Your Portable Lifeline

• •

In This Chapter

▶ Making sense of the different battery types

▶ Outwitting your battery

▶ Lugging an extra battery — heave ho or heave no?

▶ Judging the run time of your battery

• •

*N*othing could be more boring in a book about notebook computers than the chapter on batteries, right? What is a battery, anyway? Just a big, overweight concoction of chemical goop. Highly toxic goop, too — fortunately the dangerous stuff comes completely sealed in a thick layer of plastic that (hopefully) prevents leakage.

Batteries are not sexy like microchips, so go ahead and skip right past this chapter. You won't insult me, your humble author, because I know that, someday, sometime, you'll come running back.

Perhaps you're flying across the continent and your battery, which you were sure was fully charged, conks out 15 minutes after reaching cruising altitude. Perhaps you're riding that bullet train to New York, that great idea for the important proposal seems so clear in your mind, and you just need to jot it all down, and then poof! Good-bye.

Then you'll come running back to this chapter, you won't be cursing that microprocessor chip. And you won't be cursing your computer's memory chips, or its display screen, either. No, that little chemistry set that occupies roughly one-sixth of the entire volume, and sometimes as much as one-quarter of the weight of your computer is what you'll curse: the battery.

Battery Technology Makes a Difference

Here's a rundown of the rechargeable battery technologies available for notebook computers. I spare you the chemical details, but note that batteries have evolved on a clear path of improvements in the overall efficiency of the battery. Battery efficiency, technically, is measured by the amount of energy per unit of volume (size) and per unit of weight.

- **Nickel-Cadmium,** also known as *ni-cad* batteries, are the oldest rechargeable battery type you find in laptops. Ni-cads are the least efficient rechargeables — they're heavy and don't store as much electricity, per unit of weight and volume, as newer battery types. Ni-cads also suffer from the *memory effect* — if you recharge a battery numerous times after just half an hour of use, eventually the battery will only last for half an hour, even though it may have once had a run time of two hours. The memory effect is why you are supposed to run ni-cad batteries all the way down before you recharge them — not terribly convenient for computer use.

- **Nickel-metal hydride,** sometimes written as *Ni-mh,* is currently the most common battery technology found in laptops. Ni-mh batteries are more efficient than ni-cad, especially for their weight, and they are less susceptible to the memory effect.

- **Lithium-ion,** or *Li-ion,* is the newest and most efficient battery technology, both in weight and volume. Lithium-ion batteries are more expensive compared to the other, older technologies; however, they're not only more efficient for both weight and volume than ni-cad or nickel-metal hydride batteries, but also more intelligent — some newer technology, called *smart batteries,* have microchips built in that can report back the exact amount of remaining charge.

If both weight and run time are more important to you than cost, look for a computer that uses one of the newest lithium-ion rechargeable batteries.

Run Time: the Only Feature That Really Counts

The amount of time you can run your particular computer with its particular battery — *run time* in technical jargon — depends not just on the goop inside the battery, but on the size of the battery, the power consumption of the computer itself, and what kinds of tasks you tend to perform with it.

Run time is not as simple a measurement as, say, how long a light bulb lasts before it burns out — it's affected by quite a few different variables, like

- ✔ your processor type
- ✔ how often you access the hard disk
- ✔ how bright you set the screen
- ✔ the power used by your computer's memory chips
- ✔ how many plug-in cards you have installed
- ✔ how much of your computer's processing power is being used
- ✔ what type of power management system your computer uses
- ✔ how often you save files
- ✔ whether you use suspend/resume, or boot up each time you start
- ✔ whether you use the CD-ROM drive to listen to music while you work

These variables affect the power consumption, and thus the battery life, for your computer. You can, of course, read more about power consumption, management, suspend/resume features, and how these variables affect your computer's use of the juice in Chapter 4.

Two computers using identical batteries may get different run times due to differences in any of the factors in the previous list. But perhaps even more important are the manufacturers' decisions about what size and weight battery to use in each computer. Ultimately, the run time that each computer offers represents a decision the manufacturer makes about the computer's overall size, weight, and cost.

Unlike flashlights and portable tape players, the batteries found in notebook computers are not standardized. With a few exceptions, each manufacturer takes delight in creating a battery that it thinks is optimized for that particular computer (and totally impossible to use with any other computer) — fitting a specific space, and achieving a certain run time.

Consider a battery's run time before you buy a notebook computer. You may find battery life more important, in many instances, than many of the other features that are always mentioned in computer ads — processor speed, memory, and so on. For notebook computers, run time ranges from about $1^1/_2$ to 4 hours per charge, with most models lasting for about 2 to $2^1/_2$ hours.

Take manufacturer claims for a computer's battery life (run time) with a grain of salt. Testing procedures vary, and the manufacturers have an obvious incentive to exaggerate.

Should You Buy an Extra Battery?

Most notebook computers come supplied with a single rechargeable battery — additional batteries are optional. Should you buy one, or more?

The answer all depends on the kind of work you do, how critical your work is (that is, how bad life will be if your computer conks out before you can get to AC power), and how much run time you get from each charge. You may also want to consider the cost, size, and weight of the battery, too.

Many people, myself included, use notebook computers in places where AC power is readily available — on a dining room table, on a deck or patio, and so on. If you mostly use your notebook in places with AC power, then the one battery that comes with a portable computer should be all you need.

On the other hand, if you fly cross-country on a weekly basis, make presentations out of your office all day, or use your notebook to do lights or run electronic music gear at concerts where the length of a soundcheck can drain a battery dry, then you probably want to buy at least one additional battery just to have as an emergency backup.

If you do purchase a second battery to use as a backup, be sure to keep it charged.

Buying Extra/Replacement Batteries

You may need to buy a new battery to use as a spare, or to replace the original battery. (As a battery ages, it holds less and less charge — meaning the amount of run time you got the first time you used the computer on a freshly charged battery is longer than what you get two years down the road. You typically get 400 to 1,000 charge and drain cycles out of a rechargeable battery.)

The major battery manufacturers — Duracell and Eveready — have attempted to standardize the batteries used in notebook computers, but only a fraction of the industry has adopted the standard battery designs, shown in Figure 3-1. Most computer manufacturers prefer to create custom batteries for their laptops.

Every notebook and laptop computer manufacturer offers additional batteries as optional accessories for their computers. As an alternative, a cottage industry of mail-order replacement battery catalogs has emerged in recent years, often offering lower prices for products of very similar, if not identical, quality to the name-brand batteries. Mail-order operations are particularly helpful for owners of orphan notebook models — computers whose manufacturers have gone out of business. See the Appendix for a list of replacement battery mail-order companies.

Figure 3-1:
An example
of a
standardized
computer
battery —
it's a DR-36
(Duracell-
compatible)
battery
pack from
Eurocom.

When you switch batteries, you usually have to first power down the computer, swap the batteries, and then reboot. But if your computer is set up with the suspend-to-disk function, you can save a lot of time by invoking it before you swap the batteries, and then resuming your work almost immediately afterward. See Chapter 4 for more details.

Some notebook computers have two battery compartments, allowing you to double your run time by carrying an extra battery instead of a floppy or CD-ROM drive. See "Dual Battery Compartments" in this chapter for more details.

Almost all notebook computers (but don't take my word for it — check the instructions!) allow you to *hot swap* batteries while the computer is running on the AC adapter. When the first battery is about to run out, you plug the computer into the AC adapter. You can then remove the depleted battery and replace it with another charged-up battery. Then, by disconnecting the AC, you continue working from the second battery, without ever having to shut down and reboot — the hot swapping part refers to the fact that you never shut off the computer.

Before you hot swap batteries, always save the file you are working on, just in case the computer accidentally loses power and wipes out during the battery switchover.

If you do end up replacing your battery, you do the earth a great service if you dispose of the old, worn-out battery at a recycling center. If you dump your battery into an ordinary landfill, the battery will eventually leech its chemicals out and cause serious water pollution. Similarly, incinerating a battery puts dangerous chemicals in the air. Instead, you can turn your old batteries over to a local recycling center. In fact, many businesses specialize in tearing apart old batteries and salvaging and reusing their chemicals. Most local sanitation transfer stations and landfills offer a battery collection service. Also, the Radio Shack retail chain lets you bring in dead rechargeables to most stores for recycling.

Charging Your Battery with the AC Adapter/Charger

You have no way of "quick charging" your notebook computer's battery in just a few minutes. Most modern battery systems take roughly one to two times the amount of time to charge the battery as the battery lasts in your computer under normal use. That is, a two-hour battery typically takes two to four hours to recharge.

Every notebook computer comes with a system for recharging its battery and for running on AC power. Usually, both functions are combined into a single accessory, called the *AC adapter/charger.* About the size of a can of soda, except rectangular, adapter/chargers usually have two long wires extending from them — one that plugs into a standard AC outlet like you'd find in any room in your house, and one that plugs into the back of the computer. Sometimes one and occasionally both cords are detachable, to make packing them easier.

The size and weight of the AC adapter are important considerations when you buy a computer. For example, you wouldn't want to buy a computer because it weighs three ounces less than another model if its AC adapter weighs 25 pounds. (Don't worry — most AC adapter/chargers weigh much less.)

The AC adapter converts between the high-voltage AC (alternating current) from the wall and the low-voltage DC (direct current) the computer needs. The electricity throughout the U.S. is 110 to 120 volts AC, but in other countries it is commonly 230 to 240 volts. Fortunately, most AC adapters are designed for international use and work at 100 to 240 volts, sometimes with a little switch on the side to make the change. In addition, you may need an inexpensive plug adapter to use foreign electrical outlets — see Chapter 8 for more about traveling with your computer.

Charge status lights

How do you know when your computer's battery is fully recharged? Just about all charging systems include a status light that indicates what's going on. Sometimes this light is built onto the AC adapter unit, and sometimes it's on the computer (often next to other status lights). Occasionally, both the computer and the charger have a status light. Every manufacturer uses a slightly different system to indicate charge status, so you may have to dig into your instruction manual to figure it out. Typically, the charge status light blinks while the battery is charging, and then stops blinking (turns solid) when it's fully charged.

Some AC adapters also have a light to indicate when they are plugged into the wall outlet, even if no charging is taking place.

Charging while working

Most AC adapter systems are designed so that you can charge the battery while you are using the computer with the adapter. However, charging while you use the computer typically takes much longer than charging when the computer is turned off. If the battery normally takes two hours to recharge, you can expect it to take eight or more hours to recharge if you are using the computer at the same time.

Most AC adapter systems also recharge the battery while your computer is in the sleep mode almost as quickly as when the computer is turned off. And if your computer is in the suspend-to-disk mode, you can recharge at the same rate as when the computer is turned off. Chapter 4 gives you the lowdown on sleep and suspend modes.

Making "hot connections"

Most new notebook computers allow you to make a *hot connection* to the AC power adapter, meaning that you can plug the power cord into the back of the computer while the computer is turned on. But don't take my word for this! Some computers, especially older models, reboot if you attempt to make a hot connection, and a few models can actually be damaged by it.

Similarly, with most computers, you can unplug from AC and switch to battery power in the middle of work. Hot connecting like this is a very important feature if, like me, you're a klutz who is prone to accidentally tripping on the power cord and pulling it out from the back of the computer. If the computer lacks the ability to hot switch between battery and AC power, it reboots when the AC cord is unplugged, and you lose all your work completed since the last time you saved it.

Car Power for Your Portable

The AC outlet is not the only place where you can power your computer by plugging in. If you are in a car, you can use the cigarette lighter socket. If you spend serious time traveling by car with a notebook computer, consider powering and recharging the computer from this socket — especially if someone else is doing the driving. You have two options, summarized in the following table:

Option	*Cost*	*Advantages*	*Disadvantages*
DC to DC converter	Under $100	Compact, lightweight	Must be replaced if you change computer brands
AC power inverter	$40 to $120	Can be used with other household devices requiring around 100 watts	Bigger, heavier (Smaller units may not supply enough wattage)

How Long Does the Battery Last between Charges?

You can estimate the amount of run time you'll get from your battery three different ways:

- ✔ Testing it yourself
- ✔ Ratings published in independent magazine reviews
- ✔ Manufacturer claims

The list is organized in the order of the reliability of the information. When you test the computer yourself, you use the exact programs and work habits for which you need battery life information (you are actually using the computer to test it — the test and the use have become one — very Zen!), thus providing the most precise indication.

Battery Meters, Running on Empty

Just about all notebook computers incorporate a battery meter to tell you how much remaining run time the battery has. Typically, the battery meter takes the form of a bar graph display with five or six segments, indicating the charge. Though they look similar to a car's gas gauge, as shown in Figure 3-2, battery gauges are usually far less accurate. The meter in the figure indicates that roughly 60 percent of the charge (three out of five bars) remains.

Figure 3-2:
The bar-
graph
battery
meter.

When you first turn your computer on, the battery meter very often registers as having a near-full charge, regardless of its actual condition. Then, if the battery isn't really fully charged, a minute or two later the charge seems to quickly disappear, and a more accurate, lower reading shows up on the meter.

But even after things settle down, take battery meter readings with a grain of salt. Get to know your computer's meter, especially how much time you have left when it's down to the last one or two segments on the bar graph.

I've known notebook computers to indicate 40 percent charge level right up until nearly the very end. Then within a matter of a few minutes, their meters would go from showing 40 percent charge to signaling the low battery warning.

So-called *smart batteries* (much smarter than smart bombs, in my opinion) are the exception to the unreliable meter rule. Smart batteries are already being used in camcorders, and will no doubt appear in notebook computers in the years to come. Smart batteries actually have built-in microchips that sense how much charge the battery has left and report this amount. (Sony calls this technology, which they pioneered, *Info-lithium*.) With a smart battery, you always know right down to the minute how much charge remains.

The Windows 95 operating system also incorporates an onscreen battery meter that you can install in the Control Panel — see Chapter 4 for more details and the installation steps.

Many rechargeable batteries exhibit two mysterious phenomena known as *self-recharge* and *self-discharge*. *Self-recharge* means that on their own they build up a bit of charge after they were apparently depleted. Not much charge — sometimes your computer barely begins booting up and then conks out again. Wait about an hour after your battery is depleted, and then try turning the computer on again. If you're lucky, it works for another couple of minutes — not much, but in some situations, knowing this trick can come in very handy. You may have just enough time to save your file to floppy disk and take it to another computer to finish your work.

All rechargeable batteries lose their charge, over time, through a process called *self-discharge*. The amount of self-discharge depends mainly on the battery technology. Ni-cads are the worst — after a month they may lose most of their charge just by sitting around. Nickel-metal hydride batteries are somewhat better — typically, they lose about a third to half of their charge after a month. The newer and more expensive lithium-ion batteries are the most resistant to self-discharge — they lose only about three to five percent of their charge after a month. Because of self-discharge, try to recharge your battery as close to the time you need it as practical.

Dual Battery Computers

The battery that lasts for an eight-hour workday is the holy grail of notebook computer manufacturers and designers. Unfortunately, such a battery is still off in the future. But recognizing that some users really need to just keep going and going on battery power all day, some notebook computer manufacturers offer an innovative dual battery option.

The dual battery feature allows you to remove one of the computer's disk drives — usually the floppy drive, sometimes the CD-ROM — and replace it with a second battery that fits perfectly into the same slot.

Depending on the computer, you may be able to switch between these batteries without powering the computer down and rebooting (as you normally need to do when you switch batteries with single-battery computers). Switching components while your computer is up and running is called *hot swapping*. The ideal hot-swapping computer allows you to remove a drive and replace it with a battery, all while the computer stays up and running. You can even switch disk drives — for example, from a floppy to a CD-ROM — in a hot-swappable computer.

You may also hear PCMCIA/PC Cards referred to as hot-swappable — see Chapter 22 for more details.

The CMOS Battery — the Other Battery

Though you usually think of your computer as having just a single battery (except for dual battery models, of course), in fact, all notebook computers actually have a second built-in battery. This second battery, commonly referred to as the *CMOS battery,* is a small button battery similar to the kind used in wristwatches.

The CMOS battery keeps the computer's built-in clock running, but more importantly, it maintains a tiny bit of very important digital memory called the CMOS memory. (CMOS stands for *Complimentary Metal Oxide Semiconductor* — you can just remember the acronym and forget the actual term.) The CMOS memory contains the computer's setup information and tells the computer what kind of disk drives are installed. Without that information, a Windows-based computer is unable to boot up, because it needs to read from the hard drive to load the operating system. If your computer doesn't know what kind of hard drive it has, the computer can't read anything from it.

Macintosh computers also include a CMOS battery to keep the clock and certain other functions stored in memory, but it works a bit different as far as the disk drives are concerned. The disk drives in Macintosh computers run on a system called *SCSI* (Small Computer System Interface) which allows the drives to identify themselves when you turn on the computer, instead of the computer looking at the CMOS memory to find the drives. With a Macintosh, about the only thing that happens when the CMOS battery dies is that the system clock reads the wrong time.

Thus, this tiny battery is mighty important. In theory, it's supposed to last for seven to ten years. Many notebook computers get retired long before the CMOS battery wears out (you may see them lying around on the beach in Miami). But these little batteries have also been known to die prematurely, leaving the owner of the computer in quite a bit of stress.

When the computer loses its CMOS memory, you can't even boot from an emergency floppy disk (such as the kind anti-virus software commonly creates for you). Instead, you have to go into the computer's setup software — typically you get there by pressing the Delete or F1 key immediately after powering up the computer. In the setup utility, you need to enter all the technical information about the computer's disk drives.

Write down or print out your computer's setup information and keep it in a safe place, just in case your CMOS battery ever dies. You don't need to understand what any of this information is or means — just *precisely* copy it down from the setup menu. Pay particular attention to every detail relating to the hard drive. You may need to scroll through several screens of information to get it all. Simply boot up your computer and press Delete or F1 right after you power it up. Then go through all the screens you encounter, being careful not to change anything, and either write it all down, or print it by hooking your computer up to a printer and pressing the Print Screen key (sometimes a function key on notebooks).

If the unthinkable happens and your computer's CMOS memory wipes out due to battery exhaustion, even if you can successfully resuscitate the computer by reentering all the setup information, it lasts only for as long as you keep the power on. Turn off the computer, and the setup information gets wiped out again — until you replace the CMOS battery.

Unfortunately, with most notebook computers, replacing the CMOS battery requires opening up the computer. Though not the most complicated thing you can do with a notebook computer, most computer owners would probably prefer to leave this operation to a qualified technician. But before you take the computer into the service shop, look in the instruction manual to see if it says anything about replacing the CMOS battery. On some models, you can get to the CMOS battery in an easily accessible compartment without taking the computer apart.

Chapter 4:

Power Management: Squeezing Every Last Drop

. . . .

. . . .

*I*f your notebook computer seems to be turning itself off even when your battery is fully charged, you may wonder what's going on (or off), and why. That's where the computer's power management system comes in. Power management helps you squeeze every last minute of run time out of your battery.

What Is Power Management?

Power management provides a system for shutting off power to many of the components of the computer — such as the screen, hard drive, and ports — usually on an individual basis (and hopefully when you're not using them). On a more global basis, power management also turns off the entire computer, putting it in various *sleep modes* until you need to use it again.

Most power management adjustments are *time-out* adjustments, meaning that if you do not use the computer for a certain amount of time, say five minutes, the computer goes into *sleep mode,* also commonly called *suspend mode.* Other time-out adjustments can affect only one component of the computer; for example, if you don't access the hard drive for a minute, the hard drive automatically powers down.

Suspend and resume

The *suspend mode* helps you lengthen the amount of time you can keep your computer running. Suppose that you're sitting on an airplane, occasionally working on your computer and occasionally talking to the guy in the seat next to you who absolutely must show you all his vacation pictures from Miami. Say that you're alternating between these activities in five-minute bursts. If, every time you stop to talk and check out his sunburn, you turn off your computer, and then reboot it to resume working, you end up booting up your computer a half dozen times over the course of an hour. The amount of energy used by the computer to boot up (which involves intensive use of the hard drive to load the operating system into memory) is probably more than the power that you save by shutting down for five minutes at a time. However, with the suspend mode, you get the best of both worlds — you save power when you aren't using the computer without having to use the extra power to fire it up again.

In suspend mode, the computer remembers what you were in the middle of doing and then hibernates and uses much less power than normal (or zero power, in the case of *suspend-to-disk,* as I explain in a later section). The exact manner by which a computer goes into its suspend mode can vary significantly from one model of computer to another.

Suspend-to-RAM

Suspend is like suspended animation in a science fiction movie. When you use *suspend-to-RAM,* the most common suspend method, your computer is kept barely alive on the absolute minimum power. When your computer goes into the suspend-to-RAM state, it first loads into memory the exact point where you leave off. It then shuts down power to most of the computer's parts, with the exception of the memory register that now holds your place.

In the suspend-to-RAM state, the computer continues to use up battery power, but at a much slower rate than if it were fully powered up and awake. Consequently, a computer that can typically achieve two hours of run time on a full battery may be able to remain in sleep mode for 24 hours. However, that's assuming you start with a battery that's fully charged — more often, because you don't turn on the computer just in order to suspend it, you have much less than a full charge available when you go into suspend mode.

When you wake the computer up, you are almost instantly back where you left off when you suspended — your same program and whatever you were working on is waiting for you to continue.

Suspend-to-disk

Most notebook computers offer a choice of suspending to RAM or disk. The RAM setting, as I describe in the previous section, is usually the default — the information where you left off is saved into electronic memory. *Suspend-to-disk,* on the other hand, stores your placemarker onto a portion of your notebook's hard drive and then powers down completely. When you power back up, you find yourself in the exact place you left off — same software, same document, ready to go. The real difference is that RAM requires a bit of power to store your placemarker, whereas the disk requires no power at all.

Suspend-to-disk is a great feature, but setting it up can be a complicated affair. Unless your computer comes with a suspend-to-disk feature already installed, I don't really recommend trying to set it up unless you have a good deal of experience with hard drives. Installing a suspend-to-disk feature usually involves a complex setup procedure in which you must *partition* (create divisions that the computer recognizes as separate drives) your computer's hard drive to create a separate area for the suspend mode — it's a complex procedure that can do devastating damage to information on your hard drive if you mess up.

Despite my warning, when the suspend-to-disk feature is all set up and working properly, it's fantastic. While in suspend-to-disk mode, your computer uses absolutely zero power. You can even remove the battery while your computer is in suspend-to-disk mode and replace it with a recharged battery, without losing the place where you left off. Theoretically, you can suspend to disk for months at a time if you want. The main disadvantage of suspend-to-disk is that when you want to resume your work, the computer takes longer to get back up and running — typically about 10 to 20 seconds — instead of the five seconds (or less) that it takes to power back up from suspend-to-RAM.

The reason that waking up from suspend-to-disk takes a bit longer is that the computer stored the point where you left off onto the hard drive, and must read the information off the drive and back into memory. Though time consuming, waking up from suspend-to-disk usually takes a lot less time than rebooting from scratch.

Another very minor disadvantage of suspend-to-disk is that you must permanently set aside a small portion of your hard drive for holding the suspend-to-disk data. You can't use this part of the hard drive for any other purpose.

Note that all computers offering suspend-to-disk also offer suspend-to-RAM, but not the reverse. For some models, suspend-to-RAM is referred to as *sleep,* whereas suspend-to-disk is called *hibernate.*

Some notebook computers let you have both suspend-to-disk and suspend-to-RAM available so that, for example, after five minutes the computer suspends to RAM, and then five minutes later, if the computer still isn't being used, it suspends to disk. Other computers require choosing one or the other, as I cover in more detail in the "What are all those adjustments?" section later in this chapter.

Suspending your computer manually and waking it up again

Most notebook computers include a button or a function key (see Figure 4-1) that lets you manually put the computer in suspend mode anytime you want. My favorite computer design includes a separate button, usually labeled Suspend/Resume. The advantage of having a separate button is that it's easy to find. The disadvantage of a special button with some models is that you must press the same button to resume your work — if you forget that you left the computer in suspend mode and press the On/ Off button by mistake, you may accidentally turn the computer off and lose your work. Ouch! Better-designed suspend/resume systems suspend with the Suspend/Resume button and automatically resume when you press either the Suspend/Resume button or any other key.

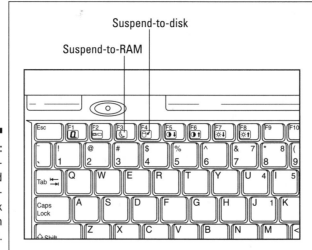

Figure 4-1: Suspend-to-RAM and suspend-to-disk function keys.

On computers that resume when you press any key on the keyboard, I recommend using the Escape key, because if you press it several times, you won't accidentally be typing letters or commands into the application when it wakes up. You can also move the mouse to wake up your sleeping computer, but you need to be careful not to accidentally click on anything, especially with the tricky touchpad systems (see Chapter 2).

Besides automatically going into suspend mode after a period of inactivity (typically five minutes), some computers also automatically suspend whenever you close the cover. Other models turn the display off when you close the cover, but do not go into suspend mode. Shutting down the display typically reduces the drain on the battery by about 20 to 40 percent, whereas suspend-to-RAM typically reduces power consumption by 80 to 90 percent.

When you come out of suspend mode, the computer takes just a few seconds to pick up exactly where you left off. Of course, a few seconds is a lot more convenient than having to wait for the computer to reboot, then launching the application you were using (such as a word processor or spreadsheet), and then locating the particular file you were working on.

The computer's screen may flash on and off a couple of times when you press the resume key before things settle down and the hibernating bear comes back to life. Be patient — no matter how long the wake-up takes, it's faster than rebooting.

Locating Your Notebook's Power Management Controls

If you run Windows 95, the Control Panel is the first place to look for your computer's power management controls. The Windows 95 operating system includes an icon in the Control Panel for Power, with a picture of a battery and an AC power plug. The Power icon (if your computer has it installed) is the easiest way to activate power management features, although it does not offer access to the full range of adjustment that the computer probably makes available elsewhere.

Double-click the Power icon in the Control Panel, and you see a submenu that lists three broad choices for power management: Advanced, Standard, and Off, as shown in Figure 4-2.

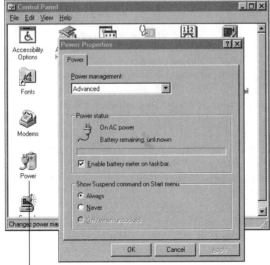

Figure 4-2:
Windows 95
Power
Management
menu.

Power icon

✔ The **Advanced** setting is the most aggressive, meaning that the computer's components shut down most frequently at this setting. However, you can often change the exact parameters that get implemented in the Advanced mode, using the adjustments that I describe just a bit later.

✔ The **Standard** setting represents the manufacturer's defaults for power management. Typically, the Standard setting puts the computer in the sleep or suspend mode if you don't do any typing or mouse movements for five minutes.

✔ The **Off** setting simply disables power management entirely — the notebook computer operates essentially like a desktop machine, with all systems powered up and ready to use all of the time as long as the machine is turned on.

The Windows 95 Power Manager, represented by the Power icon, and the control that it offers are just the tip of the power management iceberg. Most power users (pardon the pun) also dive into the underlying power management controls that are directly accessible via the computer's function keys.

Enabling Your Windows Power Management Support Features

Although Windows 95 includes a power management control feature, it doesn't automatically get installed on all computers. Go into the Control Panel — if you don't see an icon that looks like the battery and an AC power plug shown in Figure 4-2, then you need to install the power management feature yourself. Installing the Windows power management feature also installs the Windows battery meter feature, which lets you know how much juice you have left. Be aware, however, that the Windows battery meter does not work with all computers (see the last step in the following numbered steps).

To install the Windows power management feature, follow these steps:

1. **Choose Start⇔Settings⇔Control Panel.**

   The Control Panel appears.

2. **Click the System icon in the Control Panel.**

   The System Properties dialog box appears.

3. **Click the Device Manager tab that appears along the top.**

4. **Click the + sign next to System Devices.**

5. **Double-click the Advanced Power Management support icon listed under System Devices.**

   The Advanced Power Management support Properties dialog box appears, as shown in Figure 4-3. If you don't see this icon listed, your computer cannot provide this feature.

6. **Click the Settings tab.**

7. **Click the box next to Enable power management support so that a check mark appears in the box (do *not* click the three boxes listed below; leave these options unchecked — see Figure 4-3).**

8. **Click OK to close the Advanced Power Management support Properties panel.**

9. **Click OK to close the System Properties panel.**

10. **Click the Power icon in the Control Panel, and you are offered the option to put the battery meter symbol on the taskbar (along the bottom).**

    The battery meter may not work immediately, in which case you see a question mark in the taskbar, usually in the lower right corner of the screen. After a day or two of use, it should appear — if not, the system may not be compatible with your computer.

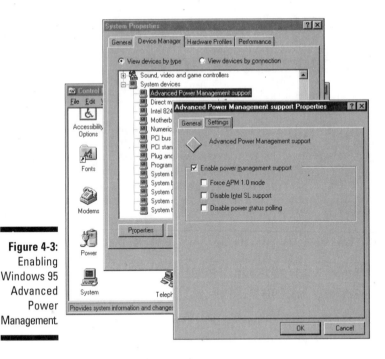

Figure 4-3:
Enabling
Windows 95
Advanced
Power
Management.

Finding Your System Power Management Controls

Your computer's own power management controls, which you can usually find described in some detail in your notebook computer instruction manual, operate on a more fundamental level than the operating system. They're part of your computer's function that's active even before the operating system (for example, Windows) gets loaded. These power management settings are part of the computer's *BIOS* (Basic Input/Output Software), whose main function is telling the computer how to read from the hard drive so that it when it boots, it can load the operating system.

With some computers, you may not be able to access the power management features while running Windows (especially Windows 3.*x,* and to a lesser extent, Windows 95). Sometimes, the power management features are accessible only just as the computer is booting up, as part of the *CMOS Setup menu.* You can access the CMOS Setup menu an instant after you first turn on the computer — when the message `Press Delete (or F1) to run Setup` appears on the screen. The CMOS Setup utility looks something like Figure 4-4.

CMOS stands for *complimentary metal oxide semiconductor,* which is a type of technology used in fabricating *integrated circuits* (the guts of all modern electronic devices, including your computer). Actually, CMOS is now used in many other chips in a notebook computer, because it uses less power than other technologies.

In the early days of computers, CMOS worked much more slowly than other types of integrated circuits and was therefore used only for applications where minimal power consumption was absolutely imperative. Keeping the computer's setup information retained in a tiny bit of memory is one such application — for both notebook and desktop applications — and because CMOS memory was always used for this application, over a period of time it became known as the CMOS setup screen. A tiny on-board button battery (like the ones you put in watches) keeps the CMOS memory powered up for several years.

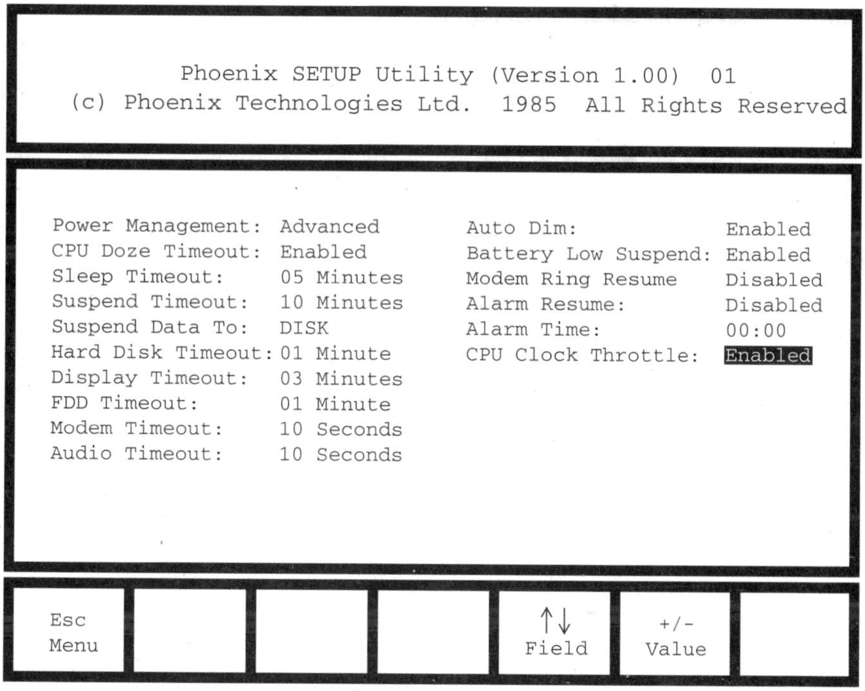

```
            Phoenix SETUP Utility (Version 1.00)  01
       (c) Phoenix Technologies Ltd.  1985  All Rights Reserved


    Power Management: Advanced      Auto Dim:             Enabled
    CPU Doze Timeout: Enabled       Battery Low Suspend: Enabled
    Sleep Timeout:    05 Minutes    Modem Ring Resume    Disabled
    Suspend Timeout:  10 Minutes    Alarm Resume:        Disabled
    Suspend Data To:  DISK          Alarm Time:          00:00
    Hard Disk Timeout: 01 Minute    CPU Clock Throttle:  Enabled
    Display Timeout:  03 Minutes
    FDD Timeout:      01 Minute
    Modem Timeout:    10 Seconds
    Audio Timeout:    10 Seconds



    Esc                                   ↑↓         +/-
    Menu                                 Field      Value
```

Figure 4-4:
A typical
CMOS
Setup utility
screen.

✔ Beware of going into the CMOS Setup utility. Think of this as your *last resort* for finding the computer's power management settings. If you mess with adjustments in the CMOS Setup utility other than the power management settings, you can experience catastrophic results — such as the inability to read anything off the hard drive.

✔ If you *do* go into the CMOS Setup utility, then before changing anything, first write down *all* of the settings, and keep this information in your computer carrying case. Pay particular attention to the drive settings (such as type, cylinders, heads, and so on).

What are all those adjustments?

When you go into CMOS Setup and start working with the power management setup utility, as I describe in the previous section, you find a set of far more detailed adjustments that let you apply power management to individual components, as well as customize the suspend mode. A typical list of power management settings includes the following items (the exact names for these settings may vary depending on your particular computer model):

✔ **Power management mode.** The choice here is usually among Always, Never, or Battery Power Only. The Battery Power Only setting allows you to set the power management features so that they kick in only when you're actually running the machine using the battery — this is the setting that I recommend. Otherwise, when you're plugged into AC, you find your screen blanking out unnecessarily. (Granted, you *do* save money on electricity by letting the machine suspend on AC, but you're literally talking about pennies, if that much.)

✔ **Power management.** This setting is usually a choice between Standard (or Default) settings, and Custom (or Advanced) settings. To make the rest of the adjustments in this list, you need to choose the Advanced or Custom option.

✔ **Suspend time-out.** Usually adjustable in one-minute increments from one minute up to half an hour. Suspend time-out determines the period of inactivity (no keys pressed or mouse actions) that trigger the computer to go into suspend mode. For suspend-to-RAM time-out, I recommend choosing five minutes; for suspend-to-disk time-out, ten minutes (if that setting is available); and for display time-out, four minutes.

✔ **Hard drive time-out.** Adjustable from one second to several minutes, or Disabled. After the hard drive is powered down, it may take a second or two to wake up for any hard drive stuff — a minor inconvenience. I recommend using one second.

✔ **Floppy drive time-out.** Adjustable from one second to several minutes, or Disabled. After the floppy drive is powered down, it may take a second or two to wake up if you need to read a floppy — a minor inconvenience. I recommend setting this option to one second.

✔ **Processor speed.** Typically, you can adjust the Processor speed between High and Low speed. The setting lets you reduce the clock speed of your computer's microprocessor so that it can operate at lower power. (If you enable battery-only power management and you adjust your processor speed to low, your computer runs slower and uses less power when you run off the battery, but automatically runs faster when AC power is plugged in.)

✔ **Auto throttle.** The choice for Auto throttle is between Enable and Disable. Rather than reducing processor speed across the board (as the Processor speed adjustment does), Auto throttle constantly adjusts the processor speed to match the needs of the task at hand. When the computer is not working, the processor's clock slows down. In theory, this operation is invisible; in practice, it may add a very slight delay to some operations. I recommend that you choose Enable.

✔ **Display time-out.** Usually adjustable from about 10 seconds to 30 minutes, or Disabled. The display system uses up more power than any other part of the computer. If you enable the Display time-out feature, you reduce your computer's power usage by 20 to 40 percent when the screen powers down.

✔ **Auto dim.** Choose between Enable or Disable. Auto dim automatically reduces screen brightness whenever you're operating on battery power. When you run off AC power, the screen brightness is back to normal. Enabling the Auto dim feature may typically add about 5 to 10 percent to the amount of run time you get per battery charge.

✔ **Auto suspend on low battery.** The choice is usually between Enable and Disable. When enabled, the computer automatically goes into suspend mode (suspend-to-RAM or suspend-to-disk) when the battery gets low. Better models first provide an audible warning before automatically suspending (see next bullet item). On some computers, the choice of whether the auto suspend is suspend-to-disk or suspend-to-RAM is made in the Auto suspend on low battery choice, or in a nearby choice called **Suspend to**. On other computers, you choose the type of suspend (to disk or to RAM) elsewhere in the computer's setup menu, and whichever you choose there applies when the computer auto suspends on low battery. Note that to use the suspend-to-disk feature, the computer must already be set up for this function with a disk partition — see the "Suspend-to-disk" section earlier in this chapter. I recommend that you choose Disable.

✔ **Audible battery warning.** The choice is between Enable and Disable. If you enable the Audible battery warning, the computer sounds an alarm — usually a beep or series of beeps — when the battery starts getting low. Some models offer two levels of warning, beginning with slow beeps and then getting faster when just a few minutes are left.

✔ **Suspend to.** Choice is between RAM and Disk. It determines where the current data you're working on gets stored when the computer goes into suspend mode. I describe the difference between the two modes near the beginning of this chapter in the "Suspend-to-disk" and "Suspend-to-RAM" sections. Most computers require you to select one or the other, in which case you usually see this choice in the CMOS Setup menu. However, some models allow both suspend-to-disk and suspend-to-RAM to be directly available via different function keys, in which case you *don't* see this choice in the power management setup screen.

✔ **Modem ring resume.** If you leave the computer in suspend mode with its modem connected to the telephone line (see Chapter 5), enabling this setup feature automatically wakes up the computer (resumes) when the phone rings so that the computer can answer the call — useful if you want to use the computer to receive faxes.

✔ **Audio time-out.** Usually adjustable from about 10 seconds to 30 minutes, this feature automatically powers down the computer's sound system if you don't use it for the amount of time you choose.

✔ **Modem time-out.** You can usually set this feature from 10 seconds to 30 minutes. Modem time-out automatically powers down the modem when you don't use it for the amount of time you choose.

You may wonder how I arrive at the settings — they all seem pretty arbitrary. When I'm writing, I want time to think, and daydream, and to make quick trips to the kitchen and bathroom. For me, a four-minute time-out on the screen is a good compromise that allows quick trips without wasting power. When I'm feeling more aggressive, such as on a plane flight, I set the display time-out to one minute and suspend-to-RAM to two minutes. I always like to set screen time-out and suspend-to-RAM one minute apart so that if I do not want the computer to suspend, I can first catch the display switching off and then press the Escape key to reactivate it. Because restarting the display takes less time than resuming from suspend-to-RAM, setting the computer up this way minimizes my inconvenience.

I recommend setting the hard drive and just about all other time-outs to the minimum setting, usually one second. The time needed to wake up the hard drives and ports is negligible. Try the most aggressive settings (shortest time period), and if you don't notice any deterioration in performance, leave them that way.

Most of my personal experience using notebook computers has been for word processing and online/Internet access. The best power management settings for you depend on the applications you run most, and you need to think about how you may better adapt and change the settings I suggest so that they fit your needs.

Enabling the Auto suspend on low battery feature is a mixed blessing, so I don't usually recommend it. Depending on how the other power management features work, you can get some funky behavior from your computer. The worst offenders are computers that just suddenly suspend without any warning — the auto suspend kicks in *instead of* the usual low-battery beep warnings. The problem here is that you never get a chance to just save your work in the normal way and shut down the computer. What happens if you're in transit and can't get to an AC power outlet for half a day or more? Unless your computer is set up to automatically suspend to disk, you lose all your work since the last time you saved it (or since the last time the software you were using at the time automatically made a backup). More polite notebook computers first provide warning beeps for several minutes and then go into the suspend mode. During those few minutes, while the beep is sounding, you have enough time to save your work onto the hard drive and to shut down whatever software you're using.

The only time I recommend enabling the Auto suspend on low battery feature is when your computer offers suspend-to-disk, *and* it comes already configured for you, *and* you get warning beeps for a couple of minutes before it automatically suspends. In this case, be sure that you know how to resume from suspend-to-disk mode. Usually you just press the Power button (once!), but don't take my word for it — check your computer's instruction manual.

Finding settings may require detective work. Not all computer manuals are as easy to read as this book.

Practically all notebook computers *do* offer power management adjustments, but you may need to do some detective work to find out where they are. Try looking in the manual's index, if it has one, under *Power management.* The work is worth the effort.

How Much Time Do I Have Left?

As I describe in more detail in Chapter 3, the battery gauges built into most notebooks are notorious for their *inaccuracy* — sometimes these meters indicate that you have more than a 50 percent charge, and then, just minutes later, the low-battery warning comes on. Chapter 3 also outlines the newer lithium-ion battery technology, which provides more accurate readouts of remaining juice.

Of particular concern when you use advanced power management features is not just how long the battery lasts in general, but more specifically, how much time you have left after the low-battery warning starts sounding (or flashing, or both).

Of course, as with run time in general, the exact amount of time you have remaining depends on what you're using the computer for, if you're using any of the disk drives a lot, and how bright you've adjusted the screen. After you test it for yourself, doing the kind of work you normally do, you get a pretty good sense of how much juice remains when the low-battery warning comes on.

So how do you test it? Easy — just leave the computer running when the warning starts, and look at your watch or a clock to keep track of how much time is passing (not your computer clock, by the way, because it disappears when you need to read it).

The temptation is just to leave the computer on, without doing any work, because when the battery finally does conk out, you lose all the work that you were doing since your last save. However, I don't recommend that approach. You want to test the computer under actual use. Keep working normally after the low-battery warning comes on, except that you start saving your work every minute. That's right — every 60 seconds. True, saving that often uses up the battery at a faster rate than normal, but when the battery finally does conk out, you lose only one minute's worth of work. And when you're really in that high-pressure situation you *want* to save your work every minute so that you don't lose anything.

- ✔ The closer your battery gets to being exhausted, the more often you want to save your work.

- ✔ Having had numerous very frustrating experiences with computers freezing up and having had to to reboot while I was in the middle of writing, I highly recommend setting your software's automatic backup function to automatically save your work every two or three minutes. This helps minimize the damage if and when catastrophe strikes.

Chapter 5

The Modem — Your Laptop's Mouth and Ears

. . . .

In This Chapter

▶ What a modem does

▶ The difference between data and fax

▶ Modem speeds and compression standards

▶ Dialing with a modem

▶ Dealing with basic modem problems

. . . .

*T*he modem provides your connection to the outside world. Modems convert the bits of data that computers use into audio signals that can be sent over ordinary phone lines (that's the rushing waterfall sound, often called the *warble,* you hear when they connect). In fact, the warble is what gives modems their name in the first place — modems convert data into sound (*mo*dulate), and sound back into data again (*dem*odulate). Cool, huh?

Using a modem, you can connect to other computers, the Internet, or online services such as AOL and CompuServe. With many new modems, often called *fax/modems,* you can also send and receive faxes. Some models have voice capability which allows you to use your computer as a voice mail system, and still others include an Ethernet adapter, fax, and modem all in the same device.

The Straight Dope on Fax/Modems

Suppose that you want to send a document to a colleague. lı you send the document as an e-mail, your colleague receives a computer file — it can be a standard word-processor file, for example — that can not only be read, but can also be modified and saved on a computer disk like any other file.

But if you send that same document via fax, the story is very different. A fax, in essence, is a crude black and white picture. When you receive a fax, even by computer, all you get is a picture of the document. The computer doesn't know that the first letter in a document is the letter *T,* for example — all it knows is that it received a picture containing dark and light areas in a particular pattern.

You can, however, convert a fax into a text file for a word-processor using *Optical Character Recognition* software, or OCR for short. And although fax signals and computer data signals (the type used for Internet and online communications) are similar in that they use audio to transmit digital signals over the phone lines, they use completely different standards or *protocols,* and represent fundamentally different animals. Just because a guy who speaks Arabic and a gal who speaks Japanese can both use the phone, doesn't mean they understand each other. For communicating between two computers, e-mail is simpler, more efficient, and more reliable. In chapter 14, I cover this and all the other fax stuff you need to know in glorious detail.

Different ways modems fit into your computer

Modems come in four forms:

- ✔ **Built-in modems** are part of the computer itself. In the early days of laptop computing, built-in modems were very common. Nowadays, some notebook computer models continue to come equipped with a permanently installed fax/modem system. The advantages of such built-in modems are that everything comes already installed and set up for you, and the modem doesn't tie up any of your PCMCIA expansion slots. The disadvantage is that the modem may not offer the fastest speed currently available and cannot be easily replaced (although you can usually switch to a PCMCIA/PC card model when you want to upgrade).

- ✔ **External modems** take the form of boxes ranging in size from about a pack of cigarettes to about four slices of bread. They hook up to the serial port found on the back of just about all computers. Their advantages are that the same modem can be easily moved between both desktop and notebook computers, and that they provide visible indicators showing the status of modem operations. However, for use with notebook computers, even the so-called *pocket modem* models, which are battery-operated, are big and bulky when compared with fax/modem cards.

✔ **Internal modems** are large printed-circuit cards designed to work with desktop computers — these *cannot* be used with notebook computers.

✔ **Fax/modem cards,** also called PCMCIA card modems, or sometimes just PC card modems, are small, slim, lightweight cards designed specifically to plug into the standardized expansion slots. Their advantage is convenience — they fit right into the computer. The only disadvantages, and they are minimal, are that you don't get status lights, as with external models, and they drain a small bit of power from the notebook computer's battery (typically less than 3 percent of what the rest of the computer uses).

Fax/modem cards

The fax/modem card is the most common way to equip your mobile computer with telephone communications. The cards are almost all the same size (roughly equal to three credit cards stacked together) and weight (about two ounces), and conform to what's technically called the *PCMCIA Type 2* standard for plug-in cards. (PCMCIA stands for a trade organization that standardized the expansion slots on notebook and laptop computers so that the same cards could be used with many different brands of computers — see Chapter 22 for more details on PCMCIA/PC card stuff.)

Most of a modem's technical characteristics are determined by its internal *chipsets* (that is, the electronic guts of the modem). Besides communicating at the stated speed, such as 33.6, all modems also have internal chips that perform data compression — effectively reducing the amount of data that needs to be sent, thus increasing the *throughput* (the amount of raw, uncompressed data that goes into the modem and out the phone line per second). Most modems come with numerous offers for free trials of online services and Internet Service Providers (ISPs), and often include bundled software for faxing (see Chapter 14).

Connectors count

Though PCMCIA/PC card modems all look alike, one physical difference is the way the phone cable attaches to the card. This connection is sometimes called the DAA for Data Access Arrangement. Most PCMCIA/PC card modems have a special multipin socket, and come with a special adapter cable that has a standard telephone plug on one end and a special plug to fit into this socket on the other end, as shown in Figure 5-1. The better modem models have clearly labeled locking clips to keep the connection between the cable and the modem card solid. With lower-quality modems, the cable can easily slip out of the socket, thus breaking the phone connection.

Figure 5-1:
Most
PCMCIA/PC
card
modems,
such as
these from
Epson and
TDK, come
with a cable
for a
standard
phone jack.
The Epson
card shown
has an
Ethernet
connection.

TIP

If it's not already clearly labeled, use a permanent pen to mark the top side of the modem's connector, so you don't try putting it in upside-down.

Alternatively, some PCMCIA/PC card modems come with a pop-out phone jack, shown in Figure 5-2. Megahertz, the modem manufacturer who first created it, calls it XJACK. Hayes calls their version the EZjack. The advantage of XJACK (and similar systems featuring a built-in phone jack) is that you never have to worry about losing or misplacing the special adapter cable. This type of jack works with any standard modular telephone cable, the same kind you probably have in your house. (In tech parlance, the modular phone plug is called an RJ-11 connector — try whipping that little term out at your next barbecue.)

Modem speed

People probably upgrade their modems more than any other part of their computers, because just about every year, it seems, the technology improves and allows ever faster data speeds. As this book was going to press, the rate of 33,600 bits per second (that's 33.6 Kbps) was commonplace, and the 56 Kbps rate was being introduced.

Figure 5-2:
These
PCMCIA/PC
card
modems
from
Megahertz
(model
XJ4288) and
Hayes
(model
Optima 288)
have pop-
out phone
jacks.

All modems are compatible with other slower modems — a feature that the tech-heads like to call *backwards compatible*. When two modems first connect to each other, during a procedure that technicians refer to as the *handshake,* they negotiate the highest data rate that both are capable of handling.

All the various modem speeds, as well as compression standards (see the next section) are described by an obscure set of technical standards administered by the International Telecommunications Union, an agency of the United Nations. These are what the numbers like *V.34* that you see plastered all over modem packaging and advertisements are all about. The "Modem standards" sidebar later in this chapter gives the technical lowdown, if you're interested.

When the newest modem speeds are first introduced, they are usually not yet standardized throughout the modem industry and therefore do not yet have an ITU classification. Sometimes two or more manufacturers compete with different standards until an international standard is established. If your main use for a modem is calling into an Internet service provider, you may not realize the benefit of a new modem speed when it's first introduced. To communicate at the fastest speed, the modems on both sides of the phone line must both be capable of handling the high speed. Online services and Internet service providers usually take as much as a year or more to upgrade their networks to the newest technology. Unless you are calling in to a service that specifically offers access at the fastest speed your modem is capable of, the extra speed is a waste of money.

Modem standards

Most new modems provide compatibility with just about all the following technical standards (as this book was going to press, the 56 Kbps speed was not yet standardized):

- Bell 212A (1200 bps U.S. modem standard)

- Bell 103J (300 bps U.S. modem standard)

- CCITT V.17 (14,400/12,000 bps fax standard)

- CCITT V.21 (300 bps fax standard)

- CCITT V.22 (1200 bps modem standard used outside U.S.)

- CCITT V.22bis (2400 bps international modem standard — the word *bis* is French for *second,* meaning a revised version)

- CCITT V.27ter (4800/2400 bps fax standard)

- CCITT V.29 (9600/7200 bps fax standard)

- CCITT V.32 (9600 bps modem standard)

- CCITT V.32bis (14,400/12,000/9600 bps modem standard)

- CCITT V.34 (28,800 bps modem standard)

- CCITT V.34+ (33,600 bps modem standard. Note that V.34+ is currently the highest standardized modem speed — the newer 56 Kbps speed had not been standardized yet when this book was going to press, though modems operating at 56 Kbps are widely available. This is the main *V-dot* standard to look for when buying a new modem.)

- CCITT V.42 (error control for 2400 and 9600 bps)

- CCITT V.42bis (compression scheme with 2:1 to 4:1 efficiency. Along with modem speed, this is another important standard to look for in a state-of-the-art modem. Fortunately, most models have this.)

- V.FAST (28,800 bps)

- MNP 2–9 (Microcom Networking Protocol–Nine progressively more sophisticated error correction and data compression levels, with up to 4:1 efficiency)

- MNP 10 (Microcom cellular telephone error correction standard. Because cellular phone connections tend to be noisier than regular wired phone connections, the data is more likely to have an error during transmission, and consequently the information is more likely to need to be repeated, thus slowing down the operation. MNP 10 is a special error correction protocol that reduces the size of data packets, so that less information needs to be repeated when an error is detected, thus improving the overall speed of communications.)

When shopping for a new modem, the main things to look for are V.34+, V.42bis, and MNP2 to 10, along with the not-yet-standardized 56 Kbps feature.

Compression

Data compression reduces the number of bits that need to be stored or transmitted, by describing repetitions in the data more efficiently. For example, suppose that the data I need to transmit is a series of zeros — let's say 200 in row — saying *200 x 0* is obviously a lot more efficient than saying *0000000000000000000.* . . That, in a nutshell, is how all data compression systems work.

Modems have their own special methods for compressing data as they transmit it from one end of the phone connection to the other. With the higher-speed modems, to gain the benefit of modem data compression, the modems on both ends of the connection must both use the same compression standard. In general, compression ratios of about 2:1 to 4:1 are the most you can achieve using modem-based compression. The 4:1 ratio, incidentally, is how a manufacturer of a 33.6 Kbps modem may claim a 134.4 Kbps throughput rate. Take such claims with a grain of salt — the maximum compression ratio is very rarely achieved.

You cannot further compress a compressed file. So if you're downloading a zip file from the Internet, for example, the fastest your modem operates is the basic bit rate that it negotiated in the *handshake* (see "Modem speed" earlier in this chapter) when you logged on. A zip file — and the same goes for JPEG, MPEG, RealAudio, VDO video, or any other data that's been compressed already — has already had all the excess data squeezed out of it. Your modem, regardless of how expensive and whiz-bang it is, can't squeeze any more.

Other modem features

Besides faster speed, some modem models may offer other desirable features such as:

✔ **Speakerphone** allows hands-free phone conversations — this feature is usually available only on external modem models, because it requires building a microphone and speaker into the unit and placing them in a position where you can speak into the unit, which would be difficult with a PCMCIA/PC Card.

✔ **Simultaneous voice and data** allows you to speak with someone while exchanging data.

✔ **Voice mail,** available on many external modem models, is useful for anyone needing extensive voice messaging. But you have to leave your computer on all the time or in a suspended mode that wakes up when the phone rings. You may also experience a slowdown whenever the computer answers a call while you're working (ditto for using the computer to receive faxes). And imagine the nightmare if for some reason you have to reboot the computer while an important message or fax is coming in! Generally, if you plan to receive a good number of faxes or voice mail messages, you're usually best off buying separate, stand-alone answering and fax machines. Voice mail requires a modem with voice capability, along with software that always come supplied with such voice-capable modems.

✔ **Cell phone protocol.** If you plan to use your notebook computer's modem with a cellular phone, select a model that has MNP 10 cellular error correction protocol (see the sidebar "Modem standards" earlier in this chapter). The MNP 10 cellular error correction protocol helps speed things through the relatively low bandwidth analog cellular channels. Another cellular modem technology, CDPD, is intended specifically for use with digital cell phone service (see Chapter 21 for more details).

✔ **Sleep state.** One other small difference among PCMCIA/PC card modems is in how much power they use in the sleep state — when the computer is on, but the modem is not being used. Most manufacturers rate sleep state power drain as a percentage of full power, making it difficult to compare (unless you also know the power drain when the modem is in use — in other words, percentage of what?). To eliminate power drain from the modem altogether, you can pop the modem out of its slot when you aren't using it.

✔ **Flash ROM.** The Flash ROM feature lets you call the modem manufacturer's bulletin board (or visit their Web site) to periodically update the modem's internal software called *firmware*. The main use for Flash ROM is to eliminate software bugs; but most modem users never notice any bugs and don't even bother with updates. However, with some Flash ROM modems, you can upgrade to faster modem speed just by calling the manufacturer's phone number! Cool stuff.

Installing the Modem: Plug and Pray!

A modem is usually easy to install, but still the best way to buy a modem is to get it already installed in the computer by the dealer who sells you the modem or computer, thus sparing you any installation hassles. Physically installing a PCMCIA/PC card modem into a notebook computer is easy enough; but on the software side, you can run into problems that prevent the modem from working properly. If you do get the store or dealer to install it, make sure that the technician also configures the computer to recognize the modem, and if possible, demonstrate to you that it works.

Fortunately, Windows 95 manages to make the operation reasonably painless. Windows 95 incorporates its own version of the software that recognizes PCMCIA/PC cards when you insert them. You know that the software recognizes the modem in the PCMCIA/PC card slot when you hear two short beeps. You hear those beeps every time the computer boots up if you have a PCMCIA/PC card installed.

The easiest way to install the modem in Windows 95 is to insert the PCMCIA/PC card modem before the computer boots. Then, as the Windows screen appears, you get a message telling you that the system has detected new hardware and will automatically configure it for you. If you're lucky, Windows finds an exact match for your modem in its list of modem manufacturers and models. However, in the worst case, it doesn't know which make or model modem you have, and you can't find it by looking through the list. And so you have to try selecting another model in this list (such as Generic Hayes-compatible), or install a new driver from the floppy disk that usually comes supplied with new modems. For more detailed instructions on installing a new driver and for troubleshooting tips on PCMCIA/PC card installation, see Chapter 22.

If your particular modem isn't listed, try other models with the same speed from the same manufacturer. If you're installing a modem for the first time, have your computer try dialing into an online service, such as AOL or CompuServe, to test it out. Software to use one or more of the online services usually comes preinstalled on most new computers.

Usually, by trying several of the generic options, you can get the modem up and running, as shown in Figure 5-3.

Figure 5-3:
If Windows 95 does not recognize your modem model, try a Standard Modem Type, or find another model from the same manufacturer.

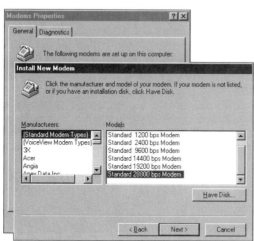

If you use an earlier version of Windows (3.*x*), you may first have to install a special type of software called *Card and Socket Services,* which essentially teaches the computer how to recognize the existence of the modem when it boots up. See Chapter 22.

Do not connect a modem directly to an office telephone system — it doesn't work and may actually damage the modem. See Chapter 19 for instructions on connecting to office phone systems.

Tone and pulse dialing

All modems, like most telephones, come equipped with two methods for dialing a phone call — tone and pulse. You can figure out which kind you have very easily — if your phone plays a tone when you press a number key, you are using a tone system. If you get a series of rapid clicks when you press a number key, you are using a pulse system. The capability of a modem to switch between pulse and tone dialing systems allows the modem to automatically dial telephone calls in most situations. However, you may run into office and hotel telephone systems that use completely different, and incompatible, dialing methods — see Chapter 19 for help in such situations.

If you can use it, tone dialing is almost always preferable to pulse dialing because it's faster and has the advantage that you can listen on an extension phone while dialing out. (Listening in is useful for troubleshooting problem situations — see Chapter 19 — though usually you don't need to pick up the phone because your computer's speaker lets you hear the modem as it dials.)

You can choose between pulse or tone dialing in your modem software. In Windows 95, the modem software is usually the Dial-Up Adapter, accessible by choosing Start⇨Programs⇨Accessories⇨Dial-Up Networking. Some online services, fax software, and communications programs have their own modem dialing software.

You may encounter rare situations where you need to use both pulse and tone dialing in the same call. For example, suppose that you're dialing out from a phone system that works only with pulse, but you're making a fax call to a fax machine that is on the same line as an answering machine, and the answering machine says that you must press a special key (typically the asterisk key) to get a fax-receive tone and activate the machine. In such a case, leave the modem set to pulse for dialing out, and then pick up an extension phone (with tone dialing) after the call goes through, and use the extension phone to press the necessary keys.

Compatibility with foreign telephone systems

Some foreign telephone systems use various incompatible tone dialing systems. Fortunately, in most foreign countries, the pulse dialing system is available. Pulse dialing is just about universal — it's based on the original dial-type or rotary telephone design (which is why we still call it *dialing a call,* even though the actual old-fashioned rotary telephone dials are very rare these days). In recent years, many countries have adopted the same tone signals (a.k.a. Touch Tone) that are used in the U.S., so my advice is to switch to pulse dialing only if you have trouble with tone dialing. Pulse dialing is the same in all countries, as well as the U.S.

The system used for dialing — pulse or tone — is not the only factor that determines modem compatibility with a foreign telephone system. Many countries use different tone signals to represent the dial tone and ring signals, so you may have to use the manual dialing technique described in Chapter 19. TDK makes a PCMCIA/PC card modem, called the Global Class PC Card, shown in Figure 5-1, which specifically addresses these differences — it can be programmed to deal with the dial tones and ring systems in most countries, and is available in both PC and Macintosh (PowerBook) versions.

Besides having technical compatibility with foreign systems, you also need to connect the modem to the foreign country's phone jack. The modular (RJ-11) phone jacks that are now ubiquitous in the U.S. are not nearly as universal overseas, and literally dozens of different types of plugs and jacks are used in other countries. You can usually purchase an adapter in the foreign country you're visiting, but if you want to play it safe, or if you travel a lot overseas, you may want to purchase a kit of foreign telephone adapters, such as the WorldPak sold by Power Express (see the Appendix). Alternatively, you can use an *acoustic coupler,* as I explain in Chapter 19, to avoid the need for plugging into the phone line altogether. Also see Chapter 8 for more travel tips.

Call waiting

Nothing wreaks as much havoc with modem and fax communications as the beep tone you hear when you have the call waiting feature and you receive an incoming call. Call waiting, in case you're not familiar with it, is a service available on most phone lines that lets you know when another call is coming in — instead of hearing a busy signal, the second caller hears ringing, and you hear a beep on the phone line while you're talking to the first person. A great idea, except that those polite beeps can ruin faxes and can disconnect you from an online service.

Fortunately, you can easily deactivate the call waiting feature before you dial out. For most phone services, turning off the call waiting feature is as simple as dialing a few numbers before you place a call that you don't want to be interrupted. If the phone line you're using to dial out has call waiting, you can store the deactivation number as part of the dialing sequence in the software that you use for dialing into your Internet service provider and/or online service.

With tone dialing, the deactivation code is

```
*70,
```

With pulse dialing, the deactivation code is

```
1170,
```

The comma makes the modem pause a moment before proceeding with the rest of the phone number. Simply insert ***70,** or **1170,** (depending on your phone system) in the appropriate box in your modem software in front of the number you want your modem to dial.

Some dialing software has these call waiting deactivation codes already programmed in and offers a special box for call waiting that you check to insert the code. With other software, you must enter the deactivation code in the Prefix area.

Modem status lights

One minor advantage of external modems over PCMCIA/PC card modems is the availability of status lights. Status lights can be helpful in troubleshooting problems when things aren't working properly. If you plan to use your notebook computer from a lot of challenging telephone situations, you may consider getting a model that has these status lights:

MR – Modem Ready: The modem is turned on and connected to the computer.

CD – Carrier Detect: The modem has detected the signal from another modem or fax machine.

OH – Off Hook: The modem has seized control of the phone line — the first thing that happens when it begins to dial a call.

AA – Auto Answer: The modem has been instructed to automatically answer incoming phone calls.

RD – Receive Data: This light flashes intermittently as the modem receives.

SD – Send Data: This light flashes intermittently as the modem sends.

TR – Terminal Ready: The modem has established communications with your mobile computer — the modem equivalent of a printer being online. Also called DTR.

HS – High Speed: The modem is operating at the fastest speed it can.

Chapter 6

Portable Peripherals, Expansion Stations, and Local Services

- -

In This Chapter

▶ Lugging extra gear

▶ Printing on the road

▶ Printing and scanning with local services

▶ Plugging into expansion stations

- -

*A*s you enter the world of portable computing and become dependent on it, you may be tempted to carry along portable versions of all the creature comforts you're accustomed to at the office, such as a printer, a scanner, and maybe an extra disk drive or two. Deciding how much, if any, of this extra stuff you really want to lug around is what this chapter explores.

This chapter covers most of the other portable devices that you can hook up to your computer, as well as the local services that you may want to use when you're on the road with a laptop. And it covers a device intended for hooking up your notebook when you're back in the office — the *docking* or *expansion station.*

Printers

Without a printer, your notebook computer can at times seem useless. If you're in business and you need to deliver a proposal, your clients usually expect to see a paper document, not e-mail. Sometimes you can finesse such situations by using your computer's modem to send a fax to a recipient, or perhaps you can use a fax machine as a printer and fax to yourself — see Chapter 14 for more about the wonderful world of faxing. However, you often find yourself in other situations where you need to produce a hard copy of a document.

You have two options for printing documents while you're on the road: You can carry a printer along with you, or you can use a local copy place or desktop publishing service with computers for rent. I cover copy places and what they offer in "Local Self-Serve Computer Places," later in this chapter.

The least expensive way to carry a portable printer is simply to choose one of the lightest weight inkjet printers you can find. You can't fit a standard inkjet printer in your briefcase, but if you are on a road trip with your computer, a home inkjet printer may be the way to go.

For a little bit more money than a standard inkjet, you can purchase a specially designed portable printer. All portable printers use inkjet or thermal (that flimsy fax paper stuff) technology. Because of the size and weight of laser printer components, they cannot be built as portable devices. The absolute smallest models are thermal printers which weigh barely more than a pound and are battery operated. However, the resulting printouts are inferior to plain paper copies because of the special fax-type paper. They're useful when you need a printout for your own reference or to give to a coworker, but you certainly wouldn't want to deliver a proposal to a potential client on thermal paper.

By making a regular photocopy of a thermal printout, you can convert it to regular plain paper. The text appears slightly fuzzier, but overall, it is probably an improvement.

At minimum, a portable printer folds up into a reasonably compact shape — usually about half the size of a cereal box, which may or may not be small enough to fit in your computer case or briefcase. In addition, you may find that some portable printers have flapping plastic parts that don't quite pack up as neatly as one would hope — especially true if the printer has an automatic sheet-feeder feature, which also adds quite a bit of size and weight. However, without a sheet feeder, you have to feed in each piece of paper by hand — a laborious and tedious process if you're printing a 20-page document.

Inkjet printers print onto plain paper. You can make the printed output look slightly better by printing on specially coated inkjet paper, available at all computer stores and most stationers.

Some portable inkjet printers are battery-operated, but my advice is to stick with AC-powered plug-in models unless you absolutely need battery power (such as to print in a remote jungle). The reason is that the rechargeable batteries for portable inkjet printers are sometimes heavier than the battery that powers your computer, adding up to quite a load.

Scanners

If your idea of a scanner is a big, clunky piece of equipment that looks like a copy machine, you need to pay another visit to the computer store. Those big scanners — called *flatbed scanners* — are still widely used in desktop publishing and are still great for home and office use. Two much smaller, lighter forms of scanners are available and are far more appropriate for your portable scanning use.

Portable page scanners

Portable page scanners are usually about a foot wide and a few inches in each of the other dimensions — roughly the size of a roll of aluminum foil. If you ever need to send a fax of an actual paper document that you don't already have stored on your hard drive (such as a drawing), portable page scanners are a fantastic accessory. The typical portable page scanner can accommodate an 8.5-inch wide page, fed through a slot in the middle of the scanner.

Portable scanners usually hook up via the parallel port or a PCMCIA/PC card for notebook PCs, or via a SCSI connector for Macintosh computers. Some advanced PC notebooks have built-in SCSI, and by buying an additional SCSI PCMCIA/PC card, you can add SCSI capability to just about any notebook, if you need it. The main advantage of SCSI is that you can connect numerous devices to the same port — see Chapter 2 for more information. Some models hook up to the new USB (Universal Serial Bus) port, as shown in Figure 6-1.

Figure 6-1: This Logitech PageScan USB scanner handles 8 ½ x 11-inch pages and hooks up to the new USB port found on some notebooks.

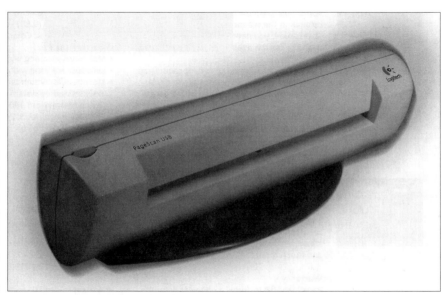

Many scanners come with *OCR* (Optical Character Recognition) software that lets you feed in a printed document and convert it into a word processor file that you can edit.

The main differences between these scanners, besides the way they hook up, are their resolution (measured in dots per inch — 400 to 600 is typical), whether they are color or black and white, how they are powered (AC, battery, or from the computer itself), and the supplied software that comes bundled with the scanner. Besides OCR, many models also include photo editing software, and some include document archiving systems to help you create a paperless mobile office.

Yes, technically a computer, scanner, and printer do make a copy machine of sorts, but using these devices to make copies can be a tedious and slow process — a useful convenience in an emergency, but not really a viable way to crank out a lot of copies from a hotel room.

Card, photo, and wand scanners

The more compact types of scanners cannot handle letter-sized pages and are designed for scanning smaller items. Depending on what kind of projects you're working on, these scanners can be very useful road warrior accessories. Besides the differences in the type of scanner, as I cover in the next few sections, the main things that distinguish one model from another are the size of the scanned area, the maximum resolution — typically in the ballpark of 300 to 1600 dots per inch (dpi), whether the scans are in color or black and white, and the software that comes supplied with the scanner.

Business card scanners

Business card scanners are designed specifically to scan in business cards (threw you for a loop there, huh?) and come with special *OCR* (Optical Character Recognition) software that automatically extracts the name, title, company name, phone number, and so on, and places the information in an electronic address book or contact manager file of your choice. If your work includes assembling a bunch of business cards and entering them all on a mailing list, business card scanners are great — the provided software can even print up mailing labels for you.

These special-purpose scanners are about the size of a fat paperback novel and have a slot where you feed the card through. They weigh about a pound, making them a reasonably portable option, though you usually need to plug them into AC power, because most models are not battery-operated. These scanners are usually limited to black and white — even when you feed a color business card through, the scanner creates a black and white copy of it.

Note that what makes these scanners really special is the software that comes supplied with them. It goes beyond ordinary OCR (see Chapter 14 for more about OCR) and actually figures out which item is the name, which is the title, which is the street address, which is the city, and so on. This software is remarkably intelligent, and accuracy is usually in the 90 to 95 percent ballpark (you still have to proofread the information). You purchase this software separate from the scanner as well — CardScanner from Corex is a good example.

Photo scanners

Photo scanners are intended for adding color or black and white photographs to documents or Web pages that you create. Photo scanners can also double as business card scanners, and many models include the OCR software needed for that purpose.

Photo scanners are about the size of a small tissue box and typically handle photographs or documents up to about 4 inches wide. (The length can usually run quite long, because the scanner just keeps feeding it through — in the unlikely event that your photo measures 4 inches x 40 inches, for example, many models can accommodate it.) Like the business card scanners, photo scanners have a slot where you feed the photograph in, and then a motor pulls it through. Weighing about a pound, these scanners are reasonably portable, but they usually require AC power. Just about all photo scanners generate color images, but you can always feed black and white material through too, and the supplied software usually lets you scan in black and white to reduce the size of the image files.

Wand scanners

Wand scanners, also known as hand scanners, are the most compact and lightweight — about the size of a big remote control for your television. They're different from the other scanners I mention in this section because the object you scan doesn't feed through automatically. Instead, you drag the wand across the document by hand (see Figure 6-2). Wand scanners typically come with a special plastic tray that helps keep your dragging smooth and with software that lets you scan larger areas by automatically combining a series of sectional scans (you can thus scan a full letter-sized page if you're in a crunch).

Wand scanners are the most suited for portable use — besides their small size and light weight (just a few ounces), they also require no hookup to AC power. Often, they get their power from the computer itself (through the parallel port), and don't even need batteries. The least expensive versions are black-and-white, and better models are color.

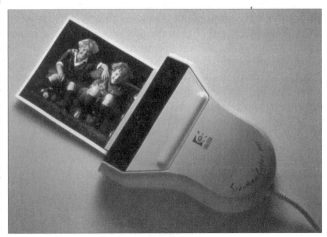

Figure 6-2: The Logitech ScanMan Color 2000 wand color scanner requires you to drag the wand across the picture or other item to be scanned.

Even though you can scan in full-sized pages, I suggest that you don't rely on a wand scanner to scan full pages very often. They are much better for small objects like magazine columns and photographs.

Disk Drives

Several optional disk drives are available as attachments to your notebook computer. You may find that an extra or additional disk drive is useful for a variety of purposes, such as software installation, transferring files to and from other people, and backing up your hard drive.

For use with a notebook PC, purchase a drive that connects to the parallel port — that is, unless you're in the unusual circumstance of owning a notebook with a SCSI connector, or you have an Apple PowerBook. Otherwise, you have to spend extra money on a special SCSI adapter card. Note that with SCSI, however, many of the drives listed in this section work more quickly, so if you have this connection available, use it.

Floppy drives

The smallest notebook computers, sometimes called *subnotebooks,* do not have a built-in floppy drive. Instead, subnotebooks come supplied with an external floppy drive that you connect to your computer with a short cable that plugs into a *proprietary connector* (unique to the manufacturer) on the back of the computer.

Sometimes notebooks with a built-in floppy drive also offer a proprietary connector, to which you can hook up a second (external) floppy drive or an external CD-ROM drive (see the section "External CD-ROM drives" later in this chapter).

At the very least, you need a floppy drive to install new software (unless the software is on CD-ROM, in which case you need a CD-ROM drive). And if you're like me, you also need it to store files. Whenever I work with a subnotebook computer, I always take the floppy drive with me wherever I go.

External CD-ROM drives

If your notebook computer does not have a built-in *CD-ROM* (Compact Disc–Read-Only Memory) drive, you can add one as an external accessory. Many portable CD-ROM drives have their own battery power and can double as portable audio CD players, and they're about the same size as their audio-only brethren (but cost a bit more). If the CD-ROM drive draws its power from the laptop computer, you get less run time between battery charges when it is connected. Weight is typically in the one- to two-pound ballpark. The drives most often hook up to your computer via the parallel port, but some models connect via the PCMCIA/PC card slot, as shown in Figure 6-3.

Figure 6-3:
This Panasonic KXL-783A portable CD-ROM drive is 8x speed and hooks up using a PCMCIA/PC Type II card.

If your computer lacks not only a CD-ROM drive, but also lacks audio inputs, outputs, and speakers, look for a CD-ROM drive that also has a built-in multimedia audio system. A CD-ROM drive with built-in multimedia features spares you the hassle of installing a separate sound card and should prevent annoying device conflicts.

Removable hard drives

Most modern notebook computer designs incorporate removable internal hard drives, thus allowing you to upgrade to a higher capacity down the road, or to replace a faulty or crashed drive without junking the computer. If your internal hard drive just slides out from a panel underneath or on the side of the computer, you may be able to replace it yourself (see Figure 6-4).

If you replace an internal hard drive with a different model from what you originally had in your computer, you need to go into the computer's setup program (CMOS) to tell it about the new drive. Changing the CMOS settings is a fairly advanced operation that you may want to leave for your local computer guru or technician. In addition, if you are simply upgrading your drive, you also have to be willing to reinstall all the software you use. If you suffered a hard drive crash, then you have to replace everything anyway (I hope it never happens to you).

Figure 6-4:
A removable hard drive, from Simple Tech-nologies.

Note that you usually have to order the new hard drive directly from the manufacturer of your notebook computer. Although the guts of the drives are standard devices made by the usual hard drive manufacturers — Seagate, Western Digital, Maxtor, and so on — they are usually contained within a custom hookup arrangement and/or plastic shell that varies slightly for each brand of computer.

Besides upgrading, you can also use multiple drives to hold different data — such as different presentations. If you use multiple drives, they should all be identical (same size and model) so that you don't need to change any of the CMOS settings when you switch drives. With most computers, you need to first turn the computer off, then switch drives, and then turn the computer back on. But some models allow *hot swapping* — meaning you can actually change disk drives while the computer is up and running.

Removable cartridge hard drives

Removable cartridge hard drives, with cartridge capacities generally in the range of 100MB (megabytes) per disk up to as high as 1GB per disk, are very popular with the desktop publishing industry, multimedia production, and graphic artists. They provide a convenient way to move large files around — such as high-resolution color photo scans and audio files — and to make backups of important files on your hard drive. Iomega's popular Zip disk system is probably the most well known removable cartridge hard drive system; Syquest is their main competitor. For really large storage needs, Iomega's Jaz drive cartridges hold 1GB each (that's 1000MB). Removable cartridge hard drives are so popular that many copy places and other outfits that offer hourly computer rental now have one or more of the removable hard drives for customer use.

 Remember not to confuse a *removable cartridge* hard drive with an *external* hard drive. Both can be connected or removed from the computer. The difference lies in the details: Cartridge systems are also sometimes referred to as removable hard drives, and have a disk or cartridge that can be removed from the drive. Standard external hard drives have no cartridges, as I explain in the next section.

External hard drives

You can also add a second hard drive to your notebook computer via the parallel port, a PCMCIA/PC card connection, or a SCSI port if your computer has one. Although removable in the sense that you can connect and disconnect the drive at will, the disks themselves cannot be changed within the unit — that's how a hard drive is different from the removable cartridge hard drive described in the previous section (confusing, I know).

You can buy hard drives that plug into your computer's parallel port or PCMCIA/PC card slot from most well-stocked computer stores. Besides offering faster data transfer speeds, the PCMCIA/PC card connection also has the advantage of being *hot swappable* — meaning you can unplug one drive and plug in another while the computer is up and running.

A parallel-port-connected hard drive provides a very easy way to keep backup copies of large amounts of data. If your external hard drive is the same size as your notebook's built-in hard drive, you can just copy the entire contents of your internal hard drive every time you want to make a backup. This lazy approach saves you the effort of picking which specific files to back up — just back up everything, and breathe easy.

Flash memory cards

Okay, technically speaking, Flash memory cards are not really disk drives at all — they are solid state memory cards. However, you can use them for the same applications as disk drives — to store information even when the computer is turned off, and even when the cards are removed from the computer. So discussing them here makes sense.

Flash memory cards come in two sizes: The standard PCMCIA/PC card size, shown in Figure 6-5, and the smaller CompactFlash size, shown in Figure 6-6. The smaller CompactFlash cards can fit into an adapter and plug into a standard PCMCIA/PC card slot. Flash memory cards typically hold from 2MB to about 40MB of data — the bigger PCMCIA/PC card variety have the higher capacities, whereas CompactFlash cards typically hold just a few megabytes. Many digital cameras (see Figure 6-7) use flash memory cards to store images — depending on resolution and card capacity, you can get from around 10 to 100 pictures on each memory card. The Panasonic CoolShot KXL-601A stores 96 pictures with 320 x 240 resolution, or 24 pictures with 640 x 480 resolution, on a single 2MB CompactFlash card. With the PCMCIA/PC card variety, you can simply pull the card out of the camera, put it in your notebook computer, and import the photographs right into your document.

Flash memory cards are different from ordinary RAM because they use special types of memory chips called *nonvolatile* memory. These chips retain their data regardless of whether power is turned on or off, and are thus similar to disk drives. Because they are solid-state (no moving parts), they are much faster than disk drives, both for reading and writing information.

Figure 6-5:
This PCMCIA/PC card Flash memory card from Simple Technology holds 40MB of data.

Figure 6-6:
An 8MB Compact-Flash memory card fits into a PNY VersaCard Adapter to plug into a standard PCMCIA/PC card slot.

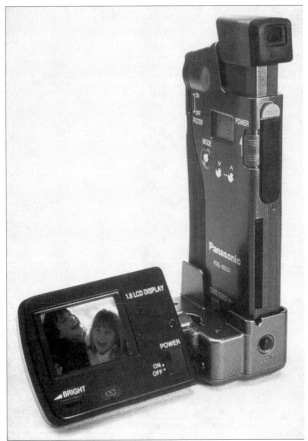

Figure 6-7:
The
Panasonic
CoolShot
KXL-601A.

Keyboards, Mice, and Monitors

Using a notebook computer while sitting on an airplane or in a library is one thing; using the computer from a vacation home, dorm room, or dining room table is quite another. Many people end up using a portable computer from a more or less fixed location, and only occasionally go mobile with it. After awhile, you may start wondering why you don't just use a desktop computer — especially if your notebook's keyboard is uncomfortable, its pointing device is frustrating, and its screen is fuzzy and small.

Fortunately, you can address all three of these problems without buying a new computer, simply by plugging in an external keyboard, mouse, and display to your laptop.

Keyboards are big but comfortable

If you do a lot of writing with your notebook computer from the same place, and if your hands or wrists ache after long writing sessions, I highly recommend that you buy an external keyboard to plug into your computer. Practically all notebooks have a special jack on the back or side to plug in an external keyboard — typically, it's a PS/2 jack, which is round with five little holes, as shown in Figure 6-8. External keyboards can cost as little as $20; special ergonomic models can cost several hundred dollars.

Figure 6-8:
The PS/2 type keyboard/ mouse jack is found on just about all notebook PCs.

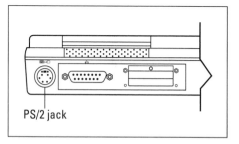

PS/2 jack

If you have an old keyboard with a big round connector that doesn't fit in your laptop's jack, you can buy an adapter at any computer store for about $5 that converts it to the right plug (PS/2 style) for your computer.

A mouse is a small thing to lug

If you're used to working with a traditional mouse on a desktop computer, the pointing device built into your notebook computer can be the most annoying part of your new portable friend. Some pointing systems are so irritating to use, you never really get comfortable with them.

Fortunately, with most notebooks, you can easily plug in an external mouse and use it instead of the built-in pointing device. A regular mouse can cost as little as $15 to $25, and is compact and lightweight enough to carry with you everywhere. Some models have been especially designed for notebook use (see Figure 6-9). If you don't mind the slight clumsiness of having to plug the mouse in each time, you may find that it is a great low-cost way to improve your overall enjoyment of using your laptop.

Figure 6-9:
The
MouseMan
is available
in both PS/2
and serial
port
versions,
and weighs
under four
ounces.

External mice for PC-compatibles come with two types of connectors:

- PS/2 keyboard connection (round)
- 9-pin serial port connection (trapezoid)

Almost all notebooks can accommodate the serial port version. With the PS/2 mouse version, you can plug the mouse into the PS/2 keyboard jack. However, if you also want the keyboard jack for an external keyboard, then you usually need to use the serial port for the mouse. Some notebook models have two PS/2 jacks in the back, one for a PS/2 keyboard, and one for a PS/2 mouse connection. Some other models come with a special adapter that plugs into the single PS/2 jack and provides separate connections for a mouse and keyboard.

The Apple PowerBook notebook computers have a similar-looking, but different (and of course incompatible) port for both an external keyboard and mouse, called the ADB port (Apple Desktop Bus). The ADB port is designed for connecting both an external keyboard and mouse at the same time — most external keyboards designed for use with Macintosh computers feature at least one extra ADB port, into which you can plug the mouse.

If your computer is running Windows 95 and doesn't immediately work with the external mouse after you hook it up, go into the Control Panel and click on the Add New Hardware icon, and let the computer search for the mouse (this process may take several minutes).

Microsoft makes a mouse intended for use with desktop computers, called the *bus mouse*, with a connector that looks very similar to a PS/2 connector, except that it has 9 pins, instead of the usual 4 or 6. It does not work with notebook computers, because it requires a special card that plugs into a desktop computer slot.

A monitor is a big thing to lug

Add a regular desktop type monitor, external keyboard, and mouse, and you have the functional equivalent of a desktop computer. Some notebook computer users hook up a big (15- or 17-inch) external monitor when using the computer at the home base, such as at the office, in a dorm room, or at home.

You can plug an external monitor into the VGA jack located on the back of most notebook PCs. Besides external monitors, a host of other display devices are available to plug into this jack. Take a look at Chapter 17 for more information on displays and projectors.

Expansion Stations and Port Replicators

Rather than having separate computers for desktop and portable use, you may be persuaded by the logic of buying just a single computer for both purposes, especially if you're the one footing the bill for all your computer equipment. With the addition of an expansion station or port replicator to your rig, you can get the full functionality of a desktop machine from your portable computer.

Expansion, or docking, station

The *expansion station* (or *docking station* — I call it an expansion station in this book), offers a way to add the standard plug-in cards intended for desktop computers to your laptop. I'm not talking here about the standard PCMCIA/PC cards that plug into notebook computers — rather, I'm talking about cards that go inside desktop machines. On PCs, these cards are usually called *ISA* (Industry Standard Architecture) or *PCI bus* cards (Peripheral Component Interconnect; *bus* refers to any electronic pathway). Note that not all expansion stations have ISA or PCI bus slots, and when they do, they usually have just one or two of them.

Some ISA and PCI bus cards offer highly specialized functions that you can't find in a PCMCIA/PC card version. For example, I use a PCI bus card for digital video editing. Most people don't need such cards, and so an expansion station is just a convenient way to connect an external keyboard, display, mouse, printer, and AC adapter in one easy, slide-it-right-in step, without having to fish with all the different cables.

Expansion stations are *proprietary devices* — each notebook manufacturer makes its own, and they generally don't work with other brands (or sometimes even other models from the same brand).

Some expansion stations also offer the ability to recharge a second battery outside the notebook computer. Many expansion stations also have built-in CD-ROM drives, as shown in Figure 6-10.

Figure 6-10: This expansion station from Toshiba has a built-in CD-ROM drive, and stereo speakers built into its sides.

Port replicator

A *port replicator* offers a lower-cost alternative to the expansion station, and is great if you don't need any slots for ISA or PCI bus cards, and just want the ease of a single connection when you bring your computer to your primary work space. Basically, the port replicator attaches to a single proprietary connector on the back of the computer, and through this connection, it provides the same connections for a full-sized keyboard, mouse, monitor, printer, and serial port that you have on the back of the computer itself. The advantage is that you don't have to fuss with five cables and figure out which thing goes where. You can leave all your external devices connected to the port replicator, and then simply connect the port replicator to your computer whenever you want.

✔ With most port replicators, you still have to plug in the AC adapter and phone line separately.

✔ Some port replicators and expansion stations also provide an additional serial port connection, or game port connection, that you don't find on the computer itself. On rare occasions, you may need two serial ports — such as to hook up an external mouse and external modem simultaneously.

Local Self-Serve Computer Places

I'll never forget the very first time I went traveling with a laptop computer, and had a deadline to meet on the road. I was in Amsterdam in the summer of 1985. My computer was a 12-pound laptop that ran the CP/M operating system (kind of like a horse-drawn carriage compared to Windows), and after finishing a magazine article I had due using its primitive but effective word processor, I needed to print it up. I walked into a Radio Shack store that I luckily found there, and begged a salesman to let me pay him to hook up my computer to one of their printers. He wouldn't take my money, but we spent about an hour talking about the future of computers (the salesman was amazed by my laptop machine, which was more sophisticated than Radio Shack's own pioneering portable computers).

Needless to say, rental computer places have sprung up everywhere since that day in 1985.

Nowadays, practically every big city has one or more of these businesses that specialize in printing and scanning for the desktop publishing industry. Especially near colleges, you find places with computers that you can rent by the hour and that are hooked up to printers and scanners that you can use for additional charges.

Though in many cities you have a wide choice of local shops that offer these services, the Kinko's chain of photocopy stores is a real (and dependable) pioneer in offering computer services in most of their copy shops.

Using local copy places and computer rental places for scanning and printing, you can actually use your notebook computer to produce professional documents for publication as brochures, ads, and so on. Professional high-resolution color scans — generated by *drum scanners* that cost thousands of dollars — generally cost about $10 to $20 each, and produce files that are several megabytes in size.

For much less money, you can often rent the use of a lower-resolution *flatbed scanner* by the hour — prices typically run about $20 per hour — and the quality is more than adequate for publishing newsletters, Web pages, and many other applications. Resolution is typically in the range of 600 to 800 dpi (dots per inch). You can save the file in any of several different file formats and then import it into any word-processing program such as WordPerfect or Word.

Chapter 7

Compact Alternatives

- -

In This Chapter

▶ The incredible shrinking computer

▶ Making sense of your compact alternatives

▶ Comparing operating systems for the various compact alternatives

▶ Pen-based computing

- -

*E*ver since pocket-sized computing devices became technically possible in the late 1980s, manufacturers have applied a variety of somewhat confusing and often overlapping terms to describe their wares. Here's a brief explanation of these terms:

✔ **PDA – Personal Digital Assistant.** This term is one that Apple helped coin when they introduced the Newton pen computer and that is now used by several other manufacturers. In its full glory — which has not yet really been achieved — the PDA is supposed to store notes and phone numbers and act as an intelligent agent that can access the Internet and accomplish tasks, such as finding the best airline flight for you to take (like an electronic travel agent). Anyway, PDAs tend to have the most computing power and are comparable to handheld PCs (HPCs) in the amount of computing power they have (processor speed and memory) and the types of tasks they can perform (word processing, address book, e-mail, and so on).

✔ **Pocket Organizer.** Manufacturers who use this term to describe a device are making clear that the device is not really a full-fledged computer. Electronic pocket organizers don't claim to be anything more than address books, appointment schedulers, and to-do lists.

✔ **HPC – Handheld PC.** This term was coined by Microsoft when they introduced the Windows CE operating system and is therefore usually applied only to devices that run Windows CE, even though the term can obviously be more generic. What makes HPCs different from all the rest is the fact that they conform to the common Windows CE operating system, and so the experience of using numerous different brands of HPCs (see Figure 7-1) is essentially the same (see Windows CE in "Proprietary OS versus Windows CE," later in this chapter).

Figure 7-1:
Handheld
PCs, such
as this one
from LG
Electronics,
often have
a miniature
keyboard, a
touch-
sensitive
screen, and
a stylus as
the pointing
device.

- ✔ **Palmtop computer.** This term applies generally to any computer that does not have a standard-sized keyboard. In a way, *palmtop computer* can describe this entire list of devices, but most often, it describes the next size smaller than a sub-notebook computer. A palmtop has a Pentium-type processor that can run Windows 95 (not Windows CE) and a built-in hard drive. Some models weigh under two pounds.

- ✔ **Pen computer.** This denotes a computer, usually pocket-sized (but not always), that has a touch-sensitive screen that you use to select functions and data and handwriting recognition capabilities (see "Handwriting Recognition: The Holy Grail?" later in this chapter).

- ✔ **Pocket computer.** This generic term can apply to all these devices — anything smaller than a subnotebook. I prefer to use this term to describe the entire category. Unlike handheld PC (HPC), it doesn't imply any particular operating system; and unlike PDA, it doesn't imply some grandiose new lifestyle role. A pocket computer is simply a computer that fits in your pocket. Of course, that may depend on how big your pockets are.

Weight, Size, and Juice

The main advantage of all pocket computers, of course, is that they are smaller and lighter than even the smallest subnotebook computers. Many models fit comfortably in the breast pocket of a jacket and weigh less than one pound.

Because pocket computers use less powerful processor chips, have less memory, and no disk drives, they tend to use less power than their note-book-sized brethren. But more than anything else, they save power in their displays. Sometimes pocket computer displays are not even backlit, and when a backlight is available, it usually stays on for just a minute or two and then automatically turns off. These factors contribute to much longer battery run time than notebook computers — pocket computers typically get around 50 to 100 hours of use on a set of batteries. So unlike notebooks, which always run from rechargeables, pocket computers are usually pow-ered by standard throw-away AA or AAA batteries.

A Full-Sized Keyboard

Pocket-sized computers all have keyboards that are too small to type on comfortably. These keyboards are fine for entering names, addresses, phone numbers, and brief notes, but don't try writing a report or term paper.

A regular full-sized keyboard, such as what you find on a desktop PC and on most notebooks, has 19 millimeter spacing between the main alphabet keys. Some of the advanced palmtop computers — with Pentium processors and full computer functionality — have 12 millimeter spacing, which is very cramped but may be workable for touch typing if you have small hands. Most pocket computers have keys that are spaced just 8 to 10 millimeters apart, which practically dictates using the one-finger hunt-and peck ap-proach to typing.

Pocket-Sized Screens

The displays you find on pocket-sized computers are quite different from notebook and subnotebooks. They have lower resolution, typically 320 x 240 pixels or less, and they are monochrome, not color. Text typically appears as black against a green background.

In spite of these drawbacks, pocket computer screens commonly have one feature that bigger, more expensive notebook computer screens lack: They are touch-sensitive. A touch-sensitive screen eliminates the need for a pointer device like a mouse or touchpad — you can tell the pocket com-puter what you want to do by just pressing the choice right on the screen itself. Most models come equipped with a stylus that you can use to press on the screen, but you can also use your fingertips.

Computing Muscle

For the basic task of word processing, you can do just fine with much simpler processors than those in notebook computers. Some of the more compact pocket computers actually have all the processing power you need — the problem is that their keyboards and screens are too small.

Some of these pocket computers include facilities for you to retrieve and send e-mail messages. Of course, they can't handle file attachments or other more advanced e-mail functions, but for sending and receiving basic text messages, they may meet your needs.

 Check out the details very carefully if you buy a pocket computer for e-mail. Many models require that you purchase a separate modem, and the built-in modems tend to run more slowly than on notebook computers — not much of a concern, unless you receive lengthy messages.

So if the only real needs that you have for a portable computer are to keep track of appointments and contacts, to jot down occasional notes, and to send and receive e-mail, one of the pocket-sized models may be just the ticket.

If you want to do anything more, however — such as writing reports, working with spreadsheets, browsing the Internet, accessing databases — then you need at least a subnotebook computer to do it.

Proprietary OS versus Windows CE

Prior to 1996, each brand of pocket computer used its own proprietary operating system. If you purchased a Sharp Zaurus, a U.S. Robotics Pilot, or an Apple Newton, for example, you could run only programs written specifically for that type of pocket computer. Most people who buy these devices don't ever buy any additional software anyway — the built-in contact management, scheduler, and notepad software is usually sufficient. Almost all these devices come with some means of linking up to a desktop or notebook computer, via infrared or serial port connection, so that, for example, you can transfer a memo that you write on your pocket computer to your desktop machine.

Windows CE

In 1996, Microsoft introduced the Windows CE operating system. Windows CE (CE is widely believed to stand for Consumer Electronics) is like Windows lite — it's designed specifically to run on less powerful computers, for portable applications (see Figure 7-2).

What makes HPCs different from other pocket computer systems is that they conform to a common standard. Just as desktop PCs and laptop computers were originally standardized on the DOS, Windows, and Macintosh operating systems many years ago, pocket organizers are now going through that same transformation.

You benefit from a common software standard in a number of ways. First, you don't have to worry about getting stuck with a future orphan technology that may be abandoned a year or two down the road. Second, you're assured that the time and effort you spend entering names and numbers won't be wasted a few years later when you buy a newer, spiffier model. You should be able to transfer the data over to the new machine. Third, the common standard encourages development of new software by third-party publishers.

Windows CE includes several applications that should satisfy the needs of most users without any additional software. It includes Pocket Excel (spreadsheet), Pocket Word (word processor), Inbox (e-mail), and personal information software (calendar, address book, tasks) — each of these can exchange data with more powerful desktop versions of the software. You also get Pocket Internet Explorer, a stripped-down version of Microsoft's Web browser — realistically, Pocket Internet Explorer (or PIE as it's called) is not really compatible with many Web pages, due to the lack of color, smaller screen size, and the inability to add plug-ins like RealAudio and Java.

Figure 7-2:
The Windows CE operating system is available on numerous brands of handheld PCs, such as this one from Casio.

If you need additional software, the common Windows CE operating standard for numerous brands is a big advantage because it spurs software development by independent third parties — just as keeps happening with software for desktop PCs. If you want to go beyond the basic software that comes included, you can most likely find what you need in the Windows CE format. Symantec's PC Anywhere, for example, is available in a Windows CE version — this program allows you to control your desktop computer from a remote location (see Chapter 13). And WyndMail for Windows CE, an e-mail program, works in conjunction with a wireless PC card (PCMCIA) radio modem (the U.S. Robotics Megahertz AllPoints — see Chapter 21). These sorts of nifty third-party products are not generally available for the pocket computer platforms.

Microsoft claims that another advantage of Windows CE-based pocket computers is that they are easier to learn how to use, because their interface resembles one most computer users already know — Windows 95. To be fair, however, the other pocket computer systems are quite easy to learn, too.

Understandably, the hardware companies that have spent considerable resources developing their own pocket computing software — most notably Apple and Sharp — are not jumping on the Windows CE bandwagon just yet. . . .

The manufacturers of Windows CE pocket computers include Casio, Compaq, Hewlett Packard (whose previous Palmtop PC model was unusual in that it ran a light version of DOS), Hitachi, LG Electronics (GoldStar), NEC, and Philips. Some models come with built-in modems whereas others have modems optionally available. (Most accept standard PCMCIA/PC cards — the same kind that notebook computers use, so you can add a modem and use the HPC to send and retrieve e-mail, or to fax.) Other differences among brands include keyboard layout, the inclusion of a backlight, processor speed (typically 25 to 50 MHz) and the amount of memory (usually in the 2MB to 6MB range).

Because notebook computers and pocket computers use the same PCMCIA/PC card modems, if you have both types of mobile computers, you can save money by swapping one card between the two. This also makes an upgrade to newer, faster modem technology cheaper.

Sharp Zaurus

Sharp is the world's leading manufacturer of LCD screens, and probably as a result, the company really pioneered the pocket computer/organizer product category with the Wizard and Zaurus series. Sharp was the first to offer *digital ink* — the ability to write notes directly on the screen, and have them saved as picture files. However, the current Zaurus models are not up-to-date. They have excellent built-in software for contact management, appointments, jotting notes, and sending e-mail (some models even have a built-in fax/modem, as shown in Figure 7-3). They have everything going for them except one detail: They're not on the Microsoft Windows CE bandwagon, and from my vantage point, Windows CE is the writing on the wall.

Sharp has also been a leader in putting infrared ports in both its pocket computers and its notebook units. If you purchase the same brand for both your pocket organizer and notebook computer, you're assured of the ability to transfer data between the two without wires. Sharp's address book system has a sophisticated synchronization system goes one step beyond the usual ability to find whichever version of the file is newest (see Chapter 9). With the Zaurus contact manager system, you can actually add new names on both your notebook computer and on your Zaurus pocket computer, and then when you synchronize, each device sends the new entries to the other.

The Zaurus theoretically has the most advanced screen technology of all pocket computers — which should come as no surprise, considering Sharp makes more than half of all the LCD screens used in notebook computers. The most advanced version of the Zaurus has a color screen and comes with accessories that turn it into a digital camera and Web browser. I say *theoretically*, because, at least when this book was going to press, Sharp hadn't yet brought this advanced color Zaurus model to the U.S. — so you may have to finally take that trip to Japan to get one.

Figure 7-3:
Sharp
Zaurus ZR-
3500X has a
built-in fax/
modem.

U.S. Robotics Pilot

The U.S. Robotics Pilot is innovative in that it has no keyboard — it's designed to be operated from the touch screen. However, the Pilot has no handwriting recognition software, so all entries are made using an on-screen soft keyboard or the digital-ink memo pad system. The Pilot uses a connecting cable to share data with a PC. In other respects, it is a pretty basic pocket organizer with address book, to-do lists, appointments, and expense registers.

Psion Series 3

Psion was a real pioneer of pocket computing and still has a following, though it is questionable as to how long they can continue to offer their own proprietary operating system rather than switching to Windows CE. The most advanced Psion model, the 3C, includes an IrDA port for transferring data and printing on compatible printers. And with an optional modem, it has the ability to receive attachments along with ordinary e-mail as well as send faxes. It also has reasonably sophisticated word processor and spreadsheet programs built in.

Apple Newton MessagePad

The Newton probably has more computing power built into its slightly bigger-than pocket-sized case than any of the other devices in this chapter. Its price tag matches its power — you can actually find notebook computers for less money.

What makes the Newton MessagePad (see Figure 7-4) special is that it offers true pen-based computing. Not mere digital ink, but actual handwriting recognition. You can scribble notes into its address book, calendar scheduler, or notepad, and about a second or two later, it converts your handwriting into standard alphanumeric text. The 6-inch diagonal screen — almost as big as the entire unit — has a hefty 480 x 320 resolution, and like all the computers in this chapter, it is monochrome (not color), with text appearing as black against a green background. A backlight can be optionally turned on for operation in the dark. The Newton MessagePad also has a built-in infrared port, two PCMCIA/PC card slots, and a serial connector for hooking up a keyboard or transferring data.

The Newton has attracted a loyal following over the past few years, and by all accounts, the handwriting recognition keeps getting better. The Newton comes with an accessory keyboard — a full-size keyboard that I can actually type on. The whole computer, including this keyboard, weighs exactly two pounds.

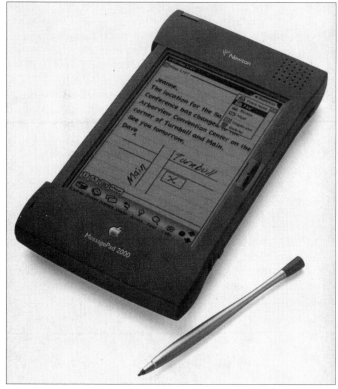

Figure 7-4:
The Newton
MessagePad
2000.
Courtesy of
Apple
Computer,
John
Greenleigh,
photo-
grapher.

A cable and Windows 95 software supplied with the MessagePad allow fairly easy transfer of files over to a PC or to a Macintosh computer. Note that the MessagePad's operating system is completely independent of the Macintosh operating system — the only software the Newton MessagePad runs are programs written specifically for it.

Of all the pocket-sized devices mentioned in this chapter, it's the only one I would recommend to anyone who intends to use the machine for writing anything longer than a brief memo — but note that though lightweight, the extra keyboard is hardly pocket-sized.

Apple eMate

Technically, the Apple eMate (model 300) is not a pocket computer — it's about the same size as a small notebook (see Figure 7-5), and at about 4 pounds, just a bit lighter. However, the eMate resembles other pocket computers in a number of ways. Like the other devices listed in this chapter, the eMate lacks both a hard drive and a floppy drive. Everything gets stored in solid-state memory. The eMate actually uses the same operating system as the Newton MessagePad — in fact, to be technically accurate, Newton is the name of the operating system, and the handheld device that most people call *the Newton* is actually called a MessagePad in Apple jargon, as I describe in the previous section. In any event, the eMate has almost the same display screen as the MessagePad — at 7 inches diagonal, it's slightly larger than the MessagePad, but still considerably smaller than most notebooks. Like the MessagePad, it's monochrome (black on green), has 480 × 320 resolution (half of normal VGA), and is touch-sensitive. Also, it doesn't have a pointing device — you touch the screen directly to tell it what to do. And like the MessagePad Newton, the backlight can optionally be switched on.

Unlike the handheld Newton MessagePad 2000, however, the eMate 300 does not include handwriting recognition software. Instead, it comes with several other programs that its handheld cousin lacks — including a word processor with more power than the notepad function, a drawing program, spreadsheet, and graphing calculator. These programs are all geared to the needs of students.

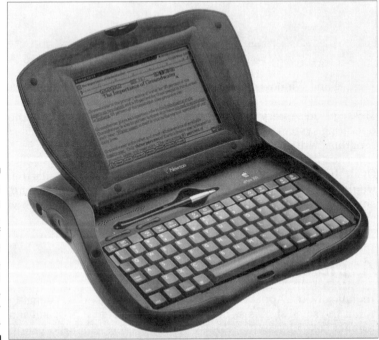

Figure 7-5: The Apple eMate 300. Courtesy of Apple Computer, John Greenleigh, photographer.

The primary market for the eMate is not the ordinary consumer, but school systems. Apple has designed the eMate to be a rugged unit that students can, for example, check out of a central supply room for use during a science laboratory class. However, it also makes a great kids' computer. Like the pocket unit, the eMates include a serial port and an infrared port so that students can send data to a printer or to a teacher's computer for grading. File transfer software for both the Macintosh and Windows 95 operating systems is also included.

If you're in the market for a regular notebook computer, with a hard drive, color screen, and a wide choice of available software, the eMate isn't really in the running. This is not a computer for a sales manager who needs to crunch spreadsheets, prepare sales reports, and display multimedia presentations. Then again, neither are any of the other computers in this chapter. The eMate has the same kind of computing capabilities that smaller pocket units have, and packages them in a bigger, more rugged case with a full-sized keyboard. For students and educational use, and as a kids' computer, eMate is a clever niche product.

Handwriting Recognition: The Holy Grail?

The ability to convert handwritten notes into standard computer text that can be edited in a word processor and printed on a printer has been the holy grail of pocket computing for several years. When Apple launched its Newton line back in 1993, they promised that it would do just that — but most users were disappointed by the initial results. The newer Newton models (such as the MessagePad 2000) actually do quite a good job of recognizing handwriting — if you're willing to discipline the way that you write characters on the touch-sensitive screen.

The problem with handwriting lengthy documents is twofold: First, even when recognition is 95 percent accurate, which is roughly where I estimate Apple's Newton 2000 to be after some training to figure out how to write on it, you still end up with one error every three or four words (a typical word has five characters, so 95 percent accuracy translates into one error per four words). My second complaint is relevant to anyone who already knows how to touch type: You may not realize it, but typing — even if you're a comparatively slow typist, as I am — is still quite a bit faster than longhand writing.

About three or four years ago, pen computing was the hottest thing happening in portable computing. Though technically nifty, these computers never really gained a foothold in the consumer marketplace — they have instead become industrial products that get sold for *vertical applications* (where a company buys hundreds or thousands of units to equip a fleet with its own custom software). For example, a shipping company may use these computers to fill out order forms, or an automobile manufacturer may use a pen-based system as a repair mechanic's tool to run diagnostic tests on a car's on-board computer — in fact you probably see something like this now and again. Some retail stores even use a pen-based system to get your signature for credit card purchases. (For more on stuff like this, look up AllPen Software in the Appendix — they put together custom packages, and also sell a Web browser for the Newton operating system.)

Pen computing does have one other big advantage over keyboard-based computing: The device can be made much smaller, because the manufacturer gets to save all the real estate that would normally be devoted to the keys.

Also, pen computing is more than just handwriting recognition for letters and numbers — it's also a way of controlling the computer to edit the text you enter. On the Apple Newton MessagePad 2000, for example, writing a ^ (caret) symbol moves the insertion point (cursor) to the spot where you write it. Drawing a zigzag line through a section deletes it.

All pen-based computers offer a *soft keyboard* as an alternative to handwriting recognition. No, a soft keyboard isn't a pillow with buttons — rather it's a software-based keyboard that pops up on the screen. A picture of a standard-layout (QWERTY) keyboard or a simpler ABCD keyboard appears on screen, and by touching the computer's stylus to these keys, you can type in letters and numbers without the error-prone handwriting recognition. Such soft keyboards are absolutely essential when you want to enter punctuation symbols accurately.

Use the soft keyboard for entering phone numbers and other numeric data — it's just as fast as handwriting, and more precise.

Chapter 8

Traveling with a Laptop

· ·

· ·

*P*erhaps more than anything else, laptop computers are about freedom. With a portable computer, you are free to do your work practically anywhere. With a laptop computer, you can take your work (or your computer fun) anywhere. You can make use of all the unproductive time you spend riding on airplanes, trains, or buses (cars too, as long as you're not driving.)

But I wouldn't be honest if I did not also report the down side to all this freedom. I call the first concern of a laptop relationship *lugging,* and though most models are small and reasonably lightweight, a notebook computer constitutes one of the most annoying pieces of luggage you ever have to handle.

Your second concern when traveling with a laptop is security, both in terms of theft and protection from damage. Notebook computers are fragile and costly items that are worth protecting, or sometimes, worth *not* bringing along on a trip.

And finally, who cares whether your laptop is heavy, broken, or stolen if it's useless anyway because you ran out of power and can't even turn it on? Well, you probably realize that all you need to do is plug in your adapter/ charger and things are okay again, but how do you plug in on the road? You can sneak into someone's back yard, find the outdoor power plug, and crouch in the bushes until you're charged up, or you can read this chapter and avoid the possibility of being arrested as a Charging Tom.

The Joy and Misery of Lugging Your Laptop

Granted, packed in its carrying case with perhaps a floppy disk and charger, your notebook computer is not particularly big — at least compared with a suitcase or backpack. But when you toss even a lightweight six-pound notebook in a day pack, you feel it. By the end of the day, you may be ready to curse this hi-tech brick you're lugging — especially if you don't even get a chance to use it.

And then you have the inevitable worries — after all, a notebook computer is both very valuable and very delicate. When you travel with your laptop, you need to maintain a constant awareness of the possibility of both theft and breakage.

In the first two chapters of this book I speak a bit about how all portable computers are essentially a compromise: How much of the functionality of a full-size desktop computer are you willing to live without, for the sake of portable convenience?

The initial choice you make — about what's an acceptable size and weight — influences your decision every time you debate whether to bring the computer along. And ultimately, I guarantee you, you have times when you wish that instead of opting for a notebook-sized machine, as most people do, you bought one of the smaller and lighter palmtop models I describe in Chapter 2.

Traveling with a notebook computer is a bit of a balancing act. You need to consider

- ✔ Your desire to take the computer with you everywhere versus the reality that you may not have time (or be too distracted by other, more fun activities) to work.

- ✔ The freedom to do your work practically anywhere versus the trap of working non-stop — even when you're on an outing and supposedly spending time with your family and friends.

- ✔ The possibility of theft and damage — your laptop may become a burden if you need to keep it with you at all times. Having to keep your laptop safe can limit your spontaneity and flexibility.

- ✔ The need to keep the battery recharged versus the desire to have unlimited portable computing power wherever and whenever you want it.

Of course, only you can decide when to take your laptop computer along, and when to leave it behind (and where you can safely leave it).

Figuring the total weight

Ultimately, when you travel with a computer, the total weight — not just the computer itself, but also all the accessories you're lugging — is what counts. Unless you're just going on a day outing, you probably don't carry your computer very far without also lugging along its AC power adapter/charger. You may even be thinking about bringing along a second battery, or perhaps even a portable printer — all these things increase the weight.

My advice is to be wary about taking much else along besides the computer, the AC adapter, a few extra floppies (assuming you have a floppy drive), and perhaps your phone cords and adapters. Among the worst weight offenders are the instruction manuals for your computer and the software you use. after you are comfortable with your computer and can leave instruction manuals behind, you can cut down on travel weight quite a bit by leaving them at home. (Of course, you still want to bring this book with you.)

Security considerations

Be street smart when you travel with a computer — especially when you're nowhere near a city street. Beaches are particularly problematic because your computer can't swim with you. When you are at a public beach you want to

 ✔ Keep the computer with a large group of people where at least one person stays there at all times.

 ✔ Conceal the computer by leaving it in a cheap-looking tote bag while you go swimming and don't start using the computer until after you're finished.

I can tell you from personal experience that it's no fun asking your traveling companion to take turns swimming because you want someone to stay and watch the computer. Swimming together is always more fun, and safer, too.

Of course, not everyone lives near the beach. Consider other real-life security situations that may come up:

 ✔ You're in a café or airport bar alone, working with your computer. You want to go to the bathroom and then resume working. Is the computer safe to leave on your table? Should you ask a waiter or waitress to watch it? Will it be confiscated by airport security who assume everything left anywhere is a bomb?

✔ You're attending a day-long conference or convention at a hotel, and you want to check your computer at the bell desk. But they insist you sign a waiver stating that they're not responsible for computers (like, uh, so they have permission to sell it to a pawn shop?). Should you sign it, or lug the computer around all day?

✔ You're staying in a hotel with a laptop computer and a rented car. The hotel says not to leave valuables in the room, but when you ask whether you can leave your computer at the front desk where they keep valuables for valued guests, they say that their safe deposit boxes are too small. What should you do? Here are your choices:

   A. Leave the computer in the room, but attempt to hide it (under your underwear, for example — a spot that no maid has ever dared visit).

   B. Check the computer with the bell desk every day when you go out, and pick it up when you return. Tip the bellhop each time.

   C. Take the computer with you when you go out, and leave it in the trunk of the car (packed in foam, or lots of underwear!).

   D. Take the computer with you and lug it around everywhere you go all day and night. Don't ever let it out of your sight.

I have no right answer to this problem. At various times, I have exercised all these options. A couple of times, while traveling in Europe, I left my computer in a rented locker, sometimes for days at a time, and took it out only when I needed it to write.

Call me neurotic (my wife sure does!), but in some hotels I've been known to take the computer out of the room until after I knew for sure that the maid had cleaned it, and then leave the computer in the room for the rest of the day.

For me, the best solution all depends on a vibe about a particular place that suggests that one course of computer security precaution makes more sense than another.

If you keep a laptop in a dorm room or in an open office, you can buy an accessory lock, available at larger computer stores, that tethers your laptop to a tabletop via a thick metal cable, much like a bike lock.

Information security

Besides worrying about the physical security of your computer and its lost value should it be stolen, may I also suggest concern for the information you're carrying in the computer. This concern may cut both ways — you certainly don't want to lose the information in the computer, and you also may not want anyone else's prying eyes to examine your files.

Periodically making backups of your notebook computer's hard drive is a good idea, and an especially good one if you are about to go traveling with it. Losing the monetary value of the computer is one thing — losing the value of the information you have on it is another. The best backup strategy, though the most cumbersome, is to make a backup copy of the entire hard drive, using another hard drive, or an external tape or removable disk system. If you don't have access to any such devices and can't readily copy large amounts of your hard drive, then at the very least make floppy disk copies of your documents, spreadsheets, and address books.

When traveling, periodically make copies of your important files on floppy disks, and store these floppies separately from the computer, to serve as emergency backup files. If your computer doesn't have a floppy drive, you can use e-mail to store emergency backup files — just send yourself (or coworker) a note, and attach copies of the files you want to back up.

Establishing a password for access to your notebook computer — in both Windows 95 and Macintosh — prevents unauthorized users from seeing anything on your computer. This is particularly relevant in dorm rooms and open offices. (Be sure that you don't forget your password!)

To active the password feature on Windows 95 notebooks, follow these steps:

1. **Click Start⇨Settings⇨Control Panel to launch the Controls Panel, which appears as a panel filled with icons for such things as modems, display, mouse, printers, and so on.**

2. **Find the icon the Passwords icon (it looks like a set of keys) and double-click on it.**

   A new Passwords Properties dialog box appears.

3. **Make sure that the Change Passwords tab at the top is selected (click on it if it isn't selected).**

4. **Click on the Change Windows Password button in the top half of this dialog box.**

   A new, smaller dialog box appears, as shown in Figure 8-1.

5. **If you are installing a password for the first time, leave the text box next to Old password blank.**

6. **Make up a password, and enter it in the New password text box.**

7. **Enter the exact same password, again, in the Confirm new password text box.**

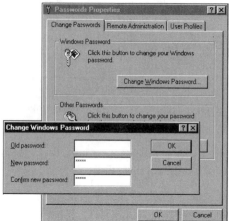

Figure 8-1:
The
Windows 95
Change
Windows
Password
dialog box.

8. **Write down the password you have created on a slip of paper and put it in your wallet, or other place, for safekeeping.**

9. **Click OK.**

   An alert box appears that says, "The Windows password has been successfully changed."

10. **Click OK, then click the Close button on the Password Properties dialog, and then click the X in the upper right corner of the Control Panel to close everything up.**

    The next time you boot up the computer, Windows 95 requires you to enter the password.

11. **To cancel the use of a password, repeat steps 1 - 10, except for steps 5, 6 and 7, in which you need enter the password you want to stop using in the Old password box, and leave the two fields for New password and Confirm new password blank.**

Packing your notebook for stealth and protection

Think how often you are jostled, bumped, run into, or otherwise aggravated when you travel. Be it by other people in public places, in buses or cars, or just walking around and knocking into things, you and your computer both stand to be bumped now and then. I don't recommend that you wear any kind of football pads for standard travel, but your computer may benefit from the following precautions:

✔ Do not put it in the trunk of a car, for example, unless you pack it in thick layers of foam (as in the original box it came in) or other cushions. I always carry my notebook computer on the seat of a car and strap the computer in place using the seatbelt.

✔ Be careful about putting things on top of your computer. Always place the computer on *top*. Avoid putting any weight on top of the computer, because pressure on the screen can break it.

✔ When you take the notebook to a beach or a park, be careful not to allow sand or dirt to get into the keyboard, floppy drive, or the jacks in back. The more rugged notebook models have covers to protect the jacks.

✔ Do not allow cab drivers or luggage handlers to toss your computer.

✔ Always take your computer as a carry-on on an airplane, to prevent it from getting bumped around or stolen.

 Whenever I can, I carry my computer in a regular-looking knapsack rather than in a standard-issue computer case that tells would-be thieves what's inside. Usually I wrap the computer with a sweater or jacket or other soft items — they provide an extra layer of cushioning for the computer and something to wear if I get cold.

(Not) attracting attention

Whenever you use a computer in a public place — a park, a beach, a restaurant, a café, a library, an urban plaza, a plane, a train, and so on — you may attract the attention of people who happen to be nearby.

Only you can decide how comfortable you feel when you use a computer in any particular situation — I have no hard and fast rules to guide you. I can tell you that the bigger (and noisier) the computer, the more attention you're likely to attract — the palmtop/handheld PC models I describe in Chapters 1 and 7 have a clear advantage when you want to be discreet.

You have two things to be concerned about when you are noticed with your laptop: theft and the feeling that people are staring at you because what you're doing (using a notebook computer) is so unusual. Granted, this feeling isn't an issue when you're waiting for a connecting flight in Atlanta. But if you make your way to the less developed parts of the world and start using your laptop on a beach or in an outdoor restaurant, for example, you may find yourself the object of a good deal of curiosity.

Finally, note that some notebook computers have been especially designed for your abusive behavior, known as *ruggedized* computers. Panasonic has been a leader in this area, offering a line of computers that they claim is drop-proof. You pay a premium for this feature, but gain a certain peace of mind. Unfortunately, to date, no one makes a theft-proof computer.

Passing your laptop through the x-ray machine

As you go through an airport to your plane, you pass through the x-ray security check area and you may wonder if the x-rays are safe for your notebook computer. The official answer is yes — it's safe. Fortunately, if you suffer from this neurosis, the airport security personnel will usually indulge your fears and let you take your notebook through the checkpoint without x-rays, as long as you can demonstrate that the computer turns on and the screen lights up. (This is their way of verifying that you haven't gutted the insides and replaced them with plastic explosives.) So the moral is: If you're neurotic about x-rays, be sure your battery isn't dead when you go into an airport.

AC Power for Your Portable

When you travel with a laptop computer, you become very aware of the battery's charging needs, especially if you fly or take trains a lot, and use the computer while in transit. Of course, you want to begin every trip with a fully charged battery, but sometimes that's not enough.

Suppose that you're catching two two-hour flights with an hour stopover in the city where you change planes. You use the computer for an hour-and-a-half on the first flight, and the battery is almost completely drained. Yet you still have to work to do on the second flight. What do you do?

Your answers depend on your own style, work habits, and preparedness. The more you depend on your notebook computer, the more you find yourself in restaurants, or other people's offices or homes, asking whether it's okay to plug in your AC charger and get your battery in shape for the next leg of your trip. And the more your battery runs out in the middle of your work, the more you wish you had a second or third battery to take along with you (see Chapter 3 for more battery stuff).

If you travel internationally, plugging into AC power becomes a bit more complicated. Fortunately, just about all AC adapters for notebook computers are designed to work with a wide range of input voltages, so you usually do not have to worry that the electricity in a foreign country is different from that at home. AC power in the US and several Asian and South American countries is 110 to 120 volts, but in most of Europe, Africa, and parts of Asia, it's 220 to 240 volts.

Just look at the fine print on your AC adapter to be sure that it's suitable for use in foreign countries without a voltage converter. It should say, "100 to 240-volts, 50/60 Hz" — meaning you can use it practically anywhere.

Usually, the 240-volt systems operate at 50 Hz, whereas the U.S. power and most other 120-volt systems run at 60 Hz. This difference is important for some motorized equipment but doesn't affect portable computer equipment, because what the AC adapters do, in essence, is convert the alternating current to DC (which is like 0 Hz — it doesn't alternate).

Different plugs

The fact that you can use your AC adapter/charger with any AC voltage, however, does not mean that it just plugs right into the wall anywhere you go. Although the AC adapter may be compatible with the local voltage, you also need to make its plug compatible with the local wall sockets. The two flat blades used in the AC plugs in the U.S. are actually not very popular around the world — in most countries, the wall outlets are designed for plugs with two round pins. So you need a converter that adapts your AC plug to fit the local wall outlets.

You can buy a kit for about $10 at Radio Shack containing adapters to convert U.S.-style plugs to the most popular plug types used around the world . You also may try a luggage and travel store, if you have such a thing near you. Be sure to buy just a simple plug adapter, and not a voltage converter!

Finally, note that if you look very carefully at the two flat blades on your AC adapter plug, you may observe that one is slightly wider than the other. A plug like this is called a polarized AC plug — polarized plugs are safer than the earlier style with both blades the same size. Fortunately, the problem is rare — most AC adapters for computers come with non-polarized plugs, which fit in any outlet. But if you do encounter the problem, get an adapter — most hardware stores can sell you an adapter for older, non-polarized wiring.

Different voltages

What if your computer's AC power adapter works only with 110 to 120 volts? Then you have to get a *transformer,* which converts 220/240 to 110/120. You can buy a power transformer at Radio Shack, and most other general electronics stores. Prices range from about $20 to over $100, depending on how much power — measured in watts — a particular model is capable of handling. Notebook computer AC adapter/chargers typically require 150 to 200 watts, but don't take my advice — check the fine print on your computer's AC adapter, or the instruction manual, to determine the wattage. In addition, if you plan to use a portable printer or other device at the same time, add the wattage of the additional device to your total.

- ✔ Sometimes the number of watts needed by the power supply is not listed directly on the computer's AC adapter/charger. Instead, you must calculate it based on the voltage and the amperage. The number of watts is equal to the number of volts × the number of amps. For example, if the AC adapter says, "110-volts, 1.2 amps," then it requires 132-watts (that's 110 V × 1.2 A = 132 W).

- ✔ Sometimes the letters V, A, and W are used as abbreviations for volts, amps, and watts, respectively.

Phone Connections: Worthy of an Entire Chapter!

I bet that the most frustrating aspects of your travels with a computer — unless it gets stolen — are your attempts to plug into the unfamiliar phone systems and connect to an online service, the Internet, and/or your office or home computer system.

The unbounded joy you can experience with phone connection presents a variety of specific challenges. Fortunately, you can overcome most of them rather easily, but I need to have an entire chapter to go through all the possible problems and remedies.

Oh, yeah, that's the heart and soul of Chapter 19.

Part II
Staying Connected

In this part . . .

This part is about what to do if your notebook is *not* the only computer in the world you care about. If you have other computers in your life —such as a desktop computer at your office, or an online service or the Internet on the side, or even a bevy of fax machines — you need to know how to get access with your portable computer. In the next few chapters, I show you all you need to know to connect to the basic stuff like e-mail, fax machines, the Web and Internet, and other desktop computers for file transfers and remote computing.

The connections available to your mobile computer run from the mundane — such as the ability to send a fax to a circa 1985 fax machine (see Chapter 14) — to the truly mind boggling. Some gadgets are straight out of a James Bond movie — check out the wireless modems that can tie your notebook or pocket computer into the Internet while you camp in the Catskills in Chapter 21. You can even use remote computing software to connect to your desktop computer and access its files and software.

This part really gets down to some of the cool, road warrior stuff that makes owning a portable computer so much fun.

Chapter 9

Exchanging and Synchronizing Files Between Two Computers

. . . .

In This Chapter

▶ Keeping your notebook and desktop computers in sync

▶ Using the Windows 95 Briefcase

▶ Using LapLink

▶ Connecting two computers with an infrared (IrDA) port

. . . .

*I*f you work with two different computers — for example, a desktop computer at your office and a laptop when you travel — you need to be able to exchange data between them. Transferring data between computers is the key to bringing your work from the office along with you when you travel or taking your work home with you. Ahh, yes — who doesn't want to take more work home? (Are you sure that you want to know how to do this stuff?)

Moving Files with Floppy Disks

The easiest way to move files between two computers is by using a floppy disk. You simply save, or transfer from the hard drive, the files from your first computer that you want to move onto a floppy. Then remove the floppy from the first computer, stick it in the second computer, and open the file(s) to use them, or transfer them from the floppy to the second computer's hard drive.

The floppy method may not seem like the most technically elegant way to move data around, but believe me, it's the fastest and most hassle-free approach in many cases. If, for example, your needs are limited to working on a couple of word-processor documents or a spreadsheet, a floppy works just fine. Transferring files via floppy disk also has the advantage that the two computers don't need to be anywhere near each other — you can leave your notebook computer at home, for example, and bring back files from the office on a floppy in your shirt pocket.

Floppies have one big limitation: The amount of data each disk can hold is limited to 1.4 MB. For word-processor documents and small- to medium-sized spreadsheets, 1.4MB is plenty of room. (The manuscript for this entire book, for example, may fit on two or three floppies.) Start adding photographs and other graphic elements, however, and forget it — the amount of data goes through the roof and you need to consider one of the other methods in this chapter.

Windows 95 Explorer

You can use floppy disks to transfer files between computers without ever using a file manager program. You simply save the file onto a floppy when you're in the word processor, spreadsheet, or whatever other program you use, and then open it on the second computer with the appropriate software.

However, suppose that you have four files — a word-processor document, a spreadsheet, a digital photograph, and a graphics file containing your organization's new logo — and you need to copy all four to a second computer. You may spend quite a bit of time opening up each of the programs used to create these files just to make a copy on a floppy disk.

Instead, you can use a file manager program such as Windows Explorer and copy entire groups of files simultaneously. You can even copy entire directories (folders) containing dozens or hundreds of files. Using a file manager program, you can even *clone* an entire hard drive — making a copy of everything on it (assuming, of course, you have a second drive with equal or greater capacity ready to receive the data).

To copy files to a floppy disk, follow these steps:

1. **Choose Start⇨Programs⇨Windows Explorer.**

   Windows Explorer pops up. On the left, you see a list of the disk drives on your computer. On the right, you see the contents of whatever drive or directory (folder) you highlight in the left panel.

2. **Find the file(s) you want to copy by selecting the directory, subdirectory, or sub-subdirectory (and so on) in the left panel, until you see the file(s) listed on the right.**

   Whenever you see a plus symbol (+) next to a directory, you can click it to see the subdirectories stored within it.

3. **Click and hold the file in the right-hand panel that you want to copy to the floppy.**

   To select several files to copy at once, hold down Ctrl while you click each selection (see Figure 9-1). Or, for a group of files that are listed right next to each other, first click on the first file in the list, and then hold down Shift while you click on the last item in the list.

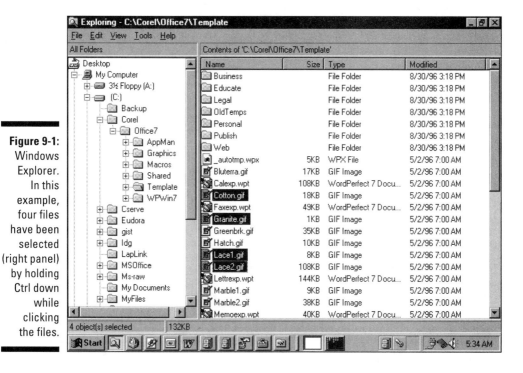

Figure 9-1:
Windows
Explorer.
In this
example,
four files
have been
selected
(right panel)
by holding
Ctrl down
while
clicking
the files.

4. Drag the file(s) over to the floppy drive icon (where it says $3^1/_2$
Floppy (A:) **in the left panel) and release the mouse button.**

The file is copied to the floppy. You can check the contents of the
floppy to make sure that your files made it there okay by double-
clicking the floppy drive icon in the left panel. Any files on the floppy
disk appear in the right panel.

In Explorer's View menu, try switching among the four different views for
the right panel — Large Icons, Small Icons, List, and Details. One view may
better suit your preferences than another.

Mac-PC file transfers

If you use computers running both the Macintosh and Windows 95 operating
systems, you probably transfer files between them using floppy disks or
removable hard drives such as Iomega's Zip or Jaz systems. Even if you're
only on one side of the operating system fence (the vast majority of users
are currently in the Microsoft camp), you may find yourself in situations
where you need to move files across platforms. If you do anything with
desktop publishing, you almost certainly need to transfer files between
Macintosh and PC platforms.

The current state of computers is a bit like a one-way mirror: Most newer Macintosh models (using the PowerPC chip) can see both sides. Macintosh computers (including the portable PowerBooks) not only read Windows and DOS files, but, with optional software, can also run Windows 95 and DOS programs — essentially emulating a PC. The reverse, however, is not at all true — if you place a Macintosh floppy disk in a Windows 95 computer, you get an error message saying that the disk is unreadable.

You have two ways around this problem. The easiest is to use the Macintosh computer to write to the floppy disk in PC format — an option that's readily available when you save files. The second approach is to purchase special software for your PC notebook that allows its floppy drive to read Macintosh-formatted disks, such as Pacific Micro's Mac-In-Dos for Windows 95 or DataViz's MacOpener.

To transfer files from the Macintosh to the PC platform, your PC must be able to read not only the disk format, but also the file type in question. The safest bet is to use software made by the same company on both sides. For example, if you need to do desktop publishing work, and you use Adobe PageMaker for Windows 95 on your PC, then if you use PageMaker for Macintosh on your Mactinosh computer, you can generally minimize any problems with file transfers. In the worst case, you may need to convert a word-processor file to simple ASCII text — without any font or typestyle information — to move it across the Mac-PC bridge.

If the Macintosh and PC in question are both connected to a local network, you can transfer files via the network and not even bother with disks.

Moving Files via E-Mail

You can also use e-mail over the Internet as a way to move files from one machine to another — even if the two machines are right next to each other. Simply send an e-mail with the files you want to transfer as attachments from the first computer, and then pick up the e-mail and attached files on the second computer. Using this procedure, you can break past the 1.4MB limitation of floppy disks and send larger files. You can also transfer files across platforms, such as from Windows 95 to Macintosh. Just remember that at phone line access speeds, you may have to wait up to an hour to send a 2MB file — and then the same amount of time *again* to pick it up with the second computer (see Chapter 12 for more about e-mail).

Connecting Computers Together

If you have a notebook PC and a desktop PC, you can connect them together for direct file transfers. With a direct connection, you can transfer files that are bigger than the 1.4 MB limit of floppy disks, and access hard drives directly without the hassle of fumbling with a bunch of little floppies. Cable and infrared connections provide the fastest way (up to 2 MB per second) to transfer large amounts of data between computers.

If you have a subnotebook computer that does not have a built-in floppy drive, hooking up the cable to transfer files from/to your desktop machine is just as easy as hooking up the dangling floppy drive attachment.

LapLink for Windows 95

I am a real fan of the Traveling Software LapLink program — of all the useful mobile computing products I mention in this book, I can't think of anything I'd recommend more. LapLink has been there practically since Day One of laptop computers, and has always kept pace with new developments — for example, the latest Windows 95 version incorporates wireless infrared (IrDA — InfraRed Data Association) data transfer. Most importantly, LapLink is much easier to use than the file transfer system built into Windows 95.

LapLink for Windows 95 comes supplied as a kit that includes connection cables for both serial and parallel ports, and software that works with the supplied cables as well as with infrared and telephone connections. After you activate the software, it starts seeking a connection to the other computer via the type of hookup you specify. The parallel port connection and infrared connections are best because they achieve the fastest data rates — you need to use the slower serial connection only if the parallel or infrared connections are unavailable.

You supply a name for each computer, which lets you easily see which computer is which (over the years, having tested numerous notebooks for magazine reviews, I recall several choice pet names I gave to various computers). You can hook up any two computers this way — laptops, desktops, or whatever. (A couple of times I had to frantically copy files from one notebook I had reviewed to another notebook that recently arrived, just moments before a FedEx employee came to pick up the older unit and return it to its manufacturer.) For the sake of clarity though, rather than saying *the first computer* and *the second computer,* I refer to them here as the *desktop* and *notebook machines.*

When you first launch LapLink on your desktop computer, a window appears, showing the contents of the computer's hard drive. This window looks very similar to Windows Explorer, and you can use it the same way you use Explorer to copy files between the hard drive and floppy disks on the same computer. However, LapLink's real power gets unleashed when you connect it to another machine.

Next, you launch LapLink on your notebook computer. (You run exactly the same program on both machines.) Just as with the desktop machine, a directory window appears, showing the contents of the notebook's hard drive.

Then, a few seconds later, you get a message on both computer screens indicating that the connection to the other computer has been detected. A moment later, a second panel appears on the screens of each computer, showing the name and drives and directories (folders) of the other computer (see Figure 9-2). If a computer — such as a desktop machine in an office — is hooked up to a network, the network drive letter(s) are displayed as well, and your notebook can thus have access to a network without the need for a special Ethernet card.

To copy files, you just drag them from one panel to another — the procedure works a lot like Windows Explorer (see the first section in this chapter), except that with LapLink, you see two different computers represented simultaneously. You can use either computer to control the action — it doesn't matter which — and you can switch between issuing commands from one or the other.

LapLink provides *two-way synchronization* that automatically copies the most recent version of a file, or any new files that you created since the last time you connected the two computers. You can designate specific directories (folders) to synchronize in this way.

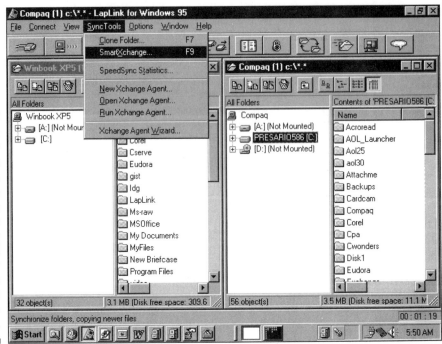

Figure 9-2:
LapLink for
Windows
95. You can
move files
between
computers
by dragging
and
dropping, or
with more
automated
synchroni-
zation tools.

You can also use LapLink as a file manager for copying between disk drives on the same computer — you can even use it to *clone* an entire disk drive (copy the entire contents).

Do not attempt to copy installed software from one computer to another (unless you're cloning the entire drive). It usually doesn't work because the installation process involves special drivers that get installed in Windows 95 (see Chapter 15). Instead, limit your use of LapLink to copying documents and files that you create with your software.

LapLink also lets you use your notebook computer to remote control your desktop computer via a dial-up connection — see Chapter 13.

Windows 95 file transfer — Direct Cable Connection

As a lower-cost alternative to LapLink, you can purchase a commonly available connector cable called a *null modem cable* (usually about $20), and use the Direct Cable Connection software that comes with Windows 95 to transfer files between a desktop and a notebook PC. You can also use a parallel transfer cable, similar to the one that comes with LapLink, and commonly referred to as a *LapLink parallel cable*. Parallel cables are harder to find but worth seeking out because they allow you to transfer files much more quickly.

You cannot use a regular parallel printer cable to connect two computers via their parallel ports — you need a special parallel port file transfer cable. Fortunately, an ordinary printer cable has different types of connections on each end, making it impossible to use to connect two computers. And if you think that you're clever and try to hook up an adapter to the printer end of the cable to make it fit the computer's port, it doesn't work. The two computers end up trying to send data over the same wires. The special LapLink type parallel transfer cable has one computer's send wires connected to the other's receive wires, and vice versa.

Unlike LapLink, which allows both computers to work from each other, Direct Cable Connection requires that you designate one computer the *host* (typically your desktop computer) and the other as the *guest* (typically your portable computer).

If you don't see Direct Cable Connection listed in Accessories, you can install it from the Windows 95 installation software. Just choose Start➪ Settings➪Control Panel and then double-click on Add/Remove Programs. On the Add/Remove Programs dialog box that appears, click Install and then follow the wizard.

To establish a Direct Cable Connection in Windows 95, follow these steps:

1. **On your laptop computer, choose Start⇨Programs⇨Accessories⇨ Direct Cable Connection.**

2. **In the Direct Cable Connection dialog box that appears, designate your laptop as Guest by clicking the radio button.**

   Typically your desktop machine is the host — the host has the files that you want to access. (However, if you want to copy files from your notebook to desktop, then designate your laptop as host and your desktop as guest in the next step. For clarity's sake, the rest of this procedure assumes your desktop machine is host and the notebook is the guest.)

3. **Click Next.**

   Another dialog box appears.

4. **Select the type of connection you want to establish in the** `Select the port you want to use` **list box.**

5. **Connect the cable to your notebook.**

   The following steps are all performed on your host (desktop) computer:

6. **Repeat Steps 1 through 5 on your desktop machine, except select Host for the desktop.**

7. **Enable the file and printer sharing function by choosing Start⇨ Settings⇨Control Panel.**

8. **In the Control Panel, double-click Network.**

9. **In the Network dialog box, click the Configuration tab at the top.**

10. **On the Configuration tab, double-click File and Print Sharing.**

11. **In the File and Print Sharing dialog box, make sure that both check boxes — one labeled** `I want to be able to give others access to my files` **and the other** `I want to be able to allow others to print from my printer(s)` **— are selected (have checks in the boxes).**

12. **Click OK.**

    You arrive back on the Configuration tab in the Network dialog box.

13. **Click OK.**

14. **Reboot the desktop computer.**

15. **Use Windows Explorer to designate which directories (folders) you want the host computer (desktop) to share with the guest computer.**

    You get to Windows Explorer by clicking Start⇨Programs⇨ Windows Explorer.

16. **Find the directory(ies) that you want to make available for sharing from the list on the left panel (you may need to scroll down, or click on a + button to see subdirectories). Click the first directory that you want to share so that it is highlighted.**

17. **Choose File➪Properties.**

    The File Properties dialog box appears.

18. **Click the Sharing tab.**

19. **Select the Shared As radio button.**

    Note that if you want to make an entire hard drive accessible for file transfers, you have to repeat this process for each directory of the C: drive.

20. **Click OK.**

21. **Activate the connection on the host (desktop) computer by choosing Start➪Programs➪Accessories➪Direct Cable Connection.**

22. **Return now to the guest (notebook) computer, and activate the connection the same way, by choosing Start➪Programs➪ Accessories➪Direct Cable Connection.**

23. **In Direct Cable Connection, click View Host on the guest computer (notebook).**

    The guest computer opens a window showing the shared directories, and you're able to copy them to the guest (notebook) computer by dragging and dropping, just as in Windows Explorer (see "Windows 95 Explorer" earlier in this chapter).

Personally, I think that this process is way too cumbersome, compared to the ease of LapLink.

Staying in Sync

Most *file synchronization tools* are based on the premise that though you may use two different computers, you work on only one of them at a time. You leave the office for a long weekend, for example, and take your work with you on your laptop computer, while your desktop machine remains idle. When you begrudgingly come back to the office on Monday, you have revised versions of the files you took home on Friday on your notebook computer.

Synchronization software basically compares the dates and times that files with the same names were last modified, and then replaces the older version with the most recent version at the location (computer, folder, or disk drive) that has the older version. Most synchronization tools, such as the SmartXchange feature that comes with LapLink and the Windows 95

Briefcase, work in both directions — in other words, if one computer (or disk drive) has a few files that are newer, and the other computer also has newer versions of other files, the newest versions are each transferred to the other machine with the older versions. This provides a great way for two computers to maintain the most recent versions of all your work. Figure 9-3 shows the SmartXchange function in LapLink for Windows 95 that compares the files in the selected directories in each computer, and transfers new files and newer versions to whichever computer needs them.

Figure 9-3:
The LapLink dialog box for copying new files.

 Use the My Documents directory (folder) to store all the files you create on your desktop machine. You can always create subdirectories (folders) under the My Documents folder if you have a lot of files you need to store. That way, when you need to synchronize your work on two computers, you can synchronize the entire directories (folders) rather than selecting the individual files.

 File synchronization has one big limitation: It works only if one computer's file remains *dormant* while you make changes on the other. Suppose, for example, that while you're off traveling with your notebook computer, a coworker continues to make changes in a file on your desktop machine — the same file that you're working on while you're away. When you return, you now have two different versions of the file, each with revisions that need to be entered in the other version. This limitation is a big part of the reason why local networks are set up in organizations — the same files can be shared and worked on by various people, without ending up with a zillion different versions.

One exception: Some pocket computer address book systems, such as the Sharp Zaurus, come with software for synchronizing the address book with a copy stored in a computer, and automatically combine the listings in both so that new entries made in either machine are added to both files.

Most HPC (handheld PC) and PDA (Personal Digital Assistant) devices come equipped with a cable for connecting to your computer's serial port and exchanging data. The included software usually lets you transfer files back and forth or back up data (see Figure 9-4). The synchronize feature is very useful if you keep the same address book files on both your handheld computer and your notebook or desktop computer. See Chapter 7 for more information on the various HPC and PDA options.

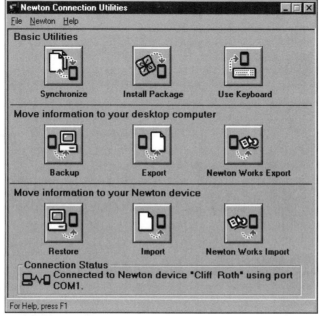

Figure 9-4: Apple's Newton comes with Connection Utilities (software and cable) for exchanging data with Windows 95 computers.

I tend to rename files every time I change them substantially, with filenames like VERSION1, VERSION2, and so on. I thus altogether avoid having different versions of files with the same name on two different computers. I never have to wonder which computer or disk has the newest version of a project I'm working on — I can tell just from the name.

Even if you follow my advice and keep renaming your document files when you change them, you may still come across many situations where you want to keep the files in two computers in sync. Suppose that you go on the road with your notebook and enter a bunch of new names, addresses, and phone numbers in your contact manager software, or enter new bookmarks in your Web browser. Synchronization can automatically update those files for you when you return back to your desktop machine.

Synchronizing with LapLink

If you want to keep files in your notebook and desktop computer synchro-
nized, I urge you to get a copy of LapLink — it really makes synchronizing
two computers amazingly easy. It is vastly superior to the Windows 95
Briefcase that I describe in the next section. The only reason I've included
instructions for the Windows 95 Briefcase is that I made a promise on the
back cover of this book to help save you money — but this is one case
where the savings may not be worth it.

Follow these steps for synchronizing two directories (folders) using LapLink
for Windows 95 (version 7.5):

1. **Connect the two computers together using the LapLink parallel or
   serial cable, or if both computers have infrared (IrDA) communications, point the red windows toward each other at close distance (less
   than two feet).**

2. **Launch LapLink on the *desktop* computer by double-clicking its icon
   (on the desktop's computer's desktop screen, so to speak), or by
   choosing Start⇨Programs⇨LapLink.**

   The LapLink window opens on your computer.

3. **Launch LapLink on the *notebook* computer by double-clicking its
   icon (on the notebook computer's screen) or by choosing Start⇨
   Programs⇨LapLink.**

   The two computers recognize each other within a few seconds after the
   programs start. When they do, the screens on both computers show
   two panels, listing the directories of each computer's hard drive ($C:\backslash$).

   If you see no panels, or only one panel, try choosing Connect⇨
   Connect over Cable, or Connect⇨Connect over Wireless. If that doesn't
   work, choose Options⇨Port Setup and make sure that the relevant
   connection port, such as LPT1 for the parallel cable, is enabled. If it
   isn't, highlight the port and place a check mark in the Enable Port box.

4. **Select one computer to work on, and don't touch the other one for
   the rest of these instructions. Using whichever computer you choose,
   select the directories (folders) from both computers that you want to
   synchronize. Use the left half of each of the two windows (represent-
   ing the local and remote computers) to find the directories, and
   select the directories.**

   The file folder icons next to the two selected directories (one on each
   computer) appear open. You can also select the C:\ at the top of the
   directories if you want to synchronize the entire hard drives fo both
   computers.

5. **Click SyncTools (using the same computer that you used to make the directory selections in the previous step).**

6. **Click SmartXchange.**

   A dialog box appears showing the selected directories on the source and target computers. Because the transfer is two-way, by default, these terms are really irrelevant — LapLink copies files in both directions, based on which computer has the newer (or only) version of each file within the selected directories (refer to Figure 9-4).

   If you prefer to copy files only in one direction — such as when you return from a trip with your notebook — and want to copy new files you've created to your desktop, then click Options, put a check mark next to One-way transfer only, and make sure that your source and target machines are listed correctly. (If they are not listed correctly, close the panel and reverse the sequence in which you select the two directories in Step 5.)

7. **Click OK.**

   The file transfer process begins. When complete, a dialog box showing the number of files transferred, the number of bytes transferred, and the time it took appears.

8. **Click OK to end the synchronization process.**

Synchronization is based on the date and time that files are saved, as determined by the clock on the computer that saves the file. When you use synchronization, you need to make sure that both computers' calendars and clocks are set correctly — otherwise you may accidentally replace a newer file with an older one, simply because the dates or times were messed up. When LapLink first establishes a connection between two computers, it makes sure that their clocks are in sync — if they're not, it displays a warning message and suggests that you choose one or the other as the correct date and time.

Synchronizing with the Windows 95 Briefcase

The Windows 95 Briefcase is intended specifically to help you move files back and forth between a notebook and desktop computer. You can use it with floppy disk copies of files or with the Direct Cable Connection. The Windows 95 Briefcase compares the date and time that the selected files were last modified and keeps track of which disk, directory, or computer holds the most recently updated version of a file.

I've explored a lot of nooks and crannies in Windows 95, and the Briefcase feature has to be one of the all-time most confusing — even though the My Briefcase icon that appears on your desktop looks so inviting. A Briefcase at first glance resembles a folder or directory, but actually it operates more like a tracking system. It both holds the newer versions of files that you're working on and remembers where older versions of those files are stored, so that it can automatically replace earlier versions with newer ones. You can create as many Briefcases as you want — the default one, called My Brief-case, is always preinstalled on Windows 95 on notebook computers.

You place files in the Briefcase the same way you move files to any other location or disk drive. It functions like a transfer station. Say, for example, that you're packing up for a weekend with your notebook computer, and want to take files from your office computer home with you to work on using your notebook. Follow these steps:

1. **Launch Windows Explorer (choose Start⇨Programs⇨ Windows Explorer).**

   Windows Explorer appears.

2. **Highlight the files you want to work on over the weekend in the right panel, and click and drag them over to the My Briefcase icon on the left panel of My Explorer.**

   The My Briefcase icon may be toward the bottom on the left-hand side of Windows Explorer.

3. **Click Desktop on the left panel so that the My Briefcase icon appears in the right panel.**

4. **Insert a formatted floppy disk in your desktop computer's floppy drive.**

5. **Click and drag My Briefcase in the right panel to the 3^1/$_2$ Floppy (A:) icon on the left panel.**

6. **After the computer is finished copying files to the floppy, close Explorer by clicking the × in the upper right corner.**

7. **Remove the floppy disk from the desktop computer, label it My Briefcase, and pack it with your notebook.**

8. **Go home! (Don't forget your notebook computer — weekends are for work, not fun!)**

9. **When you're ready to start working at home, insert the floppy disk in your notebook computer and open the files on the floppy disk using whatever word processor, spreadsheet, or other program you ordinarily use.**

   The files are listed in the My Briefcase folder in the floppy disk.

10. **Save your work as exactly the same file (don't change the filename or location on the floppy disk).**

When you get back to your main computer or desktop machine and you need to update your files, here's how to do it using My Briefcase:

1. **Put the floppy disk with the new files (stored in its Briefcase folder) into the desktop computer.**

2. **Choose Start⇨Programs⇨Windows Explorer.**

3. **Click the 3¹/₂ Floppy (A:) icon in the left panel.**

4. **Click and drag My Briefcase in the right panel to the Desktop in the left panel.**

5. **Double-click My Briefcase on the desktop.**

   In the right panel, you see a list of all the files that you took with you over the weekend.

6. **Highlight the file(s) you wish to update, or skip to Step 7 if you want to update all files listed.**

7. **Choose Briefcase⇨Update All or Update Selection.**

   The Briefcase menu is at the top of the Explorer screen, to the right of File, Edit, View, and Tools. It appears only when you've selected (high-lighted) a Briefcase.

   The Briefcase gives you the chance to confirm file replacements. A message appears, letting you know that newer versions of files have been found.

8. **Click Update to replace the original files on the desktop computer with the revised files from the floppy (see Figure 9-5).**

For moving just a couple of files between a notebook and desktop computer, the Windows 95 Briefcase is probably more trouble than it's worth. However, if you're juggling a half-dozen or more files, and each is stored in a different directory (folder), and you don't want to try to remember where each file is, then the Briefcase can be a terrific help because it keeps track of where all the original files were stored.

Infrared Linking

The infrared link is the absolute coolest, most futuristic way to get two computers to talk to each other. You can connect with no cables whatsoever — just place the two computers near each other, and let them go at it. An invisible beam of light, similar to the type used in wireless TV remotes, provides the connection between the two computers.

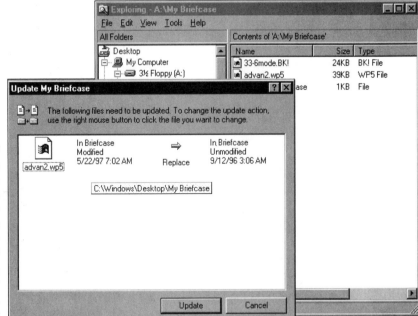

Figure 9-5:
The
Briefcase
automatically
updates
older
versions of
files with
newer
ones.

IrDA is the official name for the standard infrared protocol — it stands for *Infrared Data Association,* the group that came up with the protocol. You find an IrDA port built into many new notebook computers, and some laser printers (especially Hewlett-Packard models). With an IrDA-ready printer and a computer with an IrDA port, you just place the notebook computer in front of the printer to send a file to print.

If you're not sure whether your computer has an infrared port, look for a dark red plastic window along the front or rear panels.

To use the IrDA port with a printer, you must select it as the activated port that the computer uses to talk to the printer. In Windows 95, follow these steps:

1. **Choose Start⇨Settings⇨Control Panel.**

   The Control Panel appears.

2. **Double-click Printers.**

   The Printers dialog box opens.

3. **Double-click Add Printer.**

   The Add Printer Wizard dialog box appears.

4. **Click Next.**

5. **Click the Local printer radio button (so that a dot appears in the circle), and then click Next.**

6. **Select the manufacturer from the left panel and model of your printer on the right panel, and then click Next.**

   If your particular printer is not listed, and you have the drivers disk that came with it, then click Have Disk and follow the instructions. If it's not listed and you don't have the disk you need, you can try installing a similar model from the same manufacturer. Or try calling the manufacturer's customer service number to get the disk, or visit their Web site to see whether the driver is available for download.

7. **Click Next.**

   A dialog box appears, listing available ports, including the IrDA port if your computer has one.

8. **Select the infrared port and click Next.**

   A new dialog box appears with the printer name (leave it as is) and a choice to install this as your default printer connection.

9. **Click Yes if you want to make this the usual way that you print documents from your notebook computer.**

10. **Click Next.**

    A new dialog box appears, asking whether you want to test it out.

11. **Click Yes if your printer is nearby and turned on (the infrared ports on your computer and printer should be no more than two feet apart, and facing each other).**

12. **Click Next.**

    The printer is installed in the Printers group. (In some instances, Windows 95 may ask you to find the original installation disks that came with the computer.) If you clicked Yes in Step 9, Windows sends a test page to your printer and asks you whether it printed correctly. Click Yes if it worked okay. If it doesn't print, click No and check your printer's instruction manual to see what you need to do to activate its infrared port to receive the signal from your computer.

You can install both an infrared connection and a traditional printer cable connection for the same printer by installing the same printer twice. Simply run through the previous steps once and install the printer with one connection, and then run through them a second time and install the second type of connection. You have to choose one as the default, but you can easily switch between the two systems using the Printer Name box that commonly appears in software such as Word for Windows or WordPerfect 7 when you try to print a document.

You can also use IrDA wireless connections and LapLink or other file transfer software to transfer data between two computers. Both computers, of course, need to be equipped with IrDA ports. If you need to exchange data between two notebook computers with IrDA, this is clearly the easiest (and coolest) way to go. However, most desktop computers do not have an IrDA port, so if you want to use infrared connections, you need to purchase a special adapter for the desktop machine. IrDA adapters connect to the computer's serial port and cost about $100 to $150 — two examples are the Puma Infrared Desktop Adapter, and Extended Systems' JetEye (see Figure 9-6). An infrared adapter, such as the JetEye from Extended Systems, as shown in the figure, (the mouse-like device in front of the monitor) connects to the serial port of your desktop computer and facilitates wireless file transfers with your IrDA-equipped notebook.

What if you're so enamored by the idea of infrared data transfers that you want to do them even though your notebook computer does not have an IrDA port? Easy — you just hook up two of the IrDA adapters: one to your notebook and one to your desktop PC. Extended Systems sells a file transfer kit, just for this purpose, that includes two adapters and a copy of LapLink (see the Appendix to locate manufacturers).

Figure 9-6:
The JetEye
from
Extended
Systems.

Chapter 10

Portable Communications Overview

. . . .

In This Chapter

▶ Understanding the portable communications possibilities

▶ Retrieving e-mail on the road

▶ Figuring out what you need for each form of communication

▶ Using Telnet

. . . .

*T*he possibilities of two computers linked together is rich with science fiction scenarios of computers taking over the world, making more computers, and eventually making humans obsolete. As powerful as your notebook computer may be by itself, you can do much more with it when you hook it up to other computers, be it through the phone line, a local network, or wireless connection systems. (However, I can say without a doubt that, much as I like science fiction, connecting two notebook computers does not get you started building your own computer breeding farm.)

Your connection may be to a very specific machine, such as your desktop computer at your office, or it may be to something much more amorphous, such as the Internet or an online service that puts you in touch with not just one computer, but vast networks of computers. Either way, connecting your computer to other computers is about *communication*.

This chapter provides a quick guide to the fantastic possibilities for mobile communications. The latter part of this chapter explains what terminal emulation and Telnet are all about.

Three important points to keep in mind as you consider your communication and connection options:

> ✔ You can often accomplish the same thing in several different ways —
> for example, you can retrieve e-mail from a remote location using
> remote computing software, the Internet, or a direct dial-in connection.

✔ Setting up accounts and installing software is time-consuming and can be tedious. If you already have a desktop computer with a functioning Internet or online service connection, you minimize connection and setup hassles by simply installing the same software and accessing the same accounts with your notebook computer. With online services and Internet accounts, you are not limited to a single computer, just a single *account*. You can equip your notebook computer with the same accounts as your desktop machine without having to pay anything extra.

✔ Connecting your notebook computer to big networks, such as online services, is usually much easier than connecting it to just a single computer because online services supply their own easy-to-install and configure software.

What Do You Want to Do?

With your portable computer, you can accomplish some of the same communications tasks in a bunch of different ways. One or another method may already be familiar (and hopefully easy) to you.

E-mail

You can access your e-mail in more different ways than just about anything else, so I devote the marvelous and much-ballyhooed Chapter 12 to the subject. If your e-mail account is with an online service, or if your portable computer is the only computer you use for e-mail, getting set up is easy. If your e-mail account is with an Internet Service Provider, configuring your portable computer to access the same account as your desktop machine can be a bit more complicated. And if you want to use your portable computer to receive the same e-mail that you get on a desktop machine that's on an office network, you have the most complicated task, as well as the most options.

Web surfing

Surfing the Web is both recreation and research for many computer users. The two most common ways to access the Web from a portable computer are via a dial-up connection to an Internet service provider (ISP), or through an online service such as America Online or CompuServe (see Chapter 12). If you use a computer in an office with a local area network, you may also be able to tie in with an Ethernet adapter to gain access to the Internet (see Chapter 20). In some unusual circumstances, you may be able to access the Internet more easily using remote computing — essentially using your desktop machine to access the Internet, and relaying the images your desktop computer sees to your notebook computer (see Chapter 13).

Remote computing

Remote computing software lets you literally use your notebook computer to do just about everything your desktop machine can do, including gaining access to any Internet or online connections available on your desktop machine. You can also use remote computing software to grab files from your desktop machine, or even run large applications that normally run slowly on your notebook. With remote computing software, your notebook computer operates like a remote control, telling the desktop machine what to do — I give you all the details in Chapter 13.

Conferencing

Video conference software lets you see the person you're talking to. You need a separate miniature video camera and video capture card — small accessories that you can easily carry with a notebook computer. For best results, use exactly the same setup on both sides of the conference, and have two phone lines available simultaneously — use one to talk via an ordinary voice connection, and the other to send the digitized video using your computer's modem. Another type of conferencing, sometimes called *whiteboard conferencing,* allows you and someone else to mark up the same document simultaneously. ProShare software from Intel is the leader in this category. As with video conferencing, you get the best results if you have two phone lines available so that the voice signal has its own line independent of your computer's modem.

Faxing

If your portable computer has a modem, you can probably send and receive faxes. Sending a fax is considerably easier than receiving one, especially if you are at a hotel where all incoming calls first go through a switchboard. Chapter 14 tells you all you need to know to fax like crazy and not get burned.

Chatting

If you ever find yourself alone in a strange town with nothing but your notebook computer and perhaps a hotel TV as entertainment, you may find making new friends in distant places a fun way to pass the time and gain some semblance of social contact. Thousands, perhaps millions, of people from all parts of the globe spend hours every week occupying computer chat lines, where many good friendships and even some marriages have been formed.

Chat is basically a text-based affair — you and others type messages into computers, and everyone in a chat *room* sees what everyone else is typing. The three general places where you can find chat are

- **Online services.** Chat service is actually one of the things that makes online services better than straight Internet accounts. Online services have literally dozens of discussions taking place round the clock.

- **Internet.** You may need special plug-in software for your Web browser, such as Internet Relay Chat (IRC), and you need to know the addresses of specific sites that offer chat rooms.

- **Bulletin board services (BBSs).** Essentially like text-based mini-online services that you can dial into, BBSs function on their own with no connection to the Internet. Most BBSs also incorporate a chat feature so that you can dial in to one and chat with anyone else who also dialed in (technically this isn't a bulletin board — it's chat, but it's a feature commonly found in BBSs). Of course, you can also read and post messages on the computer bulletin boards.

What Software Do You Need?

Each aspect of communications with your computer entails using a different program — a possible source of confusion. However, don't assume that you have to go out and buy a ton of software just to communicate — the Windows 95 operating system actually includes many of the functions I cover in this chapter, each within a separate program that you can launch. (In fact, within the software community, the most common complaint against the Microsoft behemoth is that they absorb entire product categories and include them within the operating system.)

So why buy a standalone version of the software if a slightly stripped-down version is included free in Windows 95? Full versions of software typically offer more advanced and often easier to use features than what you get with your computer. But the main reason, in most instances, is probably familiarity: If you're already used to a particular program — say, because you use it at your office and you want to put the same thing on your laptop, or because you got an earlier version of it several years ago — then inertia dictates that you stay with the program unless you can save a bundle of money by switching.

As an arbitrary ballpark estimate, figure on taking about two hours to learn to use most new communications programs. You may need to take another hour or more to figure out how to transfer customized settings and databases such as address books, favorite places, bookmarks, and so on.

Here are the main types of communications software you probably want to have on your notebook computer:

- ✓ **Web browser.** If you want to surf the World Wide Web — which is what most people think of as the Internet — you need a Web browser. (Actually, the Web is just one part of the Internet — it also includes file transfers, e-mail, newsgroups, and Telnet terminal communications.) Netscape Navigator and Microsoft Internet Explorer (included with Windows 95) are the most popular. You need to obtain a Web browser if you're accessing the Internet through a no-frills Internet service provider. Most of the larger nationwide ISPs and all online services provide you with a free copy of a Web browser when you sign up.

- ✓ **Online services.** Most online services — for example, America Online, Prodigy, and CompuServe — have their own proprietary interface for accessing their services, and then launch a separate Web browser program when you want to access the Internet through their service. This software is always free when you sign up and forms the basis of the ubiquitous free trial offers that clog up your mailbox every week.

- ✓ **E-mail.** If you already use an e-mail program on your desktop computer, and you want to use your notebook to retrieve the same mail while you're away, I highly recommend that you use the same program on your notebook machine as on your desktop. Using the same software on both machines makes matching configurations a lot easier, and that helps prevent slip-ups — such as mail being erased when you wanted to save it. Windows 95 includes Microsoft Exchange, and Netscape Navigator includes Netscape Mail. But Eudora, a standalone program, is probably the most popular e-mail program.

- ✓ **Faxing.** The ever-popular fax is the crudest way to send data — instead of talking to another computer, your portable computer talks to a comparatively idiotic fax machine. However, fax technology is also just about *everywhere* — if you need to get a document to someone fast, and that person does not have a computer, fax is the way to go. Almost all modems can support faxes and come bundled with fax software. Windows 95 includes Microsoft Fax (in Accessories), which is very simple compared to the niftier standalone products like WinFax and EclipseFax.

- ✓ **Data communications.** Windows 95 includes two programs for data communications — Hyper Terminal, for use with traditional bulletin board-style dial-up services, and Telnet, for emulating terminal-style communications over the Internet (see "Telnet/Data Communications" later in this chapter). Most advanced users prefer standalone products such as Crosstalk (from Attachmate) or ProComm (Quarterdeck).

What Can You Connect To?

Your notebook computer can connect to other privately owned computers, to private networks, or to public networks such as the Internet. In this section, I present an overview of the types of connections you can make with your portable computer.

Online services

Online services have been around since before the Internet. More recently, as the Internet has become public domain, they have adapted by offering both their own exclusive services as well as access to Internet services like the Web and Telnet.

For notebook computer owners, the online services offer ease of use, when compared with Internet access through an ISP (Internet Service Provider). Online service software installs easily on your computer and automatically connects you to the proprietary features of the online service, as well as to the Internet, with minimum hassle. Additionally, when you log in for the first time, you feel like your online service provides a centrally organized home base — a place from which you can branch out to explore. A straight Internet subscription has no such central hub.

If you bought a notebook computer in the past few years, it probably came with software for one or more of the online services, such as America Online, CompuServe, and Prodigy. If it has Windows 95 installed on it, then the software you need for Microsoft Network — which is like a cross between an ISP and an online service (see Chapter 11) — is already on your computer (just double-click The Internet icon on your desktop, and follow the instructions).

The Internet

When you plug into the Internet, you can literally connect to the entire world from wherever you are with your portable computer. You can use the Internet to send and receive e-mail, and to view Web pages on all kinds of topics, including travel and reservation info. An Internet service provider (ISP) gives you a phone number, username, password, and other information so that you can use your notebook computer's modem to dial in and access the Internet. You can also access the Internet using an online service (see Chapter 11). Most people use the Internet for two purposes — to send/receive e-mail, and to access the World Wide Web, using a Web browser. You can also download software — much of it for free — and log onto remote computers (using Telnet, explained in "Telnet/Data Communications," later in this chapter).

Wireless services and networks

Without a doubt, wireless communications offer the sexiest, most fun way to link your portable computer to the outside world. You can choose from numerous forms of wireless communications, each covered in more detail elsewhere in this book:

- ✔ **Infrared (IrDA)** lets you connect a portable computer to a printer, or two computers in the same room for file transfers or remote computing.

- ✔ **Cellular modem** lets you access anything with your portable computer that you normally would access via a dial-up phone call.

- ✔ **Pager (one-way and two-way) messaging services** deliver wireless e-mail. Two-way systems let you respond instantly to messages that you receive.

- ✔ **Wireless local network** for an office or campus allows you to keep your portable computer always connected to the network, and thus to the Internet and e-mail, via microwave radio signals or infrared light.

Bulletin board systems and teletext services

In the early days of online services, back before Windows caught on and DOS was still king (or Mr. DOS to you), computers had no pictures, no point-and-click mouse operation, no sound beyond a simple beep. Online communication was limited to text messages that could be typed. Such simple text-based systems have fallen by the wayside for the big online services, but you can still find smaller online services, and people and organizations who run bulletin board services (BBSs) that are based on the old teletext communications.

Though technically crude, BBSs have two big advantages over the more dazzling Web page style of presenting information. First, because the data is limited to text, information comes through the phone line much more quickly than with graphics-laden Web pages. (BBS technology was designed for 300 bps and 1200 bps modem speeds, so with today's 33.6 Kbps modems, they are lightning fast.) Second, BBSs are universally accessible. They are humble. They do not play a *keeping up with the Joneses* game of ever-escalating technology (unlike the Web, which perennially requires ever more plug-ins and the latest browser to view the most elaborate sites). Teletext can thus work with older, more humble computers — such as the type you may encounter when visiting less developed countries.

To access BBS services, you need terminal emulation software, as I explain in "Terminal emulation," later in this chapter.

Computer-to-computer

Ironically, what would seem like the easiest computer connection of all —
from one computer to another — is actually the most complicated, assuming that you're doing it over the phone line. For starters, you have software
to deal with on both sides of the equation — you must take responsibility
for properly configuring not just one, but two computers. The best way to
link two computers that are right next to each other is via a direct cable or
wireless infrared connection, as I explain in Chapter 9, because this provides
the fastest data transfer speeds and is very easy to accomplish using
software such as LapLink.

One method for sending e-mail back and forth between two computers is to
use communications software on each side, such as Crosstalk (Attachmate)
or ProComm (Quarterdeck). You must configure one computer to receive the
phone call — automatically or manually, if someone is there to receive the
call (assuming you are calling in with your notebook from a remote location). This type of software also lets you type messages back and forth,
as well as send files.

A more sophisticated way to link two computers via telephone is by using
Remote Access software, which essentially lets you use your notebook
computer as a remote control to operate your desktop machine — see
Chapter 13.

Sending and receiving files as e-mail attachments using the Internet or an
online service as the intermediary is usually much easier than using any
kind of direct computer-to-computer software. Also, when you transfer files
via the Internet, the two computers can connect at completely different
times — if you're in Asia and need to send a report back to the office in
North America, you don't have to wake anyone up to do it; the mail will be
there in the morning. Only transfer files over a phone line directly between
computers if you have a specific reason to do so, such as security concerns
or lack of Internet/online access on one side of the connection.

Telnet/Data Communications

When you access an online service, you use their own special software that
displays their screens. When you access the Internet, you use a Web
browser such as Netscape Navigator or Internet Explorer. These types of
software represent the most sophisticated forms of computer communications, because they provide users with a graphic interface — a method of
doing things that involves pointing and clicking. Some smaller online

services, for stock trading and research, also provide their own special interfaces that you use when you access the particular service. But the smallest online systems, bulletin board systems (BBSs), many college/university computer systems that you can log onto remotely, and most other computer systems offering dial-up access, use a much simpler text-based system for communicating, called *terminal emulation*.

Terminal emulation

Terminal emulation is a throwback to an earlier era of computing. Back in the 1970s, when remote computer terminals had no processing power built in, these so-called *dumb terminals* were basically a display screen and keyboard that could send text back and forth to a mainframe computer on a network.

Terminal emulation is also commonly referred to as *teletext* — meaning text sent over the telephone line.

You have two approaches to using your notebook computer as a terminal. The first is to establish a direct telephone connection to the computer or network that you are remotely accessing. A university computer system, for example, may have local phone numbers that you can dial to access the network. A private bulletin board service, for example, provides a special number for modem connection. The software you need to access any of these types of services is commonly called *data communications software*. It typically includes terminal emulation, as well as modem dialer functions. The most well-known examples are Crosstalk, HyperAccess, and ProComm. However, if you use Windows 95, you may not need to buy anything extra — Hyper Terminal, included in Accessories, provides adequate terminal emulation for most people's needs.

Telnet

Telnet is the second approach to teletext communications. Rather than connecting to the computer you want to access via a direct modem connection, you use the Internet. Of course, from a notebook computer, you usually dial in anyway — whether to the Internet or to a special computer. But Telnet offers a way to provide terminal emulation-type access to any other computer on the Internet, without having to set up dial-in phone lines for each end of the connection.

Telnet-compatible programs are commonly included in communications software, such as Crosstalk and HyperAccess. If you're running Windows 95 on your notebook computer, you already have a Telnet program — it is just buried in the Windows directory (folder).

To launch the Windows 95 Telnet program,

1. Choose Start⇨Run.

The Run dialog box pops up.

2. Type C:/Windows/Telnet **in the text box.**

3. Click OK.

Like all other programs that lack icons on your Windows 95 desktop, you can create one for Telnet, if you use it frequently. Follow these steps:

1. Choose Start⇨Programs⇨Windows Explorer.

The Windows Explorer pops up.

2. Click the directory (folder) in the left column, and then locate the program TELNET.EXE **in the right column and select it with the mouse.**

3. Choose File⇨Create Shortcut.

A shortcut icon appears at the bottom of the list of files, but you have to scroll down to see it — it looks like a duplicate copy of the listing you highlighted, only it lets you know that it's a shortcut by calling itself Shortcut to Telnet.exe.

4. Click and drag this shortcut onto your desktop.

Reduce Windows Explorer to less than full-screen in order to be able to drop the shortcut onto your desktop. When you let go of the mouse button, the icon gets big like the other icons on your desktop.

Telnet programs, such as the one in Windows 95, assume that you're already connected to the Internet. From a notebook computer, you can use Dial-Up Networking to accomplish this connection (see Chapter 11). When you run Telnet (by double-clicking the shortcut on your desktop) and click on Connect in Telnet, it's to connect to a specific computer server that's on the Internet. For example, by choosing Connect⇨Remote Access, and then typing **well.com** under Host Name, you are connected via Telnet to The Well, a legendary West Coast counterculture-oriented bulletin board service from the pre-Internet days, offering zillions of discussions on politics, music, drugs, culture, and so on. After you get there, you have to subscribe (pay) to use the service — thus proving that not everything on the Internet is free.

Chapter 11

Using Online Services and the Internet to Be a Better Road Warrior

*Y*ou may find yourself in plenty of situations where you want to connect to the Internet or online service. You may just need to send and receive a bit of e-mail (more on that in Chapter 12), or maybe you have the overwhelming desire to buy or sell stock in the middle of the night. Or maybe you want to *chat* (type messages back and forth) with friends you've made online.

In any event, if you're on the go with a portable computer, I highly recommend that you subscribe to an online service or a nationwide ISP so that you can do all these things from wherever you may find yourself.

Choosing between an Online Service and an ISP

In the early days of personal computers and modems, you could use a modem to dial in to a bunch of services to get information or exchange e-mail with other members of that same service, for a monthly fee. Called *online services,* these businesses started out as purely text-based, with the remote computer acting as a *dumb terminal* (see Chapter 10) that could display and transmit text messages only — no images, no animation, no MIDI versions of the *Beverly Hillbillies* theme. Gradually, these services developed cool-looking graphic interfaces so users could point and click menus and icons. Then the Internet came along, and the biggest online services — America Online, CompuServe, and Prodigy — had to adapt. So they started incorporating the Internet within their services. And then Microsoft launched its own online service, called Microsoft Network, based entirely on the Internet and the Windows 95 operating system.

Today (at least as this book goes to press), you can connect to four big online services — America Online (AOL), CompuServe, Prodigy, and Microsoft Network (MSN) — each of which offers two main features within their service, namely:

- ✔ **Access to their own proprietary content.** This can include news services, shopping services, games, chat rooms, and a host of other possibilities.
- ✔ **Access to the Internet.** This includes e-mail to members of other online services or Internet accounts, the Web, newsgroups, and so on.

In the case of the original three big online services (AOL, CompuServe, and Prodigy), the graphic interface for the service is also proprietary — in other words, instead of using a standard Web browser, such as Netscape Navigator or Microsoft Internet Explorer, you use special software provided by the online service to access it. Microsoft Network is different, in that you access the proprietary areas of the service the same way that you access the Internet — using a Web browser. (Conventional wisdom says that the other services will also switch to creating Web-compatible content for their proprietary areas in the near future.)

All these services charge about $20 per month for unlimited access to both their proprietary areas and the Internet.

An Internet Service Provider, or ISP, is a business that has little or no proprietary content and simply provides access to the Internet. These businesses sprang up after the World Wide Web started becoming a phenomenon in the mid-1990s, and after the creation of the Web browser as a standard software item that most computers can run.

Many ISPs are mom-and-pop local operations, but you can also connect to several nationwide ISPs, including PSINet, NetCom, NetworkMCI, and AT&T WorldNet. For use with portable computers, I highly recommend one of the nationwide ISPs over the mom-and-pop variety, for the simple reason that whether travel brings you to Miami or Cincinnati or Las Vegas — or any other major U.S. city — you're likely to find a local access number for these services. Some of the ISPs, especially smaller, local companies, charge a bit less than the online services — as little as $10–15 per month if you pay in advance for a year's worth of service (paying $120 to $180 in a lump sum). However, most large nationwide ISPs charge about the same as the online services.

If you are deciding between signing up with an online service or a straight ISP, I highly recommend that you go with one of the online services. In the early days of online services offering Internet access, they were atrociously inferior to making a direct connection to the Internet via an ISP. However, today you find almost no difference — the online services provide as good access to the Internet as you get from an ISP. Plus, with online services, you get all their additional proprietary content, which includes extensive chat areas to meet with other users. And if you have trouble getting things up and running, the online services offer customer support numbers to call. (Some mom-and-pop ISPs have notoriously poor hand-holding for customers with problems.)

The online services also provide a certain feeling of being centered, a kind of home base that's a familiar element when you're on the road. Unlike the Internet, which has a sort of random, chaotic quality, online services are organized, with information grouped together in categories. As shown in Figure 11-1, the Internet is just one of several places you can go when you are a CompuServe user.

I must also admit a personal bias here: I have been a member of CompuServe since 1984, and I have good friends who are in the business of creating the proprietary content for the online services — both on the editorial and technological sides. Besides wanting to keep my friends working, I also think that the online services deserve a lot of credit for pioneering the whole online concept prior to the Internet. They offered the very first places to go with a laptop computer and a modem.

Figure 11-1: The opening screen for CompuServe. Note that the Internet is just one of several things you can do. The other buttons all lead to CompuServe's own proprietary content.

Internet button

Accessing the Internet through Online Services

Online services offer a one-stop, does-everything solution to installing and configuring the software you need to access the Internet. A single installation program handles dialing into the online service and establishing the connection, your connection to the Internet and the Web (remember, the Internet is separate from the online service's proprietary connection), a Web browser, and your e-mail.

Don't attempt to copy an online service's program files from your desktop machine. Instead, reinstall the software from the original installation disk(s), and then copy your address book and/or bookmark information (by copying the specific files or by reentering the information). Besides the obvious files in the directory created by the online service, these programs just have too many other tentacles in Windows 95 — installing special drivers, dial-up programs, and other files — that also need to be copied.

If your notebook computer doesn't have a CD-ROM drive and your online service's software came in CD-ROM format, you can request a floppy disk version by calling the online service's customer service department. Alternatively — or if you have a subnotebook computer with neither floppy nor CD-ROM disk drives — you can use the CD-ROM drive in your desktop computer and a file transfer system such as LapLink to copy the installation files to your notebook computer's hard drive and then run the installation program (see Chapter 9).

The exact way you dial in and access the Internet varies with the different online services. CompuServe, for example, automatically installs and configures the Windows 95 Dial-Up Adapter accessory (see "Windows 95 Dial-Up Networking" later in this chapter), whereas America Online has its own dialing software. The details of each service are sure to change as newer versions of online service software are released and as Web browser software evolves.

Though the first attempts to offer Internet access through online services were sluggish and didn't fully work all the time, today the Internet access you get through an online service is virtually identical to what you get with an ISP.

Accessing the Internet through ISPs

Installing the software you need to access the Internet through an Internet Service Provider can be relatively easy or a big pain in the neck. AT&T WorldNet, for example, at one end of the spectrum, provides you with an installation disk that handles everything automatically, making it just as easy as an online service. At the other end of the spectrum are the no-frills mom-and-pop ISPs that simply give you a sheet of paper with a bunch of obscure code numbers on it, and you need to enter all the information manually.

With such minimal services, you may not even get a Web browser or e-mail software included. Fortunately, Windows 95 includes a copy of the Internet Explorer browser, and Microsoft Exchange mail software which you can use with such services.

At minimum, you need to install and configure a couple of individual software components to access the Internet through an ISP:

- ✔ **The dialer.** This is the software that calls up the telephone number, establishes a connection, and logs into your ISP's computer.

- ✔ **The Web browser.** This is usually Netscape Navigator or Microsoft Internet Explorer, and it allows you to surf the World Wide Web.

- ✔ **E-mail.** Eudora is the most popular e-mail software, and it's available in Windows and Macintosh versions. If you are a Windows 95 user, you can use the included Microsoft Exchange. Some browser programs, such as Netscape Navigator, have e-mail software built in so that your e-mail appears integrated with your Web access. See Chapter 12 for more info.

In addition to having a browser installed on your notebook computer, you may also want to add the plug-ins that you normally use on your desktop machine (if you have one), such as RealAudio, VDO (video), Shockwave (animation and multimedia), NetShow (Microsoft's multimedia player), and new ones that spring up.

If your office computer is connected to the Internet via a high-speed connection and you need to download a lot of plug-ins or a new browser version from the Internet, try using your office machine to download the installation files, and then copy them to your notebook using a program such as LapLink (see Chapter 9).

Windows 95 Dial-Up Networking

If you use a notebook with Windows 95 to access the Internet via a telephone connection, you probably use the Windows 95 Dial-Up Networking accessory. Dial-Up Networking is one of the most confusing aspects of hooking up to the Internet, and if you ever have problems getting things to work right, it probably has to do with the Dial-Up Networking program.

Software from some online services and ISPs attempts to set up Dial-Up Net-working for you. However, sometimes you have to go into Dial-Up Networking manually to finish making the settings — especially if you have a funky phone line situation with an outside line access code (usually 9), or something similar. Other times, you can't change the phone number or other parameters in Dial-Up Networking because the parameters in that particular installation of Dial-Up Networking are actually being controlled by an online service's software (as happens with CompuServe's WinCIM 3.0.1 software).

If you have problems with Dial-Up Networking and your ISP or online service, try some of these tricks:

- ✔ Go into the Setup or Options menu of your online service to change your phone number settings.

- ✔ If you also use your computer to hook up to a local network (in an office) via an Ethernet card (see Chapter 20), you may experience conflicts between the two different methods of networking. You may need to disable one form of networking to get the other one working. Dealing with similar conflicts is covered in Chapter 19.

- ✔ Dial-Up Networking is not in the Windows 95 Control Panel, where you expect to find it. You get to it by choosing Start⇨Programs⇨ Accessories⇨Dial-Up Networking.

If you experience difficulty connecting to the Internet with your modem and you feel confident that you have the modem properly installed and recognized by Windows 95, follow these step-by-step instructions for setting up Dial-Up Networking (Note that if you're setting up your notebook computer for Internet access for the first time, the process may actually involve two different installations — first for the Dial-Up Adapter, and then for the TCP/IP protocol.):

1. **Choose Start⇨Settings⇨Control Panel to open the Windows 95 Control Panel.**

2. **Double-click the Network icon.**

   The Network dialog box appears.

3. **Click the Configuration tab on top, if it's not already selected.**

4. **Look for** Dial-Up Adapter **in the list box that says** The following network components are installed:.

   If the Dial-Up Adapter is *not* present, then follow these substeps:

   a. Click Add.

   The Select Network Component Type dialog box pops up.

b. **Select the Adapter icon.**

c. **Click A̲dd.**

The Select Network adapters dialog box pops up.

d. **Under M̲anufacturers, click Microsoft (scroll down the list if you need to).**

e. **Click Dial-Up Adapter in the Network Adapters column, as shown in Figure 11-2.**

f. **Click OK.**

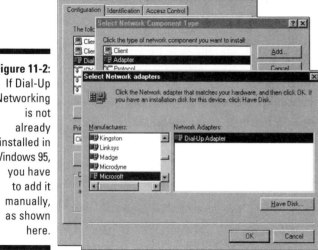

Figure 11-2:
If Dial-Up
Networking
is not
already
installed in
Windows 95,
you have
to add it
manually,
as shown
here.

5. **Back in the Network dialog box, make sure that the TCP/IP protocol is listed in the same box where the Dial-Up Adapter is listed (under the heading that says** The following network components are installed:**).**

If the TCP/IP protocol is *not* listed, follow these substeps:

a. **Click A̲dd.**

The Select Network Component Type dialog box pops up.

b. **Select the Protocol icon.**

A *protocol* is like a language that computers use to exchange information.

c. **Click A̲dd.**

The Select Network Protocol dialog box pops up.

    d. Click Microsoft (scroll down the <u>M</u>anufacturers list on the left).

    e. Click TCP/IP in the Network Protocols column.

    TCP/IP stands for *Transfer Control Protocol/Internet Protocol* — this protocol is what allows all computers on the Internet to talk to each other.

    f. Click OK.

    g. Most Internet Service Providers automatically obtain an IP address for the TCP/IP protocol, in which case you can skip this step. But in the unlikely event that your service provider specifically tells you that you must specify an IP address, here's how to do it: With the TCP/IP protocol highlighted in the Network dialog box (under the Configuration tab), click <u>P</u>roperties.

    The TCP/IP Properties dialog box appears.

    h. The IP Address tab should already be selected (if not, select it).

    i. Click the radio button that says Specify an IP address **and enter the IP address provided by your ISP, online service, or network administrator, along with the Subnet Mask, in the fields provided.**

    j. Click OK to close the TCP/IP Properties dialog box.

  6. Click OK to close the Network dialog box.

  7. Click the × in the upper right corner to close the Control Panel.

Next, to set up the Dial-Up Adapter for your particular Internet Service Provider, follow these steps:

  1. Choose Start⇨<u>P</u>rograms⇨Accessories⇨Dial-Up Networking.

  2. Double-click Make New Connection (or alternatively, choose <u>C</u>onnections⇨Make <u>N</u>ew Connection).

  3. Enter a name for your new connection.

    Probably the best name is something like **ISP connection** or the name of the particular service you plan to use this connection for (such as **Joe's Internet Service** — the default is **My Connection**). Verify that your modem appears in the field that says Select a modem. (If not, click the down arrow on the right, scroll through the list until you find your modem, and then double-click it. If your modem isn't listed, you need to install it — see Chapters 5 and 23.)

4. Click Next.

5. Enter the Area code, Telephone number, and Country code for the ISP in the appropriate text boxes.

6. Click Next, and then Finish.

Voila! A new icon now appears in the Dial-Up Networking window, with the name that you assigned.

7. Double-click this new icon for the new connection you just created.

A new Connect To dialog box appears.

8. Enter your User Name and Password for your ISP account in the Connect To dialog box.

9. Click Save Password to avoid entering your password each time you dial in.

Note that this action saves you the hassle of having to remember and type in your password each time you want to get on the Internet, but it has a security disadvantage: If someone steals or borrows your computer (as may happen in a college dorm room), they can gain access to your Internet account (and possibly read your e-mail, spend your e-cash, and so on). Personally, I accept this risk, but others may prefer to err on the side of caution.

10. Click Connect if you have your modem plugged into a regular phone line and you are ready to go.

If you're using an office or hotel phone system and need to first dial a prefix or disable call waiting, or — heaven forbid — need to use pulse dialing, then first click Dial Properties in the Connect To dialog box, and then enter the information where appropriate. See Chapter 19 for more information about these options.

If you have Dial-Up Networking configured and working properly (no sweat after all those steps, huh?), and your modem is plugged in and working, then you're ready to connect to your ISP. When you click Connect, you first hear a dial tone, and then you hear the software dialing your ISP. When your ISP's modem picks up the call on the other end, you hear a sound like rushing water (often called the *warble*), and then you see messages on the screen such as `Verifying user name and password`. At the end of the process, a small box appears on the screen saying something like `Connected at 28,800`. This number indicates the actual speed of the connection you've established, which is usually a little slower than your modem's maximum speed. You can now launch your Web browser or e-mail program.

Finding a Local ISP or Online Service Phone Number

The Internet can theoretically save you oodles of money by letting you exchange unlimited amounts of e-mail with people in other cities and foreign countries without paying any of the long distance charges you usually pay for a phone call or fax. However, watch out for one big catch: To save money, your connection to the Internet must be a local phone call. A local phone number is the only way you can keep that attractive $20 per month unlimited service plan from becoming a much higher bill.

You may find that signing up with a big nationwide Internet service provider or online service has a huge advantage over smaller, more local and regional services providers. A big nationwide service provider offers hundreds of different phone numbers, spread all across the U.S. Just about every big city has a local number you can call — also known as a *Point Of Presence* or *POP,* in Internet techie jargon.

Some online services — most notably, CompuServe — offer local numbers internationally as well, which are great if you expect to travel in Europe. For more help finding a local number for AOL, CompuServe, and other online services, and for help with changing the phone number using their software, see Chapter 19.

So how do you find other phone numbers for your ISP outside your local area? With online services such as CompuServe, AOL, and Prodigy, they are available directly from the customer service area. With the major ISPs, such as PSInet and AT&T WorldNet, you may be able to get them from their home page Web sites. If you can't find the number you're looking for on the home page, call the customer service telephone number, or send them e-mail and request a complete list. Of course, the numbers change periodically, so make sure that you have a current list before you zip off on an around-the-world journey.

What if your service provider doesn't have a local number in the town you're visiting? Whether or not you want to shell out the long-distance dough is your call, and it depends on how badly you really need Internet access and how much you have to pay for the long distance charges. In most cases, setting up a new account just to send a couple of e-mail items during a weekend getaway is a lot of work and not really worth the effort. On the other hand, if you're spending the summer in a remote cabin, finding a local number may be a good idea.

How do you find a local service provider? Look for ads in local newspapers and entertainment weeklies. You can also use the Internet itself to find service providers — use a search engine and enter the name of the town (or the name of the biggest town in the same local calling area), the plus sign (+), and the word **Internet**, or the phrase **Internet service**.

After you find a new number or set up a new account, see Chapter 19 for more information about changing the configuration of your software.

Note that two other options exist with many nationwide online services and ISPs:

- ✔ **1-800 number access.** Typically for about a $6 to $10 per hour surcharge, you can get a toll-free number to dial into from within the U.S. Of course, at those rates, costs mount quickly if you do lot of Web browsing or chatting, but for quick e-mail access, the toll-free numbers are great.

- ✔ **Bite the bullet and pay.** This option is the laziest, and makes sense only if you expect to be online for a few minutes, for example, just long enough to send or receive a quick e-mail. Just bite the bullet and pay for a long distance call to your service provider in your hometown. Unfortunately, you *still* usually have to change your dial-up settings to include an area code. See Chapter 19 for more help in this area.

Maintaining Multiple Services and Accounts

Serious travelers often spend a good amount of time in two places. Maybe you travel to a specific town on business fairly regularly or maybe you work in public relations or the news media and you need access to a variety of these services to keep track of market trends or some such thing. In these types of situations, you may want to configure your notebook computer to access multiple online services and/or ISPs.

If you travel extensively and rely heavily on the Internet, you may want multiple services just to hedge your bet on finding a local phone number. The exact towns with a local number vary for each service provider, so by maintaining two (or more) accounts, you're more likely to find a local access number when you're visiting small- to medium-sized towns. Big cities, of course, are pretty universally covered by all the major online services and nationwide ISPs.

For connecting to multiple ISPs, you can create an additional new connection for a second or third service provider by clicking Make New Connection in the Dial-Up Networking program group, and following the numbered steps in the previous section, "Windows 95 Dial-Up Networking."

After you connect to your second ISP, you can usually retrieve your e-mail from the first account just by leaving the settings in your e-mail program (such as Eudora) the way they are. See Chapter 12 for more info.

Portable Web Browsing

As amazing and vast as the Internet is when you're home, it can be even more cool when you're away.

The world becomes both smaller and more familiar when you travel with the help of the Internet. Unlike TV stations, radio, and newspapers, the Internet is the same wherever you go. The bookmarks you create in your Web browser work anywhere, whenever you connect to the Net. All your favorite and informative Web sites are just as accessible from a hotel room across the country as they are when you're home. The Internet allows you to have a home of sorts in cyberspace where you can always check in, and where you are always reachable, no matter where you are physically. In addition, the Internet can directly aid your travel, by helping you make reservations, track flight information, and schedule meetings with people you plan to visit.

You can order merchandise or read up on just about any topic you can think of. And when you're alone in an empty hotel room, the World Wide Web can be as much of a companion as the TV set — if not more, because the Web is interactive.

Bargain fares on the Net

The Internet offers many resources to help you find bargain airfares and other travel arrangements. For college students and backpackers looking for the most economical way to travel, courier flights offer an attractive, no-frills option. As a courier, you use a ticket that was purchased by a shipping company for the sake of the luggage allotment given to each passenger — the shipping company needs a warm body to fill the seat to satisfy the legal requirements of the ticket. (No, you don't have to *carry* anything — this is all taken care of by the shipping company in advance — but you are strictly limited to carry-on luggage only, so having a really compact and lightweight mobile computer is absolutely essential.) You can also find all sorts of

discounted airfares and accommodations via the Web, and you can partici-
pate in auctions where travel arrangements are sold to the highest bidder.
The following sections describe some sites that offer various forms of travel
bargains.

✔ Besides the individual sites run by each of the major airlines offering
up-to-the-minute flight arrival times, Yahoo! maintains a site with
current flight availability and on-time information called Yahoo Travel
at `http://travel.yahoo.com/travel/`.

✔ The major online services (AOL and CompuServe) also offer access to
two proprietary reservation systems, called EasySaabre and
TravelShopper, that can book air travel, hotels, and car reservations for
you, and charge your purchases to a credit card number. Also, because
these systems are on online services, they may offer a bit more security
for credit card transactions than Internet travel services.

Air Courier Travel

Run by the International Association of Air Travel Couriers, this site gives
you the opportunity to become an air travel courier and fly cheaply to most
major cities around the world. Remember that you usually cannot bring any
checked luggage with you.

`http://www.courier.org/`

Air Ticket Shopper

You can shop for the best air ticket by filling out a form with an air ticket
quotation request that is then sent to four different travel agents (at no cost
to you). But note that you may end up dealing with travel agencies across
the country, or even in another country.

`http://www.bestadv.com/airshop/`

Internet Travel Network

Here's how the Internet Travel Network works: Watch the Low Fare Ticker
on the screen. When you see a good flight price that interests you, click the
fare to enter the reservation system and find out whether the fare is available when you wish to travel and book your trip. You can also subscribe to a
fare notification service that notifies you via e-mail when the price to a
particular destination dips below a threshold that you specify.

`http://www.itn.net/`

Net SAAver Fares

By subscribing to the American Airlines Net SAAver mailing list, you get e-mail notices of specially discounted travel opportunities and fares to different destinations each week. Every Wednesday, Net SAAver sends you the latest list of discounted fares for travel within the U.S. and between the U.S. to Canada. You can also subscribe to an e-mail list for international travelers.

```
http://www.americanair.com/aa_home/net_saavers.htm
```

TISS

The TISS Travel Information Services site (TISS stands for Travel Information Software Systems) offers access to the lowest published regular airfares directly from airlines. You fill out a form for where you'd like to travel and get back instant flight fares with a travel agency that is offering that particular rate. You can then book the flight straight from your computer.

```
http://www.tiss.com/
```

Help in a strange town

Whether you're just visiting for a weekend or relocating for the next year, the Internet can be a resource for finding out more about the place where you are. Check out these possible sources:

- ✔ Local government or chamber of commerce
- ✔ Local newspapers

Recognizing the possibilities that the Web offers as a local advertising medium, a number of companies, including Microsoft, have started building local guides or city guides on the Net. At their best, these are an Internet equivalent of a local entertainment weekly, complete with local columnists and personalities. Many, however, are simpler compilations of lists, such as movie schedules and restaurants, and are run en masse from a single central facility with minimal local staff (if any).

Most of the guides listed in this section have started by focusing on a few major cities, but have ambitious plans to extend their coverage to all major markets. Just how far they will go with those plans, like most things on the Internet, depends on what the Net itself is doing in the future and the popularity of these initial offerings.

Yahoo! Get Local

Yahoo!'s city guides provide classifieds, sports scores, weather forecasts, and local Web resources.

```
http://local.yahoo.com/local/
```

CitySearch

CitySearch has local staffs in each of the seven cities it serves so far, and provides well-organized information, as shown in Figure 11-3.

```
http://www.CitySearch.com/
```

SideWalk

Produced by Microsoft, each city that SideWalk covers (just two so far) has a large local staff. If you're visiting Seattle, this is definitely the site to check first.

```
http://www.SideWalk.com/
```

City.Net

A very inclusive site of where to eat, sleep, and meet people in many U.S. cities. You can also book hotel reservations by becoming a member.

```
http://www.city.net/countries/united_states/
```

Figure 11-3: CitySearch is one of several Web sites devoted to providing local information including news, events, maps, restaurants, and listings for movies, art, music, and so on.

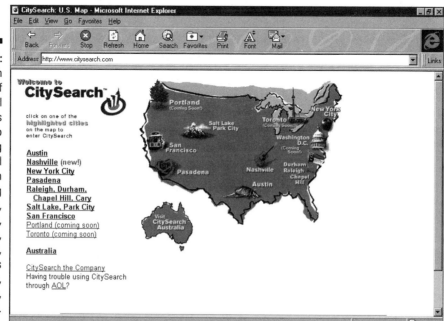

CityInsights

Reporting on restaurants, entertainment, shopping, hotels, and services only in San Francisco, Chicago, New York, and Boston.

http://cityinsights.com/

USA CityLink

This Web site maintains links to sites that provide information about cities useful to anyone just wanting to visit or learn more about a specific place.

http://www.usacitylink.com/

TimeOutNet

Covering most major international cities and some major U.S. cities, this site has entertainment listings and links to other city-oriented sites.

http://www.timeout.co.uk/

Dive In

Cities include Jacksonville, Los Angeles, the Twin Cities, Phoenix, Portland, and Seattle.

http://www3.divein.com/divein/html/01_national_home.html

Intellipages

This site is a city guide combining local directories, news, and community information.

http://www.intellipages.com/

Company intranet

Besides accessing the Internet and online services, another type of network exists that you may need to visit using browser software on your notebook computer — the corporate *intranet*. An *intranet* is a local network set up within an organization to function with the look and feel of the Internet, but that is accessible only to members of that organization.

When you're traveling, an intranet may have useful information, such as contact information for branch offices or databases from which you need to extract information. Intranets may also be used for video conferencing (to hold meetings between branch offices, for example), for providing training videos and training multimedia, or for making company-wide announcements.

Technically, an intranet is really just a specific form of Local Area Network —
a topic I cover in more detail in Chapter 20. However, because the network is
organized around Internet standards, you use the same tools (mainly a Web
browser) that you use to access the Internet to access the intranet.

News services

You can find so many news sources available on the Internet that I have a
hard time even summarizing the variety of what's out there — it's like
describing the non-fiction section in a bookstore. Practically every
major publication these days maintains a Web site, offering a selection of
current articles or sometimes an online version of the entire publication.
When you travel with a notebook computer, local newspaper Web sites
provide a great way for you to keep up with local news events and sports
from your hometown. You can be halfway around the world, yet keep track
of your hometown high school basketball team.

All three of the major national newspapers in the U.S. — *The New York
Times, The Wall Street Journal,* and *The Washington Post* — maintain Web
sites offering much of what's in the print versions. Other major sites for U.S.
news are operated by the CNN and MSNBC cable networks, and by ABC
News. Other sites of interest include ESPN's sports site, the Mr. Showbiz
entertainment site, TV listings at Gist (great if you're in a hotel room
at midnight, have no local paper, and want to know what's on TV), and
high-tech news from C-NET.

Financial services

Online brokerage services that let you buy and sell stocks from your computer can have several advantages over using a traditional broker. You can
access the service 24 hours a day, 7 days a week. Commissions are usually
lower — you often find the deepest discounts at online stock trading
systems because the automated service is cheap to operate. Of course, the
assumption of these services is that you know what you want to buy and
sell, and aren't seeking the advice of a personal stockbroker. These services
tend to be very impersonal, though sometimes they are run by the same
companies that run traditional brokerage services.

Options in this category include QuickWay from Quick and Reilly (available
via CompuServe), E*Trade (available via Internet and online services), and
E-Schwab from Charles Schwab (available on the Internet).

Many banks also offer electronic banking services. In addition to letting you transfer money between accounts and check your balances and statements, these services usually offer something that's very useful to people who are on the road for long periods of time: The ability to cut checks by remote control. You can be traveling in India, for example, and by hooking into your electronic banking service, you can get your bank in New York to write a check to your landlord to pay your rent. Of course, you have to have money in the account to cover it.

Research

As a general-purpose research tool, the Internet is beyond compare for both its vastness and ease of use. Imagine making a new business contact while on the road and being able, from your hotel room, to learn all sorts of information about that contact's company by looking up both what the company says about itself and what others say.

Imagine researching college term papers or a doctoral thesis, not in a stuffy library, but from the deck of your sister's beach house in the Florida Keys. The possibilities of Internet research are so vast . . . the hard part is getting the sister with the beach house.

Many university libraries have vast online resources that are at your disposal, free of charge, offering unprecedented research capabilities from anywhere in the world.

Not all search engines are the same. WebCrawler, for example, offers numerous advanced search tools and customizable options that are more likely to turn up information on a specific obscure string (such as you may search for in a research situation) than some of the more commercially-oriented search engines. Try using several different search engines when researching a specialized topic.

Note that if you're doing academic research and need to tie into a university computer system, you may sometimes need to use terminal emulation software to gain access. See Chapter 10 for more about data communications and the Internet's Telnet protocol.

Chapter 12
Mobile E-Mail

. . . .

In This Chapter

▶ Figuring out what you need to get e-mail on your mobile computer

▶ Configuring e-mail for a second computer

▶ Retrieving e-mail on the road

▶ Getting e-mail from an office computer system using your notebook on the road

. . . .

E-mail is without a doubt the most universal and popular way that people communicate using mobile computers. Though the vast majority of the portable e-mail action takes place on notebook computers, e-mail is one application where you can also get away with using smaller pocket computers, especially if the messages you need to send and receive are fairly short.

Using e-mail has definite advantages, such as:

- ✔ Enabling you to stay in contact with your home office, with clients, with friends, and with others connected to the Internet or an online service

- ✔ Providing a cheap, fast, reliable means of communications

- ✔ Giving you a convenient way to access mail — a way based on your schedule rather than others'

And the great thing for mobile computer users is that your e-mail address need never change, no matter where your travels take you. With e-mail you are available globally, and you can access it locally.

Getting Up and Running with E-Mail

In addition to a modem (see Chapter 5), you generally need two things to get up and running with e-mail on your mobile computer:

✔ **Some kind of online service, Internet Service Provider (ISP), or office network with a phone number you can dial into.** You can use an account with a commercial ISP or online service provider, a dial-in connection to your office computer system, or a dial-in connection to a campus network.

✔ **E-mail software.** For example, Eudora, Microsoft Exchange, or any of a dozen other programs, including ones that are provided by online services when you subscribe.

If you subscribe to an online service such as AOL or CompuServe, e-mail software is included as part of the service's software that you receive when you sign up. E-mail software is also usually included in the Web browser software that you use when you access an ISP. Examples include Netscape Navigator, which has its own e-mail program, and Microsoft Internet Explorer, which uses Microsoft Exchange (included with Windows 95).

However, many Internet users prefer to use a separate, more powerful program for e-mail, such as Eudora, which is currently the most widely used e-mail program.

When you sign up with an online service or ISP, or even with an office or university network, you almost always get an e-mail account to which you can receive mail. Usually, the address for this account is based on the username that you select when you establish the account, and the name of the ISP or online service. If the username is `joeblow7` and he or she is using the `applesandbananas` ISP, the address is:

        `joeblow7@applesandbananas.com`

Figuring Out Your Approach to E-Mail — Multiple Accounts and More

You have several different approaches you can take to get your e-mail with your mobile computer. The exact way you get your e-mail depends on what type of e-mail account you have (through your business or college or organization, from an online service, or from an ISP), what sort of dial-up connections your office computer system has (if you have one at all), and what sort of long distance telephone charges play into your setup. I describe your various options in the next several sections — skim through them to see which situation(s) apply to you, and then make your selection (if you have a choice) based on what seems easiest, and what results in the lowest phone bills.

What if you already have an e-mail account, say at the office where you work? What you probably want to do is just configure your notebook computer to receive the same e-mail that you get at the office. You may never even use the e-mail address that comes with your dial-up service provider — you simply use the online account to get on the Internet and connect to your office e-mail. Of course, to do this, your office e-mail system needs to be hooked up to the Internet with mail hosting — check with your company's computer systems administrator to make sure.

You may end up with several different e-mail addresses because of the various accounts that you need to set up with online services in order to obtain local access to the Internet in different places you visit. And each account most likely comes with an e-mail address. Your e-mail life is bound to be much simpler if you give out just one e-mail address, and use other accounts only to access your one chosen account that you use for e-mail. (See Chapter 11 for information about setting up accounts with multiple online services.)

You have an online service or ISP e-mail on another machine

You have the easiest time configuring your mobile computer for e-mail if you already have an account with an online service or ISP on another computer, and you use that account as your sole connection. Just copy the same software that you use on your desktop machine onto your notebook, and copy the account number and password information as well. You can use the same account with as many different computers as you want as long as you connect with only one at a time. See Chapter 11 for more detailed information on changing phone numbers and finding a local access number.

Your office has a dial-in Internet (TCP/IP) connection

Among all the possible scenarios for gaining access to your e-mail on your office computer system, the best is when your organization's network is both connected to the Internet and offers its own dial-in phone number. You most often find this luxury with big university computer systems, and other large organizations with many employees, or users that need to gain remote access to the computer system.

However, most smaller organizations do not have dial-in phone numbers for their computer networks — because they don't want the expense of the phone line(s), don't want the security risk of having intruders calling in, or simply because no one has needed it prior to you.

If the local area network you use at work or school is hooked up to the Internet (that is, you can receive e-mail from anywhere in the world, and/or can use a Web browser), ask your organization's network administrator whether you can get dial-in access for your mobile computer. If the answer is yes, then you need to know your account name and password — these are most often the same as when you're in the office. You can then use the same software you use at your office to access the office network's dial-up connection.

Most network administrators limit dial-in access to the mail server, in which case the only thing you can do with your dial-in connection is retrieve and send e-mail. However, in some cases, the dial-in connection may be set up so that as soon as you dial in, you have access to all the network resources that you would normally have access to from inside the office. The only difference is that because you are using a phone line, you may find the connection a bit slower than what you're used to in the office. In this scenario, your office computer system essentially functions as an Internet Service Provider — by dialing into the office network, you may be able to get onto the Internet without any additional accounts.

Now that's a pretty good (and free) setup, isn't it? Unfortunately, most organizations don't provide it, due to the security risk.

Your office has no dial-in, but has an Internet connection

If your office computer system is connected to the Internet (you have Web access and/or can receive e-mail from people all over the world), but has no dial-in phone number of its own, then you may have a cool option. You can probably retrieve your office e-mail from a mobile computer by connecting to the Internet through an online service or ISP, and then setting your e-mail program to pick up mail from your office e-mail server at its specific Internet address.

Pretty powerful stuff, eh? One beauty of this setup is that you may have to pay only local phone charges for your Internet access — no big savings if you're just going out of town for a weekend, but if you spend the summer with your uncle in Italy, finding a local number may amount to substantial savings (see Chapter 11).

I say that you can *probably* use this setup, because you are ultimately at the will of your organization's network administrator. Technically, the fact that your local network is connected to the Internet means that the network can be set up to allow you to access its e-mail server and pick up your mail via the Internet. However, some network administrators choose to disable this capability for security reasons — to prevent would-be hackers from attempting to gain unauthorized access to employee e-mail. You can talk to your organization's network administrator to find out for sure, or you can ask around among other members of the organization to see whether anyone else is picking up their e-mail remotely.

When you speak to your network administrator about getting e-mail remotely, be sure to ask for all the relevant information you need to configure your e-mail software, including account name, password (this may be different from your usual network login password), POP (Post Office Protocol — how you pick up mail via the Internet) account, and SMTP (Simple Mail Transfer Protocol) server name.

Perhaps the most complicated thing about receiving your office e-mail through the Internet is the fact that you are now juggling two sets of usernames, passwords, and e-mail accounts. Follow these basic steps:

1. **Connect to your online account or Internet Service Provider.**

   You use one username and password to connect to your online service, such as AOL or CompuServe, or to your Internet Service Provider (ISP). (See Chapter 11 for more info.)

2. **Configure your POP (Post Office Protocol) e-mail program in your online account or ISP to pick up mail from the Internet address for your organization's e-mail server.**

   You can get the information you need (as listed in the following bullet list) by either launching your office e-mail software and looking at the configuration settings, or by talking to your office network administrator.

   - Most e-mail programs use POP, but check to make sure that your e-mail program uses it. Programs that do include Eudora, Netscape Navigator, and Microsoft Exchange.

   - The Internet address for your organization's mail server is sometimes called an *IP address* — you can get it from your network administrator if you can't find it listed in your software configuration at work or school.

   - As with all e-mail software, you also need your username and password, in this case you want to enter the username and password for your *office* e-mail system, not your username and password for the ISP or online service you are using as a "bridge" to get access to your office e-mail.

   - The *POP account name* that you may need to enter in the e-mail software combines your username and the Internet address, such as joeblow7@applesandbananas.com. See Figure 12-1 for an example.

   - You may also need to enter an SMTP (Simple Mail Transfer Protocol) address, usually the same as your POP account name minus your username, such as applesandbananas.com. See Figure 12-3 for an example.

   3. Get your mail using the POP (Post Office Protocol) e-mail program, now set to go out and pick it up from your office e-mail server.

   Through the magic of the Internet, the e-mail software goes out and grabs the e-mail from your office server, even though you are connected to the Internet somewhere completely different and through a completely different server.

You can find detailed, numbered steps to help you configure Eudora and Microsoft Exchange for this procedure in the "Receiving E-Mail on Two Different Machines" section in this chapter.

Your office has no outside connection

Suppose that your office has its own internal network, but offers no dial-up access, and the network has no connection to the Internet whatsoever. Your office is just a little electronic island in the sun. You may even use a basic *peer-to-peer* network, in which several computers in the office are hooked up to a printer, but you have no central server — each computer in this type of network is as much at the heart of the network as any other computer. Your coworkers in the office use the network to send each other e-mail, and while you're away, you don't want to miss out. How do you retrieve your e-mail?

With one big warning, you are an excellent candidate for remote computing, as I cover in detail in Chapter 13. You have to install the appropriate software on both a desktop machine in the office, and you have to equip the desktop computer with a modem, if it doesn't already have one.

Installing remote computing software on any machine in a network makes the entire network vulnerable to electronic invasion by computer hackers. This threat may be the reason why your network is not connected to the outside world. If your office network isn't connected to the Internet because it's a small office and no one has bothered to do it, and the slight risk of using remote computing is acceptable to the powers that be in your organization, then by all means go ahead and set it up (see Chapter 13). However, if your organization has made the decision to keep its network totally separate from the outside world as a safety precaution, don't subvert that policy. The wrath of the network administrator is a powerful one.

As a safer alternative (from a systems security standpoint) to remote computing, you can establish an account with an online service or Internet Service Provider, and then have your desktop machine at the office automatically forward your e-mail from the local network to your external address (see "Forwarding E-Mail" later in this chapter). You still need a modem for your desktop machine, and you still make the local network slightly vulnerable to electronic attack, but at a much lower risk than with remote computing. The reason the risk is less is that your desktop modem isn't *answering* calls — just making calls, and only to a specific phone number (for the online service or ISP).

If this solution all begins to sound a bit complicated, you have a far less technical approach that always works in a pinch: Call your office, and ask someone there to read your e-mail to you. Someone you trust. Pretty low-tech, but effective and reliable.

Receiving E-Mail on Two Different Machines

Once you figure out how you need to connect to your office or school network, either directly or via an online service or ISP, and you configure your e-mail software to pick up and send e-mail to and from that network, you are all set to pick up your mail from your office or school account. You can use a program like Eudora, or Microsoft Exchange e-mail software that comes built into Windows 95, or the e-mail software that's usually included with Web browsers such as Netscape Navigator. However, you have some-thing else to think about.

When e-mail addressed to you comes in, it is first received by a *mail server* (a computer that lies at the center of your mail system), and then you pick it up with your mail program with your computer acting as a *client* (most networks consist of *server* and many connected *clients* — an arrangement you can think of as a hub and many spokes of a wheel). In some systems, the mail resides on the server even after you read it — in other words, if you have a desktop and a portable computer, all of your mail is available at all times to both computers, no matter where you are and when you connect. This situation can be thought of as *server stored mail.*

However, another system which you can think of as *client stored mail,* works like this: Every time you log on to read mail, the server spits out all the mail it has for your address to your client computer, and then the mail is deleted from the server (unless you tell it not to, as I explain in the next section). You store the actual messages on your desktop or portable computer. The problem that can arise with this situation is that if you are out of town with your portable computer and you pick up your mail, you then don't have your mail available on your desktop computer when you get back — you must either coordinate your two computers or run the risk of your mail becoming a disorganized mess.

Figuring out where your messages are stored

When you configure the e-mail software on your notebook computer, you usually have several choices regarding what happens to the e-mail on the server (the computer that collects your e-mail) after you retrieve it. These choices are

- ✔ **Leave mail on the server after you retrieve it**

- ✔ **Delete mail from the server after you retrieve it** (and store it on the client — be it your desktop or notebook computer)

- ✔ **Automatically delete your mail from the server after a specified number of days**

I strongly advise you to leave the mail on the server — you need to configure this for the e-mail on your laptop computer as well as on your desktop computer. That way, you don't run the risk of having an important message get deleted from the server, and then not having it available because you picked it up with your other computer. I set both my desktop and laptop computers' e-mail software to automatically delete messages from the server after 120 days — I figure if after four months I haven't gotten to an e-mail, I probably blew it anyway.

Most e-mail software allows you to limit received messages to a specified size — this feature prevents you from suddenly spending hours downloading a multi-megabyte file over the phone line, and is very useful as a setting for your notebook computer when you're on the go. However, remember that you must later retrieve the full message from the server, or it will be deleted after the specified period of time (assuming that you activate the delete-after-so-many-days feature).

The Microsoft Exchange program built into Windows 95 includes a special feature called Remote Mail, intended especially for use with laptops. Remote Mail's main advantage is that it lets you scan through the list of e-mail waiting for you on the server, without actually taking the time to download all the messages. If you receive a lot of e-mail or very big files, this approach can save you serious online time. The idea is that you retrieve just the messages you need while on the road, and then look at everything else after you get back to the office and have a quick LAN (Local Area Network) connection. The Remote Mail screen lists the name of the sender and subject for each message — you then mark which ones you want to download remotely. Note that Remote Mail does not work with all e-mail systems — your safest bet, if you want this service, is to sign up with the MSN online service (Microsoft Network). You can see how to install Remote Mail in the "Microsoft Exchange and Remote Mail Settings" section in this chapter.

You can get essentially the same flexibility that Remote Mail offers with just about any e-mail software by limiting the size of the files you retrieve to a very small amount, such as 1KB. As long as you do not delete the e-mail from the server, you can retrieve all the messages in full after you get back to the office, and you can selectively retrieve only the messages that you need while you're on the road.

In some rare instances, such as when you have to deal with older networks or small networks that are not connected to the Internet, the e-mail may work on a strictly client-stored basis. In these systems, your desktop machine receives e-mail directly from other computers on the network, without ever being stored on a central e-mail server. In such cases, remote computing is your best bet for retrieving e-mail — see Chapter 13.

Note that when you send e-mail from two different computers, such as an office machine and a notebook, the e-mail software in each retains a separate list of outgoing mail. You don't have any master file containing all your outgoing mail, unless you go through the trouble of creating one using the synchronization techniques I cover in Chapter 9.

Configuring Eudora Pro and setting it to store messages on the server

Eudora is probably the most popular Internet e-mail program — Qualcomm (Eudora's publisher — see the Appendix) claims over 18 million users. Following is a quick guide to setting up Eudora to keep your incoming e-mail on the server so that you can pick it up easily from both your desktop and mobile computer, without losing any important mail. As I describe in the "Figuring Out Your Approach to E-Mail — Multiple Accounts and More" section, you need to copy the POP and SMTP information exactly as it appears in your desktop installation, or obtain this information from the network administrator at your office or school, or from your Internet Service Provider. Just follow these steps:

1. **Launch Eudora by double clicking its icon on the desktop.**

2. **Choose Tools⟹Options.**

   The Options dialog box appears with icons on the left for numerous options categories, as shown in Figure 12-1.

3. **Click Getting Started in the Category menu on the left.**

4. **Enter the POP account (the address provided by your e-mail service, ISP, or network administrator), your Real name, and choose Winsock as the Connection Method (assuming you're retrieving e-mail from an Internet service provider or an online service with full Internet compatibility).**

Figure 12-1:
The Options
dialog box
in Eudora
(version 3.0).
Note the
Category
column on
the left.

If that's not the case, check with your network administrator or e-mail provider for configuration specifics.

5. Click Personal Information in the Category list on the left.

A new set of blank fields appears in the Options dialog box.

6. Enter your e-mail address as your Return address.

Note that your e-mail address is not the same as the POP (Post Office Protocol) account information (unlike the e-mail address, the POP account includes the name of the mail server, as shown in Figure 12-2).

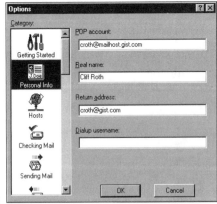

Figure 12-2:
The
Personal
Info
submenu in
Eudora.
Note that
POP
account is
different
from Return
address.

7. Click Hosts in the Category list on the left.

Again, a new set of fields appears in the Options dialog box.

8. Enter the <u>P</u>OP (Post Office Protocol) account (if it is not already listed) and <u>S</u>MTP (Simple Mail Transfer Protocol) account information, as shown in Figure 12-3.

Figure 12-3:
The Hosts submenu in Eudora. Note that SMTP information is different from the POP account.

9. Click Checking Mail in the <u>C</u>ategory list on the left.

   A new, much more complicated-looking set of fields appears in the Options dialog box.

10. Some of the settings in the Checking Mail section of the Options dialog box depend on your particular needs, but I recommend the following settings, as shown in Figure 12-4, for these reasons:

   • You don't want the computer to check for mail automatically unless you're tied into a network, so I set Check for mail <u>e</u>very 0 minutes.

Figure 12-4:
Eudora's Checking Mail options.

- **Skip messages over 250KB** to help screen out big files (such as graphics attachments) that you don't need to look at right away.

- **Send on check** delivers any messages that are stored in the Outbox whenever you tell your computer to check for new mail. This option saves you the time and trouble of remembering to send messages out and is helpful even if you don't ordinarily use the Outbox — if the computer ever has a problem sending a message, checking this box ensures that it will try again the next time you retrieve your mail.

- **Save Password** so that you're not prompted for it each time you check for your e-mail. (*Note:* If you leave your mobile computer out where others can use it, you may want to leave this box blank for security's sake, and enter your password whenever you retrieve e-mail.)

- **Leave mail on server** so that you can also have access to it from your desktop computer. This way, when you pick up messages using your notebook computer, they are still available on your desktop computer as well — the main point of this section, remember?

- **Delete from server after** 120 **days** — if you are traveling around the world, which takes only 80 days, 120 days should be long enough to make sure that you get the access you need to your e-mail from both your mobile and desktop computers.

- **The Determine first unread message by** option is relatively minor — it determines whether or not a dot (indicating whether a message has already been read) appears in the Status column. My preference is **First message not read by this machine** — this choice shows me what I have and haven't yet read using the particular computer I'm on. The other two choices (**Status: headers** and **POP3 LAST command**) base the decision of what's been read on the message headers, or on whether new mail has been sent since the last batch, respectively.

- **I suggest leaving Delete from server when emptied from Trash unchecked.** This choice is the superneurotic approach: Even if I move mail into the Trash box on my notebook computer (to delete it), knowing that a copy of it is still available on the server is comforting, in case I make a mistake.

- **The Authentication style selection** (Passwords, Kerberos, or APOP) is information that you can get from your network administrator or e-mail provider. However, if you must make an educated guess, go with Passwords (and if it doesn't work, you have only the two other options to try).

11. Click Sending Mail in the Category list on the left.

Another dialog box appears.

12. **Verify that your Return address and SMTP server are correct, and make sure that the boxes next to Immediate send and Send on check are checked.**

13. **Click OK.**

    Congratulations — you've just configured your e-mail so you can receive it on the road and still have it available on your desktop computer when you get back. You're well on your way to being a true road warrior.

Microsoft Exchange and remote mail settings

I highly recommend that you use Eudora Pro or other e-mail software rather than the Microsoft Exchange e-mail client software that's built into Windows 95. Eudora is much, much easier to use, and also offers more features and options that are especially useful to notebook computer users, such as the ability to automatically delete e-mail from the mail server after a specified period of time.

Nevertheless, Windows 95 includes Microsoft Exchange e-mail, and it's the least expensive way to enable notebook PCs for e-mail. To get ready to use Exchange with your basic e-mail settings, follow these instructions:

1. **Choose Start⇨Settings⇨Control Panel.**

2. **Double-click Mail and Fax.**

    The MS Exchange Settings Properties dialog box pops up.

3. **Click the Services tab if it is not already selected.**

4. **Select Internet Mail from the list of Services (if Internet Mail is not listed, click Add and select Internet Mail, and then click OK).**

5. **Click Properties.**

    The Internet Mail dialog box appears.

6. **Enter your account information: Full name, E-mail address, Internet Mail server, Account name, and Password, as shown in Figure 12-5.**

    You must copy this information precisely from your desktop computer or get it from your network administrator.

7. **Click the Connection tab on top.**

8. **Click Connect using the modem (make sure that your dial-up connection is listed in the box below this option — if not, you must set up Dial-Up Networking, as I explain in Chapter 11).**

Figure 12-5:
The
Properties
dialog box
for
Microsoft
Exchange
Internet
Mail.

9. **Click OK (near the bottom) to close the Internet Mail Properties dialog box.**

10. **Click OK to close the MS Exchange Settings Properties dialog box.**

Microsoft Exchange, all by itself, is enough to retrieve and send e-mail. However, as soon as you retrieve e-mail with your notebook computer, it is deleted from the mail server. In other words, you don't have access to it from your desktop computer after you get back into the office. To get around this problem, you must use the Remote Mail feature to retrieve e-mail, as I explain in the following steps:

1. **Launch Microsoft Exchange by double-clicking the Inbox icon on the Windows 95 desktop.**

   The Microsoft Exchange program launches.

2. **Choose Tools⇨Remote Mail.**

   If Remote Mail appears grayed out, meaning it's not available, see the Warning icon at the end of these numbered steps.

3. **In Remote Mail, choose Tools⇨Connect and Update Headers, as shown in Figure 12-6.**

   Sound confusing? It is. This Remote Mail Tools menu is separate from the Tools menu in MS Exchange. By choosing the Connect and Update Headers option, the program retrieves just the *headers* (the name of the sender and subject of each message) from your e-mail server, while leaving the actual message text on the server.

4. **After Remote Mail gives you a list of the headers, highlight the message(s) you want to read.**

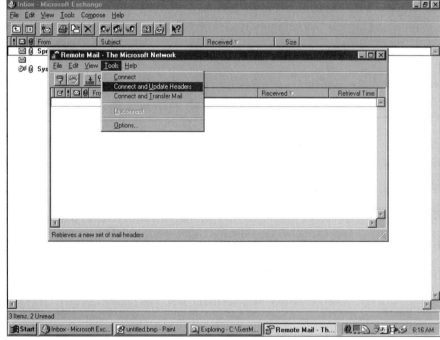

Figure 12-6:
Microsoft
Exchange
and Remote
Mail —
Connect
and Update
Headers
option.

5. Choose Edit⇨Mark to Retrieve a Copy to retrieve a message while leaving it on the server (so that you can later pick it up from your desktop machine as well).

6. Choose Tools⇨Connect and Transfer Mail (or Transfer Mail if you're still connected to the service provider).

7. Choose Tools⇨Disconnect to end the connection manually.

Or, you can follow these four steps:

Choose Tools⇨Options

Click the Transport tab

Select the Disconnect After Transferring Mail from Remote Mail option, as shown in Figure 12-7, to set the program to automatically disconnect after your pick up mail. The options selected in Microsoft Remote Mail leave you connected after you download the message headers so that you can select which ones to transfer. Then after you transfer the messages, your computer disconnects from your e-mail account.

Click OK.

You return to Remote Mail.

8. Double-click each e-mail message you want to read.

Figure 12-7:
The
Transport
dialog box.

✔ The Remote Mail feature can be tricky to get working with online services or ISPs other than Microsoft Network. You must already have MS Exchange installed with a Personal Folder and Personal Address Book. After installing these elements, you may need to reboot the computer to get the Remote Mail option to become available in the MS Exchange Tools menu.

✔ Eudora does everything Remote Mail can do, and it's much easier.

Pocket Pagers Receiving E-Mail

Most e-mail software, including Eudora, can sound an audible alert whenever new e-mail arrives. In order to hear it, of course, you have to leave your computer connected to the Internet all the time. If you need to be alerted to important e-mail as soon as it comes in, you can have your e-mail automatically forwarded to an alphanumeric pocket pager. You can actually read the e-mail right off the pager, using services available from RAM Mobile Data (see the Appendix).

Alternatively, instead of having all your e-mail go to the pager, you can selectively give out the pager service e-mail address to just those people who you want to hear from in your pocket. You can also equip a pocket computer with a wireless modem, to create the equivalent of a pager that both receives and sends full-scale e-mail. See Chapter 21 for more information about wireless e-mail.

Using Voice E-Mail

Imagine calling your office and having your secretary read you your e-mail over the phone. That, in essence, is what a service offered by CompuServe provides — except instead of a secretary, it's an automated computer voice. You can use it with your CompuServe account's e-mail only.

CompuServe's voice e-mail system works for receiving messages only — not sending — and it can handle only straight text messages (not file attachments). Imagine — if an attached image file is worth a thousand words, your ear is likely to fall off if you have to listen to the whole thing.

Forwarding E-Mail

You may find yourself in numerous situations where you want to have your e-mail forwarded. Here are some typical reasons why you may want your e-mail forwarded:

- You change jobs and get a new e-mail address from your new employer.
- You change Internet service providers and want mail that was sent to the old account to follow you to the new.
- You move to a different city and find that you have to change service providers in order to have a local access number at your new location.

Though these reasons are all perfectly valid, having e-mail forwarded is not such a simple thing — e-mail forwarding features from an ISP or online service are one of the lamest aspects of the Internet today.

Don't get me wrong — technically, forwarding service is easy enough for any online service or ISP to offer. However, in practice, it isn't done very much. From the point of view of online services and ISPs, offering mail forwarding service is a bad idea. Obviously, if you're having your e-mail forwarded, you're using someone else's service to pick it up, thus taking business away. If you've ever rented a private mailbox (not a post office box) from a service like Mailboxes, Etc., the situation is similar — after you close your account, you can no longer forward e-mail. With most online service providers, the situation is even more severe — they don't forward e-mail for you even if you keep your account active.

However, you can readily forward mail from one account to another manually, but then you are still paying for and using two separate accounts. In any case, if you need to do so, just retrieve the mail, select all the messages, and select the Forward To option and send them on to the account where you want them to go.

For an automated solution, you can purchase software, such as E-mail Connection (from ConnectSoft — see the Appendix), which can forward mail for you automatically. Essentially, this software makes all the calls and connections for you. It automatically dials into all your e-mail accounts with various service providers, retrieves the mail from each account, and forwards it all to a single e-mail address you specify. You don't save any money this way — you must keep all the accounts active — and you may have to pay for long distance charges to pick up e-mail in distant cities. However, it can save you a lot of time.

As I say earlier in this section, from a standpoint of the technology, e-mail forwarding service is possible from any server computer that administers an e-mail system. In fact, mail forwarding service is a standard feature that's always included in the setup software used by the computer system administrator to run the entire e-mail system! The problem is getting the person or company in charge to agree to do it for you. . . .

As a matter of policy, most online services and ISPs do not forward e-mail for you. However, if you change jobs, you may have much better luck talking to the system administrator at your former employer — just one of many reasons why you may want to remain on friendly terms with this person. If you can talk the system administrator into forwarding your e-mail to your new e-mail address, your new job can be that much easier. Alternatively, you may be able to convince your system administrator to respond to e-mail with an automated message listing your new address, without actually doing any forwarding. This method at least alerts anyone who tries to contact you at the old address to the fact that you've moved.

Using the Outbox While Traveling

Most e-mail software revolves around an Inbox and an Outbox. The Inbox is where you see all the messages that arrive for you and where you double-click a message to read it. When you send messages from a desktop computer, or while your mobile computer is connected to your ISP or online service account, you don't need to use the Outbox — just click *create new mail* (or *compose new message,* or something like that), list the recipient, write your message, and click Send.

However, suppose that you're on an airplane, on a train, or in a park, and you want to write e-mail to send out at a later time — say when you get back to your hotel room. The Outbox is the solution to your problem. It accumulates messages to send out the next time you go online. You can deposit a whole pile of messages while you're not connected to any e-mail account, and then when you finally do connect, spew them all out into the electronic yonder.

Fortunately, the Outbox usually works automatically. Just click Send in the usual way after you create a message, and if the e-mail software can't send it out immediately (because you're not online), it puts the message into the Outbox automatically and then sends the message out the next time you're online.

Chapter 13

Remote Access to Your Office Computer

● ●

In This Chapter

▶ Accessing your desktop machine when you're away

▶ Setting up phone lines and modems for remote control

▶ Choosing between remote computing and other methods

▶ Dealing with your network administrator

▶ Considering security

● ●

*I*f you have a desktop computer that you use at your office or home base, and a notebook computer that you take on the road, you probably run into situations where you want to have access to your desktop machine from a remote location. If you run a small business, you may need to look up an invoice or other old files that you don't carry with you. If you work in an office with a network, you may need to gain access to the network through your desktop machine because the network's central server offers no direct dial-up access.

Remote communications software can usually help you in your remote times of trouble with three services:

> ✓ **File Transfer mode.** You can transfer files over the phone line between your notebook and desktop computers.

> ✓ **Remote Control mode.** You can actually operate the desktop computer from a remote location.

> ✓ **Chat mode.** You can exchange messages between the two computers.

 Before latching onto remote communications technology as your savior, be advised: If your desktop computer is hooked up to a network, you must obtain the permission of the network or systems administrator before you set up remote computing software. If you get permission, your network administrator probably wants to set the software up for you, or at least oversee the installation. Remote computing can be a major security liability for a big computer network — see "Informing Those Who Need to Know," later in this chapter.

Remote Accessing Your Computer

Remote access computing is one of the most powerful communications tools in your portable computing arsenal. With remote access, you can call up your desktop computer from anywhere and grab or drop off files, use programs, or even chat with someone on your desktop computer.

All the available remote access programs work about the same. You need to install the software on both computers (your notebook and your desktop), and then you need to designate one computer as the host and the other as the guest. Someone can use the host — typically the desktop machine — for other purposes while the software waits for the phone to ring. When the modem answers your remote call, the remote access software kicks in and takes over the desktop computer, and whoever may be using your desktop is locked out.

PC Anywhere from Symantec is probably the most well-known remote access software, but my favorite is LapLink — the same program you can use for transferring files using direct cable (or infrared) connections, as I describe in Chapter 9. LapLink, in my view, is like the pocketknife of mobile computing — you can pretty much whip out the necessary tool for any situation. Actually, PC Anywhere and LapLink have met in the middle. Many moons (and versions) ago, LapLink was purely for local connections and PC Anywhere was only for remote computing. Now, each program offers both functions, and PC Anywhere comes with a LapLink-style parallel transfer cable for synchronizing files. Other software choices for remote computing include Microcom Carbon Copy, and Triton Technologies CoSession for Windows (see the Appendix for contact information). PC Anywhere has a version available for the Windows CE platform so that you can actually remote control your desktop machine using a small handheld PC. Besides offering file transfers and remote computing, most of these programs also facilitate chatting between the connected computers.

Remote control of your computer

The remote control mode is unquestionably the most exciting and powerful aspect of remote communications. The ability to operate your desktop machine by remote control effectively gets you past the phone line bottleneck that makes sending data so slow — you can work on large files that would otherwise take hours to send via phone connections, or use programs that are installed only on your desktop computer.

The trick is that the only data your desktop computer sends to your notebook is what to display on the screen. All the actual computing takes place on the desktop computer, and your notebook just receives images of what the screen looks like. You can point and click something on the notebook computer, and that menu action is executed on your desktop machine. The system works like a remote controlled toy car — you don't actually sit in the driver's seat, but it goes where you want.

When you use the remote communications software in the remote control mode, the screen on your guest (notebook) computer *refreshes* (updates) once every several seconds. The host (desktop) computer screen appears as a window in the remote access software on your (guest) notebook computer. In actual use, operating the host computer by remote control this way is amazingly easy and intuitive. The only difference, compared with actually being at the host computer, is a slight time delay for you to see your commands being executed.

Remote communications allow you to use a low-priced notebook to control a beefed-up desktop. You can thus run programs that require more memory, disk space, or processing power than your notebook computer has. Remote access can also solve the problem of keeping the desktop machine updated with the most recent version of a file — instead of copying the file from one computer to the other, you do all the work and save the file on the desktop's hard drive, using the notebook as a remote control.

The down side of using remote access software for this sort of remote control — rather than just basic file transfers — is that the phone bill you receive for staying connected while you do your work can get pretty fat. Spend an hour running software on your desktop computer, and you have to pay for an hour-long call.

You may be able to save money on your phone bills and add to the security of your remote computing setup if you have your host computer automatically call you back at the phone number where you are connecting with your notebook computer. This *callback* feature is standard in remote communications software. If you need remote access from only one specific location, such as your home, you can program the remote communications software to always call back the same number, as shown in Figure 13-1. In the example, the software is set up to automatically call back a specified number (212-555-1212) when you initiate remote access — this arrangement is perfect if you always use your notebook from the same location. In addition, the call is charged to your office computer instead of your personal phone.

Figure 13-1:
The LapLink
remote
access
security
provisions
allow you to
establish
login names
and
passwords
for remote
commun-
ications.

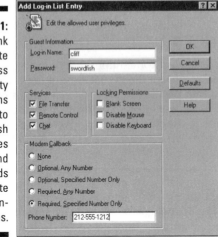

 No one else in your office should attempt to use your desktop computer while you're accessing it from your notebook (most software lets you lock out the keyboard and mouse when you call in — activating this feature is a good idea). In addition, you have to leave your desktop computer on all the time, with its modem set to answer incoming calls — if coworkers use your desktop computer while you're away, you have to let them know that the computer is no-touchy (unless they really know what they're doing, and know how to reset the computer to answer your call if they have to reboot).

 If your desktop computer is connected to the Internet via a high-speed T-1 office connection, and you need to do a lot of intensive Web browsing from a remote location with your notebook, you can use this remote control system to obtain high-speed Internet access with your notebook. The time the remote communications software takes to send new screen images over the phone can be significantly faster than the time new Web pages take to download over a modem. However, if you use this system, you sacrifice the ability to view animation and other quick-changing features of a Web page. Because the remote control software essentially sends a snapshot of the host computer's screen every few seconds, you may miss anything that changes in less time, or doesn't remain on the screen after it first appears.

 Because each remote communications program uses its own exclusive driver system, the programs are all mutually incompatible with each other — you cannot keep two or more of these programs functioning properly on the same computer.

Transferring files

For file transfers, most remote control software offers a *remapping* system for the various drives, so that, for example, you can *map* (as it's called) the C: drive on the host computer as the F: drive on your notebook. You can then use Windows Explorer to copy files back and forth between the two drives.

Transferring files can be useful if all you need to do is drop off a document on your desktop computer. You can then have a coworker pick it up as necessary if you have a deadline to meet and you are out of the office. Conversely, you can pick up a document from your desktop that you need to work on while you are away.

By using the remapping feature in remote communications software, you can even install new software on your notebook computer from a CD-ROM drive on your desktop machine.

Chatting

All remote communications programs also offer a chat mode, for typing messages back and forth between the two computers. You can thus be in a hotel room or dorm room, while chatting with someone in your office or with a friend far away — your own two-person chat room. Besides oddball situations, this may be useful when you need to communicate with someone without making a lot of noise, or to communicate with someone who has a hearing or speech impediment. The chat feature is also useful when you're already logged onto your desktop machine, and you need to get the help of a coworker (whom you've conveniently asked to keep on eye on the screen of your desktop computer to see what's going on when you call in).

Of course, you can always call the coworker and talk over the phone like a normal human being, but because you're usually limited to just one phone line when you're on the road with your notebook computer, calling on the phone requires that you break the computer connection, make a voice call, and then reestablish the computer connection to complete the task that you were working on when you called. In a situation like this, the chat feature may spare you a migraine or two.

What You Need for Remote Access

Here's what you need to set up remote control access to your desktop computer from your notebook:

✔ **Remote control software** (such as LapLink or PC Anywhere) installed on both the desktop machine and on your notebook computer

✔ **Two modems** — one for your desktop computer and one for your notebook computer

✔ **A regular (nondigital) dedicated phone line** that you can leave your desktop computer's modem connected to all the time you are away

Ideally, the phone line you use with the desktop computer has nothing else hooked up to it — no fax machine, no answering machine, no phone-controlled back massagers. Additional devices may interfere with your modem's ability to answer your remote computing calls whenever it rings — you may call in wanting to connect with your notebook computer, and then you have to duke it out for phone time with your obstinate fax machine who thinks that it's his job is to answer the phone. In addition, you're best off if your phone does not have any call-waiting features, or if it does, you can disable them, because the call-waiting beeps can wreak havoc with data communications.

If you have call waiting on your desktop computer, you can disable it by using the remote computing callback feature (as I describe earlier) and including the Disable call-waiting code in your callback number. That way, you can connect to your desktop, hang up, and then have your desktop call you back at your remote location and establish the connection without fear of interruption. You need to check with your local phone company to find out what the Disable call-waiting code is for your area.

Your desktop (host) computer must have a regular outside telephone line — not a digital office phone line — for remote computing to work. As I explain in Chapter 19, you can get an adapter that lets you use a modem with a digital office phone system. However, these adapters require you to be present when you use the modem — they do not work with the crucial auto-answer feature that makes remote computing possible.

When you first set up remote computing, you may find it helpful to have two phone lines available in the room where your desktop computer lives. Use the second phone line for your notebook computer, so you can figure out how to use the remote access software while watching both computer screens at the same time. And if things don't work perfectly on the first try, you're in a much better position to troubleshoot the situation with both computers right there in front of you. If you have only one phone line available — such as if your desktop computer is in your home or in a small office — then try prevailing upon a friendly neighbor next door to use their phone line with your notebook to test out your remote access setup.

For advanced users, setting up remote access may take about two hours, including installing the software on the two computers, configuring the host and guest, and testing it out to make sure that the host answers calls properly. However, setting up a remote access system can take more like half a day. Do not hesitate to call the remote access software company's technical support line at the first sign of trouble. This stuff can be tricky.

Remote access, by virtue of using two modems simultaneously, is just about the most complicated thing you can do with your notebook computer and its modem, so be sure that you have your modems up and running correctly. The best way to check your modems out is to get on the Internet and make sure you are receiving Web pages without trouble.

Passwords and Security

The biggest drawback to remote computing — besides the complexity of setting up your desktop computer to receive calls from your notebook — is the security issue. By setting up your desktop computer so you can conveniently call in and have access, you also expose this computer to every petty computer hacker looking for kicks, or, on a more serious note, corporate espionage.

All remote communications programs offer several security options for the host computer — such as not allowing the guest computer to delete files on the host, or requiring that the guest provide a password before allowing access.

As shown in Figure 13-2, the security screen for LapLink for Windows 95 (version 7.5) lets you choose which services are available to remote computers (File Transfer, Remote Control, and Chat), and whether a login name and password are required to access the host computer. In the example shown, Anybody is selected, meaning that the desktop computer has no password protection. The Locking choices (not selected) allow you, using a notebook computer from a remote location, to prevent someone in the office from seeing what you are doing while engaging in remote computing (Blank Screen), or to deactivate the host computer's mouse and/or keyboard so that no one else can use the computer while you're accessing it over the phone line.

To protect the host computer at a small business or home office — where you really have no reason to think that a hacker or anyone else would ever even bother trying to break in — the password protection built into remote communications software probably provides as much security as you need. But don't kid yourself — if your host computer contains extremely valuable information, or if for some reason you think that you may be targeted by a hacker, the password protection is the electronic equivalent of a dime-store padlock.

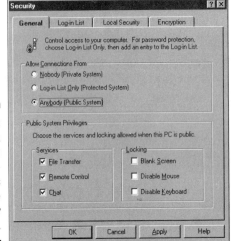

Figure 13-2:
The LapLink
remote
communica-
tions
software
security
screen.

Hackers can write programs that automatically try tens of thousands of different password possibilities. To thwart such efforts, some remote communications programs offer a security feature that disables the system after numerous attempts are made with incorrect passwords. But a dedicated hacker, or espionage agent, has all sorts of tricks up his or her sleeve, so no security setup is absolutely safe.

Rather than leaving the host computer on 24 hours a day to receive your calls, you can arrange with someone else in your office to turn on the computer, or activate the auto-answer feature, only during certain hours when you know that you need it. For the absolutely tightest security, you can first call your office over a regular voice phone and ask a coworker (or your spouse or roommate, in the case of a home office) to turn the host computer on. Then, as soon as you're finished, call again and ask your partner to turn the computer off. Of course, if you travel through Asia and need access at three in the morning in the U.S., this system may be a bit inconvenient for the person helping you.

An alternative to having a live human turn the computer on and off is to put the computer on a timer, and have it automatically turn on at a certain time of the day and shut off an hour or two later. You can plug the host computer into a standard lamp timer — available at any appliance store. You have to configure the remote communications software on the host computer so that it automatically launches in auto-answer mode whenever the computer boots up. Note that when the computer shuts off like this, you don't exit Windows in an orderly way — unless, that is, you use the remote control software to exit Windows on the host computer prior to disconnecting. (If you do, the computer no longer answers incoming calls until the timer forces it to reboot. Some people use this technique, without a timer, to disable remote computing on the host computer after finishing a project, to minimize the security risk.)

Informing Those Who Need to Know

One of the main reasons that people who work in offices like to set up remote communications to their desktop computers is to gain access to the local area network (LAN) while on the road. Most remote communications programs include special features to help facilitate this, such as Automatic LapLink Start Up in LapLink, which lets you logon to your Windows 95/NT office network by remote control (see Figure 13-3). By checking the box for Automatic LapLink Startup in your host computer's remote control options, you can enter your login information via your notebook computer before the desktop computer boots up — just as if you were at the office working on your desktop computer.

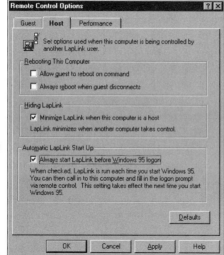

Figure 13-3:
The LapLink
Remote
Control
Options
dialog box.

However, from a security standpoint, accessing a local network through remote computing software is a two-way street. Just as you, using your notebook computer, have access to your desktop machine as well as the entire network it's connected to, so too does any hacker.

From the point of view of a network administrator overseeing dozens or hundreds of computers in an office, allowing even one person to establish remote communications for his or her computer may open Pandora's box. After one person does it, someone else wants it. And then someone else. And before you know it, you have a dozen or more computers in the office, each with their own remote access setups (and phone numbers). And then, inevitably, as the remote communications gets taken for granted, someone forgets to put password protection on his or her particular desktop computer and some hacker, randomly dialing every phone number in your company, discovers a way in to your network. There goes the security game — within minutes, your organization's entire computer network may be ruined, and thousands of documents containing crucial information may be wiped out.

If you and your network administrator are at loggerheads over the installation of remote computing on your desktop machine, you can offer a compromise as a last resort: Disconnect the desktop machine from the local network whenever you're out of town. This may not satisfy all your remote computing needs, but if you only need access to files and programs on your desktop machine's hard drive, then this arrangement provides it without threatening network security. You can configure most remote communications software to limit access to specific drives, but to be absolutely sure that you (or the network staff) can physically pull the plug out of the network jack in the back of your desktop computer. Of course, with this approach, you're making the entire contents of your desktop computer vulnerable to attack by hackers and snoopers, but so long as it is disconnected from the LAN, you aren't endangering anything else in the office.

If your only need for remote access is to pick up e-mail, you may have easier and more secure options than remote access — see Chapter 12 for more info. Use remote access only when no other, more secure alternatives to access your office network (such as direct dial-up or Internet access) are available.

Chapter 14

Faxing with Your Portable Computer

*I*magine that you're working out of a hotel room, you just finished preparing a document on your notebook computer, and you need to fax it to a client. You can go downstairs to the hotel business center, if your hotel is swank and with-it enough to have one, and print out the document (oh, yeah, the hotel business center has to have a printer, too) and fax it there. Or you can do everything from your hotel room, simply by using your computer as a fax machine.

Almost all modems sold these days also have fax capability, as I cover in Chapter 5. If your computer already has a way to hook up to the phone line, you can probably use it to send and receive faxes.

So what do you need to start faxing? Besides a modem, you also need special fax software. Fortunately, such software is almost always *bundled* (included free) with a new modem. The quality and ease-of-use of the bundled software may vary tremendously, however. If you do a lot of faxing, you may wish to purchase more sophisticated fax software, such as WinFax or EclipseFax. Often the stripped down or *lite* version of the fax software bundled with some modems is missing some features you may find handy. Computers that come with built-in fax/modems usually include their own versions (see Figure 14-1). The litest version of all comes bundled with Windows 95 — it's called Microsoft Fax.

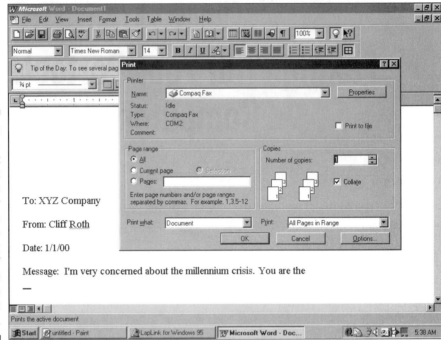

Figure 14-1:
To send a
fax, select
the fax
software as
the printer
(in this
case, the
Compaq
built-in fax/
modem)
from within
your word
processor.

If Microsoft Fax is already installed on your Windows 95 notebook, it shows up in the list of available printer names when you choose Print in your word processor. If it's not available, you can easily get confused looking for it, because although it winds up as a printer driver, you do *not* install it as a printer driver. Follow these steps to install it:

1. **Choose Start⇨Setup⇨Control Panel to open the Control Panel.**

   You see numerous icons for mouse, display, modem, and so on.

2. **Find the Add/Remove Programs icon and double-click it.**

   The Add/Remove Programs Properties dialog box appears. Along the top of this dialog box are several tabs.

3. **Find the Windows Setup tab and click it.**

   A list of various Microsoft programs appears.

4. **Use the scroll bar on the right, if necessary, to find the Microsoft Fax component. Click the check box next to Microsoft Fax to put a check mark in it, as shown in Figure 14-2.**

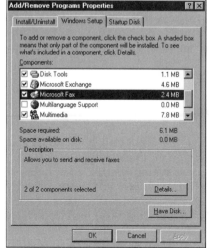

Figure 14-2:
Installing
Microsoft
Fax from
the Add/
Remove
Programs
Properties
dialog box.

5. Click OK at the bottom of the screen to complete the installation.

Understanding the Difference between Data and Fax

Although your modem can convert both faxes and data (such as e-mail) signals into audio signals for transmission over the phone lines, fax and data transmission are two completely different animals. They each employ a different language to transmit over the phone lines, and they almost never come together (two exceptions are *Internet fax relay* and some *fax mailbox* systems, both described in the last section of this chapter). A fax is essentially a picture of a document that is transferred over the phone lines as a language that fax machines or fax/modems can understand. Data, such as e-mail or a document file, is transferred via modems in a language that only computer modems understand.

Data is more efficient to send than a fax — it takes less time and gets transmitted more reliably. Furthermore, when you transmit data, such as e-mail, you have the opportunity to easily modify documents you receive, as well as forward them to others, with no deterioration in quality. Faxes, by contrast, look worse each time they get re-faxed to someone else, and are far less flexible — you have to employ Optical Character Recognition (OCR) software, as I describe later in this chapter, and convert the fax into an editable document in order to change any of the fax's contents.

Faxes, however, have one really big advantage over e-mail: They're universal. Practically every business in the world has a fax machine. Although in some circles and professions, e-mail is everywhere, it is far from universal. Faxes *are* universal in business, and nowadays, many homes have fax machines, too.

Sending faxes: easy

Unlike e-mail, fax software works very differently for sending and receiving faxes. Though confusing at first, you practically have to use two completely different pieces of software, depending on whether you plan to send or receive a fax. In general, fax software is easier and more reliable to use for sending faxes than for receiving. The age-old adage, "It is better to give than to receive," applies even for the mobile computer user.

In the Windows 95 (and 3.*x*) and Macintosh platforms, the software for sending faxes is installed as a printer driver. You create your fax document with whatever word processor or spreadsheet program you ordinarily use, and when you want to send it as a fax, you choose the Print command from within that program. Then, if it's not already the default, you select that particular printer (the fax software acting as a virtual printer) from the list of installed printers. You next select the recipient(s) — entering the receiving fax phone number(s) manually, or selecting them from your address book, or selecting a group of recipients for a fax broadcast — and tell the software to go to work. First, it creates the fax pages from your document, then it attaches a cover page (you have a wide choice of styles, as explained later in this chapter), and then it dials the number(s) and starts faxing.

Fax software provides a great way to broadcast the same fax to multiple recipients. You can maintain a list of all your customers, for example, and then pick out just the ones in a particular state or region to send a fax to. You can even go beyond the built-in address book capability of your fax software and use contact manager software (such as GoldMine or Act!) to organize your fax broadcasts.

Most fax software offers a Page Preview option that lets you see more precisely what your fax is going to look like before it goes out. If the formatting of your document is important — such as when you send a proposal to a potential client — Page Preview is a crucial feature.

Before faxing out a really important document to a client, you can first send the same document to a colleague, and then call and ask whether it looks okay. Or, if you're staying at a hotel or near a copy store, you may want to fax it to the closest fax machine and take a look at it yourself.

For sending faxes, most fax software is usually quite reliable. If the machine on the receiving end has problems (such as out of paper), the software alerts you, and like a regular fax machine, it can automatically redial every few minutes until the fax goes through. The same is true if your computer picks up busy signals on the receiving end.

The problems you're most likely to encounter when sending faxes are general modem difficulties, such as not being able to dial the call. See Chapter 5, which covers modems, and Chapter 20, on phone problems, for help in getting your fax/modem up and running.

Adding a cover page

Most fax software offers numerous options for attaching a cover page to the documents you send. Libraries of 100 or more predefined cover pages are often included with fax software — just fill in your name, company name, address, and phone numbers, and in a matter of minutes, you have a custom cover page that you can use again and again.

In addition, the cover page you create with fax software usually includes an area where you can write brief notes, just as with a regular paper fax. If you feel ambitious, you can also import your company logo as a graphics file to create an even more customized cover page. You need a scanner if all you have is the company logo on paper, or maybe you can get someone in your company to give you a copy of the logo file on a disk, if one exists.

If you're confused by or dissatisfied with your fax software's cover page, select the Do not send cover page option, and then in your word processor, simply create your own cover page as the first page of the document you want to send. A fax cover page can be as simple as your name, organization, and your voice and fax numbers. You can then fill in the recipient's name, fax number, the number of pages, and a brief message as necessary.

Many people send cover sheets without attached documents in order to relay short, written notes, such as a foreign address with a complicated spelling, or maybe a list of a couple of phone numbers. Although most fax software does allow you to send cover sheets by themselves, here's my advice: The easiest way to send a one-page fax is by printing from your word processing software. You can use your word processor to create a cover page and then send this as your fax document without attaching any additional cover page created by the fax software.

Fax software also usually includes the ability to store a signature file, that is, a picture of your signature, and then place it onto letters and other documents before sending them out. Using a signature file makes your fax look like you actually signed a sheet of paper. You can create a signature file by scanning your real signature and then saving it as a graphics file. Or here's a trick: Fax yourself your own signature (that is, use your computer to *receive* a fax that contains your signature) and then use the Select, Cut, and Paste tools in your fax software to crop the signature and save it as a graphics file. Nifty stuff. To minimize degradation of your signature, try writing it with a thick black marker pen, and make it *big*. Then, after you receive it, and cut and paste it, reduce its size to something that fits between the close of your letter and your name.

Receiving faxes: not so easy

You can receive as well as send faxes with just about all fax software and fax/modems, but you may find receiving faxes quite a bit trickier than sending them. Even after you figure things out, you generally find that, although useful in some circumstances, receiving faxes on your computer can prove to be more trouble than going to the local copy store or hotel fax machine.

For receiving faxes in Windows 95, you must choose Start⇨Programs and select your fax software. If you work with an earlier version of Windows, simply click your fax software in Program Manager.

Most fax software offers two modes of receiving: manual and automatic. The manual mode assumes that you have already picked up the phone and heard that you have a fax coming in (at least you're pretty sure that none of your friends hiss and beep at you). The automatic mode makes the computer work much like a regular fax machine — when the phone rings, the computer automatically answers each call, and if it detects a fax tone, it goes into fax receive mode. Some PCMCIA/PC modem cards also include a voice mail feature — turning your notebook into an answering machine. Such cards usually distinguish automatically between incoming fax and voice calls (but this feature is prone to make errors, especially when receiving faxes from some older fax machines).

The incoming faxes are stored on your computer's hard drive. Depending on the resolution you select, and the amount of material printed on the page, each faxed page occupies roughly 10 to 20KB of hard drive space, so you can store about 50 to 100 pages in 1MB of hard drive capacity — a pretty efficient use of space. You can use any printer — including the portable variety I discuss in Chapter 6 — to print the faxes you receive onto regular paper.

Problems receiving faxes

For receiving the occasional fax, your notebook computer can be an incredible convenience. But for continuous all-day service, a notebook computer is not nearly as reliable as even an inexpensive standalone fax machine. Let me offer several warnings and tidbits of advice on receiving faxes with your notebook computer:

✔ Test out the receiving process with your particular computer, modem, and fax software before you try using it for important business documents.

✔ When you receive a fax in a hotel room, the sender first has to talk to the hotel operator to ask for your room and then wait to be connected. So instruct whoever is going to send you a fax to dial manually, talk to the operator, load the document into the fax machine, and then, after hearing the phone line ringing for your room, the sender should press the manual send button on the fax machine.

✔ Although you can leave your notebook computer in your hotel room plugged into the phone line and into the AC outlet all day to receive faxes for you, be aware of the pitfalls. If anyone else tries calling your room, they get the fax tone (unless you have integrated fax/voice mail software, which makes your computer double as an answering machine). Depending on where you stay, leaving the computer hooked up that way may make it more vulnerable to theft.

✔ Viewing faxes on your computer screen can be more cumbersome than printed pages — even curled thermal fax printer pages. Your notebook computer's screen usually can't show the entire page at once with sufficient resolution for you to be able to read it, so you end up having to scroll down to read the bottom of each page.

✔ When some fax machines send you documents, you may have to use manual receive mode to activate your computer's fax reception. The automatic receive mode sometimes waits to hear the fax initiation beep tones that most — but not all — fax machines send out. In the worst-case situation, the fax and your fax/modem sit on each end of the phone line doing nothing because each is waiting for the other to make the first move. Clicking the manual receive option in your fax software should solve this problem by sending out the hello beep.

✔ Before receiving a fax, close all other programs, or at the very least minimize them, and allow the fax to come in with nothing else going on in the computer. If you still have trouble, try minimizing or switching off any features of the fax software that let you see the fax as it comes in.

Optical Character Recognition (OCR)

To convert from a faxed document to a word-processor document, you need to use Optical Character Recognition (OCR) software. OCR software is sometimes included with the fax software that comes bundled with the modem, but more often it is optionally available in the deluxe version of the fax software (which you can often get as an upgrade from the lite version of fax software that comes bundled with most modems). OCR software is also sold separately, but you're best off using a version designed to work specifically with your fax program. OmniPage Pro from Caere is the leader in this field.

If you're familiar with the way the post office uses automated equipment to read the ZIP codes and addresses on envelopes, then you've already been introduced to the world of OCR (and its reliability problems). Recognizing which letter is which on a printed page is actually more challenging than you may think. For one thing, you can get a zillion different fonts, as well as upper- and lowercase characters. For another, pages going through fax machines are often skewed at odd angles, or transmitted upside down. Most pages mix several different sizes and styles of fonts — such as a newspaper article with a headline, or a message typed on company letterhead. And in the case of newspaper and magazine articles, the text is usually organized into columns that must be recognized by the software — otherwise you end up with one line from one column jumbled with the adjacent line from the next column over.

Fortunately, the current generation of OCR software ranges from very good to excellent at dealing with the various problems you encounter in faxed documents. Most current OCR programs can detect upside down pages, alignment problems, photographs or other nontext elements, columns, and whatever other curveballs the fax may throw. Then it goes ahead and converts the tiny picture of each letter into the computer code for that letter. As it performs this image-to-text conversion of the fax, a spell checker may be used to help limit the conversion to actual words.

After you finish proofreading and correcting the converted document, you can save it as a standard text file (ASCII) or in standard word-processor formats for Microsoft Word, WordPerfect, and so on.

OCR software generally works well, but not perfectly. You usually need to carefully proofread the converted document to find the mistakes and correct them manually. When the OCR software comes across a character it just can't figure out, it inserts a special symbol in the converted document to alert you that the software gave up figuring out that particular letter or number. More advanced OCR software lets you teach it new characters, and even entire fonts — but this process is tedious.

A few ways you can get better results with OCR software are

- ✔ Have the sender select Fine or High resolution on his/her fax machine.
- ✔ Tell the sender to be very careful not to feed pages in at an angle.
- ✔ Try to avoid using OCR with unusual, decorative fonts.

✔ Avoid *noisy* documents, such as photocopies of newspaper clips that have lots of little speckles in the background.

✔ Avoid documents with very small print.

✔ Don't try to convert handwriting unless it is very clearly and neatly printed in block letters.

Forwarding Faxes to a Fax Mailbox

Suppose that you're staying in a hotel and you're expecting a fax, but you don't know exactly when it will arrive. For the reasons cited in the "Problems receiving faxes" section earlier in this chapter, you are unlikely to want to leave your computer in the room all day to receive faxes. Even if you do, going through the hotel operator may make sending the fax more of a hassle than you can reasonably expect the sender to endure.

If you're in this situation a lot, you are a good candidate for a *fax mailbox*. A fax mailbox serves as a receiving point where people can send you faxes whenever they need to. Then, whenever you want, you can use your notebook computer to call into the mailbox and retrieve the faxes. Fax mailboxes work very much like e-mail boxes, though as explained in the first section of this chapter, the faxing and e-mail are completely different.

You have two main options for fax mailboxes: as a monthly service provided by independent telephone companies or as a fax mailbox you set up yourself by buying the necessary hardware.

Fax mailbox monthly service

As a monthly service from your phone company, fax mailboxes usually cost a monthly fee plus a certain price for each page of received and relayed fax. Most fax mailbox services also offer a toll-free number service for an additional per-minute charge (so people can send you faxes toll-free). Typical prices may run around $15 to $20 per month (plus a one-time setup fee), and anywhere from free to $1 per fax page, plus around 25 cents per minute for 800 number service. Fax mailbox service is often offered along with voice mail service, too. Most of the fax mailbox services now available are from smaller communications companies — including Answer America, FaxWeb, AlphaNet, and SureCom.

To find a fax mailbox service in your area, you can try looking in the local yellow page directory under Telephone Answering. But you find a lot more of these services by looking on the Internet, using a search engine with the key words *fax mailbox* (in one search, I found over 600 sites). The only problem with using an out-of-town service is that the fax mailbox phone number has a completely different area code from your regular phone number. For that reason, the toll free number service is a popular option — to create the slick impression that your fax number is a national, rather than a local number.

If you want to use the fax mailbox service only when you're away from your office (so you can dial in and pick up faxes from wherever you may be), but otherwise wish to receive faxes with your normal office setup, you can have your local phone company install *call forwarding* on your regular fax line. Then, when you go away, you just punch in a code on the phone line to instruct calls to automatically be forwarded to your fax mailbox number. Of course, if your fax mailbox is in a different area code, you end up paying long distance charges for the call forwarding, but the people sending you faxes are not aware that the call is being diverted to a different area code.

Fax mailbox hardware

As a long-term proposition, if you receive more than a few faxes per week, you're usually best off setting up your own fax mailbox system. With your own equipment, you can decide when to print faxes regularly and when to send them to the fax mailbox — and you get no per-fax charges. Bogen's Fax Friday electronic telephone center is the most well-known of these devices, available in several different versions, with prices starting at a few hundred dollars. Similar fax mailbox devices are also available from Muratec and other manufacturers. You can also configure a computer equipped with fax software to operate as a fax mailbox, but I don't really recommend attempting this setup unless you're a very advanced computer user (and you're prepared for what happens if the computer crashes while you're away!).

Chapter 15

Installing Software on Your Notebook

- -

In This Chapter

▶ Choosing which software to install on your notebook

▶ Getting your desktop and laptop software to match

▶ Installing compact versions of software

▶ Copying software and configuration settings

- -

*I*f your notebook computer is your only computer, or functions as your main computer where you keep most of your files and software, then you can probably ignore this chapter. However, if, like many notebook computer users, you also have a desktop computer that serves as your home base, and you use your notebook for travel and/or working at home, you may wonder how much of the software from your desktop machine you should install on the portable computer.

Installing It All!

One approach is to completely and totally duplicate the entire contents of the desktop computer's hard drive onto your notebook machine. You can use a program such as LapLink, which I discuss in Chapter 9, to duplicate files with its Synchronize function. Assuming that both of your machines are reasonably matched in terms of processor power, memory, and hard drive capacity, and that they have a minimal number of plug-in devices installed, you may be able to pull off a Synchronize operation.

However, fully synchronizing two machines is not for the faint of heart — doing so essentially replaces all the software that came preloaded on your notebook computer hard drive with software from the desktop machine. You usually have to reinstall Windows on your notebook after all the other stuff has been transferred over (Aaargh!). And if you have any devices such as modems or additional drives on one computer and not the other, you get all sorts of error messages telling you that the given device does not exist. After you transfer all the software, you inevitably need to reinstall add-on components such as a PCMCIA/PC modem. So, in a nutshell, copying the entire contents of a hard drive is an operation that only experienced users should attempt — and be forewarned, it's very messy.

A more practical approach — the one used by most notebook computer owners — is to install a *subset* of the programs and files from your desktop machine onto your portable computer. You just install the few software programs that you really need on your portable computer. To do a subset installation, what I like to call a *fresh installation,* you have to locate the original software installation disk(s) that came with each program, and re-install this software onto the notebook's hard drive.

I can think of numerous reasons to take the fresh installation approach. First and foremost, installing software with the manufacturer's disks is easy. And if you install the word-processor and/or spreadsheet program you use most of the time, you have pretty much just about everything you ever need on the notebook, unless you do some kind of specialized work with a particular program that you may also need to install.

Your notebook computer no doubt comes with some software already installed on it — at minimum, it has the operating system (Windows 95 or Mac OS) and software for using online services such as CompuServe and AOL. You may want to add an e-mail program such as Eudora (available for Mac and PC), and maybe a Web browser. In addition, the notebook probably comes with a fax program, but you may have a need for a more robust version. (See Chapter 14, which covers faxing with your portable computer, for more details on fax software.)

Keep all your original software together in a safe place, for easy access when you need to reinstall software in a new computer. As an extra precaution, make backup copies of the original software floppies, so that if they ever get damaged, you don't lose the software you purchased.

You don't need to load in everything all at once. If you're new to mobile computing, my advice is to try getting by with the few programs you use the most, and then add whatever else you think may be handy on an as-needed basis.

Hard Disk Realities: Laptop and Custom Installations

Notebook computers often have smaller drives than their desktop companions, making it impossible for you to fit all the files from your desktop unit's hard drive onto your notebook. So by necessity, you may have to choose which software items are most important to have while you are traipsing around the countryside.

Most major applications and software suites, such as Microsoft Office, Microsoft Word, WordPerfect, and so on, offer a special *laptop installation* option, sometimes just called *minimum installation*. Laptop installation provides the easiest way to install the software into a minimum amount of hard drive space. The difference can be quite significant — in the case of Microsoft Office, which is an entire suite of word-processing, spreadsheet, presentation, contact management, and other software, you save more than 50MB of disk space by choosing the minimum installation option.

The stuff that gets sacrificed when you choose the laptop or minimum installation option varies from program to program. Typically, the following items are considered optional frills that most users can do without:

- ✔ Dictionary and/or grammar check features (not spelling check features, however, which just about everyone uses)

- ✔ Predefined templates for various applications

- ✔ Tutorial programs and sample files that show you how to use the software — these are not the same as Help files, which come in handy for even the most experienced users

- ✔ Clip art collections, font collections, cover pages, and so on

What if you want to install some, but not all, of these items? That's precisely what the *custom installation* option lets you do. Besides letting you choose which features get installed, custom installation also gives you control over which directories (folders) get installed on your computer. Normally, you just allow the software to create whatever directories it wants, and install things in those directories — in other words, you don't mess with choosing directories for the installation. However, if you have the same software also installed on your desktop machine, and you have already installed that software in a special directory, you may want to create a directory with the same name on your notebook computer to keep the directory structures of the two machines matched.

When you install big software suites, such as Microsoft Office or Corel Office, you are also given a choice of which elements (applications) to install. You can leave out the spreadsheet program, for example, or the presentation software if you don't think that you need it. You can always add any of these programs later if you find that you want them — you don't have to reinstall everything else.

Most notebook computers that come with Windows 95 preinstalled include a complete set of printer drivers on the hard drive. However, if you install the operating system yourself, or make modifications to save disk space, you may be tempted to omit them. Don't. They don't occupy much space, and if you're ever on the road and need to connect to someone else's printer, you'll be glad you have them.

Software Licensing, Disk Formats, and Upgrades

Okay, I admit that I sound like a Goody Two-Shoes saying this, but at least for the record I should point out that legally, the licensing agreement for most software that you buy only allows installation on a single computer.

Of course, in practice, most individuals and small businesses can get away with installing the same software on both desktop and notebook computers, with little consequence (most corporate software purchases are explicitly for multiple installations, and should therefore cover installation in company-owned laptops). And some license agreements are for an individual user, rather than an individual computer — in which case you're legally allowed to install the software on two machines as long as you only ever use one at a time.

Legalities aside, one practical concern with installing the same software on both a desktop machine and a notebook computer is that they must be able to read the same disk format. Although floppy disks are near universal, CD-ROMs are not. If your notebook computer does not have a CD-ROM drive, try to purchase your software in floppy disk format.

If you need to install software from a CD-ROM onto a notebook computer that has no CD-ROM drive, you can get around the problem if the notebook computer has enough extra room on the hard drive to hold both the installation files and the installed program, and you have a cable connection to your desktop machine (such as LapLink — see Chapter 9). Using the connection, first create a temporary directory on the notebook's hard drive, then copy the entire contents of the CD-ROM (or all the installation files, but omit sample files, tutorials, and other unnecessary frills) to that directory, and then use Windows Explorer to find the software's installation program, usually SETUP.EXE, on the notebook's hard drive and launch it by double-clicking it. (In the worst case, you may need more than 650MB of disk space to temporarily hold the CD-ROM's contents, but usually all the files on the CD-ROM occupy far less space, and your notebook has enough room.) After the software is installed, you can delete the temporary directory you created with the installation files.

If you have a Local Area Network (LAN) connection for your notebook computer at an office or school, you may be able to install software from the network, or a desktop computer that is connected to the network. Because networks are all different, and the method you need to use may take some computer trickery, you are best off checking with your network administrator for how to install software this way.

One other technicality may haunt you if you have installed an upgrade version of a software package on your desktop machine and want to duplicate it on your notebook computer. Upgrade versions of a software product are sold at a much lower price than the same software as a standalone product. Upgrades are sold on the premise that you already have a previous version of the software installed. Or, in the case of *competitive upgrade* software, the package is sold on the premise that you already have a competitor's software installed.

What happens is that the upgrade software actually contains a full version of the program — not just a few newer patch-up files — but what makes this software different from the more costly standalone version is that it performs a check on the computer's hard drive before it installs. This check makes sure that the qualifying older version, or competitor's software, is already installed. The bottom line is that as you install the same upgrade version on your notebook computer that's on your desktop machine, you may have to first install the earlier version of the software or a competitor's program that you don't really ever use, in order for the upgrade version to properly install on your notebook computer.

Reinstalling versus Copying

In the old days of DOS, before the Windows operating system became prevalent, you could easily copy software from one computer to another. You could usually just copy the directory the software was installed in — using floppy disks or a program like LapLink with a connecting cable — from one computer to another. Nowadays, the Windows operating system has made such simple copying all but impossible. The problem is that when a program gets installed, it notifies Windows of its existence. True, the program still creates its own directory and installs a zillion files there, but the program also goes into the Windows directory, modifies the Windows setup and initiation files, installs special drivers if needed, and installs an icon for the desktop to make the program easy to access — doing all this stuff manually is a headache.

The easiest way to get software from your desktop to your notebook is to go back to the original software installation disks and install the software into the new computer from scratch — I call it a *fresh installation*.

The disadvantage of a fresh installation is that you lose whatever customization you may have on your desktop machine.

For example, I always set up my word-processor so that the default font is Arial 18 point — a big, easy-to-read font that lets me keep my distance from the screen without straining my eyes. I also have my word processor set to automatically save a backup copy of whatever I'm working on every two minutes (I've learned *that* lesson the hard way!). And I have a button installed on the toolbar to provide me with the word count (professional writers are often paid by the word). I lose these custom settings whenever I do a fresh installation of the software. However, compared to trying to copy the files that contain all this custom information and putting them in the right place, I have found that simply recustomizing the freshly installed software almost always takes less time. For most people, redoing any customization takes about half an hour, usually much less. And believe me, trying to figure out which files are needed to duplicate the way a program works can take a lot longer!

Transferring your address books and e-mail settings

Address books, contact databases such as you use in e-mail, electronic appointment books, and contact management programs, are the one exception I make to my "do a fresh install" advice in the previous section. If you have more than a dozen or so entries in your address book or contact manager software, you do yourself a favor by figuring out where these are stored in the desktop computer and copying the specific file to your notebook computer. Similarly, you can copy Bookmarks or Favorites that you've stored on your desktop computer's Web browser for easy access when you surf the Web with your notebook computer.

Fortunately, address books are almost always contained within a single file that's usually pretty easy to locate. Sometimes the software even provides you with an *export* feature (look in the File menu) specifically for this purpose. If you create multiple address books — such as one for business contacts and one for personal contacts — within the same program, each of these address books is usually saved as a separate file. First look in the directory (folder) where the program is installed, and then look in any subdirectories (subfolders). Usually, the file is clearly labeled.

You can use Windows Explorer to locate and copy your address book file(s) onto a floppy disk, and then copy it (them) from the floppy to your notebook computer. Be sure to copy the file(s) into exactly the same subdirectory (subfolder) where it resides on the desktop computer — write the name of this subdirectory (subfolder) down on a sheet of paper so you don't forget it. The software program, whether it is a Web browser or a contact management program, looks in a specific subdirectory (subfolder) of its main directory for all address book, bookmark, and similar data files — if the file isn't there, your address book or Favorites aren't available when you run the program.

If you have trouble locating the file you need on your desktop computer, one method you can use to test whether a selected file is actually the address book you're looking for is to rename it:

1. **Choose Start⇨Programs⇨Windows Explorer.** The Windows Explorer pops up.

2. **Browse through the directory for the e-mail or Web browser or whatever other program for which you want to find the address book or Favorites file.**

3. **Select (highlight) the file.**

4. **Write down the original name of the file you are testing.**

5. **Choose File⇨Rename, and add a letter or number to the end of the filename to make it different.** If you make a mistake, just press the Esc key before you press Enter to accept the name change.

6. **Close Explorer.**

7. **Now try using the program you are testing.** If the program tells you that it can't find the address book, Bookmarks, or what have you, the file you renamed is the one you need.

8. **Rename the file back to its original name using Step 5 (remember, you wrote it down in Step 4).**

9. **Copy the file to a floppy disk and transfer it to your notebook computer into the same subdirectory of the program that uses it.**

After you find the correct file containing your address book, bookmarks, or other data file, you can use the *Synchronize* function in a file transfer program like LapLink to periodically copy new entries from one computer to the other and keep all data files up-to-date. See Chapter 9 for more details.

Dial-up settings

You also need to copy the setup information for your online service or Internet service provider — including such information as the phone number you dial into, your account number, and your password. Although this information, like the address book, is also stored in one or more files, I always prefer simply rentering the information in the freshly installed software.

Note that with Internet service providers, you usually need to enter the necessary information in the Dial-Up Networking adapter in the Windows 95 Accessories group, whereas with online services (such as AOL and CompuServe) you usually enter the information in the Preferences or Settings area of the online service software.

If you use a separate e-mail program, such as Eudora, you also need to copy the setup information from your desktop machine to the notebook computer. Again, the easiest way to do this is to simply go into the Settings or Preferences area(s), write down all the information on a sheet of paper, and then retype it into the notebook computer's software.

When copying e-mail setup information, pay particular attention to the *leave on server/delete from server* choice. When you pick up e-mail with a remote computer, such as using a notebook in a hotel room, you often want to leave the mail on the mail server (the computer where your e-mail is centrally handled) so that next time you're in the office, the same e-mail will also be available on your desktop computer. (See Chapter 10 for more details.)

Part III
Taking Your Show on the Road

The 5th Wave   By Rich Tennant

©RICHTENNANT

FIRED

YOU

"NIFTY CHART, FRANK, BUT NOT ENTIRELY NECESSARY."

In this part . . .

Many people buy notebook computers specifically for making presentations. You may need to present a market forecast to potential clients. Or maybe you have an entire computer video mock-up of a movie pitch for a major Hollywood studio. Or better yet, maybe you need to run a giant two-screen computer graphics show at a huge party with blasting techno and thousands of crazed teenagers.

This part of the book is devoted to helping you find your way to, and through, using a notebook computer to put on the greatest show on Earth! — well, at least the greatest show in Cincinnati at 4:30 on Tuesday afternoon.

Chapter 16

Portable Presentations: Authoring and Storing

. . . .

In This Chapter

▶ Creating a presentation

▶ Hiring professionals to produce it

▶ Incorporating pictures and sound

▶ Storing the sometimes massive presentation files

▶ Distributing copies of presentations

. . . .

*O*ne of the coolest things about a notebook computer is using it as a show-and-tell machine. With nothing more than a laptop computer (and perhaps one of the display options I talk about in Chapter 17), you can put on a show to literally dazzle your audience.

In computer jargon, a show generated by the computer is called a *presentation* and you use *presentation authoring software* to create one. The simplest presentations appear like slide shows, consisting of a series of still frames that have your key points and ideas, tables, graphs, and images such as scanned photographs, logos, or other graphics on them. More sophisticated presentations can incorporate audio, animation, and/or video clips.

In this chapter, I give you an overview of the *process* of creating a presentation. If your audience consists of just one or two people — such as potential clients — then you can show the presentation right on your notebook computer screen. For larger audiences, you probably want to hook up some device to make the image a bit bigger — a traditional monitor, a projection panel, a TV monitor, or a projector — see Chapter 17 for details.

If this chapter really gets your juices flowing, you may want to check out books specifically on the subject, such as *PowerPoint 97 For Dummies* by Doug Lowe, or *Macromedia Director 6 For Dummies* by Lauren Steinhauer, both from IDG Books Worldwide, Inc. I briefly describe these software packages in the "Authoring Software — the Way to Create Presentations" section a bit later in this chapter.

Who Is Your Audience and What Does It Need?

Presentations come in all different levels of complexity and expense to produce. At the lowest budget level, for example, a presentation may consist of nothing more than a series of *slides* (the jargon from the now low-tech slide presentation has more or less drifted over to computer presentations) containing the names and titles of a series of people who are speaking at a conference — the slide changes to announce each new speaker.

At the other end of the spectrum, a presentation at a big corporate marketing event — say a 500-person cocktail party held in a hotel ballroom during a trade show — may consist of multiple screens showing different images simultaneously, with video testimonials from satisfied customers, custom animation revolving around the company's logo, and original music scored for the event, naked people in bubbles. . . you get the idea.

Obviously, most people seek outside help to produce such a high-impact, lavish multimedia event. So if you're looking to create a presentation, the first thing to ask yourself is whether you're going to make it yourself or hire someone else to produce it for you. Keep the following questions in mind as you decide just how good your presentation needs to be and whether to do it yourself or hire a bigshot Hollywood producer:

- How many people do you expect to see your presentation? How big an audience do you expect per viewing, and how many viewings do you expect to give for your presentation?

- For how long do you expect the presentation to stay current? How soon will it need updating? Who will do the updates, and how much will they cost?

- Are you the only person who will run the presentation, or will copies of it be distributed to others to run on their computers?

- What is at stake? Who are you trying to impress, and how much do they matter?

- What's your budget?

Authoring Software — the Way to Create Presentations

Nope. Authoring software is an entire category of programs that is devoted to creating presentations and multimedia. If you plan to put on a presentation, you want to use this special software because it can make simple text and photographs look really good on a computer screen or projected on a large movie screen. For one thing, when the presentation is running, it fills the entire screen from edge to edge without distracting menus, toolbars, or anything else. Beyond that, the authoring software contains a zillion built-in tools that make creating your presentation easy, including templates for common applications such as a sales presentation or report.

Authoring software also provides you with interesting backgrounds, such as *gradients* that create colors which fade from one edge of the screen to the next, and graphic elements like boxes and diamonds and shadows (see Figure 16-1).

All authoring software lets you use photographs (which you can scan in — see Chapter 6 for information on scanners) and *clip art* (small images that are often included with the software) to stick in your presentation. Most packages also offer easy tools for creating graphs and importing audio and video.

Microsoft's PowerPoint, shown in Figures 16-1 and 16-2, is probably the most widely used presentation authoring software, partly because it comes included in the Microsoft Office suite (which also contains Word and Excel). You may even already have this program installed on your computer if Microsoft Office is part of your pre-installed software.

Besides helping you figure out what the content of each slide needs to be — such as text, graph, table, or animation — authoring software also provides tools for creating interesting-looking transitions between slides, as shown in Figure 16-2. You can have them change with a venetian-blind effect, for example, or as a dissolve or wipe, and each new slide can be accompanied by a sound effect such as a video game laser gun, or a camera click.

Besides Microsoft PowerPoint, you have numerous other, more advanced presentation authoring software programs available to you. Macromedia Director, available for both Windows and Macintosh computers, is widely considered the mother of all authoring programs. The original version of Macromedia Director practically defined the whole authoring software category. Other contenders include mFactory, mTropolis, Corel Click & Create, Astound, and Innovus Multimedia Presentations. Such authoring software can vary tremendously in price from under $100 to over $1,000.

Besides presentations, you can also use some of these programs, such as Macromedia Director, to create multimedia CD-ROMs. This useful if you need to create very large presentations and you don't have a whole bunch of hard disk space on your notebook computer.

Authoring software packages vary in numerous ways relating to the file formats they can import — in other words, the other file formats, be they graphics, audio, video, or word processor files that you create using another program, that can be readily used in the particular authoring software. Be sure to purchase software that is compatible with any other tools you already use.

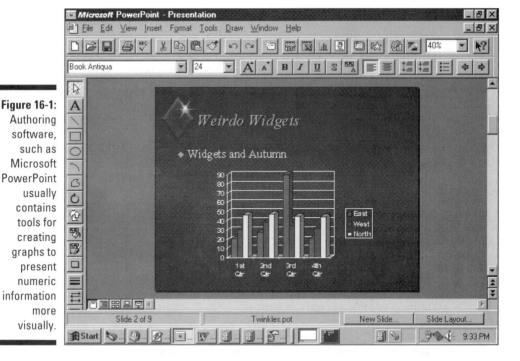

Figure 16-1:
Authoring
software,
such as
Microsoft
PowerPoint
usually
contains
tools for
creating
graphs to
present
numeric
information
more
visually.

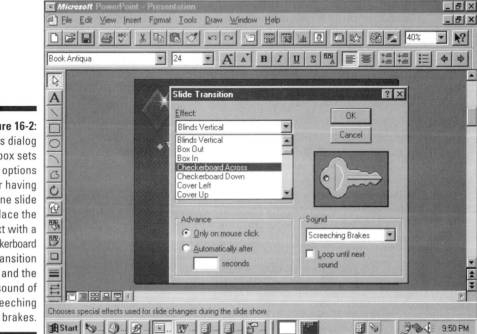

Figure 16-2:
This dialog
box sets
the options
for having
one slide
replace the
next with a
checkerboard
transition
and the
sound of
screeching
brakes.

Some presentation authoring software packages offer animation features, letting you create images that move on the screen. Animation is not all that useful for business presentations, and can be more distracting than cool, but for some situations, animation can be great.

Often, the metaphor used to represent the various *slides* in a presentation varies from package to package. Macromedia Director, for example, calls each frame a *stage* — other more multimedia-oriented authoring tools use a hierarchy of *sections* and *subsections, timelines, storyboards,* or *slides* to show the different visual elements.

Budget, talent, and creativity

Mastering the art of multimedia production, in the fullest and most creative sense, requires mastering its component fields of photography, video production, lighting, sound design, and graphic arts. You can contract someone to create presentations that cost hundreds of thousands of dollars, even millions of dollars to create. You can also produce pretty cool presentations on your own with a good authoring package. However, if your boss asks you to put together a presentation to run on a notebook computer, be sure that you both agree that what you create is going to be a relatively simple, bare-bones production unless you really invest the kind of time, software, and money needed to create the serious stuff.

One intermediate alternative between doing it all yourself or hiring someone else to take over the project is to hire specialists to shoot video, take pictures, or create artwork. You can get these specialists to deliver their work to you in the form of a file, and then import these files directly into your presentation. Be sure that if you go this route, you agree on the correct image, video, and audio file formats to use in your presentation authoring software.

Picking a way to present — automatic, manual, and interactive presentations

Most business and academic presentations are intended as a backdrop or supplement to a spoken presentation. Though you can certainly create a completely self-running presentation, with a hired voice of doom narrator and Ride of the Valkyries background music that makes your computer presentation look just like a professional videotape production, most presentations are considerably less glossy. You may use a sound effect (like the sound of squishing cheese) to usher in a new slide, but then the computer is silent to create a space for the speaker to talk.

When you create a presentation, you have a choice of having the slides change automatically, or having the slides change only when you provide a manual command such as a mouse click. Usually, having the slide show wait for your mouse click is preferable in order to keep the presentation in sync with the accompanying speech, or to provide time for any discussion or questions that may come up. Also, if you control the presentation yourself, you have the option of easily returning to a previous slide to clarify a point.

Most presentations are linear, following a straight course from beginning to end, just like a slide projector or videotape. However, at the most advanced level, a presentation may include *branching*. A training presentation, for example, may offer different segments to teach different skills. A sales presentation designed to be delivered one-on-one to potential clients can include a section where you take a look at different products in an electronic catalog, and close with electronic order-taking, in which the client or salesperson fills out an on-screen form.

Scripting such presentations (writing them out and making sure they work) is a pretty big undertaking, and you may need to create a fairly detailed outline before you even start your authoring software. However, if your company has paid to have such a presentation professionally produced, and you're in the position of having to run it on your notebook computer, my advice is to thoroughly familiarize yourself with it in advance. You not only familiarize yourself with the presentation and give a more fluid and convincing performance, but you also ensure that you catch any mistakes in the slides (see Chapter 18).

Incorporating photos, video, audio, and graphics

If you ever fantasize about being a film director, you may get a kick out of producing your own presentation. Even the most basic authoring tools, such as Microsoft PowerPoint, let you incorporate all sorts of visual and audio elements to make your presentation more dazzling.

Importing still images (photos, digital photos, video frames)

You have several ways to incorporate still photographs into a presentation. Most authoring software works with the standard JPEG file format, as well as other photo file formats. (JPEG stands for *Joint Photographic Experts Group* — they, the joint experts, decided on the JPEG format, which is particularly good for storing photographic images as small computer files.)

So how do you get a picture into the JPEG format? One way is to use regular photography and scan your prints in using a scanner (see Chapter 6). Using regular film and then scanning the photos makes a lot of sense if you want printed copies of the photographs as well. On the other hand, if you need only the images in your presentation, and for no other purpose, then an electronic still camera makes sense. Of course, if you have a decent printer, you can still print out a copy of an electronic image, but a computer printer can't match the fine detail of an actual photograph.

You can also capture still images from a videotape. You need an accessory device, for example, the popular Snappy from Play Technologies, to grab still frames from your video. (These video-capture images may not look as sharp as scanned photographs — they're best used to fit in a $^1\!/_4$-screen window, but not for filling the entire computer screen.)

Importing full-motion video

You can capture full-motion video directly on your notebook computer using an accessory like the CardCam Video In from Newer Technology, shown in Figure 16-3. This accessory is a standard PCMCIA card and plugs into the PCMCIA slot on your notebook computer. The card provides a video jack for feeding the signal from a camcorder in, and using the supplied software creates a standard Windows AVI video file, which can then be incorporated into multimedia presentations. A similar device made by Videonics plugs into the parallel port on the back of a notebook computer and accepts both video and audio signals to create a standard MPEG-format video file on your notebook computer. (MPEG stands for *Moving Pictures Experts Group* — they, the experts, decided on the MPEG file format for computer video.) You can then use the MPEG file in a presentation.

And just as digital still cameras have gained popularity in recent years, a new breed of tapeless, digital camcorders are beginning to make their mark. Hitachi has pioneered this area with an MPEG camcorder — it records video clips in the MPEG file format onto a PCMCIA/PC Card hard drive. You just pop the hard drive out of the camera and put it in your notebook computer's PCMCIA slot, and you're ready to import the video clips into a presentation. (See Chapter 22 for a whole bag of beef on PCMCIA/PC Cards.)

Remember, however, that your authoring software must accept MPEG files — not all do.

Instead of shooting your own photos or videos, you can use stock photography and video clips. CD-ROM collections of various clips with themes like *people at work*, or *modern technology* are available at most computer software stores. You can also find discs with themes like air travel and bridges, both of which are great if you run a scam selling shares of the Golden Gate bridge with a free flight to see your customers' new purchase.

Camcorder connects here

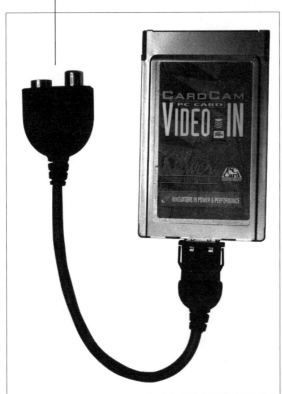

Figure 16-3:
The Newer
Technology
CardCam
Video IN PC
Card lets
you import
full-motion
video from a
camcorder
into your
portable
computer.

Importing audio

If your notebook computer is equipped with a sound card that includes microphone and headphone jacks, you can easily make audio recordings to use in your presentation. If you want to record narration, for instance, plug in a microphone and use your computer's audio recording utility, following these steps:

1. **Choose Start⇨Accessories⇨Multimedia⇨Sound Recorder.**

2. **Make sure that your microphone is connected, and then click the Record button (the one with the red dot).**

   The program works just like a tape recorder.

3. **After you are finished, click Stop (the button with the square).**

4. **Choose File⇨Save to save your recording as a standard WAV file, which you can import to almost all presentation authoring software.**

Note that computer multimedia presentations can import two general types of audio files: sound files (for example, WAV or AU), and MIDI files. Sound files are actual *digital recordings* — similar in principle to audio CDs, except they are often lower quality and don't sound as good as your typical audio CD. MIDI files are very different — these are essentially instruction sets for running your sound card, kind of like a hi-tech version of the paper rolls that were used with player pianos in a bygone era.

The advantage of MIDI files, which have the .mid file extension, is that they are highly efficient — a MIDI file containing music that lasts for several minutes may occupy under 100KB of disk space, whereas a comparable-length sound recording (WAV or AU) with high fidelity may occupy more than 10MB. Every computer sound board incorporates a MIDI synthesizer, which generates most of the video-game style sound effects (no, those aren't recordings of real laser guns firing!). The synthesizer part of the sound card can actually generate fairly sophisticated sounding music, with numerous different *voices* (instrument sounds) playing simultaneously. If you need to produce a professional quality presentation, you may want to hire a musician to create an original MIDI score. Alternately, just as you can get clip art, stock photography, and clip video to incorporate in your presentation, you can also get libraries of stock music intended for use in presentations and multimedia.

The disadvantage of MIDI files is that they can sound winky. Believe me, just because a sound card has a voice called *trumpet* doesn't mean you get Miles Davis coming out of your computer.

How Much Portable Computing Power Do You Need?

Just about any modern notebook computer can run a basic text and images presentation, and most are fast enough to run video clips as well. If your presentation includes audio, you obviously need a computer equipped with a sound card, and preferably a better way to listen than through the notebook's underpowered speakers (see Chapter 18).

If all you want to do is *run* a presentation and you're not concerned with creating it, you usually do not need to install the complete authoring software on your notebook computer — many authoring programs offer a stripped-down player program that you can copy onto your notebook along with the completed presentation. This method is a good idea for saving disk space — maybe you create your presentation on your desktop computer where you have more disk space, and then install and run it with the player program on your portable computer.

On the other hand, unless you absolutely need special graphics capability that you have only on your desktop computer (such as a scanner or video inputs), you have no problem authoring your presentations right on your notebook computer. No special computing power is needed.

If you expect to run presentations fairly regularly, you may want to consider computer features that specifically make a presentation run as smoothly as possible:

- If you need to show your audiences your presentations on your notebook computer's built-in screen, then the quality of the screen should be one of the main factors you consider when shopping for a computer. An active matrix screen is always preferable to a passive matrix (also known as dual-scan) screen, because it has better contrast. The bigger the screen, the better, too. (See Chapter 2 for the details on LCD displays.)

- Don't assume that screens with higher resolution are inherently better for presentations. Though usually this rule is true, in order to take advantage of SVGA screens with 800×600 resolution, the presentation must be created for that resolution. Most professionally-produced presentations are designed for standard 640×480 VGA resolution.

- If the presentations you run include scanned photographs or video clips, look for a notebook computer that has a screen capable of showing at least 256 colors, and preferably 32,000 or more colors. The color *depth,* as this is called, has a big influence on how good your pictures look.

- For running presentations, look for a notebook computer that has actual hardware controls for contrast and brightness instead of the function button-based software controls that are more cumbersome to use. Actual sliders make you less likely to fumble around to make the screen viewable while your audience waits. Ditto for the volume control — if your presentation includes sound, choose a notebook computer that has a real, physical volume control, not software controls. If the audio is too loud or soft, you want to be able to adjust it immediately, and the software-based controls sometimes have a delayed response.

Where Can You Store It?

A simple text-oriented presentation — even a lengthy one containing dozens of slides — usually takes up less than 1MB of disk space, and can thus easily fit on a floppy disk if you need to move it from one computer to another. Once you start including photographs and/or video, you're talking about some serious disk space. Some presentations fill an entire CD-ROM — that's 650MB!

If you run just your own presentation on your own notebook computer and you are the only person in the world who ever needs to run that presentation, then you can usually just run the presentation off your hard drive, or use an additional drive of some sort (see Chapter 6).

On the other hand, if your company or organization wants to have several people carrying the same presentation on several different notebook computers, then you need to figure out how to distribute it to all those computers, and how to distribute updates when the presentation changes.

CD-ROMs are a popular method for distribution — the discs themselves are pretty cheap (about $7 each for recordable discs), and they can just be thrown away when a new version arrives. Whoever produces the presentation needs to have a CD-ROM recorder, or *burner* as they are called by those who use them, which is different from a CD-ROM drive. Of course, the notebook computers that run presentations from CD-ROM need to be equipped with CD-ROM drives. Note that in some rare instances — especially with older notebooks playing presentations that include video clips — the CD-ROM drive may not be able to spew out data at a fast enough rate to make the presentation run smoothly.

If you experience problems running a presentation distributed to you via CD-ROM, try copying it onto your computer's regular hard drive (usually the C: drive), and then run the presentation from there.

You can also use removable hard drive systems, such as Iomega's Zip or Jaz disks, to store presentations. The Jaz disks, for example, hold 1GB (1000MB) each. Removable disks allow you to easily switch between one presentation and another, and unlike CD-ROM, have the advantage of allowing you to make changes to the presentation.

PCMCIA hard drives and flash memory cards are another storage option, offering the benefits of an added drive without taking up any additional space in your computer carrying case. Note that most PCMCIA hard drives require a Type 3 slot (the double-size slot — if your notebook has two slots one on top of each other, most hard drive cards take up both slots), and these drives tend to cost more than physically larger units. (See Chapter 22 if you are wondering what all the PCMCIA/PC Card stuff is about.)

Chapter 17

Presenting on the Road: Display Options

*Y*our notebook computer is a fantastic portable show-and-tell machine. Using your notebook computer, you can show clients sales presentations, you can estimate prices and projected profits using spreadsheet programs for clients, or you can access and display catalog information from CD-ROM or the Internet. Using a notebook computer, you can readily present a series of pictures, tables, charts, and other materials to groups of hundreds or even thousands of people.

All on that little, winky-dink screen? Okay — the screen on your notebook computer is its Achilles heel when it comes to showing things to groups of people. The 10- to 12-inch LCD (*Liquid Crystal Display*) screens on notebook computers are fantastic for private, personal use. And then you try getting even a small group of people — three or four, for example — to all have good, comfortable views of your notebook's screen, and you quickly see the problem (or *don't see* the problem, as the case may be).

Compared with the standard CRT-type display monitors used on desktop computer monitors, the LCD screens on notebook computers are markedly inferior for group viewing (CRT stands for *Cathode Ray Tube* in case you were wondering). The reason is that LCD screens, in general, are very unforgiving when it comes to viewing them at an angle. They work best when you sit directly in front of them and look directly at them. The limited viewing direction of LCD screens is why the angle of the screen relative to the keyboard is adjustable. Just try tilting the screen up or down from your optimum angle, and you see how it looks to someone peeking over your shoulder.

If you ever make presentations to large groups of people, or find yourself in any other situation where you're trying to impress a group of people with what's on your portable computer screen, consider some of the display options explained in this chapter. And obviously, if you're making a presentation to a large group of people — anywhere from ten or fifteen people up to an auditorium packed with hundreds (such as a college lecture hall or business convention) — using one of the projection systems I cover in this chapter is absolutely necessary.

The Straight Dope on Display and Projection Methods

You have numerous ways to show a presentation from your notebook computer on a bigger screen. Table 17-1 provides a brief rundown.

Table 17-1	Quick Comparison of the Displays Covered in This Chapter		
System	*Pros*	*Cons*	*Cost*
External CRT computer monitor	Ideal when presenting to small groups in a business office or computer lab	Not adequate for more than a few people	You can usually borrow someone else's monitor, so cost is usually free
Big-screen TV set	Suitable for, and often available at, hotel conference rooms, business conference rooms, and so on	Usually requires scan converter, often has a fuzzy picture	$200 to $2,000 for scan converter, and a whole lot more if you need to buy the TV as well!
LCD projector	Good for use with larger groups, lectures, auditoriums; often easily rented or supplied by better auditoriums	Can be bulky, expensive	$2,000 to $10,000

System	Pros	Cons	Cost
LCD projection panel	Lightweight and compact, especially good for classroom and lecture use, easy setup	Requires overhead projector	$1,000 to $5,000
CRT projector	The sharpest and brightest picture quality of any projection method	Very heavy and bulky to lug around, tedious setup procedure	$5,000 to $20,000

Things to Bring to a Presentation for Connecting to Various Displays

You often run into situations where you need to connect your notebook computer to one of the display methods I describe in this chapter, and the connection isn't exactly what you expect. Rather than fumble around and make your audience impatient, consider some of the following accessories. Most of these accessories are useful for all the display situations described in this chapter.

✔ **VGA cable.** Instead of using the cable that's already connected to a CRT monitor, or expecting one to come with a projector, you may prefer to bring your own VGA cable. For one thing, connecting with your own cable usually involves less crawling around on the floor, especially if you have to use someone else's computer monitor. And if you purchase a long one — say 10 or 15 feet — you have more flexibility in where you place your notebook computer while you run your presentation. Such cables cost about $15 to $20 and are available at just about any computer store. Note, however, that some inexpensive computer monitors come with a VGA cable permanently attached, so you may have to crawl around anyway.

✔ **VGA gender changer adapter.** If you give presentations fairly regularly and you often hook up to other monitors or projectors, you can save a lot of grief by keeping both male-to-male and female-to-female VGA gender-changer adapters with your notebook computer. The adapters are cheap and lightweight, and you look much more professional when you solve a monitor problem quickly from within your computer carrying case as opposed to fumbling around your client's office for the right kind of cable. Figure 17-1 shows a typical gender-changer adapter.

✔ **Screwdriver.** You may also want to carry a small screwdriver with you. Note that the VGA connector — whether on the back of a computer, monitor, or projector — is usually secured by two small screws on either side, to prevent the cable from accidentally coming loose. You have to unscrew these screws before pulling the cable away from the computer.

✔ **Signal converter.** For many televisions and some older models of projectors, you may need both a *scan converter* and an *RF converter* (see Figure 17-2). The scan converter changes the computer's digital signal into a form that a television can understand. The RF converter switches the cable type so that you can connect the television and computer video cables together. The "Hooking Your Notebook Up to a TV" section later in this chapter, explains more.

Figure 17-1:
A male-to-male VGA gender changer — useful if you have two female connectors that need to connect.

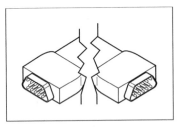

External VGA Monitors and Televisions

Absolutely the easiest way to upgrade the visual impact and visibility of your presentations to small groups of people is simply to hook up your notebook computer to a standard VGA (*Video Graphics Adapter*) monitor, the same kind most desktop computers use. Just about all PC-compatible notebook computers include a monitor output jack on the back panel. Usually the jack is a standard VGA port. The exact details of how this jack works vary (see the "Displaying on two screens at once: simulscan" section later in this chapter for more information). The purpose of the monitor jack on the back of your notebook is for hooking up to an external monitor, or to any of the other display devices, such as a scan converter, LCD projector, or projection panel, all of which I cover elsewhere in this chapter.

Obviously you don't want to lug a big CRT monitor around with you — doing so would sort of miss the whole point of using a laptop computer, wouldn't it? So the notion of hooking up to an external monitor presupposes that such a monitor is available where you're making your presentation.

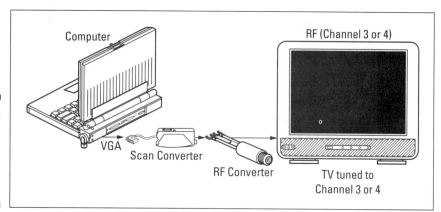

Figure 17-2:
A typical
connection
scenario
using an
older TV.

Just about all businesses nowadays have at least one computer with a color monitor; most have many more. So if you plan to make your presentation in someone's office, the expectation that you can hook up to a standard VGA or SVGA (*Super Video Graphics Adapter*) monitor nearby is a pretty safe bet, though calling ahead is never a bad idea.

To economize, yet get the benefit of both desktop and notebook computer, some users leave a regular CRT (the standard type of computer display) monitor and an external keyboard hooked up to their notebook machines all the time when they're in the office or at home, and then disconnect the notebook unit for travel. That principle is what's behind the expansion station — see Chapter 6 for more information.

Breaking down someone's computer setup politely

Be aware that as you barge into someone else's offices and start disconnecting their computer equipment, you may be intruding in a way that offsets any advantage you get from the improved display capability. Only you can gauge the comfort level of the situation — if you bum out your clients, you may end up feeling like a dweeb.

One thoughtful approach to this whole issue of etiquette is to call a couple of days in advance and ask the person you're visiting to arrange to have a monitor available, if convenient. This request leaves the decision of what size monitor, and whose to pull, to the people you're visiting, and gives them the opportunity to politely tell you if none will be available so you can make other arrangements.

Connecting to an external CRT monitor

The procedure for hooking up to an external monitor is very simple:

1. **First, to be on the safe side, make sure that all equipment (monitor, desktop computer, and notebook computer) is turned off.**

2. **Locate the cable that connects the monitor you want to use to the desktop computer.**

3. **Disconnect this cable from the back of the desktop computer.**

4. **Plug the cable into the VGA port in back of your notebook computer (see Figure 17-3).**

   In all likelihood, the connectors match. In some rare cases, you may need a gender-changer adapter, available for about five dollars at any store that sells electronics or computer stuff, to convert a VGA plug (male) to a jack (female) or vice-versa (see Figure 17-1). An exception is Macintosh computer monitors, which use a different monitor jack, and require a special adapter for connection to a VGA output (see "Connecting and adjusting your computer to weird displays" later in this chapter).

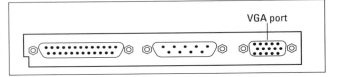

Figure 17-3: VGA port on the back of a notebook computer.

VGA port

5. **Turn the notebook computer and the CRT monitor on.**

   If you're lucky, you see the boot-up process from your notebook on the CRT monitor. If not, refer to the "Displaying on two screens at once: simulscan" and "Connecting and adjusting your computer to weird displays" sections later in this chapter.

Displaying on two screens at once: simulscan

Getting a notebook computer to display on both its own built-in LCD screen *and* on an external monitor or projector at the same time is not as easy a feat as it may seem. Not all notebook computers are capable of doing it — some require that you choose the LCD screen or the external display or projector, but not both at once. The computers that can display on both the LCD screen and an external display simultaneously often give the feature a special name: *simulscan*.

Video connections, including the VGA variety, commonly used for hooking computers to monitors cannot simply be split using the kind of Y-connector cables that you may use when hooking up a stereo system — I spare you the technicalities, but that reason is why you need the simulscan feature. If you expect to do a lot of presentations with your notebook, simulscan is an important feature to look for in any notebook purchase. Fortunately, most new notebooks have simulscan.

Notebook computers that lack the simulscan feature sometimes switch automatically to external monitor mode (with the notebook's LCD screen disabled) whenever you plug a cable into the VGA port on the back. With other models, you need to switch between internal (LCD) and external monitor modes using one of the function keys.

If your notebook computer does have the simulscan feature, it almost surely has a function key to select the operating mode, as shown in Figure 17-4. Usually you have three choices — LCD only, external monitor only, or simulscan mode. The built-in LCD sometimes dims a bit when you run your notebook in the simulscan mode. Consult your notebook computer manual for the specifics of your computer.

✔ To find the simulscan or monitor control button, look for a symbol printed on a function key (F1 to F12) that looks like a choice in screens, as shown in Figure 17-4. (This key can have one of the less readily recognized picture symbols of the function key labels, and may look like a fish, for all I know).

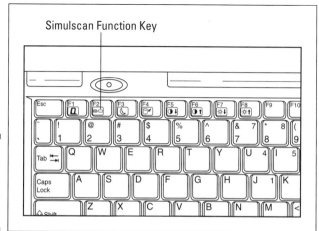

Figure 17-4:
A typical
simulscan
function
key.

✔ Often, when running a presentation on an external projector or monitor, you want to turn off the LCD screen on your laptop whenever possible to save power and extend battery life. However, you may want to keep the screen on if you need to operate the computer during the presentation. That way, you can face your audience, and still view your laptop screen and operate your computer without standing in front of the screen your audience has to see.

✔ You may need to engage the simulscan or external monitor mode to hook up *any* external display device — including monitor, scan converter, projection panel, or projector.

The very best simulscan systems — and they are very rare — actually allow you to set completely different *resolution* (the fineness of the screen's detail) and *color depth* (the number, or richness of colors the screen can display) parameters for the two displays. The next section explains how to adjust the resolution and color depth of your computer.

Connecting and adjusting your computer to weird displays

The 15-pin VGA (Video Graphics Display) connector found on the back of most notebook computers, shown in Figure 17-3, is nearly, but not quite universal. Some older computer monitors have incompatible CGA (Computer Graphics Adapter) and EGA (Extended Graphics Adapter) connectors, while monitors intended for the Macintosh computer platform have their own similar, but incompatible connections. For hookup to Mac monitors, you can buy an adapter for about $15 that makes Macintosh monitors compatible with the standard VGA ports found on PC-compatible notebooks. You can also find adapter cables available for other types of older monitor connections such as CGA and EGA, but some older monitors may not be able to handle your notebook's output resolution.

Most notebook computers have one of two screen resolutions: 640×480 pixels (most common) or 800×600 pixels (*pixel* refers to each little dot of light coming from your computer display — the more dots, the finer the resolution). Your notebook computer's default resolution is usually the maximum that its display can handle, but usually you can change this to a lower setting. Often, when 800×600 computers run CD-ROM multimedia designed for a 640×480 display, for example, the screen resolution automatically switches to the lower setting. Note, however, that these lower-resolution displays can look funky, because an LCD panel, unlike a CRT monitor, is made up of discrete dots (pixels). A computer with a 640×480 screen can show 320×240 perfectly, for example, because it has two pixels for each piece of horizontal or vertical data. But when an 800×600 display shows 640×480, the math isn't so neat, and as a result, text ends up looking not quite right. I cover screen resolution in more detail in Chapters 2 and 15.

Most notebook computers can generate a higher-resolution image through their VGA external monitor jacks than what the built-in LCD screen is capable of displaying. This feature is useful for running an external monitor with your notebook. You can usually find the adjustment in the Windows Control Panel, but be careful here — you may end up accidentally adjusting things in a way that prevents your LCD display from working at all — in which case, you can't see anything! (If something goes wrong, you may need to revert back to the emergency backup disks that Windows 95 implores you to make, or similar emergency boot disks using a utility such as Norton System Utilities from Symantec.) For advanced users (who have emergency backup disks on hand in case things go awry), get to the settings in Windows 95 like this:

1. **Choose Start⇨Control Panel to open the Control Panel.**

2. **In the Control Panel, double-click Display.**

   The Display dialog box appears.

3. **Click the Settings tab to get to the settings.**

4. **Click Change Display Type.**

   The Change Display Type dialog box appears.

5. **Click the Change button next to the Monitor Type list box.**

   The Select Device dialog box appears.

6. **Click the Show all devices radio button to get a list of available monitor types.**

7. **Select the brand of monitor in the left column and the model number in the right column. Click OK.**

   You may be prompted to insert a disk for the software driver for the monitor you have selected. See the next section, "Drivers and other details" for more information.

8. **Insert a driver disk if necessary, and follow the on-screen instructions. Otherwise, go to Step 9.**

9. **After you are finished, click Close.**

   You are returned to the Display dialog box.

10. **Click OK.**

    Your new monitor settings go into effect.

The term *VGA* (Video Graphics Adapter) refers to 640 × 480, and anything higher, such as the common 800 × 600 notebook display is called *Super-VGA* (or SVGA for short). For both VGA and SVGA, the 15-pin connector remains the same.

Drivers and other details

When you connect to strange monitors, you have a number of things you can fiddle around with to get the best display, and hopefully keep the flash and pizzazz of your original presentation.

The number of possible resolutions and colors available is a function of the *video display drivers* used in your notebook computer. The video display drivers usually have two things you can adjust: *resolution* and *color depth*. Resolution is the number of points of detail, or dots, (also called *pixels*) in the picture. The color depth is based on the number of *bits* (a bit is the smallest unit of computer data) devoted to the individual red, green, and blue signals going to each pixel. The lowest color depth is 16 colors, and the highest color depth is 16 million colors.

A third variable, called the *refresh rate*, is usually determined by your settings for resolution and color depth, but occasionally you have control of the refresh rate, too. Typically you can adjust the refresh rate from 60Hz to 72Hz (Hz is the abbreviation for Hertz, and means repetitions per second — a refresh rate of 72Hz says that the screen is refreshed at a rate of 72 times per second). The faster the refresh rate, the less perception of flicker you get with traditional CRT-type desktop monitors (but not with LCD panels, as found on notebook computers). The difference is slight, and the main reason why monitors are built to handle different rates is to maintain compatibility with the widest variety of computers and video display cards.

For example, your notebook's built-in display may be limited to 640 × 480 resolution with just 256 colors, but using the external monitor VGA port on the back, you may be able to use an external monitor at 800 × 600 resolution with 16 million colors.

Because your notebook computer and the external monitor you're connecting it to are both usually capable of handling higher resolutions than your notebook's built-in LCD screen, you may be tempted to set everything to the highest resolution for maximum display quality. However, if you're running a presentation, you actually determined the resolution for the presentation when you created it (see Chapter 16). You don't gain anything by setting the monitor to a higher resolution than the material you're trying to show. And note, as a practical matter, that some computers start acting funky at higher resolutions and color depths because the higher settings are more demanding in terms of computer processing power.

Multiscan and autosync

Most modern monitors, except for the cheapest models, are both multiscan and autosync. *Multiscan* means that the monitor is capable of displaying numerous resolutions and color depths. *Autosync* means that the monitor can sense what kind of signal it is receiving from the computer and automatically adjust itself accordingly. With older multiscan monitors that don't have the autosync feature, you have to manually change the monitor's resolution until you find a setting that is compatible with what your computer is sending out (just keep going through the choices — it's not as fun as choosing an ice cream flavor, but maybe you can go have ice cream as a reward after you figure out the right monitor setting). When the monitor and the VGA port settings don't match, the display looks like a bunch of scrambled horizontal lines.

Hooking Up Your Notebook to a TV

The device that converts your computer's VGA display to a standard TV-type signal is called a *VGA to NTSC converter* (VGA stands for Video Graphics Adapter and NTSC stands for National Television Standards Committee), or more simply, a *scan converter*. Scan converters are often battery-powered and quite compact, making them the most portable of all the display accessories discussed in this chapter. Figure 17-5 shows a typical model.

Figure 17-5: A pocket-sized scan converter, also known as VGA to NTSC converter, from AITech (model PSC-1106).

NTSC is the current system used for television in North America and parts of Asia and Africa. The other systems commonly used elsewhere in the world are called PAL and SECAM. If you're ever putting on a presentation outside the U.S. and using a TV set to display it, you need a scan converter designed for one of these alternate TV systems — some advanced scan converter models available in the U.S. have a switch that lets you switch to a foreign TV systems. The United States government recently committed itself to phasing out NTSC video, in favor of digital television over the next decade, but as this book was going to press, digital TVs were not yet even available.

Scan converters range in price from about $200 to about $2,000 (see the Appendix for a list of manufacturers), and hook up to your notebook computer's VGA port just like an external monitor. Most scan converters have *line video* output jacks — these are the same RCA phono jacks (see Figure 17-6) commonly used for hooking up stereo and audio/video equipment. I label the colors of the various jacks to help you figure them out in real life, even though the photograph is in black and white.

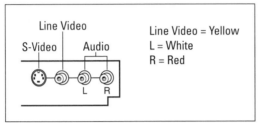

Figure 17-6:
Most big-screen TV sets have A/V line input jacks that look like these.

After you have the scan converter hooked up to your computer's VGA port, you can connect the scan converter's video output jack connects, via a cable with RCA phono plugs on each end, to the input jack on the TV. Most big-screen TVs nowadays have such jacks — the video input is usually colored yellow, and the audio inputs (to which you can connect your notebook computer's audio output, if your presentation includes sound) are red and white. To hook up the sound directly from the notebook computer to the TV set, you usually need a cable with a stereo miniplug on one end and two RCA phono plugs (usually red and white) on the other end — see Chapter 18 for more on this hookup, as well as diagrams of some of the different types of plugs commonly used in A/V hookups.

What does S-video mean?

Many video buffs believe that the *S* in S-video stands for *super*, but actually it stands for *separated*. What are separated in the S-video connection are the color and black-and-white portions of the video signal. If you ever see rainbow-like colors randomly emanating from a newscaster's tweed jacket on television, you know one problem that can occur when color and black-and-white get mixed together, as they normally do when you use the standard line video input jack. When hooking up a scan converter, you may see a very slight improvement in picture detail if you use the S-video connection rather than line-input. The scan converter and the TV set must both have the S-video connection in order for you to be able to utilize it.

Some scan converters also have an *S-video* output jack, for TVs equipped with this slightly higher-quality hookup system (see Figure 17-6). S-video is a small, 4-pin, round plug.

Other things you may need: adapters

In the unlikely event that the TV does not have these jacks, you can use an *RF converter* — sometimes built into the scan converter, and readily available at any electronics store, if not — to put the signal onto channel 3 or 4 via the TV's regular antenna connection, as shown in Figure 17-7. The RF converter usually looks like a small box, about the size of a pack of cigarettes, with two input jacks for line video and audio, a switch to choose between channel 3 and 4 (pick whichever one isn't being used by a TV station in your area), and a single antenna-type output jack (the same type used for cable-TV hookups, called an *F-connector*). If you have a really old TV that has two little screw-down connections on the back for the antenna, rather than a jack for coaxial cable, then you also need yet another adapter — commonly called a *75-ohm to 300-ohm antenna adapter*, as shown in Figure 17-8. Like the RF adapter, these are available at any electronics store.

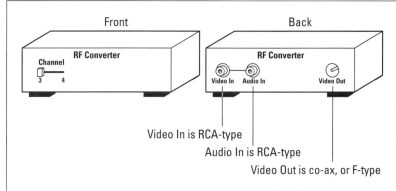

Figure 17-7:
A drawing
of a typical
RF
converter.

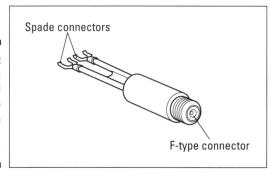

Figure 17-8:
A drawing
of a typical
75-ohm to
300-ohm
antenna
adapter.

Why the picture doesn't look as good

Even the most expensive scan converter models still don't make a TV display of a computer image look as sharp as it appears on a comparably sized computer monitor. The problem is largely with TV sets themselves. The picture tubes are not made as precisely as computer monitor picture tubes. And the way NTSC video is designed tends to blur color detail, while maintaining more precise black-and-white detail. Computer displays, by contrast, treat black-and-white and color information equally, resulting in a crisper image, especially when you view it from a close distance.

Another big problem with converting your computer image to the signal for a televison is *interlace* — a system developed back in the 1930s, when TV was just getting off the ground, as a simple way to make the picture tube not have to work as hard. All TVs are interlaced, but computer displays are almost always noninterlaced. *Interlace* simply describes the way the screen refreshes the image: If you imagine the screen as a series of lines from top to bottom, an *interlaced* screen refreshes first the odd-numbered lines, and then the even-numbered lines — the result is, the screen is actually refreshed only 50 percent each time the tube spits out a new image. On the other hand, a *noninterlaced* screen refreshes all the lines every time, resulting in the better and crisper resolution you get with computer monitors.

To deal with the conversion from noninterlaced computer VGA to interlaced TV screens, some inexpensive scan converters use just half the information from the computer signal, and repeat the same information for every two scan lines on the TV, thus reducing resolution even more. Better scan converters present the full detail of the computer's VGA signal on the TV, but this approach has a problem, too: fine horizontal lines appear to flicker, due to the way interlace works. Because of the differences in the technologies, you have no real way to get a regular TV set to have the sharpness of a computer display. Recognizing this problem, some TV manufacturers, including Toshiba and Zenith, offer big-screen TV sets that double as computer monitors with noninterlaced pictures. Rather than use scan converters, these TV sets/computer monitors actually switch between interlaced and noninterlaced operation.

Most scan converters offer a switch, usually labeled *sharpen* or *enhance*, that makes the image appear less fuzzy on the TV screen. The amount of improvement available from this switch is largely what gives the more expensive scan converters their higher price. On some units, the improvement may be negligible, or may even make the image look worse to some eyes. But overall, the difference between the cheapest and most expensive scan converters is surprisingly narrow. Yes, you do get what you pay for, but even the best models costing more than $1,000 are a disappointment when you compare them with a genuine computer display.

Sometimes you may need to use a scan converter to hook up to a projector system (described in the section "Using an LCD projector" later in this chapter). Say that you rent a nightclub for a company event, and the club has a video projector already installed. In all likelihood, the projector also accepts a direct feed from your computer's VGA port, but if it doesn't, you can use a scan converter to convert from VGA to regular video as a fuzzier-looking last resort.

Connecting to a television is easy if you follow these steps:

1. **To be on the safe side, make sure that all equipment (television, scan converter, and notebook computer) is turned off.**

2. **Get out your VGA cable and plug it into the VGA port in back of your notebook computer (refer to Figure 17-3).**

3. **Attach the scan converter to the other end of the VGA cable.**

   In all likelihood, the connectors match. In some rare cases, you may need a gender-changer adapter, available for about five dollars at any store that sells electronics or computer stuff, to convert a VGA plug to a jack or vice versa. Figure 17-1 shows a picture of such an adapter.

4. **Using an RCA phono plug cable or S-video connection (refer to Figure 17-6), connect the other end of the scan converter to the video-in jack on the television.**

   You may need to add an RF converter to this array to adapt the scan converter to the appropriate cable type for the television you are using. See the previous sections for more information.

5. **Turn on the notebook computer and the television.**

   If you're lucky, you see the boot-up process from your notebook on the CRT monitor.

If you run into any problems, read through the beginning of this section. You may need to adjust the display options, as described in the earlier section "Connecting and adjusting your computer to weird displays." If you don't get a display on your notebook's LCD screen as well as on the television, take a look at the "Displaying on two screens at once: simulscan" section earlier in this chapter.

Throwing the Computer Image on a Wall

Projecting your computer's image onto a wall has numerous advantages over the TV display approach I discuss in the previous sections. For one thing, the display is much bigger — suitable, in some cases, for an entire auditorium to view. And because projection display systems are designed from the ground up for computer signals, you see none of the fuzziness and flicker that characterizes scan converter images. The disadvantages, besides high cost, are that you must usually darken the room to get a good picture and that you must lug extra equipment around with you.

Quite a few projection options are now available for portable computers. They all have various pros and cons, as I describe later in this section. As far as connecting to displays such as the LCD projector, LCD panel, and CRT projector is concerned, however, they all work pretty much the same. Follow these basic steps:

1. **To be on the safe side, make sure that all equipment (projector or panel display, notebook computer, and so on) is turned off.**

2. **Get out your VGA cable and plug it into the VGA port in back of your notebook computer (refer to Figure 17-3).**

   In all likelihood, the connectors match. In some rare cases, you may need a gender-changer adapter, available for about five dollars at any store that sells electronics or computer stuff, to convert a VGA plug to a jack or vice versa. Figure 17-1 shows a picture of such an adapter.

3. **Connect the other end of the VGA cable into the appropriate VGA port on the projector or LCD panel.**

   You may in some cases need to obtain an adapter for BNC connections (discussed in the section "Projecting with CRT projection systems" later in this chapter). See Figure 18-6, in Chapter 18, to see what BNC connections look like.

4. **Turn on the notebook computer, projector or panel display, and overhead projector.**

   If you're lucky, you see the boot-up process from your notebook on the CRT monitor.

You may need to adjust the display options, described in the section titled "Connecting and adjusting your computer to weird displays," earlier in this chapter. If you don't get a display on your notebook as well as the projector, take a look at the section "Simulscan" earlier in this chapter.

Using an LCD projector

Weighing about 10 to 50 pounds and offering image size of anywhere from about 3 to 10 feet (measured diagonally), LCD projectors offer a lot of picture bang for the buck. Prices run from about $2,000 to as much as $10,000 (see the Appendix for a list of manufacturers; see Figure 17-9 for a typical model). LCD projectors are like the modern-day version of the slide projector or film projector, and as such, you need a semidark room, which may change how you do your presentation. Most LCD projector models hook up directly to your computer's VGA port, just like an external monitor. The least expensive projectors have only line video input and require a scan converter. Avoid these models whenever possible — they don't look as sharp as projectors with a built-in VGA input.

The advantage of the LCD projector is that you are almost completely self-contained, requiring only a standard movie screen, or even just a white wall, to project your presentation. The disadvantages are that they are fairly heavy (though far less so than a big-screen monitor or CRT projector), and that they are expensive.

LCD projectors are based on the same screen technology that's used in your notebook computer display. However, instead of illuminating the panel from behind, as on your notebook's display, LCD projectors pass light *through* the LCD color screen, and out a lens to create and focus a much larger image several feet away from the projector. The idea is almost identical to how a slide projector works, only the "slide" is an LCD display controlled by your computer. As with a slide projector, the further away the projector is from the screen or wall, the bigger the image is. Most projectors also feature a zoom lens, which lets you adjust the size of the projected image without moving it closer or further from the screen.

Figure 17-9: Sharp's XG-NV1U is an LCD projector capable of displaying both 800 x 600 SVGA resolution and 832 x 624 Macintosh resolution, with a screen size up to 300 inches (measured diagonally).

Remember that as the picture gets bigger, it also gets darker — take manu-facturers' claims of the largest possible screen size with a grain of salt. You may have to be in a completely dark room to see a decent-quality image at the maximum magnification. You can get an idea of how good the projector is at producing a bright enough image when you blow it up on a big screen by checking the amount of power its light bulb uses, measured in watts just like ordinary light bulbs. A 300-watt projector, for example, is brighter than a 100-watt model. Figure that a 250-watt bulb is typically enough to create a decent 100-inch (measured diagonally) image, and remember that this estimate depends a lot on the ambient room light (the darker the better), the efficiency of the projector itself, and the subjective decision of what constitutes an acceptable picture. If you are Batman and many of your friends are bats with poor eyesight, you can probably ignore the manufacturer's inflated claims.

You can always move the projector closer or adjust its zoom lens (if avail-able) to make the picture smaller, and thus make it brighter as well. Besides checking bulb wattage, most projectors are rated in their amount of light output, using units called *ANSI lumens*. A unit that produces 500 ANSI lumens has a brighter image than one with 200 ANSI lumens, for example. Very roughly speaking, a projector with a 250-watt bulb typically produces an image with a brightness of about 500 ANSI lumens.

Although the technology of the LCD screen used as the "slide" in LCD projectors is similar to your notebook computer, the screen inside is physically smaller. The screens don't have as many *pixels* (points of detail) as standard notebook computer display screens, so the resolution available from LCD projectors is often not as good as what you can get from a stan-dard notebook display screen.

Using an overhead projector and an LCD panel

If the presentation room has an overhead projector (the kind you can write on and use transparencies with), then an LCD projection panel offers an almost ideal way to display on a big screen. Projection panels are light-weight and easy to use.

Projection panels range in price from under $1,000 to over $5,000 (see the Appendix for manufacturers). The cheapest models are monochrome black-and-white. The most expensive models offer even higher resolution than your notebook's screen can display — as much as 1280 x 1040 pixels (dots of light), or even higher.

The projection panel, in essence, is like your notebook computer's LCD screen without the backlight. In fact, some innovative manufacturers have even made notebook computers with a detachable backlight on the LCD display so that the computer's own built-in screen can be used as a projection panel — that's the kind of stuff that makes guys like me grin. However, despite the obvious economy of this approach, most mobile computer users don't have such a computer and end up using a separate external display panel, which hooks up to the computer's VGA port just like an external monitor.

The overhead projector, shown in Figure 17-10, works by illuminating a transparent image (or LCD panel in this case), sitting on its glass table, from underneath. A pole extends up from the table, and a mirror/lens unit slides up and down along this pole. The size of the projected image grows bigger as you move the mirror/lens unit higher up the pole. A knob on the lens adjusts focus.

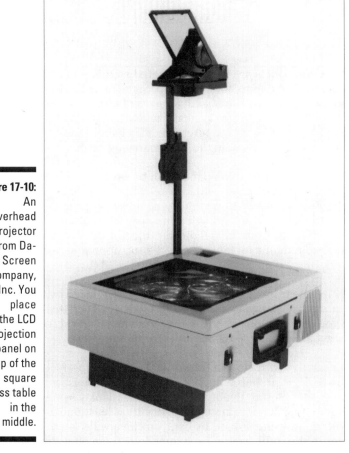

Figure 17-10:
An overhead projector from Da-Lite Screen Company, Inc. You place the LCD projection panel on top of the square glass table in the middle.

If you're familiar with using an overhead projector, you pretty much know how to use an LCD projection panel, as shown in Figure 17-11. You just place it on the projector table just like a transparency. The panel typically has only a contrast adjustment, making it very easy to set up.

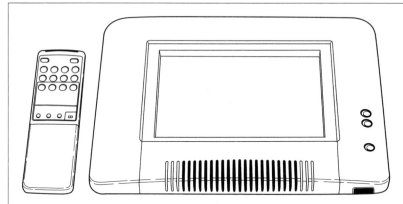

Figure 17-11:
A typical
LCD
projection
panel.

Some LCD projection panels are battery operated so that you need to mess only with a single VGA cable to hook them up. Some have built-in audio amplifiers and speakers, too. The big advantages of LCD projection panels are their weight and size — they're typically under five pounds and occupy less space than your notebook computer. You may even be able to fit your computer and a projection panel in the same carrying case.

Picture quality with LCD projection panels can be excellent, especially when you use a higher-resolution model with a notebook that is capable of putting out a high-resolution signal. The one thing you have to remember, and as every student who has ever sat through a transparency-enhanced college lecture knows, the image from the overhead projector can end up looking more like a trapezoid than a rectangle, with the top appearing wider than the bottom.

You can minimize the trapezoidal look of the projected image by raising the height of the projector and/or lowering the screen. However, the more you do, the more you end up blocking the audience's view of the screen with the projector — the Catch-22 of overhead projector technology.

As long as you can live with certain trapezoidal optical imperfections, the LCD projection panel is probably the best overall compromise among the price, portability, and picture quality of the various display systems. Most businesses, hotels, and schools are equipped with at least one overhead projector. If you're traveling around by car, you can always keep an emergency projector in the trunk, just in case they don't have one where you're visiting (they are kind of big, but are relatively cheap at just a few hundred dollars).

Projecting with CRT projection systems

The CRT (*Cathode Ray Tube*) projector, also sometimes called a *data-grade projector*, is the Rolls Royce of big screen computer display technology. CRT projectors are big, cumbersome, and expensive, but they produce the sharpest, brightest, most accurate pictures of any of the display technologies I discuss in this chapter.

If you've ever seen a two-piece (separate projector and screen) projection television system — such as the kind you see on an airplane or in a bar — then you're already familiar with the basics of CRT projectors. They have a separate picture tube for each of the primary colors of video — red, green, and blue.

Theoretically, you can project onto a white wall, but the quality of the image on a wall is a mismatch for the beautiful picture of the CRT projector. If you go through the hassle and expense of using a CRT projector, you want to use a professional movie screen with it. Often, the very places where you use a CRT projector come equipped with a screen — such as an auditorium or theater.

Not only are CRT projectors expensive (in the range of $5,000 to $20,000), big, and bulky (weighing 75 to 250 pounds), but they're also complicated to set up. Unlike LCD projectors and overhead projectors, which use a single source of light, the CRT projector has three sources of light — one for each color. Each projects its own image. Every time you move the projector or the screen, you must perform a tedious *convergence adjustment* to get the red, green, and blue images to perfectly align with each other. The more precise your alignment, the finer the image detail.

And because the CRT projector has three light sources, each with its own lens, these units usually do not have zoom lens systems. Without zoom, the size of the projected image is determined solely by the projector's distance from the screen. If you want the image to fill a particular screen, you have to precisely locate the projector a specific distance from it.

Despite these drawbacks, CRT projectors are the best choice whenever picture quality counts more than anything else. CRT projectors are commonly used for press conferences and similar events held by major corporations, for rock concerts, and in professional video installations. Most big cities have audio/visual rental houses that can rent you such a projector — often with the assistance of a technician to set it up — for a daily rate (typically a few hundred dollars). Many big hotels also have such projectors available for use in their grand ballrooms or auditoriums. Note that just about all data-grade projectors — those that have a VGA input port — are also capable of projecting regular TV-style video from a VCR. But the reverse is not true — that is, not all video projectors can also handle data without a scan converter (see the section "Hooking Your Notebook Up to a TV" earlier in this chapter if you find yourself in this situation).

Instead of or in addition to a VGA port, some data-grade projectors have separate *RGB (Red-Green-Blue)* connectors — that is, the projector has separate jacks for the red, green, and blue signals. Usually, when you buy or rent such a projector, it comes with an adapter cable that goes from this format to a standard VGA port, for connection to your computer. If not, VGA to RGB adapter cables are available from most high-end computer stores and from industrial audio/video dealers.

The RGB connectors found on projectors are usually a type of professional video hookup called *BNC connectors*. Push them in first, and then twist clockwise or counterclockwise, to connect or disconnect, respectively (see Figure 18-6 in Chapter 18).

A Light Valve Future?

Several dazzling new display technologies promise to expand your display options in the future. The science fiction dream of the screen you hang on a wall is already a reality, albeit a pricey one. Plasma displays look similar to backlit LCD panels, but plasma screens can be made much bigger than LCDs — already, screens as large as 40 inches are available, but they're currently very expensive (over $40,000).

Plasma display panels are not the kind of technology you want to carry on an airplane with you. They're not lightweight, but they are just a few inches thick, and literally hang on a wall just like a painting. In the future, such wall-mounted screens may become common in business and hotel meeting rooms. Just plug into a jack in the wall with your notebook computer, and a wall-sized presentation follows.

Light valves are another new technology offering great promise for projectors in the future. The light valve is similar to LCD technology, but is capable of providing much better contrast than LCDs, and can handle much greater amounts of light passing through it. Consequently, light valve displays can be made to look brighter and less washed out — images can have the same quality currently available from CRT projection systems, with less bulk and weight.

Chapter 18

Professional Touches for Your Road Show

*T*his chapter is dear to my heart because I have had to sit through more presentations than any sane person should — presentations are a minor occupational hazard of journalism. In this chapter, I hope to not just fill you in about some of the interesting gizmos and gadgets that you can use to make your presentations truly great, but to actually go further and inspire you to strive for excellence.

This chapter is really about the two essential ingredients for putting on professional presentations: the right accessory equipment and an *expect the unexpected* attitude.

The Wireless Mouse

If you deliver presentations to large groups of people, you may find yourself in situations where the place you need to stand when you speak is not right next to your notebook computer. Maybe your computer has to sit in the back of the room next to a CRT projector (see Chapter 17), but you prefer to speak from the front so your audience can see you. Problem: How do you advance through the slides in the presentation from so far away?

One solution is to bring along an assistant who can sit in the back or on the side of the room and operate the computer for you. Assistants are a luxury I highly recommend whenever possible — if the computer crashes or a cable gets disconnected by accident, you have someone to take care of things while you talk, dance, or tell jokes.

Unfortunately, life in the presentation fast lane is not always so sweet, and you most likely have to operate as a one-person show at least part of the time. You need some kind of accessory to control your notebook's pointing system from far away. You can hook up a trackball or other pointing system to your computer's serial port or keyboard/mouse port, and get a long 15- or 25-foot extension cord to connect it. But you know, a 25-foot cable may not even be long enough for some rooms, especially if you have to run it around rows of auditorium seating.

A wireless mouse provides a more elegant, less accident-prone solution. You have no cable stretching across the room for people to trip over. The Logitech *TrackMan Live*, for example, is a radio-based wireless trackball system that works at distances of up to 30 feet. The Mind Path *Pocket Point,* shown in Figure 18-1, uses infrared signals like a television remote control and works up to 50 feet, with an adapter, from your computer (12 feet without the adapter). The Mind Path Pocket Point provides remote control of the mouse as well as specially designated keyboard buttons, which can be used to trigger special effects via software that is included with the remote. An additional cool feature of the Pocket Point is that it has a built-in laser pointer that lets you bring attention to particular items on the screen while you deliver your presentation (assuming you are using a projection system). The Appendix has all the manufacturer contact information for these devices.

Figure 18-1:
The Mind
Path Pocket
Point.

Don't Forget the Sound

Most new notebook computers have audio speakers and a sound card to provide an audio accompaniment to your presentation. However, these built-in speakers are notoriously underpowered and often sound barely better than a tin can telephone you may have made when you were a kid. Even when you make a presentation to an audience of just one or two people, you do a disservice to your presentation's audio quality if you do not hook up external speakers.

External, powered speakers that plug in directly to your computer's audio output jack are widely available in computer stores. Some of the lower-powered units, with amplifiers in the ballpark of one to five watts per *channel,* can run off batteries. Most computer sound cards, and thus the audio output jack, are *stereo,* meaning that the left and right speakers have their own signal (channel) and produce more lifelike sound. Even these comparatively low-powered units are vastly better than most built-in speakers, and they typically cost under $30. External, powered speakers are appropriate if you need to set up very quickly and you are speaking to just a handful of people.

For larger groups, such as a classroom or board room filled with people, I recommend more powerful public-address-type systems or conventional stereo systems, with power output in the ballpark of 50 to 100 watts per channel, as I cover later in this section.

If your presentation incorporates music, consider hooking up a powered subwoofer as part of the system. Subwoofers are included in many top-of-the-line multimedia computer speaker systems, and they add quite a bit of bass (and thunderous impact) to the audio. Without the subwoofer, the main speakers by themselves usually sound slightly tinny, though still vastly better than the computer's built-in speakers. A subwoofer can really drive your points home.

Make no mistake about it — good powered speaker systems are big — much bigger than your computer. Yes, you can fit them in a suitcase, but the suitcase probably can't fit under your car seat. You may have to consider renting a system if you are flying to a presentation engagement. Unfortunately, speakers big enough to handle a decent-sized presentation don't exactly fit into the mobile computing style.

If your presentation is to just one or two people, headphones may offer a lightweight alternative to lugging big, heavy speakers. Get good-quality headphones, and bring along enough headphone extension cords and a Y-adapter splitter connection (so two headphones can plug into a single jack). Almost all headphones — even the cheapest ones — sound dramatically better than your computer's built-in speakers. However, headphones have a big disadvantage: They distance your audience from you — as if they are sealed off behind the audio equivalent of a glass wall. Furthermore, you don't really know how loud the sound in the headphones is and therefore can't gauge how loudly to speak in order to be heard over them. Headphones work best with self-running presentations that include their own narration, and are a particularly good choice if you're trying to get people to pay attention to your presentation in a noisy environment, such as a crowded trade-show exhibit area.

When you speak to groups bigger than classroom size, for example, more than about 25 or 30 people, consider using a microphone and public address system to amplify your voice. If you're already carrying powered audio speakers for your computer sound, you can mix in the signal from a tie-clip microphone. Some powered speaker systems include a second input jack and a mixer dial, just for this purpose — the mixer knob fades between two audio sources (in this case, the computer and your microphone). Alternatively, you can purchase a simple audio mixer, for under $100, that lets you combine the computer and microphone signals together. Visit a local music store or Radio Shack to find this stuff.

Some scan converters (used for hooking your computer up to a regular TV set — see Chapter 17) incorporate a microphone jack and mixer. Besides putting your computer picture on the TV, these scan converters also put the computer's sound, combined with a microphone, through the TV speakers, as demonstrated in Figure 18-2.

Note that even if your scan converter lacks this feature, you can always hook the computer's sound into the TV's line input jacks, by using an adapter cable (stereo mini plug to dual RCA phono plugs, as shown in Figure 18-3) available at any electronics store. You can then mix in a microphone if you add an accessory mixer.

For speaking to bigger crowds in auditoriums, gymnasiums, and open fields (outdoors), you need a real public address system with serious wattage. If you do lighting or computer graphics for concerts, you already know — a fat PA pumping out the block-rockin' beats always gets the attention of the CEOs. Hopefully, whoever invites you to speak in such a location has a PA system on hand. Hotel ballrooms usually have PA systems available for rental, along with technicians to operate them. If you wind up in a situation where you need to purchase your own, visit Radio Shack or a music supply store, or look under "Sound Systems & Equipment" in your local Business-to-Business Yellow Pages.

When you set up your own speaker and microphone system, always take care to place the speakers in between the place where you need to stand when you speak (typically the front of the room) and the audience, as shown in Figure 18-4. The speakers need to point toward the audience, away from you. This setup helps prevent feedback — that howling, screeching sound you hear when a microphone picks up the sound from the very same

Figure 18-2:
Using the
adapter
cable
shown in
Figure 18-3,
you can
feed the
sound from
your
notebook
computer
into a TV
monitor's
speakers.

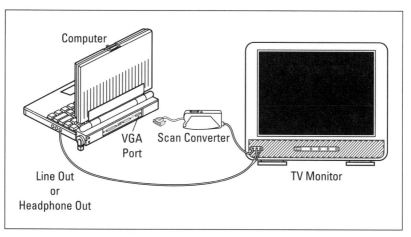

Figure 18-3:
This
adapter
cable is
useful for
numerous
hookups,
such as to
feed the
audio signal
from your
computer
into a TV
monitor.

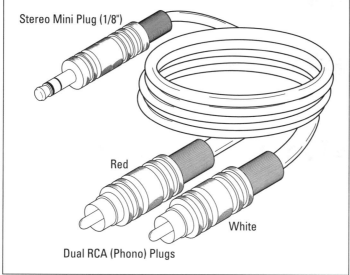

speakers to which it is delivering a signal. The best way to avoid feedback is to place the microphone and speakers so that they face opposite directions. If you hear feedback, lower the volume a bit until it stops.

Besides feedback, other more subtle audio problems can ruin your presentation, such as distortion and hum. I have seen presentations in which the voice of the person speaking sounded like an announcement in a New York City subway station. And lots of times the problem is really simple.

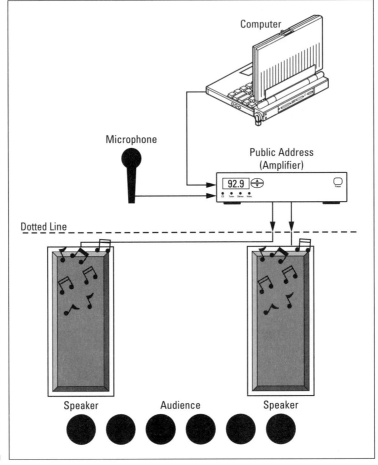

Figure 18-4:
When you set up a PA system, always position the audio speakers in between the microphone and the audience. If the microphone moves to the other side of the dotted line, you risk feedback.

- Distortion is usually caused by setting the microphone level on the mixer too high, and the master level (main volume) too low.

- A hum is often the result of a faulty cable, or a grounding problem — if your PA has a switch labeled *ground,* try flipping it to make the hum go away.

- If audio is an important part of your presentation, you may want to employ a technician who can take care of these matters. At the very least, a coworker or friend sitting in the audience to listen and trouble-shoot can be a big help. This person can let you know whether the sound is distorted or whether the picture is out of focus (and maybe even fix the problem).

Being Prepared

If you give presentations on any kind of regular basis, I'm sure that at one time or another, you've had one of those embarrassing moments when your system doesn't work or you flub lines. Even worse is if you prepare and rehearse, you know your presentation inside out, and you show up to meet your audience and realize that you can't run your presentation because you are missing a $1.95 adapter.

Cliff's recommended A/V kit bag

The exact extensions and accessories you need varies, depending on what type of equipment you use and the places you visit. If you reasonably expect to use scan converters, projectors, or hookups to other people's equipment, you may want to build a little kit bag of audio/video cables and adapters to carry along. I suggest this list:

✔ 15-foot AC extension cord

✔ a telephone extension cord

✔ VGA extension cable (if you're using a LCD projector)

✔ 15-foot phono plug (RCA-type, shown in Figure 18-5) to phono plug (RCA-type), three-wire cable with yellow/white/red audio/visual connectors

✔ 15-foot VGA male to VGA female extension cable

✔ 15-foot single phono plug (RCA-type) to single phono plug (RCA-type) cable

✔ 6-foot stereo sub-mini plug (1/8-inch phono) to dual phono (RCA-type) plugs cable

✔ 3 phono jack (RCA-type) to phono jack adapters (a.k.a. barrel style adapters)

✔ 2 phono jack (RCA-type) to 1/4-inch phone plug audio adapters

✔ 2 phono jack (RCA-type) to XLR plug audio adapters

✔ Phono jack (RCA) to BNC male video adapter, shown in Figure 18-6

✔ VGA female-to-female gender changer

✔ VGA male-to-male gender changer

Additional audio components for speaking through an amplifier:

✔ a tie clip microphone and microphone extension cable (an XLR-type microphone connector and extension cable are vastly preferable to reduce annoying hum), or wireless microphone system

✔ a small audio mixer to combine the computer's sound with your microphone

✔ an audio amplifier and speaker, or a powered speaker system, or a PA amplifier with built-in mixer

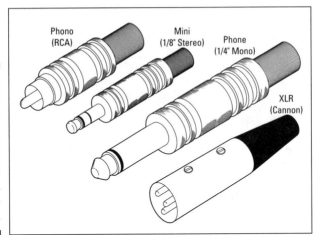

Figure 18-5: Common audio connectors. From left to right: phono (RCA), mini ($1/8$-inch), phone ($1/4$-inch), XLR.

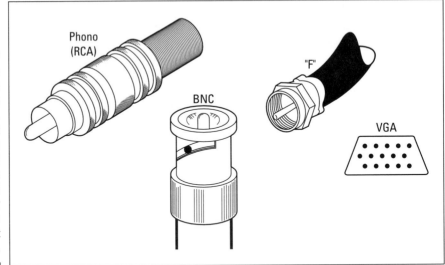

Figure 18-6: Common video connectors. From left to right: Phono, BNC and VGA (standard computer video output jack).

However, you can sidestep many problems if you take just a few precautions:

✔ **Disable the power management functions on your notebook computer while you run a presentation.** You don't want the computer going into suspend mode when you stop to answer a questions. (See Chapter 4 for more information about power management.)

✔ **Use your presentation as an accompaniment to your spoken presentation — not as a substitute.** In your speech, use slightly different words than what appear onscreen. In fact, I recommend using outlines notes rather than a word-for-word script. That way you can create a more sincere, authentic delivery.

✔ **In front of a live audience, rehearse your presentation — not only your speaking but also your use of the computer.** If you need to make the same presentation to different groups of people, schedule the first few meetings with smaller groups that are less important. Then tackle your biggest and most important audiences.

✔ **Be prepared to speak for a few minutes on the fly — in case your computer crashes or freezes.**

✔ **Pack a hardware kit bag.** Avoiding disaseters means carrying along some extra gear. See the sidebar "Cliff's recommended A/V kit bag" for a specific list of what to include in your bag.

Oops! Your Backup Plans

So many things can go wrong with presentations. That they ever run properly at all is a minor miracle. Consider the more mundane stuff, like when your battery goes dead and you can't get access to an AC plug, or when your computer crashes and when you boot up again, your presentation is corrupted and you can't access it. Then you have the video adapter you lose, the display that appears all scrambled for who knows what reason, the sound that comes out sounding like crud . . . you get the idea.

To deal with such emergency situations, and to get a good night's sleep the night before, you need to have a backup plan ready to spring into action in the event catastrophe strikes.

Videocassette

The easiest and cheapest backup plan is to record a videocassette showing the presentation and bring it along so you can play it on an ordinary VCR.

Do not pack this videocassette in your computer case — that way, if your computer is stolen, you still have your tape.

To make the videocassette, you need a scan converter to convert VGA (the computer signal) to NTSC video (standard U.S. video signal), as I explain in Chapter 17. Prices start at about $200. Follow these steps:

1. **Connect the VGA plug on the scan converter to the VGA port on your notebook computer.**

2. **Connect the video output from the scan converter to the line video input (usually a yellow-colored jack) on your VCR.**

3. **Using an adapter cable (usually a stereo $^1/_8$-inch mini plug to dual RCA-type phono plugs), connect the line audio output from your computer to the line audio inputs (usually colored white and red) on your VCR.**

   If your VCR has just a single white audio input jack, it is mono — just hook up one side of the stereo signal from the computer and leave the other disconnected.

4. **Select the Line Input on your VCR (if it has one).**

   Note that some VCRs have front and back line input jacks, usually labeled *L1* for the rear connectors and *L2* for the front.

5. **Set the VCR to the SP tape speed for best picture quality.**

6. **Put a blank videocassette in the VCR, press the record button as though you are about to tape a TV show, and start your presentation running on the computer.**

If your presentation is designed to run manually — with you clicking the mouse button to advance each slide — then you have to estimate the amount of time to wait before advancing slides as you record your emergency videocassette. If you normally speak through the presentation, try to speak just the way you normally do to time it, but I suggest adding about 20 percent as you proceed from slide to slide, to give you time to pause the tape to answer a quick question or make an additional point.

During playback of the emergency backup tape, you can pause it, if necessary, to take time to answer a question. However, remember that when you pause a videotape, the quality of the picture can vary tremendously, depending on the VCR. The cheapest two-head VCRs don't show a viewable image when paused — the screen is filled with static. Because you are probably dependent on whatever VCR happens to be lying around the place where your presentation goes awry, prepare for the worst — record the presentation with proper timing, and don't plan on using the VCR's pause button.

Incidentally, you may wonder why you shouldn't just record the presentation on a videocassette in the first place and save yourself the hassle of using the computer. Although a tape does make sense in a few instances, such as if you need to mail the presentation to someone, the picture quality on a VHS tape is markedly inferior to a computer screen, and the presentation does not look as sharp (see Chapter 17).

Backup computer

A backup computer is a bit extreme, and a bunch expensive, but for delivering a really important presentation in a situation where you won't get the opportunity to reschedule if things go wrong, you may consider having a copy of the entire presentation loaded and ready to run on a second notebook computer. Theoretically, for critical needs, you want a backup component for every single element in your presentation, including display devices and adapters, cables, power adapters, and so on.

Of course, most people putting on a presentation do not go to such extremes, but I feel it is my duty to explain this option as a way to be totally prepared. (And, along the same lines, don't just copy the final version of the presentation to the second backup computer — also run the presentation all the way through to be sure that it works properly.)

Backup software

Instead of bringing along a backup computer, you may consider bringing along a backup software copy of your presentation. That way, if you have some problem with your computer, you have a good chance of being able to still run the presentation on someone else's computer.

Besides the presentation itself, be sure to also pack a backup copy of whatever software you need to run the presentation, so you can install it on another computer if necessary.

Bringing backup copies of your presentation and software is time-consuming because every time you change the presentation, you must make an additional copy of it. Depending on how complex your presentation is and how often you change it, this procedure can range from a minor nuisance to a major hassle. If the presentation is too big to fit on a floppy disk, carrying a backup copy of it may require recording the presentation on a CD-ROM, or using a removable hard drive system, such as a Zip drive from Iomega, that you carry around with you.

Internet rescue

The Internet provides alternate approaches to maintaining a backup for your presentation. At the simplest level, you can have a new copy of the presentation e-mailed to you while you're on the road. If you're visiting an organization that has a *T-1* (a very fast type of data line) Internet connection, downloading a couple of megabytes takes just a minute or two; with a dial-up modem connection, it takes more like a half-hour.

You can e-mail a presentation to yourself, and then leave it on your mail server so that you can collect it in an emergency.

At a more sophisticated level, you can actually format the presentation as a series of Web pages. Then, when visiting a client or someone else you need to make a presentation to, you just connect to the Internet and navigate your way through your custom Web site.

The advantages of such a Web-based presentation are that numerous people in the same organization can all have quick access to the same information, without copying files over and over — making it perfect for presentations that you are constantly updating. However, if you access these pages live, while making the presentation, you are at the mercy of the Internet and whatever modem speed you can attain at the organization you're visiting. In addition, a presentation that is stored on the Internet is free for anyone to look at, so if your presentation contains confidential information, a Web site is probably not a good idea.

Your presentation appears faster if you save the Web site onto your hard drive and access the pages as files using your Web browser. Web-based presentations appear within the frame of a Web browser rather than completely filling the screen — a distracting disadvantage. (If you hire a multimedia producer, ask to run presentation software on top of your HTML Web pages to get around this problem and fill the entire screen.)

Part IV
Going to the
Next Level

The 5th Wave — By Rich Tennant

"YOU KNOW, IF WE CAN ALL KEEP THE TITTERING DOWN, I, FOR ONE, WOULD LIKE TO HEAR MORE ABOUT KEN'S NEW POINTING DEVICE FOR NOTEBOOKS."

In this part . . .

Here's where I cover some of the more advanced
things that you can do with your notebook computer. I help you deal with problems getting your modem
working (such as from a hotel room), and explain some of
the basics about connecting to wireless networks and
wireless radio systems. I also cover the expansion
capabilities that PCMCIA/PC Cards provide and wind up
with tips on the care and feeding of your computer, and a
look into the glorious future of mobile computing.

If you're ready to walk off into wild electronic yonder,
and join the ranks of the true mobile computing road
warriors, this part is your trusty sidekick.

Chapter 19

Problem Connections: Hotel Rooms, Office Phones, and International Calling

. . . .

In This Chapter

▶ Identifying problem phone situations, such as in hotels and offices

▶ Modifying configurations to adapt to new locations

▶ Dialing calls manually

▶ Gaining control over long distance billing

▶ Using acoustic couplers and other accessories

▶ Knowing when to give up and go swimming

. . . .

*Y*ou don't have to travel very far with your notebook computer before you encounter a problem telephone situation. The problem may be that you can't get to a phone jack in your hotel room, or if you can get to a jack, it doesn't seem to work right, or maybe you're in a foreign country and the jack looks like it's from another planet. In any case, you know that you want to connect to your online service or Internet Service Provider (ISP), but for some reason, you just can't get your modem to dial out.

This chapter helps you with all the problems you're most likely to encounter when you try to hook your computer modem up to unfamiliar phone lines, as well as offers advice on when to give up!

Scoping Out Your Phone Problem

Though you may sometimes find it tedious, with a bit of effort, you can overcome just about any difficult calling situation and establish your modem connection from just about any phone, anywhere in the world. In most cases, just a few minutes are all you need to figure out the problem.

Depending on how incompatible your computer is with the phone system you want to use, you may need an accessory product, such as an *acoustic coupler* or *handset jack adapter* (both are described later in this chapter), to solve the problem. In worst-case situations, you may spend hours trying a bunch of different dialing sequences.

The intricacies of getting connected when you travel vary, depending on the particular service you're trying to dial into, whether you're in a foreign country, whether a phone jack is available, and whether you're willing to pay extra for long distance calls. Each of these variables is discussed in more detail later in this chapter (also see Chapter 5 for details that relate particularly to modems and foreign travel). The first step is obviously to scope out your problem and try to figure out what is wrong so you can go about fixing it. As you work to figure out your modem connection, keep the following points in mind:

- **The status indicators that appear on your computer screen as you make a call provide useful information.** For example, if the software first gives you a message that says it's dialing and then you get an error message that says it detects no dial tone, then you probably don't have the phone line plugged in properly. Other possible problems that may arise which are indicated on screen are:

  - The number you're dialing is busy or doesn't answer

  - Your password or account name is invalid

  - Your modem is not responding.

- **Modem status lights, if your modem has them (or if your software provides them), are useful indications of modem problems.** The two most basic lights, SD and RD (*send data* and *receive data*), let you know when your modem is actually transferring information — or when it's sitting idle. When your modem is working, you see a flurry of flashes on each light as you send or download e-mail, Web pages, and so on. If neither light is on, you can bet that you have a modem problem. If only the send light is on, you may have a phone line problem.

- **Connecting to some office phone systems may permanently damage modems, so beware!** Read the section later in this chapter entitled, "Connecting to Office Phone Systems" before plugging your modem into an office telephone jack. (As I explain later in this chapter, special adapters called *acoustic couplers* and *handset jack adapters* can help you deal with this situation.)

- **Don't spend hours coaxing your computer to dial automatically, if instead, you can spend an extra 15 seconds dialing manually (see the "Manual dialing" section later in this chapter).**

When your modem seems to suddenly stop working properly and you get a "Modem not responding" error message even though it was working fine just a few minutes ago, try closing the applications you're working in and reboot the computer. Modems, more than most computer devices, seem to have a bit of the voodoo spirit and sometimes need to be reset. If you read Chapter 4, you may remember that I usually try to avoid turning my notebook computer off — instead, I suspend-to-disk whenever I'm finished working. Theoretically, I can go on working for weeks or months without ever turning the computer off, except for one problem — inevitably, my modem stops responding after a few days, and I have to reboot.

As you troubleshoot your modem situations and problems, here are some basic questions to keep in mind:

✔ **Is your modem properly installed, and is your software configured to work with it?** (See Chapters 5 and 23 for more on modems and PC card configuration, respectively.)

✔ **Is the phone line plugged in?** (Double-check all connections.)

✔ **At what point in the dialing sequence do things go awry — before dialing or after dialing?** (If things go awry before, the modem may be having problems detecting a dial tone, as I discuss later in this chapter in "Dialing without your modem.")

✔ **Do you hear the call go through and the computer on the other end pick up?** (If you do, then the problem is probably with your login information — it may simply be that you are incorrectly entering your account name and password.)

✔ **Do you need to add an area code when you travel out of your home area?** (See "Changing the area code to dial an online service long distance," later in this chapter.)

If you have problems making an online connection in a hotel room or other strange place, my first bit of wisdom is not to feel disgraced if you give up. If you're in a reasonably large city, you may find that visiting your hotel's business center or a local photocopy shop with computer access (such as Kinko's) is an attractive (and ultimately, speedier) alternative to spending time figuring out an alien phone connection. Besides, going to a business center or copy shop can turn out to be a fun social activity — you can mingle with all the other poor souls who can't seem to get their modems to dial properly.

Sending e-mail from such facilities is very easy. However, receiving e-mail using a business center may require almost as much work as trying to get the phone in your room to work with your computer because you have to enter your custom e-mail configuration information — see Chapter 10 for help with e-mail details.

Whenever you use someone else's computer to send e-mail — including friends, associates, and copy shop computers — the recipient does not see your name as the sender. Instead, the name of your friend, or the name of the copy shop appears (assuming you don't reconfigure anything). So put your name in the subject field of the e-mail, to identify it. For example, if I were sending e-mail from a friend's house, I may type in the subject field something like **From Cliff Roth — Let's meet next week.** Then be sure and remind the person you send the message to that he or she should respond to your usual e-mail address unless you are going to continue using your friend's e-mail for a while.

Dialing In from Who Knows Where

When you travel outside your home area code, you need to enter a new local number for your online service or ISP (Internet Service Provider), or set your computer up so that it can dial a long distance call.

Suppose that you rent an apartment, or stay in someone's home, and you want to check your e-mail every now and then. Because you probably only need to be online for a few minutes at a time, and the cost of each long distance call to check e-mail may be a dollar or two at most, you may not find that tracking down a local number for your e-mail connection is worth the effort. Instead, you may just want to instruct your modem to make a long distance call (rather than figure out the local call), and dial into the same number you usually use.

On the other hand, if you're calling into an online service like AOL, CompuServe, or Prodigy from a reasonably big city, you can almost certainly use a local access number and avoid long-distance telephone charges. In fact, changing numbers with online services can be very easy, as I describe in the next few sections.

Changing the area code to dial an online service long distance

The exact steps you need to follow to change the call from local to long distance depends on which online service you use. You usually find the menu you need listed under something like Preferences, Setup, or Connection. Find the spot in the appropriate menu where you enter the local access number, and add the area code for this number — not where you're located now; rather, enter the area code for the location of your online service number (it's probably the same as your home area code).

For ISPs (Internet Service Providers), you usually enter connection information in the "Dial Up Networking" portion of Windows 95 (see "Changing Phone Numbers for Direct Internet (ISP) Accounts" later in this chapter).

✔ Do not add the 1 prefix before the area code — just about all dialing programs automatically insert the 1 before the area code and number (*exception:* AOL — see "Adding an area code with America Online," later in this chapter).

✔ If you find an area code already entered in the appropriate spot, but the dialing software keeps omitting the area code and dialing the call as if it's local, then you're in a special case: Somewhere else within the software you are using, you have told the software what your local area code is — in other words, the area code of the city or town where you are based. Whenever this software sees that the area code it needs to dial is the same as your home area code, it cleverly skips past the area code information — as it should, if you are actually dialing from the same area code. However, now that you are traveling, you must find the place where you told the software what your home base area code is, and change it to reflect the new area code you are in. Then try dialing the call again.

✔ If you get stuck trying to get an area code to work, you may be able to trick the software into dialing the area code by simply inserting the area code numbers just before the phone number. In this case, you also need to insert the number 1 first, because you're fooling the modem into thinking it's making a local call (albeit, a strange, 10-digit local call).

Adding an area code to the access number in CompuServe

If you use CompuServe, for example, here are the specific steps to follow for CompuServe's standard online service software (WinCIM version 3.0.1 for Windows 95 — by the way, *CIM* stands for *CompuServe Information Manager*):

1. **Launch CompuServe by double-clicking on the CompuServe icon on your desktop.**

   The CompuServe window pops up.

2. **Choose Access⇨Preferences.**

   The Preferences dialog box appears.

3. **Click the Connection tab.**

4. **Click Configure Phone (near the bottom of screen).**

   The CS3 Connection dialog box graces your screen.

5. **Insert the area code (usually your home area code if you are trying to dial CompuServe long-distance) in the Area Code field that's located under Phone Number.**

   If this field appears to be inaccessible (gray), click the box that says Use country code and area code, and make sure that Country code is set to United States of America (1) — which is the default (see Figure 19-1).

6. **Click OK to close the CS3 Connection dialog box.**

7. **Click OK to close the Preferences dialog box.**

8. **Click Access⇨Connect to dial the new number you just entered (with area code).**

Adding an area code with America Online

To add an area code in AOL, follow these steps:

1. **Launch the AOL software by double-clicking the AOL icon on your desktop.**

   The America Online Welcome dialog box pops up.

Figure 19-1:
The CS3 Connection is CompuServe's own installation of Dial-Up Networking. Click the box shown here with a check mark, to add an area code when you leave your hometown.

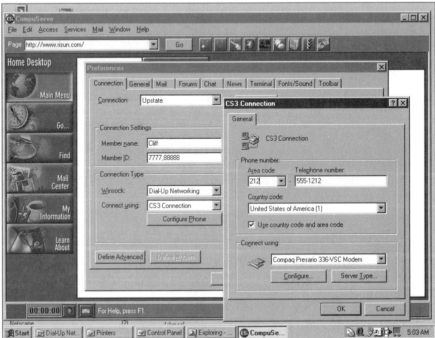

2. Click Setup in the Welcome window that first appears. (Do *not* click Sign On, as you ordinarily would.)

The Network & Modem Setup dialog box appears.

3. Click Edit Location.

The Network Setup dialog box appears.

4. In the column that says First Try, **find the field that says** Phone Number, **and type in the number** 1 **followed by the area code to the left of the phone number that's already there (as I do with** 1-212- **in Figure 19-2). Note that the phone number under First Try in the figure has had 1+area code added, but not the phone number under Second Try.**

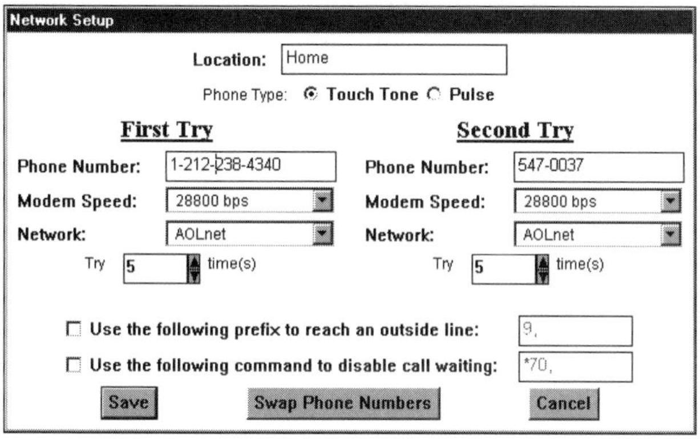

Figure 19-2:
AOL's
access
number
setup
screen.

5. Enter the maximum modem speed you can use to connect.

You may have to take a look at your modem instructions, or click Start⇨Control Panel, and then double-click the modems icon to find this information out.

6. Enter the network that you use to access AOL — the default setting, AOLNet is correct for most domestic access numbers provided by AOL.

In cases where you are not using AOLNet, you are so informed when you look up the access numbers online, or when the customer service representative tells you over the phone which numbers are available for a particular area code.

7. Repeat Steps 4 through 6 for the phone number you want to be the alternate number in the column labeled Second Try.

8. Click Save to save the settings and close the Network Setup dialog box.

9. **Click OK to close the Network & Modem Setup dialog box.**

   You go back to the Welcome dialog box.

10. **Click Sign On to dial using your new phone numbers.**

Switching to a local access number

The best way to get local (and thus cheaper) access numbers for places you plan to visit is to go online and get them prior to your departure. Okay, so this effort may require a bit more advanced preparation than some people — especially those people (like me) whose travels begin with a last-minute frenzy of activities — care to make. However, if you are serious about saving money with your out-of-town online connections, getting local access numbers is the way to go. With CompuServe, for example, you can get them from the Customer Services area. With America Online, enter the keyword **Phones** for domestic numbers, or **International Access** for cities outside your home country.

Of course, if you are less of a planner, you can get local access numbers after travels begin: Go online for the first call using your long distance access number (see previous section for help), and then look up a local number to use from that point on.

You can also call the online service's customer support number to obtain local access numbers (see the sidebar "Customer service numbers" later in this chapter). However, beware of the customer service numbers — they are notorious for their slow response, and as the online world continues to explode, you can expect these lines to remain rather busy.

This chapter assumes that you already have your computer configured to access an online service or the Internet from your hometown, and you need to change the information because you're traveling. For instructions on setting up access to these services for the first time, see Chapter 11.

Maintaining multiple access numbers

The setup menus for some services, such as CompuServe, take the possibility of travel into account and allow you to enter several different sets of dialing routines. I leave my CompuServe account set up with two dialing procedures — one I call *Local,* and the other *Long distance* (not very original names, but effective nonetheless). I live in New York City so that's my local connection. I use the long distance version to call the same number (New York area code) anytime I'm in a different area code.

Customer service numbers

Here are the U.S. customer service numbers for several major online services and ISPs. By calling these numbers, you can obtain local access numbers for the areas you're visiting. If no local phone number is available, you can ask for the toll-free 1-800 access numbers that most online services offer, but note that surcharges always apply for toll-free access. I realize that sounds weird — the *call* is free, meaning your online service pays for the call as far as the phone company is concerned, but then your online service happily passes on their 1-800 number phone bill to you.

For internationally accessible online services such as CompuServe and AOL, the customer service numbers for locations outside the U.S.

(as well as the domestic numbers listed here) are available from the Help menus, by entering customer service in the Index.

✔ America Online: 800-827-6364

✔ AT&T WorldNet: 800-967-5363

✔ CompuServe: 800-848-8990

✔ Microsoft Network: 800-336-3375

✔ MCI Internet: 800-955-5210

✔ Prodigy: 800-213-0992

✔ PSINet: 800-827-7482

Calls to 1-800 numbers are available toll-free only within the US.

Maintaining multiple access numbers in CompuServe

Follow these steps to create a new set of connection info in CompuServe (these instructions are for WinCIM version 3.0.1):

1. **Launch CompuServe the usual way, by double-clicking its icon on your desktop.**

   The familiar CompuServe program starts.

2. **Choose Access⇨Preferences.**

   The Preferences dialog box appears with numerous tabs along the top.

3. **Click the Connection tab if it is not already selected.**

4. **Click Add near the top of this panel.**

   The New Session Name dialog box appears.

5. **Enter a New Session Name in the field that appears (such as** Long distance connection, New York, **or** Harry s House **— the name should reflect the location where you plan to use this new connection info).**

6. **Click OK.**

7. **Your new connection initially has the same settings as your usual connection. To change the phone number, click Configure _P_hone.**

   A new dialog box appears with the name of the new connection listed on top.

8. **Change the numbers in the Telephone number and A_r_ea Code fields as needed.**

   Note: If the Area Code field is unavailable because the call was previously in the same area code that you were dialing from, click the box next to Use country code and area code so that a check mark appears.

9. **Click OK to close the Connection dialog box.**

10. **Click OK to close the Preferences dialog box.**

    Your new connection info is saved under the new name that you created in Step 5.

11. **Choose _A_ccess⇨_C_onnect to dial into the new number you've entered.**

Maintaining multiple access numbers in America Online

Adding a new phone number in America Online (Version 3.0) can be a bit confusing because you only have the option *before* you log on. After you're using AOL, you can't add or change phone setups. Follow these steps:

1. **Launch the AOL software by double-clicking the AOL icon on your desktop.**

   The America Online Welcome dialog box pops up.

2. **Click Setup in the Welcome window that first appears. (Do *not* click Sign On, as you ordinarily would.)**

   The Network & Modem Setup dialog box appears.

3. **Click Create Location.**

   The Network Setup dialog box appears.

4. **In the Location edit box, enter the name of your new location.**

   It can be Harry s House, New York, or Middle of Nowhere — so long as you can remember it.

5. **In the column that says First Try, find the field that says Phone Number, and type in the number of your new location. Be sure to include a 1 followed by the area code to the left of the phone number that's already there (as I do with 1-212- in Figure 19-2) if you need to make the number long distance.**

6. **Enter the maximum modem speed you can use to connect.**

   You may have to take a look at your modem instructions, or click Start⇨Control Panel, and then double-click the modems icon to find out this information.

7. **Enter the network that you use to access AOL — the default setting, AOLNet is correct for most domestic access numbers provided by AOL.**

   In cases where you are not using AOLNet, you are so informed when you look up the access numbers online, or when the customer service representative tells you over the phone which numbers are available for a particular area code.

8. **Repeat Steps 5 through 7 for the phone number you want to be the alternate number in the column labeled** Second Try.

9. **Click Save to save the settings and close the Network Setup dialog box.**

10. **Click OK to close the Network & Modem Setup dialog box.**

    You go back to the Welcome dialog box.

11. **Click Sign On to dial using your new phone numbers.**

Sometimes you may find that dialing into a different state is less expensive (because of more competitive interstate long-distance rates) than dialing an in-state number. So many different calling plans are available for interstate long distance and regional long distance that the only way to really know which call is the cheapest is to call your local telephone company and your long distance phone companies, and get the rates for the different options that are available to you. Remember, the time of day or night that you make the call is also a factor.

Changing Phone Numbers for Direct Internet (ISP) Accounts

If you get your e-mail through an Internet Service Provider (ISP) rather than an online service, your decision about paying for a long distance call versus finding a local access number, as with online services, depends on how much time you spend online in each place you expect to visit.

Note that your browser program — such as Netscape Navigator or Internet Explorer — is not where you enter your dial-up information, even though for some people the Windows 95 Dialer gets activated when you click on them. Ditto for e-mail programs such as Eudora or Microsoft Exchange. If you connect to an ISP and you run Windows 95, you change the phone number in Dial-Up Networking.

Windows 95 Dial-Up Networking

If you use Windows 95, the place to change the access number for your Internet Service Provider is in the Dial-Up Networking menu, which you get to by following these steps:

1. **Choose Start⇨Programs⇨Accessories⇨Dial-Up Networking.**

   The Dial-Up Networking window appears with various icons listed.

2. **Click the icon for your ISP so that it appears highlighted.**

   Note: When you do not already have Dial-Up Networking set up, the only icon you see may be Make New Connection. In this case, see Chapter 11 for information on how to set up Dial-Up Networking for the first time.

3. **Choose File⇨Properties.**

   A new dialog box (with the same title as the icon you selected) appears.

4. **Change the phone number information in the Telephone number field.**

5. **If you need to add an area code to what was previously a local number, click the box next to Use country code and area code, so that a check mark appears, as shown back in Figure 19-1.**

6. **Click OK to save your new settings.**

7. **Double-click the icon for the connection you just changed, to launch the dialer with the new number.**

My advice, as with online services, is to bite the bullet and pay for long distance charges if your total usage will only be a few dollars' worth over the course of your travels — but of course, this decision ultimately depends on how well you can afford the extra long distance charges, and how many times you need to go in and change the phone number. Then again, with the excellent help I give you in this book, changing your phone number is a breeze now, right?

Instead of following the procedures described earlier in this section to *permanently* change the phone number, you have a much easier way to *temporarily* change the phone number. Just launch the Windows 95 dialer program the same way you usually do:

1. **Double-click the Dialer icon for your ISP on your desktop, or double-click the Dial-Up Networking icon for your ISP after choosing Start⇨Programs⇨Accessories⇨Dial-Up Networking.**

   A dialog box pops up that shows the phone number the dialer is about to call.

2. **Simply modify the information in the Phone number field to whatever new number you want.**

    You can add a 1 and an area code, or a new local number — whatever you want.

3. **Click Connect.**

    The dialer uses this new temporary phone number for this particular call, but the next time you launch the dialer, it reverts back to the old phone number.

Finding a local ISP access number

Switching to a local access number in order to save long distance charges when you are out of town is impossible if your ISP is of the Mom-and-Pop variety — that is, a local operation with services only in your hometown.

However, if you sign up with one of the big nationwide services, such as the AT&T WorldNet Service, PSINet, or Network MCI, then you can probably find a local access number in most big cities you visit. Call the customer service number for your ISP to obtain local access numbers outside your home area. (See the sidebar earlier in this chapter for specific numbers to call to find a local access number.)

What if you can't find a local access number for your service, but you really don't want to run up a phone bill on the phone line you're using? You can use your calling card to bill the call elsewhere, but it requires making special adjustments to your dialing software, and you may have to resort to manual dialing techniques (see the "Calling card dialing" and "Manual dialing" sections later in this chapter).

Making Modem Calls from a Hotel Room

Making a modem phone call through hotel telephone systems can be tedious and frustrating, but if you expect to do a lot of traveling with your laptop, it's a skill worth mastering. Every hotel poses a different set of challenges. If you travel enough, you soon begin to recognize common themes, such as having no phone jack available, strange dial tones that the modem doesn't recognize, and the need to dial special prefix codes to get an outside line. I discuss these problems in more detail in the next several sections.

Getting an outside line (8 and 9 prefixes)

Assuming that

- ✔ your hotel room has a phone jack you can plug into (if it doesn't, see "Connecting without an Available Jack: Acoustic Couplers" later in this chapter), and

- ✔ you're willing to bill the calls to your room (you may be talking serious money here),

the procedure for getting access to your online service or ISP may be as easy as just changing the access number (see "Changing Phone Numbers for Direct Internet (ISP) Accounts," earlier in this chapter), with one additional step: Most setup menus have a field where you can enter a number for *prefix* or *outside line* — in most hotels and many businesses, the prefix is 8 or 9.

Going long distance (1 and 0 prefixes)

Typically, the hotel dialing sequence also requires the number 1 for long distance, as in this case:

```
8+1+(area code)+XXX-XXXX
```

This hotel requires an 8 to get an outside line, and then 1 + the area code and phone number.

With most software, you don't need to add the 1 before dialing a long distance number, because the dialing software inserts a 1 automatically whenever an area code is being used.

Some hotels require you to dial 0, even though the call is not going through an operator, as in:

```
9+0+(area code)+XXX-XXXX
```

In this hotel, you need to dial a 9 to get the outside line, and then 0 + the area code and phone number. You may be able to add the 0 to the dialing sequence in the Dialing Prefix area, or you may simply insert the 0 just before the phone number in the dialing software (in the Phone number field in the Connect To panel of the Windows 95 dialer, for example).

You may want to add one or more commas after the number 8 or 9 , to delay the modem slightly before proceeding with dialing out. Add commas if you notice that when you make a regular voice call, you have to wait a second or two after you press the 8 or 9 before you actually hear the outside line dial tone. Each comma you add creates a pause of about two seconds. As an example, your final phone number configuration may look like this:

8,,1-212-555-1212

Calling card dialing

Some dialing software, including Windows 95 Dial-Up Networking, lets you automatically dial the codes you need for many types of charge card calls, including major brand-name calling card services such as AT&T and MCI, and the credit card services of several foreign telephone systems such as British Telecom. Not all dialing software has this feature, however, and when it is available, the software has to know the exact service you want to use because each calling card service works a bit differently. The software may also not work properly when you dial out from a hotel because of the other tricks you often have to pull with those phone systems, such as speaking with an operator to place a call. In these instances, you need to dial manually, as I explain in the next section.

To take advantage of the automated calling card dialing in Windows 95, follow these steps:

1. **Double-click the icon for your Internet Service Provider to launch the Windows Dialer.**

   The Connect To dialog box appears. (Do not click Connect, the way you usually do.)

2. **Click D̲ial Properties.**

   The Dialing Properties dialog box appears, with a tab that says My Locations on top, as shown in Figure 19-3.

3. **Click the box next to Dial using Calling Card, or click C̲hange if you already had the Dial using Calling Card selected, and you now want to change your calling card information.**

   The Change Calling Card dialog box appears.

4. **Scroll through the list to the right of Calling Card to use, by clicking on the arrow to the right, and select the type of card you want to use.**

   Numerous telephone companies and dialing methods are listed, as shown in Figure 19-4. Note that the major long distance companies (AT&T, MCI, Sprint) each offer several different methods of dialing, including dialing prefixes and 800 number access.

Figure 19-3:
The Dial
using
Calling Card
option is in
the middle
of the
Dialing
Properties
dialog box.

Figure 19-4:
The
Change
Calling Card
panel in
Windows 95
Dial-Up
Networking.

5. **Enter your calling card number in the Calling Card number edit box.**

6. **Click OK to close the Change Calling Card panel and save your changes.**

7. **Click OK to close the Dialing Properties panel.**

8. **Click Connect at the bottom of the remaining Connect To panel to initiate your calling card call.**

Manual dialing

Sometimes, you just can't get your modem to automatically dial a number from your hotel room. All long distance calls may go through an operator, for example. In such cases, you need to dial out manually.

Anytime you spend more than a few minutes unsuccessfully trying to dial out automatically, you may want to also consider switching to the manual approach (unless you're a masochist!). Although not technically the most elegant method, manual dialing has several advantages:

- ✔ You can bill long distance calls to a charge card account even when automated charge card dialing doesn't work (see previous section).

- ✔ You can talk to operators (Oh Boy!) as needed.

- ✔ You can hear what's going on, for example, if you're even getting a dial tone, or if the line is too noisy, which may help you troubleshoot problems.

In order to manually dial, you need to have both the telephone and the modem plugged in at the same time. You probably need a *two-way phone jack coupler* to accomplish this (check out Chapter 25 for a picture of a two-way phone jack coupler), unless you have two phone jacks in the room (very unlikely).

Dialing without your modem

Even the most computer-phobic people already know how to dial manually: Just pick up the phone and place the call as you'd like to, billing it to a credit card number if you choose. What you need to do to get your computer in on the action is this: When you hear the line ringing on the other end, jump into action and tell your computer to talk to the modem on the other end of the phone line that answers the call.

If you're lucky, you may be able to just initiate the automatic dialing process the same way you usually do — even though you actually did the dialing manually — thus tricking the modem into thinking that it made the call: You hear the modem trying to dial out (over the ringing that's already taking place), and then when the call is answered, the modem proceeds with the usual *handshake* (see Chapter 5). Hang up the extension phone at this point, and pray.

Usually, when you dial manually and then instruct the modem to proceed with the call, the modem refuses to try to dial out, because it does not hear a dial tone, and you get a No Dial Tone error message. The solution, in the case of most online services, is to go into the setup area and disable the *dial tone detect* function. Essentially you're trying to fool the modem into think-ing that it's still doing the dialing, even though you're doing it manually. Note that the ability to disable dial tone detect resides in the software you use, not in the modem itself. All modems have the ability to detect dial tone, and to ignore this information when so instructed.

Disabling dial tone detect in Windows 95

If you need to dial manually to connect to an Internet Service Provider (ISP) or smaller online service while using Windows 95, follow this procedure to disable the dial tone detect feature:

1. **Choose Start⇨ Settings⇨Control Panel.**

   The Control Panel pops up.

2. **In the Control Panel, double-click the Modems icon.**

   The Modems Properties dialog box pops up.

3. **Click the General tab.**

4. **Select the modem you are using in the box labeled** The following modems are set up on this computer.

5. **Click Properties.**

   The Properties dialog box for the modem you selected appears.

6. **Click the Connection tab.**

7. **Find the box labeled** Wait for dial tone before dialing. **Click this box to remove the check mark, or press Alt+W.**

8. **You may also want to disable or extend the time-out on the next item, "Cancel the call if not connected within XX seconds." You can, for example, give yourself five minutes (300 seconds) to allow enough time for a complex call to go through several operators, or you can disable the time-out entirely.**

9. **Click OK to save your settings.**

10. **Click Close in the Modems Properties dialog box.**

11. **Close the Control Panel.**

What if I can't disable dial tone detect?

If you can't disable the dial tone detect feature (such as with AOL version 3.0), you may need to do some fancy footwork, but where there's a will there's a way. First, I assume you're in the U.S. or a country that uses a similar dial tone. In this case, your goal is to manipulate things so that, at the right point, the modem hears the dial tone — even though it may not actually do the dialing.

The key is to tell the modem to start dialing at the moment when, in the sequence of dialing out manually, you hear the normal outside line dial tone (not the hotel dial tone, if it sounds different). If the local phone system seems to ignore your modem's attempts to dial out, then fine. Simply proceed with manual dialing, and try to get the connection to go through before the modem's time-out setting kicks in. (If the modem gets no answer within a certain amount of time, usually about 30 seconds, the computer usually tries the call again a minute later.)

Creating delays with commas

If your modem's attempts to dial out interfere with the manual dialing, then you want to delay the modem's efforts until *after* you put the call through manually. You can try using commas to accomplish this. You can type in commas at the very beginning of your modem's dialing sequence and create a delay between the dial tone detect and the modem's attempt to dial out. See the tip in "Going long distance (1 and 0 prefixes)," earlier in this chapter, for more information on using commas.

Faking it

If you're traveling in a foreign country that uses a different dial tone, or if you must place calls through a hotel operator in such a way that you never hear a dial tone, and you can't disable the dial tone detect feature, then you simply have the biggest headache on the planet. Honestly, my advice in this situation is to switch to an online service or to modem software that lets you disable the dial tone detect feature. However, in an extreme pinch — and this method really is a bit extreme — you still have a way to fool the modem into thinking it has a dial tone: You can supply your own! You can actually make a recording of a dial tone from just about any phone line in the U.S. and then play it back when you're overseas so that the modem hears it and thinks it can dial out.

The best way to make such a recording, on a cassette, is with a phone answering machine. Just about everyone has heard a dial tone on their answering machine when someone hangs up. Such an accident can provide a useful recording — the modem needs only to hear the tone for a fraction of a second to begin dialing. You can use a portable cassette player with built-in speaker, or one side of a set of headphones to play the dial tone into the telephone's mouthpiece. Wacky, but it works.

Connecting without an Available Jack: Acoustic Couplers

Just as no serious backpacker would go anywhere without a pocketknife, there is one portable modem accessory device that no serious mobile computing enthusiast should travel without. This device is called the *acoustic coupler,* and it is the backup plan that always gets you connected when *all else fails*.

In the early days of modems, back in the 1960s, telephone jacks were unheard of. In fact, the entire U.S. phone system was run by a single company, and making any electrical connection to it was strictly forbidden, verboten, prohibido, no way. To get around that restriction, the earliest modems used what is called an *acoustic coupler* to send and receive the audio signals through the telephone's own microphone and speaker. Modems looked like large boxes with rubber cups for the mouth- and ear-piece of standard 1960s phones.

Without getting overly technical here, the fact that the modem's signal can be converted to audio tones and sent through a microphone and speaker is very useful if you travel with a laptop computer. The audio signal used by telephones is, in essence, a universal language that can make it across virtually any telephone system anywhere in the world.

The acoustic coupler is the device that makes all this possible. Thankfully, acoustic couplers have come down in size (as has everything else electronic), so you don't need to carry a giant box with obscene rubber cups sticking out of it. Basically, the modern acoustic coupler is an assembly consisting of a microphone and speaker that strap on to a telephone handset, so that the coupler's microphone picks up sound from the phone's speaker, and vice versa. The acoustic coupler then connects to your modem through the standard phone jack.

Whereas the original acoustic couplers of the 1960s were about the size of a tissue box and weighed several pounds, their modern-day counterparts are incredibly compact and lightweight. Most attach to the handset with Velcro straps around the top and bottom, and are considerably smaller than the handset to which they attach. The Telecoupler adapter from CP+, and the Kōnexx Koupler from Unlimited Systems shown in Figure 19-5, are among the most well known portable acoustic couplers.

If the phone line you're hooking up to has tone dialing, you can use the acoustic coupler to dial out, too. However, if you get a busy signal, you have to hang the phone up manually to redial. If the phone line has only pulse dialing (clicks instead of tones when you press a number), you have to do all your dialing manually when you use an acoustic coupler.

✔ With most phone systems, after about 20 seconds, you lose the opportunity to dial out — the dial tone disappears, and you must hang up or press the Flash button to get a new dial tone. After spending the time it takes to hook up an acoustic coupler, you usually have to manually hang up the phone and then take it off the hook again to get a new dial tone. If the phone has a modular plug, you may find it easier to just momentarily unplug the phone from the wall outlet to hang up.

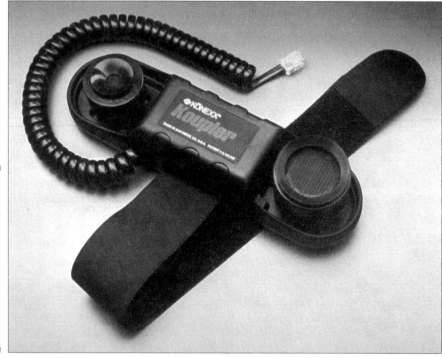

Figure 19-5:
The Kōnexx Koupler from Unlimited Systems is battery-powered, and weighs less than one pound.

✔ Acoustic couplers usually provide the only way to use your computer's modem with a pay telephone. If you're traveling on a budget, you may find that making calls from a phone booth is much less expensive than going through a hotel operator, or maybe the room you're staying in has no phone. Because acoustic couplers are rather obscure accessory products, purchase one before you take off if even a small chance exists that you may need it.

Connecting to Office Phone Systems

Beware of office phone systems! Some office telephones hook up using exactly the same jacks and plugs that you see in regular residential phone systems and computer modems, but the signals that office phones use are completely different. In many cases, they are *digital*, not *analog* (like regular home phone lines), and they sometimes use voltages much higher than regular phone connections. As a consequence, plugging into such a phone jack can actually destroy some modems. Pzzzsstt — good-bye.

Fortunately, most newer modems have been designed to protect against this calamity, so when you plug them into an office phone jack, they don't fry. However, they don't work, either.

You have two ways around this problem: Use an *acoustic coupler,* such as I describe in the previous section, or use a special *handset jack adapter*.

Handset jack adapters are designed to plug into the jack where the *handset* (that part you actually speak into) of the office telephone connects to the body of the phone — not the regular phone line jack in the wall. Then, you can plug the handset back into the handset jack adapter so it is still connected to the phone body through the adapter. The adapter then has a standard phone jack (called RJ11 in phone parlance) on the adapter for your modem. The result is a *pass-through* connection for your phone handset, and a standard phone jack for your modem so you can leave both (handset and modem) connected at the same time.

A handset jack adapter can also be useful for plugging into hotel telephones, or multiline analog telephones, as well as digital office phones. They cost about $150 — the most well known manufacturers are Kōnexx and TT Systems. Figure 19-6 shows an example. The Kōnexx Mobile Konnector is a small switch adapts it to four different types of office and hotel telephone systems. The adapter is battery-powered and weighs less than half a pound.

Modem operation with either of these types of adapters — acoustic coupler or handset jack adapter — is usually more cumbersome than with a direct phone line connection, because you need to hang up manually. With digital office phone systems and either adapter, you probably also have to dial out manually.

Connecting on an Airplane

Airplanes equipped with older telephone systems require the use of an acoustic adapter as I describe in the previous section, but many newer airplane phones feature a telephone jack just so you can plug in your computer's modem. You may need to provide your own telephone plug, so fly prepared.

Of course, the rates for these airplane phone calls are pretty steep — typically upwards of a dollar per minute, so getting on the Net just to read the online version of the Wall Street Journal can get rather expensive (especially if you can get the print copy on your flight). When you need to send e-mail, you save a bundle by doing all your writing offline, accumulating all your messages in your e-mail software's Out Box, and then sending all the messages at once (see Chapter 12). Similarly, when you retrieve e-mail from an airplane phone, dial in, pick up your mail, and then immediately disconnect the phone connection and read your mail offline.

Figure 19-6:
The Kōnexx
Mobile
Konnector
from
Unlimited
Systems.

In some rare cases, especially when dealing with older e-mail systems, this approach may be impossible because the e-mail resides on the server and doesn't actually get transferred to your computer. Similarly, when you use remote access software to look at the screen of your desktop machine as I explain in Chapter 13, for example, if you need to gain access to an office e-mail system that is not connected to the Internet and has no dial-up access, you are stuck spending some serious (and expensive) time on the airplane phone. (In this case, my only money-saving advice is to become a fast reader.)

To make matters worse, you may need to limit your modem's speed to get it to work reliably on an airplane telephone system. You can usually do so in the setup menu for the dialer program you use. As a last resort, with online services such as America Online, you can try changing the access phone number to a line that you know is limited to a slower speed (when you look up these access numbers, the modem speed is usually listed, too).

Learning to Listen

You benefit by listening for the different telephone signals if you often find yourself in difficult phone situations. In particular, pay attention to the following:

- ✔ **Internal *PBX* dial tones, such as in hotel and office phone systems, sound different from outside line dial tones.** Learn to tell the difference. (PBX stands for *Private Branch Exchange*, meaning that the phone system has an internal switchboard as well as connects to the outside world.)

- ✔ **Fast-paced busy signals usually indicate that the phone company's lines are busy, not the specific number you're trying to dial.** You are likely to get this kind of busy signal in rural areas or immediately following a natural disaster as everyone tries to reach their relatives.

- ✔ **Noise on a phone line slows down your modem communications, and in the worst case may get you disconnected.** If you hear a lot of static, and/or clicking in the background whenever you use the phone line for ordinary voice calls, beware when using your computer. With noisy lines, you may need to manually set the modem to operate at a slower rate in order to get reliable communications.

- ✔ **If you have the option, set your modem to turn the speaker off only *after* the connection is established.** That way, you are able to hear your modem as it dials out, connects, and handshakes with your online service's or ISP's modem. Both modems and fax machines have a characteristic exchange that you can listen to and get to know. Then, when something goes awry, you may be able to hear at what point things don't sound the same. You may hear, for example, if the device answering the phone seems to be a modem or fax machine, or perhaps nothing at all.

In some European countries, a system of pulses is used to meter telephone usage. When you hear periodic clicks on the phone line every minute or two, you are probably on such a system. Sometime these pulses interrupt data, or in the worst case, cause your modem to disconnect. You can purchase a special filter from PowerExpress (1-800-Batteries) called the Telefilter to eliminate modem problems from these pulses.

Giving Up

Let me tell you as one who has been there, a point exists at which you should simply give up. Send a floppy disk via an overnight express courier. Make a phone call to a friend or coworker. Consider using your computer's fax capability (see Chapter 14 for more info) if you have that working — if not, consider using the hotel's fax service or a local photocopy shop. Or visit a hi-tech copy shop, such as Kinko's, that offers online access using their own computers for an hourly rate. You may even try a cyber-café (hmm, that may be a more fun and sociable experience than spending hours fidgeting with modem settings alone in your hotel room!). Set a time limit for your troubleshooting attempts, and then give up and go take a swim in the heated hotel pool!

Chapter 20

The Office Network (LAN)

*I*f you work out of an office that has a computer network, or LAN for short, you may have times when you want to hook your notebook computer up to the network. Maybe your company has hired more people than it has computer workstations (hey, good thinking, boss!), and therefore decides to use a notebook as a new workstation for a short while. Or perhaps your company's network is *not* connected to the Internet, and the only way for you to receive e-mail is by logging on to the Local Area Network (LAN).

Before I go any further with this discussion, I want to point out that if you don't have a very specific need to connect to a LAN, and instead simply need to copy files from one computer to another, you have an easier and less expensive option. Linking software, for example LapLink, which I cover in Chapter 9, connects your notebook computer to a desktop computer for file transfers and *synchronization*. (Synchronization allows you to bring files like address books up to date on two computers.)

Furthermore, if you connect your notebook computer and your desktop machine with linking software, and your desktop machine is already on your office network, you can transfer just about anything on the network over to your notebook computer and vice versa. That way, you spare yourself the trouble of connecting the notebook up to the network with its own network adapter and all the resulting configuration hullabaloo.

This chapter is worth reading only if you really need to access the company network directly from your notebook computer — for instance, if you don't have a desktop machine or if you need to interact with other employees while working from your notebook computer.

What Is a LAN, Anyway?

LAN stands for *Local Area Network,* and most people in an office that uses one just refer to it as *the network,* kind of like how New Yorkers often refer to their town as *The City.* Prior to the rise of the Internet and online services, local networks were pretty much the only computer networks out there (in most business offices, that is — the Internet actually goes back to the 1970s for the U.S. defense industry).

Understanding what a network does is quite simple: A *network* is nothing more than a connection between two or more computers. Whenever you hook your notebook or palmtop computer up to your desktop machine, in the simplest sense, you create a two-computer network. Office computer networks typically link anywhere from a handful to several hundred different computers together.

The purpose of an office network is to allow coworkers to share the same files so that several people can have access to them at once. The network facilitates sending e-mail and documents around the office.

If your office network (LAN) is connected to the Internet, every computer on that network then has access to the Internet — you can browse the Web and send e-mail around the world. In fact, in the early days of the Internet — before all the home users started logging in — it was commonly referred to as the *network of networks* for this very reason. (See Chapter 11 for more about the Internet and how it is especially useful for mobile computer users.)

Today, many networks at businesses and schools are connected to the Internet via high-speed phone lines, such as the *T1 line,* which can send and receive data at over one million bits per second — that's 30 times faster than a typical telephone modem. I mention all this techno-stuff because one of the reasons you may want to connect your notebook machine to a local network is to take advantage of faster Internet access.

Just as you can think of your computer as consisting of two essential ingredients — hardware and software — a computer network is comprised of the wires themselves and the network operating software that makes everything happen. *Ethernet* — a technology originally developed by Xerox — is by far the most commonly used network hardware, with IBM-developed *Token Ring* running a distant second. Novell's NetWare and Microsoft's Window NT Server are the most popular network operating systems. Other systems you may hear about include AppleTalk (Apple-only networks), Banyan Vines, IBM OS/2 LAN Server, and Artisoft LANtastic.

✔ **Peer-to-peer networks.** Some local networks (LANs) are simply a bunch of computers tied together, with no single computer operating as the center of it all. Peer-to-peer networks are common in small offices where perhaps two to five computers are linked together with a printer.

When you connect your notebook to such a network, you become another peer — in addition to being able to use the printer, you can send and receive e-mail, and may have access to files on some of the other computers on the network.

✔ **Client-server networks.** Most larger office networks, connecting a half-dozen or more computers, have a special additional computer, called the *server,* whose purpose is to act as the centerpiece of the network — a hub to which the various *clients* (connected computers, sometimes called workstations) are attached. The server is where the shared files, and other resources (such as the network's Internet connection) are located. This type of network is called *client-server* — when you hook your notebook computer into this type of office network, your notebook machine becomes another client on the network.

✔ **Intranets.** Over the past couple of years, a new type of office network called an *intranet* has been gaining popularity, and many experts predict that eventually, almost all office networks will be intranets. An intranet is an office network that uses the same standards as the internet to move data around and has shared files accessible via HTML-compatible (HTML stands for Hypertext Markup Language — it is the language used to create Web pages) Web pages that can be viewed using a standard Web browser. The big advantage of an intranet over an ordinary local network is that users don't have to learn a separate system of commands to navigate the office network — the intranet and internet are both accessible using the same Web browser and e-mail programs. Technically speaking, the intranet is a form of a LAN. The difference between an intranet and a regular LAN is in what you do after you log into the network — the same general principles of *connecting* to the network with your notebook computer apply, regardless of how the network is organized.

Gaining Access to the Network (Your Network Administrator Can Help)

Just as every tribe has a chief, every computer network has a *network administrator.* In small businesses, the network administrator may just be the most computer-savvy (and perhaps unlucky) person in the office. In bigger businesses, running the network(s) is a full-time job. You are unlikely to be able to tie into an office network without first talking to (bribing) the network administrator — with one exception, which I explain in a moment.

The network administrator is usually in charge of getting new jacks (called *nodes* by network administrators — see "Finding a jack" later in this chapter) installed. If you need to hook into the network on a regular basis, try to have a node put in just for your notebook so you don't have to scrounge up a connection each time you need one.

The network administrator can also help you configure your notebook and *Ethernet card* (see "The Ethernet card" later in this chapter) to access the network, if you have any problems.

In order to log onto most networks, you need to be recognized by the system with a *username* that identifies you and a *password* that makes sure that you are you. The network administrator sets up an *account* with a username and password for each person or computer that wants to connect. Just as a network you dial into, America Online for example, has a separate account for each user, so too do local networks. A system of accounts with usernames and passwords helps provide security to prevent unauthorized access to files.

Note that the account and the node are two different things. After the system administrator sets up your notebook computer with a username, you can plug in anywhere you have a free jack (node). Similarly, in most network situations, you can enter your username and password to access your network account from any computer that is physically connected to a node.

The one way that you may be able to get a network connection on your own, without having to get help from the network administrator, is if you have a jack available, and already have a username and password to use. For example, if you also have your own desktop computer at the office and you disconnect the desktop machine from the network in order to use your notebook on the network, you should have no problem connecting with the same setup as you have for your desktop machine.

Network administrators in the wild

In this age of computer viruses, networks are kind of like hospitals that need a certain layer of insulation to keep out danger. If a network administrator doesn't want to help you tie your notebook computer into the system, that reluctance may be out of fear that you may — even unwittingly — introduce a virus. Some computer systems administrators may even frown on installing your own software — they consider each computer in the network to be one of their babies. In this context, your innocent-looking notebook computer may represent a real wild card.

The most courteous and professional way to approach the situation is to seek out the help of the network administrator or one of his/her assistants, at the very beginning, before you try monkeying around on your own.

Finding a jack

The connection to a LAN usually looks very similar to a phone jack, except that it's slightly larger (see Figure 20-1). In tech jargon, this type of jack is called an *RJ-45,* whereas a regular telephone jack is an *RJ-11.*

Figure 20-1:
The
Ethernet
network
jack looks
like an
ordinary
phone jack.

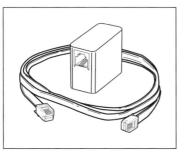

Unlike telephone jacks, with these Ethernet jacks (or other LAN jacks) you cannot just hook up a two-way splitter to create a new extension for your notebook computer. You must plug into an existing jack that's not being used. In tech parlance, each network jack is called a *node* and has a specific address on the network. Finding a node to connect to may be the biggest problem you face when trying to plug into a network.

Some networks are built with extra nodes, just for people like you who need occasional access. However, extra nodes cost money, and if a company does not have a specific use for them in mind, it usually builds its network with the same number of nodes as it has computers to hook up to the network.

If you're scavenging to find a jack to connect to in an office, find out whether anyone is out for the day (sick or away) or if anyone will be leaving early.

Installing the Ethernet card

The *Ethernet adapter card* is the hardware you usually need to connect your notebook computer to an office network. Costing about $100, these cards look just like modem cards and other PCMCIA cards — they plug into a standard PCMCIA slot found on most notebook computers. You can find models from numerous manufacturers, just like modems, and some models called *combi-cards* actually incorporate both Ethernet and fax/modem functions into a single card — a good idea if you spend time on both an office network and a phone line. (PCMCIA/PC cards are covered in more detail in Chapter 22.)

Note that Ethernet is currently the most popular network technology in the U.S. (you can see one in Figure 20-2), but competitors exist, including *Token Ring, ARCnet,* and *AppleTalk* (for Macs, of course). Each of these systems requires its own special network adapter card. When people speak of a *network card,* generically, they're almost always assuming it's Ethernet, but don't take this detail for granted — check with your network administrator if you're not sure. Instead of the RJ-45 jack, some networks use a different type of jack, called a BNC jack, and round coaxial cable instead of the flat telephone-type cable. Some Ethernet adapter cards come with special adapters for these types of connections.

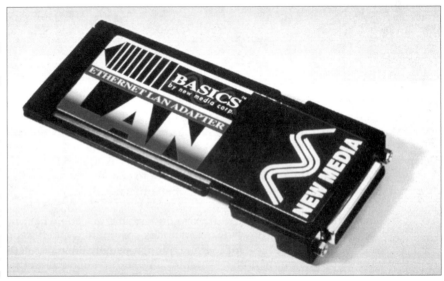

Figure 20-2:
An Ethernet adapter like this LAN card provides the interface between your notebook computer and a local network.

Before purchasing a network adapter card for your notebook computer, check with your network administrator to verify that you are indeed getting the right type of card.

Ask your network administrator whether he or she would prefer for you to get any particular brand or model of card. Getting a card that the network administrator is already familiar with is well worth a few extra dollars. When you're buying the card in a store, they all seem pretty much alike, but the right brand may mean all the difference between having a network administrator who is happy to configure the card for you or being left on your own to figure it out for yourself.

Besides getting an account (username and password) for your computer on the network, you also have to get your computer to accept the connection to the network. You first need to configure your LAN adapter card properly and then make sure that you have the right network operating system software installed.

Often, the network administrator is the person to do the configuring for you. Configuring a computer to connect to a LAN can be fairly detailed, and if someone is around to do it for you quickly and painlessly, by all means, accept the help.

If you don't have a network administrator to help you and you feel dangerous, read on: In Windows 95, as soon as you plug the Ethernet adapter card into your notebook, you get a message saying `New Hardware Detected`, and you are led through the installation process automatically. If this doesn't happen, you may have to install the necessary information manually, by selecting your particular card model from a list that Windows 95 already has, or by installing it from a floppy disk supplied by the card's manufacturer. In the worst case, if the computer still doesn't seem to talk to the card, you may have to resolve a conflict between the Ethernet card and another device in your computer — see Chapter 22 for more info.

To install the card manually, follow these steps:

1. **Choose Start⇨Settings⇨Control Panel.**

2. **Double-click Network.**

   The Network dialog box appears.

3. **Click the Configuration tab near the top of the Network dialog box.**

4. **Click Add.**

   The Select Network Component dialog box appears.

5. **Click Adapter, and then click Add.**

   The Select Network Adapter dialog box appears.

6. **Select the brand of adapter card you're installing in the Manufacturers list, and select the model in the Network Adapters list; or click Have Disk if you don't see the model you need and you got the necessary driver software from the card manufacturer.**

   If you select Have Disk, the Install From Disk dialog box pops up. **Place the disk in the floppy drive and select the file, usually** `SETUP.EXE` **or** `INSTALL.EXE`.

7. **Click OK.**

   You return to the Select Network Adapter dialog box.

8. **Click OK.**

   You see the card listed in the `The following network components are installed` list box under the Configuration tab.

9. **Click OK to close the Select Network Component dialog box.**

   At this point, the files needed for your card are copied and installed — the process may take several seconds. (***Note:*** During this process, you may be warned of a Version Conflict — meaning that the installation is about to copy an older version of a file. Usually you want to keep your existing version of the file.) After installation is complete, you receive a System Settings Change message prompting you to restart (reboot) your computer in order for the new settings to take effect.

10. Click <u>Y</u>es to reboot.

When a notebook computer recognizes a PCMCIA card, such as a LAN card, and it's configured properly, you hear two short beeps.

Getting your computer to recognize the network

Besides establishing the computer's connection to the card, you have to install the necessary network operating system software. You can find out which software you need by asking your network administrator or by looking in your or someone else's desktop computer to see which network operating system is installed there, and then matching the configuration in your notebook (see Figure 20-3).

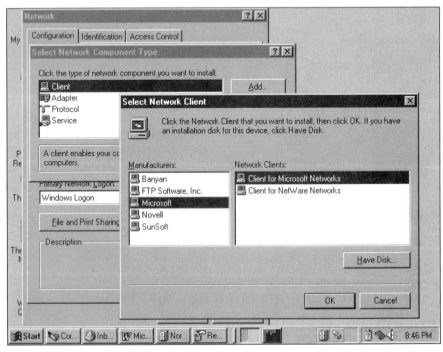

Figure 20-3: The client software you install in Windows 95 must match the network operating system that the network uses.

Follow these steps for installing network software in Windows 95:

1. **Choose Start⇨Settings⇨Control Panel.**

2. **Double-click the Network icon.**

   The Network dialog box appears.

3. **Click the Configuration tab, and look for installed components in the** The following network components are installed **list box.**

   If you see an item named "Client for [name of manufacturer] Network" where the [name of manufacturer] is the software your network administrator told you that you need, click Cancel to close the Network dialog box. You've installed the correct software.

   If the correct client software is not listed, you need to install it. Follow the remaining steps.

4. **Click Add.**

   The Select Network Component Type dialog box appears.

5. **ClickClient, and then click Add.**

   The Select Network Client dialog box appears.

6. **Select the manufacturer of the client you're installing in the Manufacturers list, and select the specific program in the Network Clients list; or click Have Disk if you've don't see the software you need and you have the necessary driver software from the manufacturer.**

   If you select Have Disk, the Install From Disk dialog box pops up. **Place the disk in the floppy drive and select the file, usually** SETUP.EXE **or** INSTALL.EXE

7. **Click OK.**

   You return to the Select Network Client dialog box.

8. **Click OK.**

   You return to the Select Network Component Type dialog box and you see the Client you selected in the The following network components are installed dialog box.

9. **Click OK to close the Select Network Component dialog box.**

   At this point, the actual installation begins, and you see a bar graph showing the progress of the file copying process. (*Note:* During this process, you may be warned of a Version Conflict — meaning that the installation is about to copy an older version of a file. Usually you want to keep your existing version of the file.) After installation is complete, you receive a System Settings Change message prompting you to restart (reboot) your computer in order for the new settings to take effect.

10. **Click Yes to reboot.**

After you think that you have a network connection, you can check to see that it works. In Windows 95, use Windows Explorer (Start➪Programs➪ Windows Explorer). Double-click Network Neighborhood to see what resources are available. Note that you sometimes don't have access to the network's central facilities, or to other people's computers, for security reasons.

Remote Networking

One instance where you can hook up to your company's network without the use of an Ethernet adapter card (see "The Ethernet card" section earlier in this chapter for details) is by dialing in from home or from a hotel room. In order to pull this little caper off, your company's network has to have special phone numbers set up for network *clients* such as yourself to call. Then, when you log onto the system, you are connected to the network at the office as though you are there, with one big exception. . . If you are used to the speed of the network when you are at work, you find a phone connection painfully slow for things like Web pages and file downloads.

Many network administrators do not like to set up dial-up network access because computer hackers typically break into the system through the phone lines to steal secrets and wreak havoc. If all you need the network for is to check e-mail, you may be able to do it via the Internet — see Chapter 10 for more about picking up e-mail over the Internet.

If your local network does not have direct dial-up access and you have a desktop computer that is permanently connected to the network, you can still gain access to the network by installing your own *remote computing software* on your desktop machine, and leaving it turned on all the time. I explain remote computing software in Chapter 13 — note that you also need a modem for your desktop machine, and a phone line to the office.

Chapter 21

Look Ma, No Wires!

*W*ireless communications let you send and receive e-mail from just about anywhere. You can connect while in a car or send a fax while stuck in traffic (hopefully someone else is driving!). You can send and receive e-mail while visiting clients, without having to bother with a phone line. And the options you have for connecting without wires are almost as numerous as the various situations where a wireless connection may come in handy.

Broadly speaking, wireless communications for portable computers come in two general forms: radio or cellular systems, and infrared light (IrDA) systems. Infrared systems are best for local connections within a defined space, such as to another nearby computer or a local area network (LAN). In Chapter 9, I tell you all you need to know to use IrDA connections for hooking up to another computer for file transfers, and in this chapter, I cover using an IrDA system to connect to a local area network. Radio systems, while also useful for local area networks, are most known for letting you connect to your e-mail or the Internet from remote areas and over distance, much as a cellular phone allows you to place phone calls where no phones are available.

One more thing to remember as you read this chapter is that a *cell* in cellular phone technology refers to a portion of a total covered area. For instance, if you live in a large urban area, that area is divided into *cells,* each with its own transmitter/receiver to handle cellular phone calls. As you drive around with your cellular phone, you are "handed off" from one cell to the next — this is how cellular phones get their name, and it is also why you sometimes experience short breaks in service as you are "handed off."

Dividing an area like this allows thousands of cellular phones, each like their own miniature radio station, to coexist over a wide area — at any given time, you are only competing for radio bandwidth with the other cell phones in your current cell.

Cellular Phones and Modems

Cellular phone technology is probably the most prevalent and basic form of wireless communication. And in addition to voice, any cellular phone can also be used to provide standard modem communication (both fax and data) from a laptop or notebook computer. All you need is a cellular phone with a modem connection or an acoustic coupler (an acoustic coupler is basically a strap-on ear and mouth for your modem so that it can do its thing through a telephone handset, as I explain in Chapter 19). With a cellular setup, you can connect to online services, the Internet, or your desktop computer from anywhere you can get cellular service.

However, keep in mind that the maximum data rate (for raw, uncompressed data) is typically around 9600 bits per second (bps), and the actual rate that you get may be considerably less.

Ideally, you have a special, proprietary adapter you can use to hook your modem up to your cell phone. The modem normally expects to connect to a telephone jack, and these adapters, in essence, fool the modem into thinking that connecting to your cell phone is business as usual. Each cellular phone manufacturer builds a slightly different jack into the phone for these modem adapters, so you must buy the exact unit that's designed for your particular phone.

- ✔ You typically get the most reliable, hassle-free cell phone modem hookups when you use a modem and cell phone from the same brand.

- ✔ If your cell phone has no special modem jack, then you can use the acoustic coupler, as I describe in Chapter 19. Note that a direct connection to the phone is always preferable to acoustic coupling and usually produces faster data speeds and better automated dialing features.

- ✔ Be sure that your modem incorporates the *MNP 10 protocol* in its arsenal of tricks. MNP 10 is a special modem protocol (you can think of a protocol as a language the devices use to talk to each other) that has been designed to improve performance in modem-cellular telephone connections. (I go into more detail on modem standards in Chapter 5.)

MNP 10 is designed to handle the frequent noise and signal dropouts that you get with cellular phones by creating smaller *packets* of data than you find with other modem protocols. (The packet size is significant because if even a slight error occurs, the entire packet needs to be repeated — if an error occurs with every second or third packet, the modem spends more time repeating information and less time sending new stuff with large packets.) On the other end of the connection, just about all major online services and Internet Service Providers install modems with MNP 10 capability.

Improving your modem speed with Modem Access

Just as MNP 10 can tweak the connection between your modem and your online service, some cellular phone service providers have tweaked their systems, adding a feature called *Modem Access* to maximize modem performance over their cellular networks. If your cellular telephone service provider has Modem Access (or something similar), you can improve upon your regular cellular data rate by about 50 percent with no additional hardware investment. All you have to do is dial a special number prior to placing the regular cellular phone call.

The number is usually *DATA (*3282). Just dial these four numbers, and then dial your ISP or online service phone number exactly as you normally do. With most cell phone companies, you still get billed at the standard voice call rates, with the advantage that your maximum data rate typically increases to 14,400 bps from the usual 9,600 bps.

CDPD

Suppose that your organization operates a fleet of vehicles that you want to tie together in a network for sending messages, creating a corporate intranet, or looking up information in databases. A special, more advanced form of cellular modem communications, called *CDPD* or *Cellular Digital Packet Data,* is available from many cellular telephone service providers specifically for this purpose. Developed by IBM and a consortium of cellular carriers, CDPD allows mobile subscribers to send data over the existing cellular voice network without interfering with voice communications. CDPD breaks data into packets and sends them over cellular voice channels during channel idle times (the brief pauses in normal voice conversations). CDPD has a transmission rate of 19,200 bps — double what you can get with a plain cellular phone connection.

Because CDPD essentially squeezes data into a more efficient use of the existing cellular spectrum, the cost of sending data can be priced lower than if you send data over a voice channel (even though you're using exactly the same frequencies). CDPD uses extensive *channel hopping,* meaning that it switches frequencies almost constantly to keep data moving in between bursts of voice information.

However, CDPD has a couple of catches:

- ✔ CDPD cellular modems work only in areas that are equipped with CDPD capability — generally large urban centers.
- ✔ CDPD is not a dial-up type of service — it is intended to provide the appearance and feeling of a continuously available online connection. The system is ideally suited for package pickup/delivery companies, vehicle tracking, credit card verification, and other applications in which the time spent dialing into a network tends to slow the process down, and you want to keep all computers on the network connected pretty much all the time.

To find out whether CDPD service is available in your area, call your local cellular phone providers. The actual hardware and software you need to get CDPD is available from third-party companies such as Software Corporation of America (see the Appendix) — but be forewarned, setting up your own CDPD network can be a hefty investment involving tens of thousands of dollars for the server base station and about $500 for each mobile client. Unless you're setting up a big network, your best bet is to try to find a local reseller of CDPD service at a substantially lower cost than setting up, running, and maintaining your own CDPD network.

The Motorola Personal Messenger 100C Wireless Modem Card (see Figure 21-1 for a similar model) is probably the best known PCMCIA/PC card that is dedicated specifically to accessing CDPD. You can use it to access the RadioMail wireless e-mail service (see "ARDIS," a subsequent section in this chapter), or to access an Internet service provider offering CDPD service in your area. Some of the radio data modems, described in the "Mobile Radio" section later in this chapter, can also provide access to CDPD cellular service.

CDPD service is harder to find than the ARDIS and RAM systems that I cover later in this chapter.

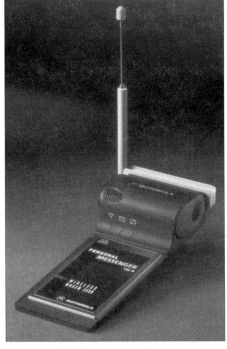

Figure 21-1:
The
Motorola
Personal
Messenger
100D
Wireless
Modem
Card.

PCS: Personal Communications Service

PCS, or *Personal Communications Service,* is a wireless communications technology that is commonly known for offering low-cost, cellular-type telephone service. Of course, as with all cellular services, you can get it only in areas where a company has decided that a market exists. PCS is the same technology behind some two-way wireless paging and information services (such as interactive stock quotes and news services), and can also be used for wireless voice mail, wireless e-mail, and wireless Web surfing.

The advantage of two-way paging is that with a two-way pager, you can notify the person who paged you that you received the page. Also, pages are never lost because the pager tells the paging system when it actually receives the page signal — with one-way paging systems, if you are out of range of an incoming page signal, the page simply disappears into thin air.

PCS telephones and computer transmitter/receivers are lower-powered than standard cellular, which combined with PCS's higher frequencies, means that the area covered by each cell site is smaller — PCS is sometimes referred to as *microcellular* technology. The main disadvantage, from a user's standpoint, is that PCS connections cannot be relied upon when traveling at speeds above around 30 mph — if you're checking your e-mail while riding a bullet train, for example, a traditional cellular phone connection proves more reliable.

But compared with cellular, PCS has one big advantage: PCS phone service is less expensive than cellular telephone service, and so for mobile computer users, it makes all your data and fax activities that much cheaper, while offering comparable data rates (typically 9600 bps).

PCS radio channels are also used in some two-way paging services, such as SkyTel. By hooking up a two-way pager to your notebook computer, you can convert it into a more sophisticated two-way e-mail system — so goes the reasoning behind Motorola's Mariner PCMCIA/PC Card. This card works as a modem/fax/LAN (Local Area Network) adapter that includes an interface for connecting to Motorola's Tango two-way pagers. The Tango pager works with SkyTel service to provide wireless two-way e-mail.

A similar pair of SkyTel-compatible pager service products is offered by Nokia. The Nokia PCS Data Card, in conjunction with the Nokia 2190 digital PCS phone, offers SkyTel access to just about any laptop or notebook computer (it's similar to the Motorola Mariner-Tango combination except that you have a phone, rather than a pager, as the transmitter device).

The Motorola and Nokia products represent the first generation, and I expect that PCMCIA/PC cards with built-in PCS radio transceivers (similar to the radio data devices described in "Mobile Radio," later in this chapter) will soon follow.

SkyTel (a paging service offered by Mtel — see the Appendix) also offers free software that you can use to access its network for both sending and receiving messages via a regular phone modem — this can be useful for sending out pager messages from a central base station and receiving delivery confirmations and responses too.

Mobile Radio

You can send and receive e-mail without subscribing to any of the special mobile radio data services, just by hooking up your computer's modem to a cell phone and dialing into your regular online service or ISP account. For occasional use, this approach is probably the easiest and simplest, and it has the added benefit that you can send faxes just as you'd normally do over a regular (wired) phone line.

However, the more specialized wireless messaging services (mobile radio data systems) have several advantages over cell-phone type systems:

✔ **More compact.** With a mobile radio system, you have a single PCMCIA/PC card plugged into your computer and an antenna sticking out directly from this card. With a cell phone, you have a cable you need to run from your PCMCIA/PC card to your phone, and then the phone itself.

✔ **Always online.** With cell phones, you have to dial into your online service or ISP in order establish a connection — this process can be time-consuming, and if you don't get through the first time, your only choice is to keep re-dialing. Mobile radio data systems keep a constant connection to your computer, offering you instant access to the radio data network to send e-mail, as well as instant notification of any incoming e-mail.

✔ **Less costly.** Cost ultimately depends on how often you use the system, but for sending numerous short messages over the course of a day, mobile radio data services can be cheaper than making a cell phone call each time you want to send a brief note.

✔ **Single bill.** When you access an online service or ISP through a cell phone, you must maintain two separate monthly-fee accounts: with the cellular phone company, and with your online service or ISP. Wireless radio data services provide both the means of communication and an e-mail account as part of the monthly fee.

Trying to make sense out of the numerous mobile data services can be challenging. I think that the biggest source of confusion comes from the fact that some services function as resellers of the basic radio networks, whereas on the other hand, you can buy service directly from the basic, underlying radio networks. All this market structure can create the illusion that dozens of these networks are out there, when in reality, only a few have licenses from the Federal Communications Commission to use the radio frequencies, and they in turn lease portions to other companies.

The radio data systems market has just two of these basic, underlying radio networks — RAM Mobile Data (it has nothing to do with the RAM in your computer) and ARDIS. Both of these services operate at about 800 MHz, using radio frequencies similar to cell phones. Within each of these two radio infrastructures, you can choose from numerous services from wireless mobile data service providers.

When you buy a wireless modem, it is *usually* designed to work with RAM Mobile Data or ARDIS. Your third option is one of the more specialized regional services, for example, Metricom's Ricochet, as I describe in the next section.

Unlike regular modems, wireless modems are designed to work with specific systems. You need to decide which system you want before you select a modem.

Most wireless modems plug into the PCMCIA/PC card slot and have an appendage attached to the PC card that hangs outside the computer. Many models have software available to work with pocket computers, such as the Apple Newton and Windows CE-based computers. This combination — a pocket computer combined with a wireless modem card — constitutes what most people would consider the closest thing to the mobile connectivity fantasy (though a bit clunky-looking, with the wireless modem bulge hanging out the back). Part of the reason these cards have the big appendage is that they contain their own batteries — models are available that can draw power from the computer battery, but you may cut your usual computer run time in half if you use one.

In addition to which radio networks they connect to, other features to look for in wireless modems include battery run time, the ability to receive and store messages while the computer is turned off, availability of status lights to indicate battery condition and other aspects of operation, and the weight and size.

RAM Mobile Data

Think of RAM Mobile Data as a completely separate backbone for the cellular phone system: RAM Mobile Data operates a two-way wireless radio messaging system that reaches about 8,000 cities and towns, covering more than 90 percent of what RAM Mobile Data calls the "U.S. urban business population." The technology that RAM Mobile Data uses is sometimes referred to as *Mobitex* — it was developed by Ericsson, a Swedish electronics company. The third-party services offered through RAM Mobile Data are sometimes called (not surprisingly) *Mobitex services*.

RAM Mobile Data sells its own e-mail service and creates custom applications for organizations needing big fleets of mobile computers. However, you're most likely to access RAM Mobile Data through one of the third-party information services that buy time on RAM Mobile Data's radio network. Third-party options are vast and include Telescan (financial information), Wireless Market Service, and Zap-It (fax/paging/e-mail). Zap-It, from DTS Wireless (see the Appendix), offers software for notebooks as well as PDA/HPC/pocket computers. (I describe PDAs, HPCs, and pocket computers in Chapter 7.) Other similar services include RadioMail and WyndMail.

GoAmerica (see the Appendix) can provide you with full-scale Internet access via the RAM Mobile Data network — you can browse the Web with Netscape Navigator or Microsoft Internet Explorer, as well as send and receive e-mail. Pricing is based on how much data you download per month.

Most of these services also allow you to send pager messages to pocket pagers and to send faxes. Pricing is lower than for comparable cellular communications — with monthly fees starting at about $10 and per-message costs running in the ballpark of 30 to 50 cents, with numerous bulk plans also available.

Modems to access the RAM Mobile Data service include the U.S. Robotics AllPoints Wireless Modem.

ARDIS

ARDIS is a competing two-way wireless system that is functionally almost the same as RAM Mobile Data, covering over 10,000 cities and towns, but offering faster connection speeds — up to 19,200 bps. Like RAM Mobile Data, ARDIS sells its own e-mail service directly to the public and also acts as host to numerous third-party service providers.

IKON MobileCHOICE, a service that works with Windows CE devices (see Chapter 7 for more info) to provide wireless e-mail, fax, news and stock quote access, and one-way paging, is the most popular ARDIS service. ARDIS also offers RadioMail which provides e-mail, messaging, voice-to-text paging (via operators who type in the message), faxing, news, and stock quotes. Software is available for a wide variety of mobile computing platforms, including Macintosh and Windows CE. (RadioMail is also available via RAM Mobile Data and CDPD, as I explain in the preceding sections, "CDPD" and "RAM Mobile Data.")

Modems to access the ARDIS service include the Motorola Personal Messenger 100D, which features an innovative status light that lets you know when a message has come in, as shown in Figure 21-1.

The Wireless Internet

As with e-mail, you don't need to do anything fancier than hook up your modem to a cellular phone to access the Internet and browse the Web, no wires attached. For occasional Internet access, the cellular approach is probably the easiest — assuming, that is, you already have a cell phone.

With a cell phone modem, under optimum conditions, you can achieve a speed of 14,400 bps (bits per second) — rather slow for looking at Web pages. Unfortunately, neither the RAM Mobile Data nor the ARDIS system offers much improvement, as they operate at 9,600 bps and 19,200 bps, respectively. CDPD, similarly, is limited to 19,200 bps. Wireless networks are really designed for sending pager-style messages and text. Nevertheless, they can offer lower-cost Internet access than cell phone connections and you save the time of dialing in.

Metricom's Ricochet is a very promising alternative, available only in a few metropolitan areas (including Northern California, Seattle, and Washington, D.C.) as this book was going to press. Ricochet is an integrated hardware/radio network service — the company sells and leases its own portable modems that tie into the Metricom Microcellular Data Network. What makes this service unique is that it offers flat-rate monthly pricing plans, just like regular dial-up Internet Service Providers. And even better, it offers much faster access speeds than you find with other services — up to 100 Kbps — even faster than the current fastest phone modems. Monthly service runs about $35.

Unfortunately, the current incarnation of the Ricochet modem is not a PCMCIA/PC card — rather, it's a cigarette pack-sized external unit that plugs into the computer's serial port. Ricochet offers support for numerous platforms, including Windows 95, Macintosh, Windows CE, and Apple Newton.

The Ricochet modems are also unusual because they can talk to each other, as well as to the Ricochet network. This is called *peer-to-peer* mode — in essence, you can create your own local network with them (range is limited to 1,000 feet maximum), even in areas where Ricochet doesn't offer Internet access.

In the future, two satellite-based Internet access systems may offer higher data speeds. One, called Teledesic (and funded largely by Bill Gates) has plans to put hundreds of satellites into the skies but will require a small dish antenna — not very portable, unless you like wearing funny hats. Motorola's planned Iridium system, however, may offer more mobile access, but probably at lower speeds. Both of these systems are expected to become available early in the 21st century.

Wireless LAN Technology

Wireless LAN systems provide excellent data throughput rates in the ballpark of 1000 to 2000 Kbps — that's roughly 100 times as fast as cellular connections. However, they have one big limitation: range. The wireless LAN is suitable only for a single office building or a campus-style cluster of buildings, such as a college or a corporate park.

Wireless LAN technology comes in two varieties: microwave and infrared (IrDA). The microwave radio system is more popular, because it goes right through interior walls to cover a large office. But as these devices currently use exactly the same frequencies as microwave ovens, they pose a bit of an unanswered safety question in my view. The infrared systems use invisible beams of infrared light, much like a television remote control. As a result, they cannot go through walls.

Either way, wireless LAN technology costs quite a bit more than traditional Ethernet installations. Instead of paying about $100 per computer or less for traditional Ethernet adapter cards, the wireless adapter cards generally run about $200 to $600 each. Of course, you save money on wiring costs, but note that the central transmitter units can cost several thousand dollars, too.

Wireless LAN systems are usually employed as an adjunct, not a replacement, for traditional wired networks. They extend the wired network so that portable computers equipped with wireless adapters can easily be on the network just like desktop machines.

Peer-to-peer wireless networks

Many wireless network adapters (both radio and infrared) can be used two ways: to connect to a central station tied into a network's server (that's called *client-server,* in LAN jargon), or to connect to each other in *peer-to-peer* mode, as it's called. Peer-to-peer mode is often limited to just two computers, and so is ideal when you're working with a partner. The two of you can exchange e-mail while sitting in on a meeting or conference, for example — kind of like hi-tech walkie-talkies.

Microwave radio LAN systems

Most wireless networking products use radio waves to carry the data, although the exact frequencies used and power levels can vary from brand to brand. All are in the microwave band, and most are currently around 2.4 GHz — a frequency that has been widely adopted by the wireless LAN industry (see the "Laptop emissions" sidebar later in this chapter). However, the Federal Communications Commission has also set aside frequencies around 5 GHz for wireless LANs, so in the future, wireless LAN technology may move to even higher frequencies. One advantage of using high frequencies is that very wide *bandwidths* can be achieved, comparable to wired LAN systems (*bandwidth* refers to the amount of information a data channel or line can carry). Another advantage is (for radio physics reasons that you don't need to worry about) that a very short antenna can be used — typically the antenna extends just a couple of inches out from the PCMCIA/PC card.

The AirSurfer card from Netwave is typical of wireless LAN adapters. It fits in a standard PCMCIA/PC Card Type II slot, as shown in Figure 21-2. It operates at 2.4 GHz and uses *frequency hopping* technology, in which the exact frequency keeps changing (this technique is also known as *spread spectrum* — see sidebar for the details). The bandwidth of the connection is 1000 Kbps (kilobits/second), and the range is typically 150 feet indoors, or up to 650 feet outdoors. Netwave Technologies also makes companion access point equipment — the central radio connection that sends and receives data to/from all the remote units and ties into a wired LAN. Other manufacturers of radio LAN equipment include Proxim, Solectek, and Applied Integration — their systems offer data rates ranging from 1000 to 4000 Kbps (see the Appendix).

Figure 21-2:
Most wireless LAN cards, such as this AirSurfer from Netwave Technologies, use microwave radio signals.

One simple application for wireless networking is to share a printer, and a company called AeroComm makes a system specifically for this purpose. The advantage of such a single-purpose wireless system is price — the cost per adapter, for each notebook computer, is under $100. If your office consists of a half-dozen people, each using a notebook computer, and your only need for a network is to share a printer, this system is perfect.

For the time being, you want to buy all your wireless LAN equipment from the same company, as each manufacturer uses a slightly different and incompatible system for transmitting data. However, that situation will probably change soon, as the IEEE (Institute of Electrical and Electronics Engineers) recently created a standard for wireless LAN systems called IEEE 802.11. So in the future, you may be able to mix and match different brands of wireless LAN cards on a network, just like you mix and match Ethernet cards today.

Infrared light LAN systems

Infrared wireless LAN (Local Area Network) systems use invisible beams of light, similar to the technology used by remote controls for TVs and VCRs, to send signals from computer to computer or between a notebook computer and a central server.

Actually, if you have two notebook computers, each equipped with an IrDA infrared port, you can establish a peer-to-peer wireless network with no additional equipment, just by activating the ports. IrDA is typically limited to a range of a few feet. For a true infrared LAN with realistic ranges, you need an infrared wireless LAN system.

Unlike the directional beams that remote controls for TVs and VCRs emit, wireless LAN systems use special optics to spread the infrared beam all around the room. The only requirement is that the room must have a light-colored ceiling to reflect the beam back down (unless you work in a disco, that requirement should be fine).

Data Technologies Corp. is one of the leading manufacturers of infrared LAN products. Their Collaborative microPCMCIA card, shown in Figure 21-3, plugs into a standard PC card slot, and provides a peer-to-peer connection to other similarly equipped notebooks, or to a wired LAN system via a special adapter. According to DTC Data Technology Corp., these wireless infrared products work at a range of up to 35 meters. Adapters are available for both PC and Apple Newton platforms.

Other manufacturers of infrared wireless LAN systems include InfraLAN Wireless Communications (see the Appendix for contact information).

Frequency hopping, or spread spectrum

Most microwave-based wireless LAN systems use *spread spectrum* technology, in which the exact frequency being used for radio transmissions keeps changing. It's as if instead of tuning into an FM radio station at 99.5, the station keeps moving every 1/10 of a second — one instant at 99.1, the next instant at 13.7, and so on.

Spread spectrum has several advantages over staying on the same frequency. Security is enhanced, because someone attempting to intercept the communications would have to keep changing frequencies to keep up. Manufacturers can also transmit at higher power levels than would be legally permissible using fixed-frequency technology, because the average amount of power being emitted at any given frequency is less than if that frequency were used continuously. Finally, spread spectrum minimizes interference problems and therefore limits data errors.

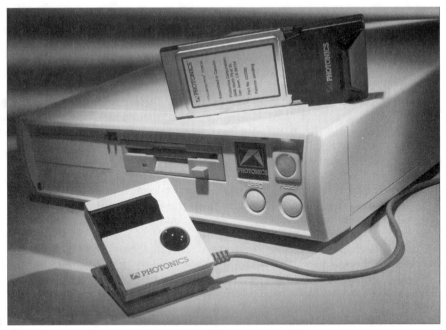

Figure 21-3:
Infrared
wireless
LAN
adapters,
such as this
card from
DTC Data
Technology
Corporation,
use invisible
beams of
light to
transmit
data.

Are Microwaves Dangerous?

Much as I like to be a cheerleader for mobile computing, I have to tell you that the scariest new technology — for anyone who worries that microwaves are dangerous, such as myself — are the 2.4 GHz wireless LAN systems. They use almost exactly the same frequency that microwave ovens use. They transmit the very same type of radio waves from which the protective screen built into the window of a microwave oven is trying to shield you.

Microwaves are generally considered more dangerous than ordinary, lower frequency radio waves because microwaves tend to make molecules vibrate and heat up. Much like a small boat bobs up and down on a lake as waves pass by, so do the molecules in living tissue vibrate as the microwaves pass by. These superfast vibrations — occurring billions of times per second — create heat from the friction between molecules as they vibrate. This friction is why a microwave oven heats from within — the center of the food is cooked just as much as the outside.

Many of the early studies that took a look into microwave danger focused exclusively on this heating phenomenon and ignored the long-term cancer risk from microwaves. Exactly what the cancer risk is remains debatable, and it lies at the heart of a cell phone safety story that prompted the publicity a few years ago (when a lawsuit was filed by a brain tumor victim who claimed the cell phone caused it). One study published in a widely respected biology journal specifically looked for cell damage to rat brains after exposure to microwaves, at levels low enough that no change occurred in body temperature. It found significant damage to the DNA, indicating a likelihood to cause cancer.

The legal power limits placed on cell phone technology — and these also apply to wireless cellular modems and wireless LAN systems — are based on avoiding the microwave heating effect. Cell phones and modems are limited to 3 watts, but most smaller units operate at about $1/2$ watt (500 milliwatts). Wireless LAN transmitters typically operate at even lower power — just 100 milliwatts (0.1 watts). A microwave oven, by comparison, typically emits about 5,000 to 10,000 times more energy, at about 500 to 1,000 watts.

That difference may sound whopping — and it explains why most people in the industry (except for a few nuts like me) consider the danger negligible. But suppose that you work with a wireless-networked computer transmitting constantly, eight hours per day, for one work-year. At the end of the year, you will have received the same amount of microwave radiation as if you defeated the safety mechanism and opened the door on a 1,000-watt microwave oven and exposed yourself at full blast for fourteen minutes.

A cottage industry has sprung up around this issue — a few small companies are selling protective shields to reduce the amount of radiation that can get from a cell phone to a user's brain. Though these shields seem like common sense, the cell phone manufacturers won't adopt it voluntarily — probably because it would be an admission that the microwaves emitted by cell phones are in fact dangerous (sound familiar?).

No such devices exist yet to help protect users from the radiation emitted by wireless LAN systems or cellular modems, and similarly, the addition of any such protective gear would probably represent an admission that a danger exists.

If you do find yourself hooked into a wireless LAN, and are concerned about the microwave danger, here's my advice to help minimize the radiation risk:

- Keep the wireless LAN adapter and antenna away from your body.

- Walk a few feet away from the computer when sending a big file. Remember that your antenna emits more power when sending files than when receiving them.

- Avoid using the LAN antenna next to reflective metal surfaces, such as an aluminum pie plate, that can bounce the signal back to you.

- Keep away from the central server antenna and transmitter equipment. These are likely to be transmitting at a higher power level than the remote (client) units, and they are transmitting constantly.

- Unplug the wireless LAN adapter card whenever you don't need it.

Wireless Privacy and Security

Any company or organization that sets up a wireless LAN needs to be aware of the security risk it is taking. The network, in essence, broadcasts all the e-mail and file transfers taking place within the organization. With the right equipment, someone in an adjacent office, or across the street, or parked in a car in the lot, can pick up all that data and capture it for nefarious purposes. Digital espionage is on the rise, and connecting to a wireless network may make you more vulnerable.

To get around this privacy problem, you can employ all sorts of encryption technology, thus engaging whomever is eavesdropping in a spy versus counterspy situation. Most wireless microwave LAN systems employ a technology called *spread spectrum,* or *channel hopping,* in which the precise frequency that's used to carry data keeps changing every fraction of a second, making eavesdroppers have a harder time keeping track.

You can also choose infrared wireless LAN technology, rather than microwaves, to keep the signal contained within the office complex. An infrared LAN system is inherently contained within a room, unless repeater units are installed. And even with repeaters, the range is only 25 feet or so — it doesn't reach the parking lot.

The security danger involves access as well as privacy. A sophisticated hacker can first monitor the wireless network to learn the usernames and passwords needed, and then access the system disguised as another user. Unlike a traditional wired LAN system, in which the hacker would need the use of a network jack (node) or phone line access, with a wireless LAN, the interloper can operate from anywhere within range.

Of course, the likelihood that someone would go to such an effort to attack your organization is probably quite low. But then again, if you just fired a mad technical genius/computer whiz, and now he's a disgruntled ex-employee, you may want to wait a few weeks before installing your wireless LAN.

Chapter 22

PCMCIA/PC Cards

. . . .

In This Chapter

▶ Identifying types of PCMCIA/PC cards

▶ Installing PCMCIA/PC cards

▶ Troubleshooting PCMCIA/PC card problems

▶ Configuring computer setups to make PCMCIA/PC cards work

. . . .

*T*he PCMCIA card, also called a PC card, opens your portable computer up to a vast array of expansion possibilities. Anytime you have a choice of ways to connect a device to your notebook computer, such as via serial port, parallel port, or PCMCIA/PC card slot, you're almost always best off choosing the PCMCIA version of the device. The PCMCIA slot usually provides the fastest and most compact connection to modems, video capture systems, Ethernet adapters, and a host of other devices (many of which I mention in this chapter). Most PCMCIA devices are contained completely within the card and slide right into the PCMCIA slot on the side of your computer.

In the early 1990s, the computer industry got together and developed a common standard for plugging accessory cards into laptop computers. Thanks to that standard — first called *PCMCIA,* later changed to the friendlier *PC card* — you can now choose from literally hundreds of different cards that work with your computer, all of which can be switched in and out as you need them, without even turning the computer off. Many handheld computers (HPCs) also accept some of these cards — see Chapter 7 for more on these nifty miniatures.

Understanding What PCMCIA Cards Do

The original PCMCIA standard was created for *flash memory cards* (a type of storage device), but it was quickly adapted for modems, auxiliary hard drives, and other devices. Today, you can get dozens of different types of PCMCIA expansion cards that you can easily plug into a notebook computer. Here's a quick rundown on the most popular types:

✔ **Fax/Modem.** Undoubtedly the most popular PCMCIA card, these let you communicate over the phone line for e-mail, Web surfing, or faxing (see Chapter 14).

✔ **LAN Adapter.** A LAN adapter hooks your notebook computer up to a LAN (Local Area Network) such as you may have in your office (see Chapter 20).

✔ **Flash Memory.** These devices are solid-state (no moving parts) memory cards that retain data indefinitely without any power (unlike your computer's RAM, which wipes out when power is removed). They're commonly used for digital photography — some camera models have memory cards you can take out of the camera and place right in your notebook computer for instant access to the images.

✔ **SCSI.** (Pronounced *scuzzy,* like the stuff that collects in the runners of sliding glass doors.) The acronym stands for Small Computer Systems Interface, and SCSI connectors are what you often need to hook up external hard drives, scanners, and other accessory products. SCSI connections are faster than serial or parallel port, and you can connect up to seven different devices to a single SCSI adapter card in what is known as a *daisy chain.* SCSI-2 is a 16-bit version of the original 8-bit SCSI protocol, and Fast SCSCI-2, a higher-speed variation, runs at 10 Mbps, twice as fast as the original. Fast and Wide SCSI-2 on 32-bit systems operates at up to 40 Mbps (it's called wide because it's designed for 32-bit data paths, instead of 16-bit). These speeds become more important when you have large amounts of data to transfer, such as may occur when running video-intensive multimedia off an external hard drive.

✔ **Audio Adapter.** Some notebook computers don't come equipped with a built-in sound card (you can determine whether yours does by looking for small jacks for headphones, microphone, and line input), and a PCMCIA/PC card audio adapter lets you record sound from a microphone and listen to sound from multimedia CD-ROMs or the Internet. You can even get more advanced audio cards that offer synthesizer sound quality not available using the standard Sound Blaster-type synthesizer chips (both Roland and EMU make such cards — see the Appendix).

✔ **Hard Drive.** Putting a second disk drive in your notebook adds storage capacity and makes swapping large amounts of information with coworkers or organizing projects involving tons of data into separate hard drives a piece of cake. PCMCIA hard drives are *hot swappable,* meaning that you can pull one out and put another in while you're in the middle of using your computer, just like changing floppy disks.

✔ **Video Capture.** For importing still frames or video clips from a camcorder, these cards have connections for regular line video (phono jack) and S-video inputs, and work with just about all camcorders. See the Appendix.

- ✔ **CD-ROM.** No, the 5-inch diameter CD doesn't magically fit into the much smaller PCMCIA card. But the external CD-ROM hooks up through a card that plugs into the PCMCIA slot rather than using the usual parallel port connection.

- ✔ **ISDN Adapter.** Similar to a modem, but for connection to higher-speed ISDN (Integrated Services Digital Network) telephone service, which offers data rates up to 128 Kbps. See Chapter 5 for more info.

- ✔ **Cellular Modem.** Eliminates the need to hook up your regular modem to an external cell phone. Cellular modems have a cellular phone built in, and they automatically dial out calls for you to send/receive e-mail and access the Internet or other online services. See Chapter 5 for more information.

- ✔ **Pager.** Allows you to receive pager messages on your notebook or handheld computer screen.

- ✔ **Wireless LAN.** Using infrared light or, more commonly, microwave radio signals, you can use a Wireless LAN PCMCIA/PC Card to connect your portable computer to a Local Area Network without wires. See Chapter 22 for more on wireless LAN technology.

- ✔ **MIDI/SMPTE Adapter.** MIDI stands for Musical Instrument Digital Interface, and it is the standard system for connecting musical keyboards, drum machines, and other electronic music equipment. SMPTE stands for the Society for Motion Picture and Television Engineers, and signifies a time code system used for identifying frames in videotapes and film. MIDI and SMPTE cards provide important connections for working with professional audio and video equipment.

Sometimes two similar functions are combined together in one card, such as in the modem/LAN card shown in Figure 22-1.

- ✔ If at all possible, get the dealer who sells you a PCMCIA/PC card to install the card for you and demonstrate that it works in the store.

- ✔ If you have to install a PC card yourself, call the manufacturer's tech support number at the first sign of trouble (these things can be a bit winky at times).

The three sizes

PCMCIA/PC cards come in three sizes, identified as Type I, II, and III. Type II has become the most common — you can currently find a cornucopia of fax/modems, SCSI interfaces, LAN (Ethernet) interfaces, sound boards, video boards, CD-ROM drives, and other accessories (and combinations of the above) that hook up in the PCMCIA Type II slot. Furthermore, though some computers may only have one PCMCIA slot, you can be sure that it accepts a Type II PC card.

Type I cards, which are thinnest, are generally the format for flash memory cards. The larger card size, Type III, is usually used for hard drives — the disk drive is actually packed into the Type III card.

Before you plug in a PCMCIA/PC card, be sure that it fits. The larger slots are always compatible with the thinner cards, but the reverse doesn't hold true — a Type II slot accommodates a Type I card, for example, but a Type II slot cannot accept a Type III card.

Most notebook computers can accommodate two Type II or Type I cards. Often the two slots are arranged right on top of one another, as shown in Figure 22-2. You can use the two slots for two Type I or II cards, or for a single, larger Type III card. The little connectors inside the slot are the same for all three types of cards — the only difference is in how thick the cards are (3.3mm, 5mm, and 10.5mm for Types I, II, and III, respectively).

Installing PCMCIA/PC cards

PCMCIA/PC cards of all three types have a similar connector on one edge of the card. Insert the card with this edge connector pointing in (toward the computer) and with the top side of the card facing up (usually the manufacturer's logo appears on top). You must press the card in firmly — don't force it — but you do need to push it a little to properly seat it in the socket.

Figure 22-2:
A typical dual TypeII/ single Type III slot on a notebook computer. Many notebook computers have two Type II slots stacked on top of each other.

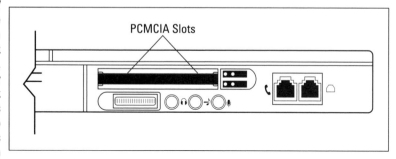

PCMCIA Slots

When properly installed, the card is flush with the edge of the computer, or inset just a bit. If you find that the card is sticking out past the edge of the slot, be sure that you have the card properly oriented (top side up). The only exception is with some microwave radio network cards that may have an antenna or other appendage sticking out past the edge of the computer (see Chapter 21).

As soon as you plug a card in, your computer emits two beeps ascending in pitch, telling you that it recognizes the card and knows how to use it (you hope). If you do not hear the two ascending pitch beeps, but instead hear a single, low-pitched beep, then the computer does not recognize the card — see the "Solving Card Recognition Problems" section in this chapter. If you already have the card installed in the computer before you turn the power on, then you usually hear the two ascending pitch beeps every time you boot up your computer.

If you don't hear any beeps and you have a volume control on your computer, make sure that your speaker volume is up. If your speaker is turned up and you still don't hear the beeps, then follow these steps:

1. **Choose Start⇨Settings⇨Control Panel.**

   The Control Panel pops up.

2. **Double-click the PC Card (PCMCIA) icon.**

   The PC Card (PCMCIA) dialog box appears.

3. **Click the Global Settings tab, and make sure that the check box next to** `Disable PC Card sound effects` **is not selected (no check appears in the box).**

4. **Click OK.**

Removing PCMCIA/PC cards

The PCMCIA/PC card slot itself always features an ejector button to pop the card back out when you want to remove it. Sometimes these buttons are a bit tricky to figure out — you may first have to pull out a lever, which then pushes in (funny as that sounds), or you may just have a simple button to push. See your computer's instruction manual if you can't figure out how the PC card ejector doodad works. (Yes, *doodad* is the official technological name for the thing.) Usually, the button's position changes slightly when a card is inserted (such as by popping out a fraction of an inch), offering an indication that the card has been physically inserted properly.

To remove a PCMCIA/PC card while your computer power is running, you need to first shut the PC card off. You have two ways to do so:

✔ Look for an icon in the Windows 95 toolbar, in the lower right corner next to the time, that looks like a card (if you don't see it, your computer may not recognize the card — see "Solving Card Recognition Problems" in this chapter). Click this icon, shown in Figure 22-3 once, and a pop-up message appears. Click the message that appears, such as `Stop Hoo-Haa PCMCIA card adapter doohickey`, for the device you wish to remove, as shown in Figure 22-4.

✔ Or you can follow these steps:

1. **Choose Start⇨Settings⇨Control Panel.**

   The Control Panel pops up.

2. **In the Control Panel, double-click PC Card (PCMCIA).**

   The PC Card (PCMCIA) dialog box appears.

3. **Highlight the card you want to remove, and click Stop.**

4. **Click OK.**

Figures 22-3, 22-4: Before removing the PC card, click the PC Card icon in the toolbar to deactivate it, and then click on the message that appears.

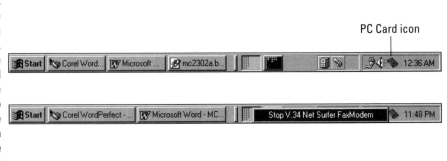

PC Card icon

PC card and PCMCIA — what's in a name?

PCMCIA stands for Personal Computer Memory Card International Association — a trade organization that was originally formed in 1989 to create a common standard for add-on memory cards. For the first few years, the sockets that accepted these cards were called PCMCIA slots. Then, in 1995, the organization officially changed the name of the cards to the simpler-sounding PC card — that's what they're called in Windows 95. But most people still refer to them as PCMCIA cards, and for those who are new to the notebook scene, the name change just adds that much more confusion.

The PC card/PCMCIA situation is also confusing because many of these cards also work in Apple PowerBook computers running the Macintosh operating system, whereas PC generally refers to the IBM-compatible Windows/DOS platform.

Finally, note that PC cards are intended specifically for portable computers — just because they are called PC cards, doesn't mean they work with all PCs. You can buy a special adapter to use these cards in a desktop computer, but unless you have some very special reason for doing so (such as to share a super-expensive card between a notebook and a desktop machine), you usually save money and hassle by just buying the card you need in the format your desktop computer uses. Accessory cards for desktop PCs come in three varieties, called ISA, PCI, and VESA. Apple Macintosh computer cards are called NuBus.

Sometimes I use the term *PCMCIA/PC card* to indicate that both names mean the same thing; other times I use *PCMCIA* or *PC card.* You say tomatoes, I say tomottoes.

All PCMCIA/PC cards are *hot swappable,* meaning that you can plug them in and take them out while your computer is turned on — a pretty cool feature indeed. For example, you can grab images through a video capture card and then upload them to your Web site with your modem card, all without the slow process of closing all your applications and restarting your computer. Don't worry about the usual advice given for desktop computers that says that everything should be turned off before making or breaking a connection. By all means, with desktop computers, this is good advice (I know from experience — I once crashed a disk drive by switching printers on the parallel port while the computer was turned on). However, with PC cards, the conventional wisdom doesn't apply.

Plug and Play

Plugging a PCMCIA/PC card into a computer running Windows 95 initiates a feature called Plug and Play, which is designed to handle the complete installation process automatically. Normally, that's exactly what happens. Shortly after you plug in the card — assuming the computer is already turned on — you get a message saying `Windows has detected new hardware`, and you're prompted to follow a series of instructions to automatically install the new card.

If Windows 95 doesn't automatically detect your new PC card, follow these steps:

1. **Choose Start⇨Settings⇨Control Panel.**

   The Control Panel pops up.

2. **In the Control Panel, double-click the Add New Hardware icon.**

   The Add New Hardware Wizard pops up.

3. **In the Add New Hardware dialog box, click Next.**

   Another dialog box opens, asking whether you want Windows to begin searching for new hardware.

4. **Make sure that the Yes (Recommended) radio button is selected and then click Next.**

   A new dialog box appears with the message `Windows will now look for your new hardware`.

5. **Click Next.**

   A bar graph appears, showing the progress on the search. At the end of the detection process, you see a dialog box that says `Windows has finished detecting hardware, and is ready to install support for all detected devices.`

   If it gets stuck in the same spot for several minutes, reboot the computer and try again, try the manual installation procedure described in the next section, or call the Tech Support department of the card manufacturer.

6. **Click the Details button in the Add New Hardware Wizard dialog box.**

   You now see the PC card listed in a box under the word `Detected` in this dialog box.

   Note: If you do not see the card listed, click Finish, and then proceed to the step-by-step instructions listed immediately after these instructions in the section "Installing a PC Card Manually."

7. **Click Finish.**

8. **If Windows 95 has the driver on hand for your card, a dialog box may appear, saying** `Systems Settings Change` **and offering to restart your computer. Click Yes if this comes up. If Windows 95 does not have the driver for your PC card, you are prompted to supply it on floppy disk — see the next section, "Installing a PC Card Manually."**

If Windows has any problem detecting your new card and if your computer has two slots, try switching the card to the other slot. This trick is not official Windows policy — in theory, the slots are supposed to be completely equal — it's just part of the voodoo that defies explanation. In any event, I sometimes notice that switching the cards works to get things going, especially with older computers running Windows 3.1.

Installing a PC Card Manually

Windows 95 comes with a library of special driver software for hundreds of different PC cards. If the card that you have plugged in is in this registry, installation is a breeze — Windows 95 installs everything you need automatically, and you are off and running like a PCMCIA chicken without a head.

However, if Windows 95 is not already familiar with the card you're trying to install — a situation that you're especially likely to find yourself in if the card is a brand-new product, then you have to supply Windows 95 with the appropriate software. Look in the box that your PCMCIA/PC card came in for a disk with a title like `Windows 95 Drivers`. If, when you go through the previous numbered steps in the "Plug and Play" section earlier in this chapter, and you're prompted to supply a disk, pick up at Step 10 in the following set of numbered steps. Or, to install the card manually — without using the plug and play features — start at Step 1:

1. **Choose Start⇨Settings⇨Control Panel.**

   The Control Panel pops up.

2. **In the Control Panel, double-click the Add New Hardware icon.**

   The Add New Hardware Wizard pops up.

3. **In the Add New Hardware dialog box, click Next.**

   Another dialog box opens, asking whether you want Windows to begin searching for new hardware.

4. **Select the No radio button (make sure that it has a dot in it) to reject the auto-detection process.**

5. **Click Next.**

6. **Select the type of device you're installing — such as modem, multi-function adapter, or network adapter.**

   Do *not* make the mistake of selecting PCMCIA socket. The trick is that you are installing a *PCMCIA Card,* not a *socket.* Choose the function that the card actually performs.

7. **Click Next.**

Depending on the type of device you're installing, Windows may again suggest automatically detecting your new hardware, or it may present a list of specific makes and models for you to choose from. If Windows suggests automatic detection again, go ahead and reject the auto-detection option. Either way, the make and model list pops up.

8. **In the makes and models list, check under the manufacturers list on the left and the model numbers list on the right to see whether your card is listed. If it is listed, click Next and proceed to Step 11. If not, click Have Disk, as shown in Figure 22-5.**

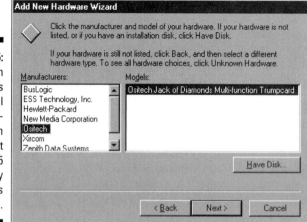

Figure 22-5: Ositech makes several multi-function boards, but Windows 95 has only one in its listings.

9. **Insert the Windows 95 Drivers disk and click OK.**

If you get a message saying `The specified location does not contain information about your hardware`, follow these substeps:

a. **Click OK.**

The error message disappears.

b. **Click Browse.**

Sometimes the manufacturers of PC cards make life even more difficult by putting the files you need in a directory (folder) on the floppy disk. A window that says `Open` appears, and on the right side, you find a list of all the directories (folders) available on the floppy disk.

c. **Look for a folder with an obvious name, such as** `Setup` **or** `Drivers` **or** `Installation`**, or just try clicking the first one and then clicking OK. If you get the error message again, try the next directory, and so on.**

If you exhaust all possibilities, give up and call Tech Support for the card manufacturer. (***Note:*** You usually need to find a file that has the `.inf` filename extension.)

10. **You may be prompted to approve suggested configuration settings, depending on the type of device you're installing. Accept whatever is suggested, unless you know of a problem.**

11. **Click Finish.**

Solving Card Recognition Problems

If you're having trouble getting a PCMCIA/PC card to work, this section is intended to help. But be forewarned — the PC card manufacturers make sure that no foolproof way exists to get every card working with every laptop or notebook computer. Also, if you are using a palmtop computer, the range of cards that you can use is usually limited to just modems.

Most of the PCMCIA/PC card problems that I have experienced came up when I tried to get two cards working simultaneously in the same computer. Usually everything works fine with just one card installed, but when a second is added, conflicts arise. The problem is that even though the computer has two slots for these cards, it may not have the available *system resources,* as I explain in the "Changing Address and Interrupt Assignments in Windows 95" section later in this chapter.

Many notebook computers have indicators on their status screens and/or appearing in the Windows 95 toolbar (in the extreme lower right corner of screen) to show when the computer senses that a card has been inserted, as shown in Figure 23-3. Note that the appearance of this icon does not mean the card is recognized and working — only that it has been inserted properly into the slot.

Usually, when you insert a PCMCIA/PC card into your computer and Windows 95 recognizes it, you hear two short beeps with ascending pitch; and when the card is removed, you hear two beeps with descending pitch. If you insert the card but the software doesn't recognize it, then you hear a single, longer-duration, lower-pitch beep.

If your operating system software doesn't recognize the PCMCIA/PC card, then it won't work. Recognizing the card goes one step beyond merely acknowledging that the card is physically present — it means that the operating system knows what the PC card needs in terms of *system resources* (see the next section).

Getting your system resources in order: addresses, COM ports, and IRQs

In order for any applications software that uses one of your PCMCIA/PC cards to know how to talk to the PCMCIA/PC card device, up to three

Windows settings must be in agreement: *address, IRQ (interrupt),* and *COM port.* As a group, these three settings are commonly referred to as *system resources.*

The simple explanation is this:

- ✔ **The address** is your computer's internal location for finding information within its memory (like over there behind that circuit, take a left at the diode, and park it in front of the thingamajig). The address refers to a special area of the computer's memory (RAM) where data is stored for the particular device.

- ✔ **The port** is the interface to the outside world for transferring information back and forth, such as the parallel port or serial port connectors on the back of your computer.

- ✔ **The interrupt** — abbreviated *IRQ* — is like a secret password that provides a way for the card to demand attention from the computer. The interrupt allows the PCMCIA/PC card to say, "Hey, stop what you're doing, I have important information for you."

All modems, LAN cards, and SCSI adapters, as well as many other (though not all) PC card communications-related devices require the assignment of a COM port number. Your computer most likely has four available, but usually COM 1 is already assigned to the serial port jack in the back.

Most problems getting a PCMCIA/PC card to work with a computer are due to conflicts between different devices trying to use the same port, address, or interrupt. Thankfully, Windows 95 automatically assigns COM port, address, and IRQ options to PCMCIA/PC cards based on which of the available numbers have already been taken up by other cards and devices at the time you first install the card.

Note that just because you don't have any PCMCIA/PC cards already installed, doesn't mean that all the possible COM port, address, and IRQ options are available. Your computer already has other devices built into your computer that take up many of the available options. These devices may include the audio system (which itself consists of various sections, each with their own address and interrupt assignments), disk drives, and so on.

To see exactly what's being used where by your Windows 95 computer, follow these steps:

1. Choose Start⇨Settings⇨Control Panel.

The Control Panel pops up.

2. Double-click the System icon.

The System Properties dialog box pops up.

3. Click the Device Manager tab.

4. Double-click the Computer icon (as shown in Figure 22-6).

The Computer Properties dialog box appears.

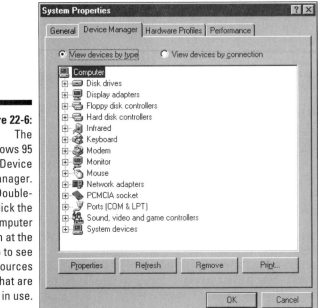

Figure 22-6:
The
Windows 95
Device
Manager.
Double-
click the
Computer
icon at the
top to see
resources
that are
in use.

5. Click the View Resources tab if it's not already selected.

6. Click the Interrupt request (IRQ) radio button to see which IRQ numbers are already being used, as shown in Figure 22-7.

7. Click Input/Output (I/O) to see which address ranges are already being used.

Note that the term *Input/Output Range,* or *I/O Range* is used in Windows 95 to refer to what accessory manufacturers commonly call the device's *address* — the same address I define in the previous section. *Address, Input/ Output Range,* and *I/O Range* all mean the same thing.

As you can see from the list in Figure 22-7, practically everything the computer uses to receive or send information — including the disk drives, keyboard, display, and mouse — have their own address and IRQ settings. Note also that the PCMCIA socket is itself considered a device and that it also has its own address and IRQ assignments. These assignments — which are technically for the PCMCIA controller chip — are completely separate from the assignments made for the card(s) that you plug into the PCMCIA slot(s).

Figure 22-7:
In this
computer,
Interrupt
(IRQ)
numbers 7
and 10
appear to
be available,
because
they are not
listed as
being
already
in use.

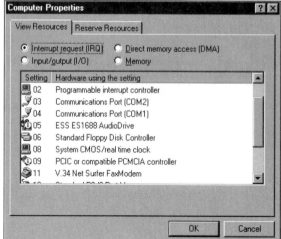

When you install a new card for the first time and Windows detects a conflict, the Windows 95 help system usually automatically guides you through the process of locating and resolving the conflict.

However, sometimes when you have a conflict, you may need to juggle the assignments for more than one device to get everything working together at the same time. This stuff can get complicated very quickly. You may need to look up the available address and interrupt codes for other devices in your system and do some switching and trading to get things working. If you are at all unsure of how to perform the steps, give your friendly neighborhood computer guru a call.

PCMCIA Compatibility

Unlike monolithic standards established by a single company, the PCMCIA/PC card standards are established by a loose consortium of hardware and software companies. See the sidebar earlier in this chapter, "PC card and PCMCIA — what's in a name?" for the lowdown.

The PCMCIA standards have evolved over the years as technology has advanced, and manufacturers maintain full compatibility with the latest version of the standards on a totally voluntary basis. At the hardware level, manufacturers regularly update certain components, such as the controller chip for the PCMCIA/PC card sockets (the brains that make them tick). Each new version of these controller chips adds new features that the latest PCMCIA/PC cards can take advantage of, but that may leave older computers in the dust. So the notebook computer that you bought two years ago may not conform to the latest set of PCMCIA standards and may not work with the newest cards.

With PCMCIA cards, you can run into many layers of compatibility issues, any one of which can prevent a card from working in your particular computer. The hardware layer (your particular PCMCIA/PC card socket) is the first step. Next, you have the software generically referred to as *Card and Socket Services*. A version of this software comes included in the Windows 95 operating system. However, if you use an older operating system (Windows 3.x or DOS), you may need to install the software manually from the utilities disks that come supplied with the computer — see the "Windows 3.x and DOS PCMCIA/PC Card Blues," later in this chapter. (This software is usually supplied both with the PC card and with the computer — usually your best bet is to try the version that came with your computer first, and then the PC card version. Note that this situation is relevant only if you are running a version of Windows other than Windows 95.)

The PCMCIA people have released four versions of the PCMCIA standard so far. Release 1.0 was the initial memory card specifications. Releases 2.0 and 2.1 added modems, mass storage, LAN, and radio network capabilities. Release 3.0, which is the most recent, adds support for multifunction cards such as LAN/modems.

Windows 3.x and DOS PCMCIA/PC Card Blues

Notebook computers with Windows 95 always boot up with the necessary Card and Socket Services software to recognize PCMCIA/PC cards. However, many notebook computers that use the older Windows 3.x and DOS operating systems include the Card and Socket Services software on a separate disk, and require you to install the software manually to activate the PCMCIA slots.

The reason why notebook manufacturers were reluctant to boot up with Card and Socket Services software automatically was that this software eats up valuable memory. Having the software installed could prevent many DOS (but not Windows) programs from running.

Some versions of DOS (6.0 and later) facilitate multiple boot-up options. Taking advantage of this feature, some DOS-based notebook computers are supplied with a boot sequence that gives you the choice of loading the PCMCIA drivers when you turn the computer on — this is the best approach for older notebooks with 486-type processors. (Alternatively, you can insert different boot disks in the floppy drive to have options for different boot sequences.)

If you have trouble getting a PC card to work in DOS or Windows 3.*x,* the first question to ask is whether the Card and Socket Services software has been loaded. You can figure out whether it has been loaded by checking these two things:

- ✔ As the computer boots up, watch the messages that flash on the screen. You probably see a series of items that relate to the PCMCIA slots — indicating special programs that are running to activate the slots and identify cards. If the messages appear too quickly to make any sense out of them, try pressing the F8 key just after the computer turns on and displays `loading MS-DOS`. Then press Enter to advance step by step through the boot-up sequence.

- ✔ Listen for beeping sounds when you insert and remove a PCMCIA card (after booting up the computer).

Card and Socket Services software in DOS and Windows 3.*x* has separate programs to help in the card recognition process. In SystemSoft's software, for example, a program called CSALLOC determines which addresses and interrupts are available for use by the socket. Another program called CARDID attempts to recognize the card. Both these programs usually run automatically when you boot up your computer — if you look closely, you see these programs being executed as computer starts up.

A third card and socket services program called CSCONFIG lets you manually assign address, interrupt, and COM port numbers for a particular card. And a fourth program, called CardView, is a Windows 3.*x* program (appearing in the Control Panel) that shows you which card is installed in each PCMCIA socket, and which address, interrupt, and COM port each is using.

Note also that another kind of conflict may occur with DOS and Windows 3.*x* memory management. Some cards (especially video-related units) require that a certain range of addresses be excluded from memory manager programs (such as EMM386, which is part of DOS and found in most boot-up sequences). Check your PCMCIA card's instructions if you are unsure.

The Card and Socket Services software included in Windows 95 and included with most computers running earlier versions of Windows 3.*x,* is published by a company called SystemSoft (they also publish an advanced PC card utility for Windows 95). Other publishers of Card and Socket Services software include Phoenix Technologies and DataBook. These companies are listed in the Appendix, and I mention them because in a near-worst-case scenario, you may have a PCMCIA card that requires you to replace your existing Card and Socket Services software with a version from one of these companies. In fact, some PCMCIA/PC cards come supplied with a version of Card and Socket Services that the manufacturer recommends for use with Windows 3.*x.*

Chapter 23

Caring for, Feeding, and Upgrading Your Mobile Computer

. . . .

In This Chapter

▶ Respecting your computer's delicacy

▶ Dealing with a spill

▶ Upgrading memory and hard drive

▶ Putting Ol' Trusty out to pasture

. . . .

*B*y their very nature, notebook and handheld computers tend to get more beat up, abused, and gunked up with grime than their more stationary desktop counterparts. The abuse is inevitable — because you carry these mobile wonders with you, they get exposed to all kinds of torture and environmental elements.

In addition, notebook computers tend to be more vulnerable even when you are *not* traveling. Consider what happens when you spill a cup of coffee on the keyboard, for example. With a desktop computer, the worst thing likely to happen is that you destroy the keyboard and need to replace it, at a cost of about $30 to $100. Spill coffee all over a notebook computer's keyboard, however, and you may destroy a lot more than just the keyboard — you may also ruin the pointer system, and if the fluid seeps down into the wrong places, the hard drive and even the motherboard may get zapped. Repair costs can run upwards of $500. People have been known to go out and buy whole new notebook computers (see Figure 23-1), following a spill, because the cost of repairs is so high — especially if your computer is more than a year old and already worth only about half what you paid for it.

This chapter is about keeping your computer running in good working condition for a long, long time. Ultimately, new technology should convince you to finally replace your machine — not a catastrophic breakdown.

Figure 23-1:
Panasonic's CF-25 Mark II is ruggedized to military specifications, and features a sealed, spillproof keyboard.

Oops! Keyboard Spills

Over the years, I have dumped more different liquids onto notebook computer keyboards than I care to remember, including seltzer, beer, wine, and coffee. The experiences have taught me some truly hard-learned lessons that I can pass on to you. My advice is the kind of stuff the computer manufacturers don't put in the computer instruction manual — in the strangely perfect world of computer designers, such spills never happen.

In the event that you spill something on your notebook, follow my damage control steps:

1. **Shut off power immediately, and unplug the computer. If your computer does not turn off but only goes into suspend mode, physically remove the battery.**

   Forget about trying to save the file you were working on — if you follow my advice about setting auto-save (see Chapter 4), your document has been saved within the past two minutes anyway, and two minutes' work is nothing compared to your entire computer.

   The greatest damage that occurs in a computer that has just received a spill comes from short circuits — the liquid conducts electricity to places that it's not supposed to go on the circuit board, and the itsy-bitsy pieces fry. If you have no electricity going through the circuits, you can avoid the damage — assuming, that is, that you eliminate the liquid before turning the computer back on.

2. **Turn the computer upside down so that the keyboard is facing the floor.**

3. **Shake the computer to try to get all of the liquid out. Keep shaking until no more liquid drips out.**

4. **Keeping the computer upside down, place the keyboard — facing down — on top of a dry towel.**

   You can use a chair to hang the computer upside down, with the display hanging down over the front of the chair, and with the keyboard resting on top of a towel on the seat, as shown in Figure 23-2.

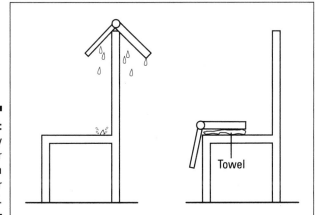

Figure 23-2: The drip-dry method for saving a computer from a spill.

Towel

5. **Leave the computer out to dry like this overnight, or longer.**

    You need to wait for the liquid inside to evaporate — ideally, if it's water, for example, evaporation leaves the computer without a trace of the mishap. Of course, other substances, such as coffee, do not evaporate as cleanly, but the residue after evaporation is still much less damaging than the liquid.

6. **Shake the computer out again after this drying process.**

    If any more liquid is evident, repeat the drying process.

7. **(Optional) If you have a hair dryer available, set it at the lowest heat setting and blow dry the keyboard, taking care not to heat things up too much.** Alternatively, you may try sucking out any remaining fluid with a vacuum cleaner, if available. A can of compressed air, as you would use to blow dust from camera lenses or film, works well too.

8. **After you feel confident that any liquid inside has evaporated, try turning the computer on and booting up. Good luck.**

If anything other than a normal boot-up process happens when you try starting your computer again after a spill mishap, turn the computer off immediately and take it to a repair center. Watching it sputter or flicker may only make matters worse.

From the moment the spill occurs, you're in a race against time. You're racing to disconnect power before the fluid can short anything out, and you're racing to reverse the direction and get the liquid flowing out of the computer as soon as possible.

What to Do if Your Computer Stops Working

Your computer may break after something obvious, like a drop or spill, or seemingly of its own accord. I have some advice on how to proceed if your computer seems to stop working. First, look for all the silly mistakes. These include:

- ✔ **The battery is not charged, or it is disconnected due to a loose connection in the battery compartment.** (Try taking the battery out and putting it back in, and recharging it again.)

- ✔ **AC Power is turned off.** Make sure that everything is plugged in, all switches are turned on, and all circuit breakers or fuses in the place you're working are okay (that is, make sure that the outlet you're using does indeed have power).

> ✔ **The display is turned off.** If you think that you hear the computer working but the screen stays dark, you may have accidentally switched the display off. On some notebook models, the screen automatically goes dark if you hook anything up to the external VGA monitor port. More often, the problem is that you accidentally pressed one of the function keys (F1 to F12) whose specific purpose is to switch between the using the screen or an external monitor (see Chapter 17 for more info).
>
> ✔ **The computer is in suspend mode.** Some computers require pressing a special button to come out of suspend mode — in the worst case, it is a function key that you're unaware of. Look up suspend/resume in your instruction manual (see Chapter 4 for more on suspend modes).

If your computer really is broken, you are probably debating the comparative merits of paying to get the computer fixed versus buying a new one. Of course, get an estimate of repair charges before junking a computer, but if you have some idea of what the problem is, your chances of getting cleaned by the repair place are less.

Hardware or Software Problem?

An old joke in computer circles says that whenever you experience problems, you call the company that made the thing and you are told that it's a software problem, and then, when you call the software company, you're told it's a hardware problem.

From a financial perspective, you can recover much more easily from a software problem than a hardware problem. Software problems can often be fixed just by reinstalling the software that's acting up. Hardware problems usually require a professional computer technician who charges you serious dough just to look at the computer and then potentially a tidy sum for parts as well.

If your computer seems to start booting up but then has a problem, you're in much better shape than if you see no signs of life whatsoever. In this circumstance — before biting the bullet and taking it in for service — you may be able to reinstall the operating system (Windows 95, typically) yourself. Some utility software, such as Norton's Utilities, includes special rescue disks just for this purpose.

If you do end up taking the computer in for service, contact the computer's manufacturer for advice on where to go. Most mail-order computer sellers offer service for their computers by shipping them back to the plant — though a bit of a hassle, I recommend this method of getting your notebook repaired over bringing it in to the local fix-it shop. After all, a notebook computer is an intricately organized and incredibly complex device — the manufacturer knows all its quirks better than a shop that may never have seen that particular model before.

On the other hand, numerous common problems tend to plague notebook computers — such as memory chips becoming loose and hard drive connections becoming loose — which hardly require the manufacturer's expertise. These problems are the computer equivalents of having a wire or hose come loose under the hood of an automobile — a reputable service shop can recognize the problem in an instant and charge for perhaps a half-hour of labor, at most, to fix it. Because notebooks get bumped around so much, they tend to experience loose connection type problems quite a bit.

So how do you know when you have an easy problem that any technician can quickly fix? That part is hard. So many things can possibly go wrong, I can't provide an easy answer to that question. The more you know about computers, the more you have a sense of what's gone wrong — try asking knowledgeable friends or coworkers. Ultimately, your best guide is the manufacturer's customer service line: They can help you identify such a problem and can often talk you through the process of fixing it yourself.

Always call your manufacturer's technical support line before bringing the computer in for service.

Screen Care

The LCD (Liquid Crystal Display — see Chapter 2) screen is the single most expensive component in most notebook computers. If you somehow break it, you usually find that buying a whole new computer is cheaper than replacing the screen.

How can you break the screen? Most likely by cracking it — from dropping the computer or from placing too much weight on top of the computer when it's closed up. I've heard one story of a screen breaking when the computer was placed behind a car seat, and then someone moved the car seat back (crunch!).

The front surface of most LCD panels is not rigid — it's somewhat flexible, as you've probably noticed. (What sane human can resist touching a glowing LCD panel?) Computer LCD panels don't use glass because glass is too heavy — instead, they use a flexible plastic. Avoid pressing your fingers on the screen surface — too much pressure, and you may damage it.

The screen's plastic cover has a special antiglare coating that is designed to minimize reflection from ambient light sources. Wiping the screen with abrasive paper, cloths, or detergent can damage this coating. Instead, wipe the screen with soft tissue paper — ideally lint-free photographic lens cleaning tissue, or cloths sold especially for this purpose, but soft toilet paper or regular tissue will do in an emergency. Avoid using soap or detergent — if you absolutely need to, use a tiny drop of very mild soap, such as a mild dishwashing soap. Never use abrasives such as scouring pads or steel wool — these permanently scratch the screen. Use a cotton-tip swab to clean around the edges and corners of the screen.

If the screen seems to suddenly stop working for no apparent reason, the likeliest culprit is the function key that you use to switch between the screen display and the VGA port. If you are absolutely certain that this is not the problem, and your computer is several years old, the screen's backlight has probably gone out. On a few models, this light is a user-replaceable part — call the manufacturer, order a new one, and follow the directions in the instruction manual. Usually, however, you have to take the computer in to a service shop to get the backlight replaced. This repair typically costs around $100 to $300.

Power Supply

The AC power supply for your notebook computer is usually a pretty hardy device requiring minimal care, but because it often winds up on the floor and has long cords that you stretch across the room, it can be vulnerable to mishaps. Take care when you remove the plug from the back of the computer to pull gently on the plug itself, not on the wire to prevent the plug from breaking off.

If you accidentally break or lose the power supply, try to obtain exactly the same part from the manufacturer. Using an original replacement part is much safer and preferable to trying to buy a run-of-the-mill replacement power supply. If you mismatch the power rating for a computer and a power supply, you can completely destroy your computer, even though the plug may fit just fine.

Alternatively, if you insist on saving the extra money, you may be able to find a similar power supply at an electronics store. You need to be extremely careful when making such a substitution. The two crucial things to keep in mind are:

  ✔ **The output voltage must precisely match the original power supply.** The number of amps, or the number of watts, is not as important — this number should be at least as high as on the original and can be higher. The voltage, however, needs to be *exactly the same value.*

✔ **The polarity of the connector plug must match precisely.** The plug has two parts: a *ring* and a *sleeve*. Usually the positive conductor is the center (sleeve), and the negative is on the outside (ring), but don't take my word for it! If you make a mistake with this, you can severely damage your computer.

Check on your damaged power supply for a polarity diagram that looks like a dot with a semicircle around it, as shown in Figure 23-3, with the dot and semicircle labeled + and – respectively, or the other way around, as the case may be. Make sure that this diagram matches the one on the replacement adapter you buy.

The power and polarity information you need is usually printed right on the bottom of the power supply, if you still have it, or you can find it in your computer instruction manual. If you're uncomfortable trying to figure this stuff out yourself, have an electronics dealer or computer store take care of it for you.

Figure 23-3:
A typical polarity diagram.

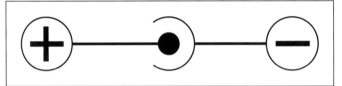

Battery

Over time and repeated charge/discharge cycles, your battery eventually wears out and needs replacement. Depending on the type of battery you use, you can expect about 400 to 800 charge/recharge cycles (see Chapter 3 for details). Storing the battery in a cool environment helps it last longer and helps it to retain maximum charge. Some people even store batteries in a refrigerator to help them keep their charge, but I think that such extreme precautions are not generally needed for rechargeable batteries. A good salami is a different issue.

Your battery also usually lasts longer if you periodically deplete it — in other words, don't run the computer on AC power all the time, with the battery perennially kept at full charge. Even if you use the computer indoors all the time, where AC power is readily available, operate the computer from battery power every now and then so it can go through a discharge/recharge cycle. Even batteries need exercise.

When it comes time to replace the battery, you can call the original computer manufacturer, or alternatively, call a battery specialty company (see the Appendix). Sometimes, through one of the various businesses that specialize in supplying replacement batteries for computers, camcorders, and cell phones, you can buy an improved battery that lasts longer than your previous one and fits in the exact same compartment.

Upgrading Your Notebook Computer

As your computer gets on in years and begins to seem outdated compared to new models — a process that begins the week after you buy it, incidentally — you inevitably start thinking about whether you need to buy a new computer or try to upgrade your existing model.

Memory

Memory upgrades are the easiest, and I highly recommend them. Unless you bought your computer fully loaded, you almost always have room for more memory in your computer. For instance, if your computer started out with just 8 or 16MB of RAM (Random Access Memory — the place where software actually runs), upgrading to 32MB usually improves performance noticeably — especially if you tend to keep a number of different applications open at the same time.

Most notebook computers include directions for adding new memory in their instruction manuals, and the procedure is considered something you can do yourself. Of course, the first step is locating the right memory for your computer. As with batteries, you can go back to the computer's manufacturer or to a third-party mail-order supplier.

Familiarize yourself with the memory upgrade options before you buy a computer. For example, you may find that to go from 8MB to 32MB requires junking the original memory (because you must install two 16MB modules); however, upgrading from 16MB to 32MB allows you to keep the original memory. In such a case, you are certainly better off buying the 16MB to begin with (not to mention the better performance you get). You may sometimes also need to purchase memory in pairs of modules, due to oddball requirements that the memory slots be filled according to a certain pattern specified by the manufacturer.

Always turn your computer's power off and remove the battery before you install new RAM. Be electrically grounded too: A static spark, if it reaches the pins on the memory modules, can destroy them. Touch a cold water pipe in your house, or the center screw that holds the faceplate on a power outlet to the wall. By grounding yourself, you discharge any static electricity your body may have accumulated.

Most newer computers automatically recognize the new memory as soon as you turn the power on and reboot. Some systems handle it all automatically, but usually you first go into the computer's Setup screen, where information such as available memory and hard drive capacity is stored.

The settings on the screen you see after installing memory are commonly referred to as the *CMOS Settings* (because they get retained in a special low-power type of memory known as CMOS — OK, you had to ask, it stands for Complimentary Metal-Oxide Semiconductor). If the computer suggests new settings based on the new memory, just approve the new settings, save, and exit, and forget what CMOS stands for!

If the computer does not suggest new settings automatically, then you may have to go into the Setup screen and change things manually. If the Setup screen does not appear automatically after you reboot, you must usually press the Delete or the F1 key just after the computer turns on — when a phrase like `Press F1 for Setup` appears onscreen. You need to find the spot in the Setup screen where the amount of RAM is specified and change it to the new value. Then save, exit, and reboot.

Though the CMOS stuff can look really intimidating and unfriendly, the procedure really isn't all that complicated. Fortunately, most computer dealers who sell memory upgrades for notebooks do the installation for you, usually for free. If you need help installing the new RAM, then you can't get the memory through mail order, of course.

Microprocessor

Most people consider the processor to be the main determinant of computer performance, and an old processor, more than anything else, seems to make a computer obsolete. Now I should point out that you may come across two completely different forms of obsolescence. The first, which I call *real* obsolescence, occurs when new software comes out that you really need to use. You need the new program to stay compatible with other software or users or to take advantage of new features that weren't in the old software. And your current computer just isn't powerful enough to run this new software properly — it's very sluggish, doesn't have the right kind of drive (such as DVD-ROM), or worse yet, it crashes constantly when you try to use it. The panic calls to tech support reveal that your machine just doesn't have enough oomph.

The second type of obsolescence, which I think is much more common and less of a problem, revolves around bragging rights. Your current computer works fine, and you don't particularly need to run any new software. However, everyone else seems to be using more powerful computers these days. So you feel the time has come to upgrade.

Unfortunately, the weakest aspect of notebook computer construction and design is that the processor is rarely upgradeable. Perhaps this quality is part of why computer dealers are doing such a booming business selling notebook computers. Unlike desktop models, when you want a new, faster microprocessor chip in your portable, you have to replace the whole thing, including display and keyboard.

This built-in obsolescence is motivated not just by manufacturer greed, but also by the competition to build notebook computers as small and lightweight as possible: Processor chips are sold in various housings. A computer manufacturer can buy a 200 MHz Pentium Pro chip in any of these various housings for use in their computers. The biggest form is in a plastic case with pins sticking out, designed for insertion in a socket (easily upgradeable). The smaller versions used for laptops are designed to be soldered directly to a circuit board and therefore aren't replaceable.

Occasionally, notebook computer manufacturers offer a socket-based chip that is user-upgradeable — or they upgrade it for you for a fee — but this upgrade path usually moves you only one notch up in performance. In other words, you may be able to switch to the next faster chip _speed,_ but not to a whole new type of processor (such as from Pentium to Pentium II).

Hard drive

The hard drives found on notebook computers seem to perennially have lower capacities than those found on desktop machines, meaning that you're likely to run out of space more quickly with a notebook than you would with a desktop machine.

Fortunately, most newer notebooks have their hard drives installed in a special compartment, like the battery, where they can be removed and replaced. (Some models even allow for _hot swapping_ of drives — meaning that you can actually change hard drives while the computer is running.)

However, from a software point of view, upgrading your notebook's hard drive can be a daunting task. Here's why: The main reason most people want to upgrade their drive is to get more space, to fit more programs and/or files. Therefore, the existing drive is already nearly full.

When you install the new drive, you have a completely blank slate. It does not even have the operating system, such as Windows 95, installed. After you get past the somewhat technical, but not insurmountable task of getting the computer to recognize the new drive (you probably have to navigate your way through the user-unfriendly CMOS Setup screen to specify the new drive's parameters), then what do you do?

You need to boot the computer from its floppy drive, or from its CD-ROM drive, using the first disk of the operating system software. Then you install the operating system. Then you can reinstall all the programs you were previously running from the old drive, and then perhaps the files you had stored on it — if you also have them stored somewhere else, such as on floppy disks.

See the problem? Not only does this process take a long, long time, but you may also lose the customizations you've created in the software you use — such as your address books, your Web browser bookmarks, the default settings in your word processor, and so on. What you really need is a method of copying the contents of the old hard drive to the new drive — the method exists, but it requires additional equipment, and forethought.

Because only one of your disk drives (old and new) can be hooked up to your notebook at any time, you need a third place where you can store the contents of the old drive while you install the new drive. Here are the possibilities of places to temporarily hold the contents of the old drive:

- ✔ **Another computer.** You can use a desktop machine with a direct cable connection and software such as LapLink (see Chapter 9).

- ✔ **An external tape backup device that hooks up through the parallel port.**

- ✔ **An external removable hard disk system.** Examples include Iomega's Jaz or Zip drives, or Syqest's SyJet or EZFlyer drives. Note that you may need to use several disks to make a backup copy of a large hard drive.

- ✔ **The central server in a computer network.** If you are authorized to store files on a network drive, you may be able to temporarily copy everything there. You don't necessarily need to have a network connection for your notebook — instead, you may be able to use a LapLink-style cable connection to your desktop computer to gain access to the network (see Chapter 20 for more information).

- ✔ **An external hard disk drive.** You can use one that hooks up to your computer's parallel port (or SCSI port, in the case of Apple PowerBooks and some PCs), or an internal or external PCMCIA hard drive.

Whichever of these systems you choose, you first have to get its software installed on the new drive before you do anything else. Here's the generic sequence you need to follow:

1. **Make a backup copy of your entire hard drive using whichever storage medium you have available.**

    Use the backup utility that comes supplied with tape drives or removable disk systems, when available.

2. **Install the new hard drive, and run the Setup utility to get the computer to recognize the new drive.**

   You may also need to run the format utility within the Setup menu to format the new drive and prepare it for first use.

3. **Install the operating system (for example, Windows 95) on the new drive.**

4. **Install whatever utility software you need for the storage system you're using.**

   This software can be what comes with a tape drive or removable hard drives, or LapLink if you're connecting to another computer.

5. **Run the Restore program in the storage system utility software to copy the information back to the new drive, or use the Copy command if you stored your old drive's contents on another computer.**

If you use the suspend-to-RAM feature in your notebook computer (see Chapter 4 for details), you probably need to make a partition in the new disk to get this feature to work again. See your computer's instruction manual for details on how to do this — it's a complicated procedure that is specific to whatever system you use and should be done immediately after a new drive is installed.

Of course, if you're replacing your old drive not because you ran out of room, but because it broke, the procedure outlined above is moot. If you can't read information from the hard drive, you have no way to copy it to the new drive, so you just have to start from scratch and reinstall all the software you use. Unless, that is, you made a backup of your notebook computer's hard drive — something I highly recommend, especially if you're running a business out of your laptop. (See Chapter 6 for backup storage options.)

Be prepared for calamity. Besides using the autosave feature to regularly make backup files on your computer's hard drive, I also suggest that as an extra super-neurotic precaution, you also make additional backup copies of the files on floppy disks. Do so every hour or two, or at least once per day, and store the floppy disk(s) in a separate location from the computer. If you have a backup system at your disposal, such as a tape drive or removable hard drive, make a backup copy of your notebook's hard drive every month. If not, keep all your program files in a safe place so you can easily gather them together for reinstallation if necessary. If your operating system software came preinstalled on the hard drive, and a backup copy was not supplied, make these disks as soon as possible — your computer usually prompts you to do so after you boot up.

Part V
The Part of Tens

" A PORTABLE COMPUTER? YOU'D BETTER TALK TO OLD BOB OVER THERE. HE'S OWNED A PORTABLE LONGER THAN ANYONE HERE."

In this part . . .

This breezy section gives you 20 specific tips — ten each on getting longer battery run time and ten great accessories for a portable computer.

Chapter 24

Ten Tips for Longer Battery Run Time

In This Chapter

▶ Getting the most out of every battery charge

▶ Exercising your battery

▶ Maintaining your battery in tip-top shape

*Y*es, you love to use the excuse that your computer's battery ran out to rationalize ordering a third alcoholic beverage and watching the in-flight movie without headphones. But just in case you really do want to keep your computer running through a four-hour flight, or if you want to work on your patio without running an AC power cord, or for any other reason you want to run on battery power for a while, this section is the one for you. Here I provide tips on keeping your computer's battery going for as long as possible. And hey, who's to say you can't have a drink and work at your computer anyway?

Activating Power Management

Your computer's battery can last one-and-a-half to two times longer if you turn on the power management system, as I explain in Chapter 4. If some of the details I cover in Chapter 4 seem too confusing, don't worry about them — just concentrate on turning on the Windows Power Management feature, as I describe in this section. If you don't already have it installed, you may need to read the installation procedure in Chapter 4. If you do already have it installed (or want to check whether you do), here's how:

1. Choose Start⇨Settings⇨Control Panel.

The Control Panel pops up.

2. **Double-click the Battery icon (if this icon is not in the Control Panel, then you need to go back to Chapter 4).**

   You get to the Power Properties dialog box.

3. **Set your power management to advanced or standard, and you are on your way to prolonged battery life.**

4. **Click OK to exit.**

Keeping the Screen Dim

The light that illuminates your computer display consumes a very large chunk of the battery's power — in essence, it's a big light bulb. So the lower your brightness setting, the less energy is being sucked from your battery, and the longer your battery lasts. The brightness control is a slider or dial under the screen or is operated by a pair of function keys — see Chapter 2. Some computers automatically dim the screen whenever they run on battery power as part of their power management features (see Chapter 4). If you ever use the computer just to listen to music from its CD-ROM drive, you may be able to turn the screen off altogether — usually with a function key — and save the juice for your tunes.

Using the Manual Suspend Feature

Whenever you take a break from your work — to eat food on an airplane, to read research materials, to look at the view — put your computer in its suspend mode. Don't wait for the power management feature to kick in and suspend automatically — you save many extra minutes of battery life by going into suspend mode manually. You can find more about suspend features in Chapter 4.

Staying Away from the Disk Drives

Because they're partly mechanical, your drives can eat up a lot of your battery's power. Of course, I also recommend that you save your work frequently to prevent catastrophe, so you must balance this conflicting advice to get the best compromise. The easiest way you can minimize drive use is to boot up only once on battery power, and then launch each program you use only once. When your computer sits idle, use the suspend/resume function instead of closing programs and turning the computer off.

You can further minimize disk access by saving just small chunks of larger files, whenever possible, and by avoiding the use of almost-full disks (if you hear the drive searching and searching to find places to store your file, you need to delete some files). You may want to periodically defragment your hard drive, too, for more efficient disk access. Note that the floppy drive usually uses less power than the hard drive, but that the CD-ROM can be a power glutton.

Recharging Just before Departure

All batteries exhibit self-discharge, meaning that if you leave them sitting around for a while after charging them up, they lose part or all of their charge. So you are best off charging up your battery(ies) just before taking off on a plane or other adventure. You can *top off* most newer rechargeables — if you last charged your battery a few days earlier, you can plug it into the AC adapter an hour or two before you leave to get it back up to a full charge.

Conversely, if you have an older laptop model that uses a nickel-cadmium battery, do not top off the battery, because this effort may result in poor performance due to the memory effect — see Chapter 3.

Removing All PC Cards

When not in use, most PC cards (also called PCMCIA cards) continue to draw juice from the battery. Even when your computer is in a sleep state or suspend mode, these cards continue to siphon off a bit of power. So if you want to squeeze every last drop out of the battery, simply pop these cards out when you don't need them. The same holds true for any removable drives your computer has. See Chapter 23 for more beef on the PCMCIA/PC card and how to insert and remove it.

Replacing the Battery

After a couple of years, your laptop battery won't last nearly as long as it once did. Depending on the particular battery technology, 400 to 800 charge/discharge cycles is about the practical limit, after which time your usable run time has probably gone down to less than half what it was when you first bought the battery. The decline in battery performance is gradual, and you may not even notice the change — by replacing the battery, you can restore the full run time your computer got when it was new. Remember to dispose of old batteries responsibly! See Chapter 3 for more information.

Exercising the Battery

Batteries, like dogs and humans, need exercise. Don't just keep your battery charged up all the time (as you are likely to do if you mostly use your laptop computer indoors and leave it plugged in). Run the computer from the battery at least once a month to keep it in shape. Otherwise, the battery may lose its ability to hold a full charge.

Avoiding Firing Up the Computer Frivolously

If all you need to do is jot down a few words or a phone number, booting up the computer can be both time-consuming and a waste of battery power. Sometimes the old-fashioned pen and paper approach makes more sense than a Pentium Pro processor. Quick notes and phone numbers are one area where pocket organizers and PDAs (Personal Digital Assistants, which I describe in Chapter 7) are clearly better than notebook computers — they boot up much faster, typically in just a few seconds, and their batteries usually last for much longer periods of time than your typical notebook computer.

Partially Recharging

Ideally, always charge the battery up all the way until the light stops blinking, the color changes, or whatever indication the computer provides tells you that the battery is fully charged. But in a pinch, you can partially charge the battery. Say that you have an hour wait in an airport before you catch a connecting flight, and you already used the computer for an hour on the first flight. By all means, sit down near an outlet and charge up. If you charge the battery for half an hour, you typically get 15 minutes to a half hour more run time.

Some exceptions are:

- ✔ Don't partially recharge older ni-cad batteries, because you reduce the amount of charge they can hold — see Chapter 3.

- ✔ Beware of chargers that have a *refresh cycle*. Found occasionally on older laptops, this cycle actually depletes the battery before charging it as a way to avoid the battery memory effect (which I describe in Chapter 3) and should never be invoked unless you have enough time for a complete recharge.

Chapter 25

Ten Computer Travel Accessories Worth Packing

In This Chapter

▶ Protecting your computer with a case

▶ Accessorizing for maximum utility (and high fashion)

▶ Hooking up to weird electricity and phone systems

*T*raveling with a portable computer that already weighs a few pounds, you usually look to keep your cyber kit bag as lightweight as possible. You must consider the value of each additional item that you toss in your bag very carefully — whether each item is absolutely necessary and how much it weighs. (Of course, if you're on the road showing presentations, you may need all sorts of specialized, and bulky, video devices — this list is intended more for general computer-in-tow travel.)

Padded case

Your notebook computer is delicate and needs to be protected both from mechanical shock and from bad weather and dirt as you carry it around. Numerous makes and models of notebook cases are available, offering varying levels of protection from mechanical shock. One innovative design uses an inflated air bag surrounding the computer (see Figure 25-1). Ideally your computer carrying case is just big enough to fit the computer, its AC adapter, and a few extra disks and cables, and has a thick layer of foam padding all around the computer. The smaller the case, the more easily you can fit it into other luggage, so you don't advertise your computer to would-be thieves. See "Ordinary Knapsack/Day Pack" later in this chapter.

Foreign AC plug adapters

AC plug adapters are cheap, lightweight, and if you travel to foreign countries, absolutely essential if you want to plug in your AC adapter/charger.

Your charger may work with foreign voltages, but the plugs themselves may not fit the foreign wall sockets, and still need to be converted — that's what these adapters do. One type of plug in particular, with two round prongs spaced about an inch and a half apart, is very widely used throughout Europe and much of the rest of the world — carrying a single adapter for this type of plug gets you through most foreign travel. See Chapter 8 for more information.

AC extension cord

If you travel to older hotels, motels, and foreign countries, you may encounter situations where your room has just a single outlet, and it's not in a convenient spot, or where every outlet is in use, and you have to unplug the lamp or the TV to plug in the computer. A simple extension cord with more than one socket solves both of these problems handily.

Telephone extension cord and coupler/splitter

Only the most modern, computer-friendly hotel rooms have more than one telephone jack. A dual-jack telephone adapter allows you to connect two modular telephone plugs into a single phone jack, thus allowing you to hook up your computer's modem and the regular telephone at the same time. This same adapter can serve double duty as a coupler, to connect together two modular phone wires (using the jacks only, and leaving the plug on the adapter not connected to anything). By bringing along an additional modular telephone cable, and plugging one end into this coupler, you get a telephone extension cord — useful if the phone jack in the room is nowhere near where you want to work with the computer when you go online.

Extra battery

If you spend a lot of travel time on planes or trains, or spend your days running presentations, consider an extra battery. It doubles the amount of run time you can get from your computer. The down side is that you have the significant extra weight to lug around, and you need to keep swapping between the two batteries to recharge them. For that reason, notebook models with two battery compartments are preferable — you can usually leave them both inside for automated dual battery recharging.

Another alternative is to carry a special charging station for the extra battery. These charging stations have a special slot where you slide the battery in and recharge it while it is outside the computer. For more on batteries and chargers, see Chapter 3.

Modem adapters for acoustic and digital connections

If your use of the notebook computer absolutely depends on being able to use your modem for telephone fax or data connections, you may want to consider two special modem accessories. The first, called an *acoustic adapter*, lets you use the modem even in places where you can find a phone but no phone jack, such as in older hotel rooms, in foreign countries, or even at a pay phone. The second type of adapter, called an *office phone adapter* or a *handset interface*, is specifically for using your computer's modem with digital office telephone systems. (See Chapter 19 for more details.)

External mouse

If you're not particularly fond of your notebook computer's built-in pointing system, you can improve things considerably (without buying a new machine) by hooking up a regular, standard-issue mouse. Both serial port and PS/2 style connections work with most PC notebooks, and prices for mice start at about $15. Best of all, mice are lightweight and occupy very little extra space in the carrying case. You can also purchase miniature trackballs (see Figure 25-2) and other pointing device accessories designed especially for laptops.

Power inverter or car adapter

If you expect to log some serious mileage in a car with your computer, a power inverter or car adapter can be a very useful accessory. Instead of having to wait to get to an AC outlet to recharge your battery, you can do so while you drive, using the car's cigarette lighter socket as the power source. Chapter 3 gives the lowdown on these two devices.

Figure 25-2:
A miniature
trackball
from
Logitech.

Ordinary knapsack/day pack

When you go on vacation with a notebook computer, you may find yourself in situations where you want to take it to a beach, park, or other public areas, and you don't particularly want to advertise the fact that you have an expensive computer in your bag. Ideally, you have a small knapsack or other bag into which you can stuff your notebook (still in its padded case). This way, you continue to get the benefit of the padding while keeping your expensive computer out of sight. Or you can improvise padding, with a long sheet of bubble wrap, foam, or perhaps a couple of sweaters wrapped around the computer. See Chapter 8 for a bit more on computer stealth and security.

Personal online/e-mail cheat sheet

Consider putting together a sheet with all the login information you need to go online, including phone numbers to dial, user names, and passwords. Include all the information you need for collecting e-mail (obtain this by copying down all the settings in your e-mail program's setup or preferences area). Keep this information on a sheet of paper — not just on your hard drive. You may also want to jot down the phone numbers for tech support for your computer, and for customer service at your online service or Internet service provider. Do not carry hefty instruction manuals just to have phone numbers handy — copy them to a lightweight sheet of paper. For security's sake, keep your cheat sheet separate from the computer.

Appendix
Where to Find All the Cool Stuff

• •

*I*f you bothered to come all the way back here to the end of the book, you are probably hooked on mobile computing. By now, you realize that mobile computing is the cutting edge of cool technology. However, being in a cool and cutting edge industry also means that businesses come, go, and move to new quarters relentlessly. This list of manufacturers and other relevant resources is intended to help you locate the products and services mentioned in this book. However, at best, it's just a snapshot of an industry that's constantly in flux — a day in the life of Mobile Computing.

In any case, this directory is divided into four main sections — Online and Internet Services, Accessories, Computers, and Software.

Plus one more oddball category that, although it has only one listing, deserves its own section: Recycling.

Recycling

You can donate your old computer to charity — remember that your old hunk of junk, if it still works, is better than no computer at all. Much of the world hasn't even seen a computer. If you are upgrading every two years to keep your rig current and always use the best technology, consider giving yesterday's machine to someone who appreciates it.

National Cristina Foundation
591 West Putnam Ave.
Greenwich, CT 06830
voice: 203-622-6000
fax: 203-622-6270
Web: http://www.cristina.org
e-mail: 72520,273@compuserve.com
e-mail: NCFUSA@aol.com

Online and Internet Services

Every service out there is a bit different and has a bit of its own personality. You can choose to go with a friendly hand-holding online service, or with the cutting edge of high-tech wireless Internet service providers.

America Online (online service)
8619 Westwood Center Dr.
Vienna, VA 22182
toll-free: 800-827-6364
Web: http://www.aol.com

ARDIS (wireless e-mail and Internet)
300 Knightsbridge Pkwy.
Lincolnshire, IL 60069
toll-free: 800-662-5328
Web: http://www.ardis.com

CompuServe (online service)
P.O. Box 20212
5000 Arlington Centre Blvd.
Columbus, OH 43220
toll-free: 800-848-8199
customer service (toll-free): 800-848-8990
voice: 614-529-1349
fax: 614-529-1610
Web: http://www.compuserve.com

DTS Wireless (*Zap-it* wireless e-mail and Internet)
10 Woodbridge Center Dr., Suite 730
Woodbridge, NJ 07095
toll-free: 888-2-GET-DTS
voice: 908-602-1144
Web: http://www.dtswireless.com

GoAmerica (wireless Internet)
401 Hackensack Ave.
Hackensack, NJ 07601
201-996-1717
Web: http://www.goamerica.net

Metricom (*Ricochet* wireless Internet)
983 University Ave., Suite C
Los Gatos, CA 95030
toll-free: 800-469-4735
Web: http://www.metricom.com

Microsoft Network (*MSN* online service)
One Microsoft Way
Redmond, WA 98052
toll-free: 800-373-3676
voice: 206-882-8080
Web: http://www.msn.com

Mtel (*SkyTel* wireless e-mail)
200 S. Lamart St.
Jackson, MS 39201
toll-free: 800-759-9138
Web: http://www.skytel.com

Prodigy (online service)
445 Hamilton Ave.
White Plains, NY 10601
toll-free: 800-PRODIGY
Web: http://www.prodigy.com

RadioMail (wireless e-mail)
2600 Campus Dr.
San Mateo, CA 94403
toll-free: 800-597-MAIL
Web: http://www.radiomail.com

RAM Mobile Data (wireless e-mail, Internet, news services)
10 Woodbridge Center Dr., Suite 950
Woodbridge, NJ 07095
toll-free: 800-726-3210
Web: http://www.ram.com

Software Corporation of America (CDPD cellular networking)
100 Prospect St.
Stamford, CT 06901
voice: 203-359-2773

Wynd Communications (wireless e-mail)
75 Higuera St., Suite 240
San Luis Obispo, CA 93401
voice: 805-781-6000
Web: http://www.wynd.com

Accessory Products

Accessorize, accessorize, accessorize. You can get almost as many different accessories for your portable computer as you can for a car. Just don't try putting one of those car air fresheners in your PCMCIA/PC card slot.

1-800-Batteries (batteries, memory, telephone, and other accessories)
14388 Union Ave.
San Jose, CA 95124
toll-free: 800-BATTERIES
Web: http://www.800batteries.com

AeroComm Wireless (wireless microwave printer sharing)
13228 West 99th St.
Lenexa, KS 66215
voice: 913-492-2320
fax: 913-492-1243

AITech (scan converters and multimedia)
47971 Fremont Blvd.
Fremont, CA 94538
toll-free: 800-882-8184
voice: 510-226-8960
fax: 510-226-8996
Web: http://www.aitech.com
e-mail: sales@aitech.com

Apollo Presentation Products (LCD panels and projectors)
60 Trade Zone Ct.
Ronkonkoma, NY 11779
toll-free: 800-777-3750
voice: 516-467-8033
fax: 516-467-8996
Web: http://www.apollo.pb.net

ASK (*Texas Instruments* LCD projectors)
1099 Wall St. W, Suite 396
Lyndhurst, NJ 07071
toll-free: 800-ASK-LCD1
Web: http://www.ask.no
e-mail: info@asklcd.com

Chisholm (LCD projectors)
910 Campisi Way
Campbell, CA 95008-2340
voice: 408-559-1111
Web: http://www.chisholm.com

Corex Technologies (card scanners)
130 Prospect St.
Cambridge, MA 02139
voice: 617-492-4200
Web: http://www.cardscan.com

Da-Lite Screen Company, Inc. (portable overhead projectors)
3100 North Detroit St.
P.O. Box 137
Warsaw, IN 46581-0137
toll-free: 800-613-2189
Web: http://www.da-lite.com
e-mail: info@da-lite.com

DTC Data Technology Corporation (Infrared LAN adapters)
1515 Centre Pointe Dr.
Milpitas, CA 95035
voice: 408-942-4006
fax: 408-942-4027
Web: http://www.betatechnology.com

Elmo (LCD projectors, projection panels)
70 New Hyde Park Rd.
New Hyde Park, NY 11040
toll-free: 800-947-ELMO

Epson America, Inc. (modems, digital
cameras)
20770 Madrona Ave.
Torrance, CA 90503
voice: 310-782-0770

Extended Systems (wireless infrared data
transfer)
5777 N. Meeker Ave.
Boise, ID 83713
toll-free: 800-235-7576
voice: 406-587-8974

Fujitsu Microelectronics, Inc. (modems)
3545 North First St.
San Jose, CA 95134-1804
toll-free: 800-642-7616

Gateway 2000 (batteries)
610 Gateway Dr.
North Sioux City, SD 57049
toll-free: 800-443-1254

Hayes Microcomputer Products, Inc.
(modems)
5953 Peachtree Industrial Blvd.
Norcross, GA 30092
voice: 404-840-9200

IBM (wireless modems)
Route 100
Somers, NY 10589
toll-free: 800-772-2227
Web: http://www.ibm.com

InfraLAN Wireless Communications
(wireless infrared LAN cards)
2940 N. Burke St.
San Jose, CA 01720
voice: 508-266-1500

Kiwi (Batteries)
2314 Walsh Ave.
Santa Clara, CA 95051
voice: 408-492-9188
Web: http://www.kiwicom.com

Kōnexx (telephone accessories including
acoustic coupler, handset jack adapter)
5550 Oberlin Dr.
San Diego, CA 92121
voice: 619-622-1400
Web: http://www.konexx.com
e-mail: sale@konexx.com

Logitech (scanners, *TrakMan* portable
trackball)
6505 Kaiser Dr.
Fremont, CA 94555
voice: 510-795-8500
Web: http://www.logitech.com/

Megahertz Corporation (modems)
4505 South Wasatch Blvd.
Salt Lake City, UT 84124
toll-free: 800-LAPTOPS

Microcom, Inc. (modems)
500 River Ridge Dr.
Norwood, MA 02062
toll-free: 800-822-8224

MindPath (wireless mouse and keyboard)
12700 Park Central Dr., Suite 400
Dallas, TX 75251
voice: 214-233-9296
Web: http://www.mindpath.com

Miram (universal expansion station that
connects via PCMCIA/PC card)
14405 21st Ave. North, Suite 117
Minneapolis, MN 55447
toll-free: 800-30MIRAM
voice: 612-404-1229
fax: 614-404-1242
Web: http://www.miram.com

Mitsubishi (*Megaview* monitors, touchscreen displays, LCD projectors)
5665 Plaza Dr.
Cypress, CA 90630
toll-free: 800-843-2515
Web: http://www.mela-itg.com/
index.html

Motorola (wireless modem cards, regular modem cards, ISDN modem cards)
50 East Commerce Dr.
Schamburg, IL 60173
toll-free: 800-894-7353
voice (wireless products): 847-538-5200
Web: http://www.mot.com

NEC (LCD projectors, monitors)
2880 Scott Blvd.
Santa Clara, CA 95050
toll-free: 800-366-9782
Web: http://www.nec.com

Netwave Technologies (wireless microwave LAN cards)
6663 Owens Dr.
Pleasanton, CA 94588
toll-free: 800-NETWAVE
voice: 510-737-1600
fax: 510-847-8744
Web: http://www.netwave-
wireless.com
e-mail: info@netwave-wireless.com

New Media Corp (LAN, modem, audio, SCSI, and other cards)
One Technology, Building A
Irvine, CA 92618
toll-free: 800-CARDS-4-U
voice: 714-453-0100
fax: 714-453-0114
BBS: 714-453-0214
fax-back service: 714-789-5212
Web: http://www.newmediacorp.com

Ositech Communications (LAN and modem cards)
679 Southgate Dr.
Guelph, Ontario
Canada N1G 4S2
toll-free: 888-674-8324
voice: 519-836-8063
fax: 519-836-6156
Web: http://www.ositech.com

Panasonic (CD-ROM drives, monitors)
2 Panasonic Way
Secaucus, NJ 07094
voice: 201-348-9090

Practical Peripherals (modems)
375 Conejo Ridge Ave.
Thousand Oaks, CA 91361
voice: 805-497-4774

ProLux (LCD projectors)
32961 Calle Perfecto
San Juan Capistrano, CA 92675-4705
toll-free: 800-3-PROLUX
Web: http://www.prolux.com

Proxim (wireless microwave LAN cards)
295 North Bernardo Ave.
Mountain View, CA 94043
voice: 415-960-1630

Sharp Electronics (LCD projectors and panels)
Sharp Plaza
Mahwah, NJ 07430
toll-free: 800-BE-SHARP
Web: http://www.sharp-usa.com

Simple Technology (removable hard drives, flash memory cards)
3001 Daimier St.
Santa Anna, CA 92705
voice: 714-476-1180
Web: http://www.simpletech.com

Smart Clips (wireless laptop theft alarms)
47 Denton Ave.
New Hyde Park, NY 11040
toll-free: 888-727-7262
Web: http://www.monaad.com
e-mail: infor@smartclips-na.com

SoftBoard (digital whiteboard for remote
computing)
7216 S.W. Durham Rd.
Portland, OR 97224
toll-free: 800-SOFTBOARD
Web: http://www.softboard.com

Solectek (wireless microwave LAN cards)
6370 Nancy Ridge Dr.
San Diego, CA 92121
toll-free: 800-437-1518

Sony (LCD projectors, CRT projectors,
wireless mouse)
3300 Zanker Rd.
San Jose, CA 95134
voice: 408-432-1600
Web: http://www.sony.com

Targus (carrying cases)
6180 Valley View
Buena Park, CA 90620
voice: 714-523-5429
fax: 714-523-0153

TDK Systems (modem cards and international modem card)
136 New Mohawk Rd.
Nevada City, CA 95959
voice: 916-478-8421
Web: http://www.tdksystems.com/

Toshiba America Information Systems
(port replicator, expansion stations)
9740 Irvine Blvd.
Irvine, CA 92618
voice: 714-583-3000
Web: http://www.toshiba/tais/csd

U.S. Robotics (wireless modems and
modems)
P.O. Box 16020
Salt Lake City, UT 84116
toll-free: 800-342-5877
Web: http://www.usr.com

Visioneer, Inc. (scanners)
34800 Campus Dr.
Fremont CA 94555
voice: 510-608-0300
Web: http://www.visioneer.com

Zoom Telephonics (modems)
207 South St.
Boston, MA 02111
toll-free: 800 631 3116

Computers

This section speaks for itself!

Acer America
399 B Trimble Rd.
San Jose, CA 95131
toll-free: 800-554-2494
Web: http://www.acer.com

Compaq Computer
10251 N. Freeway
Houston, TX 77037
toll-free: 800-345-1518
voice: 713-370-0670
Web: http://www.compaq.com

Amrel Technology (ruggedized notebook computers)
11801 Goldring Rd.
Arcadia, CA 91006
voice: 818-303-6688
Web: http://www.amrel.com

Apple Computer, Inc.
5 Infinite Loop, MS 305-3C
Cupertino, CA 95014
toll-free: 800-776-2333
voice: 408-996-1010
Web: http://www.apple.com

AST Research
16215 Alton Pkwy.
Irvine, CA 92618
toll-free: 800-293-1651
voice: 714-727-4141
Web: http://www.ast.com

Canon Computer
1 Canon Plaza
Lake Success, NY 11042
voice: 516-488-6700

Casio, Inc. (*Cassiopeia* handheld PC)
570 Mt. Pleasant Ave.
Dover, NJ 07801
voice: 201-361-5400

Chaplet Systems USA (subnotebook computers)
252 N. Wolfe Rd.
Sunnyvale, CA 94086
toll-free: 800-308-3388
voice: 408-732-7950
e-mail: chaplet@best.com

Commax Technologies, Inc.
2031 Concourse Dr.
San Jose, CA 95131
voice: 408-435-5000

Dell Computer Corp.
2214 W. Braker Ln., Suite D
Austin, TX 78758
toll-free: 800-289-3355
voice: 512-338-4400
Web: http://www.us.dell.com/smbus

Digital Equipment Corp.
Computer Systems Division
111 Powdermill Rd.
Maynard, MA 01754-1499
toll-free: 800-DIGITAL

Eurocom Corporation
148 Colonnade Rd., Unit 1&3
Nepean, Ontario,
Canada K2E 7R4
voice: 613-224-6122
fax: 613-224-2511
BBS: 613-224-2903

Everex Systems, Inc.
5020 Brandin Ct.
Fremont, CA 94538
toll-free: 800-821-0806
Web: http://www.everex.com

FieldWorks, Inc.
9961 Valley View Rd.
Eden Prairie, MN 55344
voice: 612-947-0856

Fujitsu PC
598 Gibraltar Dr.
Milpitas, CA 95035
voice: 408-935-8800
Web: http://www.fujitsu.com
Web: http://www.fujitsu/pc.com

Gateway 2000
610 Gateway Dr.
North Sioux City, SD 57049
toll-free: 800-846-2000
voice: 605-232-2000
Web: http://www.gw2k.com

Hewlett-Packard Co.
3000 Hanover St.
Palo Alto, CA 94304
toll-free: 800-752-0900
voice: 503-752-7736
Web: http://www.hp.com/go/omnibook
Web: http://www.hp.com/handheld

Hitachi Home Electronics (handheld PCs)
3890 Steve Reynolds Blvd.
Norcross, GA 30093
voice: 770-279-5600
Web: http://www.hitachi.com

Hitachi Home Electronics (notebooks)
2520 Junction Ave.
San Jose, CA 95134
toll-free: 800-555-6820
voice: 408-321-5000
Web: http://www.hitachipc.com

IBM Corp.
P.O. Box 1295
Research Triangle Park, NC 27709
toll-free: 800-772-2227
Web: http://www.pc.ibm.com/thinkpad

IBM Corp. (Networking Hardware Division)
1001 Winstead Dr.
Cary, NC 27513
toll-free: 800-IBM-3333

Kiwi Computers, Inc.
2314 Walsh Ave.
Santa Clara, CA 95051
voice: 408-492-9188
Web: http://www.kiwicom.com

LG Electronics (**GoldStar** brand)
1000 Sylvan Ave.
Englewood Cliffs, NJ 076322
voice: 201-816-2000

Micron Electronics, Inc.
900 E. Karcher Rd.
Nampa, ID 83687
toll-free: 800-700-0612
voice: 208-893-3434
Web: http://www.mei.micron.com

Mitsubishi Electronics
Mobile Computing Division
5665 Plaza Dr.
P.O. Box 6007
Cypress, CA 90630
voice: 714-229-6527
fax: 714-236-6199

Motorola
6501 William Cannon Dr. W
Austin, TX 78735
toll-free: 800-845-MOTO
voice: 602-952-3637
Web: http://www.mot.com

Nimantics (subnotebooks)
2913 El Camino Real
Tustin, CA 92782
toll-free 800-646-5005
Web: http://www.nimantics.com

Panasonic
30 Hartz Way
Secaucus, NJ 07094
toll-free: 800-662-3537
voice: 201-271-3182

Philips Mobile Computing
441 DeGuigne Dr.
Sunnyvale, CA 94088
toll-free: 888-367-8356
voice: 408-523-7800
Web: http://www.velo1.com

Psion (pocket computer)
150 Baker Ave.
Concord, MA 01742
voice: 508-371-0310
Web: http://www.psion.com

Samsung
105 Challenger Rd.
Ridgefield Park, NJ 07660
voice: 201-229-4000
Web: http://www.sosimple.com

Sceptre Technologies, Inc.
16800 E. Gale Ave.
City of Industry, CA 91745
toll-free 800-788-2878
Web: http://www.sceptretech.com

Sharp Electronics
Sharp Plaza
Mahwah, NJ 07430
toll-free: 800-237-4277
voice: 201-529-8200
Web: http://www.sharp/usa.com

Texas Instruments
P.O. Box 6102, MS 3242
Temple, TX 76503
toll-free: 800-TI-TEXAS
voice: 817-774-6001
Web: http://www.ti.com

Toshiba
Computer Systems Division
9740 Irvine Blvd.
P.O. Box 19724
Irvine, CA 92623
toll-free: 800-457-7777
Web: http://
www.computers.toshiba.com

Twinhead Corp.
1537 Centre Pointe Dr.
Milpitas, CA 95035
voice: 408-945-0808
Web: http://www.twinhead.com

WinBook Corp.
1160 Steelwood Rd.
Columbus, OH 43026
toll-free: 800-965-5287
toll-free: 800-468-2162
Web: http://www.winbook.com

Software

Throughout the book I mention various useful software packages. You can find addresses for the companies that make all the fun and fantastic software in this section.

AllPen Software, Inc. (pen computing,
Apple Newton applications)
51 University Ave., Suite J
Los Gatos, CA 95030
voice: 408-399-8800
Web: http://www.allpen.com
e-mail: info@allpen.com

Goldmine Software Corp. (contact
manager software)
17383 Sunset Blvd., Suite 301
Pacific Palisades, CA 90272
toll-free: 800-654-3526
Web: http://www.goldminesw.com

Microcom (*Carbon Copy* remote computing and file transfer)
500 River Ridge Dr.
Norwood, MA 02062
voice: 617-551-1000
toll-free: 800-822-8224

Microsoft
One Microsoft Way
Redmond, WA 98052
voice: 206-882-8080
fax: 206-936-7329

Odyssey Computing (contact managers for handheld PCs)
16981 Via Tazan, Suite D
San Diego, CA 92127
voice: 619-675-3660
fax: 619-75-1130
e-mail: info@odysseyinc.com

Phoenix Technology, Ltd. (PCMCIA/PC card and BIOS)
2575 McCabe Way
Irvine, CA 92714
voice: 714-440-8000

Qualcomm (*Eudora* e-mail)
6455 Lusk Blvd.
San Diego, CA 92121
toll-free: 800-238-3672
Web: http://www.qualcomm.com

Quarterdeck Corp. (*Procomm* data communications, *Rapid Remote*)
13160 Mindanao Way
Marina del Rey, CA 90292
voice: 310-309-3700
Web: http://www.quarterdeck.com
e-mail: info@quarterdeck.com

Symantec (*Act!* contact manager, *PC Anywhere* remote computing, *Winfax Pro* fax software, *Norton Utilities,* and *Norton* anti-virus software)
10201 Torre Ave.
Cupertino, CA 95014
voice: 408-253-9600
Web: http://www.symantec.com
on CompuServe: GO SYMANTEC
on America OnLine, Keyword: SYMANTEC

SystemSoft (PCMCIA/PC card software)
313 Speen St.
Natick, MA 01760
voice: 508-651-0088

Traveling Software (*LapLink* file transfer and remote computing software)
18702 North Creek Pkwy.
Bothell, WA 98011
toll-free: 800-343-8080

Triton Technologies (*CoSession for Windows*)
200 Middlesex Tpke.
Iselin, NJ 08830
voice: 908-855-9440

Index

(continued)

(continued)

IDG BOOKS WORLDWIDE REGISTRATION CARD

Visit our Web site at http://www.idgbooks.com

ISBN Number: 0-7645-0151-8

Title of this book: Mobile Computing For Dummies ®

My overall rating of this book: ❏ Very good [1]   ❏ Good [2]   ❏ Satisfactory [3]   ❏ Fair [4]   ❏ Poor [5]

How I first heard about this book:

❏ Found in bookstore; name: [6]

❏ Advertisement: [8]

❏ Word of mouth; heard about book from friend, co-worker, etc.: [10]

❏ Book review: [7]

❏ Catalog: [9]

❏ Other: [11]

What I liked most about this book:

What I would change, add, delete, etc., in future editions of this book:

Other comments:

Number of computer books I purchase in a year: ❏ 1 [12]   ❏ 2-5 [13]   ❏ 6-10 [14]   ❏ More than 10 [15]

I would characterize my computer skills as: ❏ Beginner [16]   ❏ Intermediate [17]   ❏ Advanced [18]   ❏ Professional [19]

I use ❏ DOS [20]   ❏ Windows [21]   ❏ OS/2 [22]   ❏ Unix [23]   ❏ Macintosh [24]   ❏ Other: [25]

(please specify)

I would be interested in new books on the following subjects:

(please check all that apply, and use the spaces provided to identify specific software)

❏ Word processing: [26]

❏ Data bases: [28]

❏ File Utilities: [30]

❏ Networking: [32]

❏ Other: [34]

❏ Spreadsheets: [27]

❏ Desktop publishing: [29]

❏ Money management: [31]

❏ Programming languages: [33]

I use a PC at (please check all that apply): ❏ home [35]   ❏ work [36]   ❏ school [37]   ❏ other: [38]

The disks I prefer to use are ❏ 5.25 [39]   ❏ 3.5 [40]   ❏ other: [41]

I have a CD ROM: ❏ yes [42]   ❏ no [43]

I plan to buy or upgrade computer hardware this year: ❏ yes [44]   ❏ no [45]

I plan to buy or upgrade computer software this year: ❏ yes [46]   ❏ no [47]

Name: Business title: [48]   Type of Business: [49]

Address (❏ home [50] ❏ work [51]/Company name:)

Street/Suite#

City [52]/State [53]/Zip code [54]:   Country [55]

❏ **I liked this book!** You may quote me by name in future IDG Books Worldwide promotional materials.

My daytime phone number is _____

IDG
BOOKS
WORLDWIDE

THE WORLD OF
COMPUTER
KNOWLEDGE®

❏ YES!

Please keep me informed about IDG Books Worldwide's World of Computer Knowledge. Send me your latest catalog.

BESTSELLING BOOK SERIES FROM IDG